NATIONAL AND
INTERNATIONAL POLITICS
IN THE MIDDLE EAST

NATIONAL
AND
INTERNATIONAL
POLITICS
IN THE
MIDDLE EAST

Essays in Honour of
Elie Kedourie

edited by

EDWARD INGRAM

*Professor of Imperial History at
Simon Fraser University*

FRANK CASS

First published 1986 in Great Britain by
FRANK CASS AND COMPANY LIMITED
Gainsborough House, 11 Gainsborough Road,
London, E11 1RS, England

and in the United States of America by
FRANK CASS AND COMPANY LIMITED
c/o Biblio Distribution Centre
81 Adams Drive, P.O. Box 327, Totowa, N.J. 07511

British Library Cataloguing in Publication Data

National and international politics in the
Middle East: essays in honour of Elie
Kedourie.
1. Near East—Politics and government
I. Kedourie, Elie   II. Ingram, Edward,
1940–
956   DS62.8
ISBN 0-7146-3278-3

Printed in Great Britain by
A. Wheaton & Co. Ltd, Exeter

TO
ELIE KEDOURIE

for his interest in
the island of Perim

Don't ever ask where the Empire's gone.
It's hush hush!

Uncle Clam,
Salad Days,
Act I

CONTENTS

MAPS

PREFACE

Elie Kedourie, F.B.A., Professor of Politics in the University of London, is sixty years old. In celebration of his birthday, these essays are presented to him by a group of his admirers overseas. None of his colleagues will be found among the authors and only one of his students. Likewise, only one of us is a close friend. Some of us have met him occasionally, many of us never: all, however, are great admirers of his work. Historians ought to be known – and ought to be able to be known – by their work rather than their personalities. Too many reputations in North America and, one suspects, in Great Britain are founded upon hustle around conferences and commissions. Professor Kedourie is known for his unforgettable essays, for the pattern of interpretation and view of the world which hold his readers spellbound, even when they strongly disagree with his opinions, and for *Middle Eastern Studies*, which recently reached its majority and which he and Frank Cass together have turned into the foremost scholarly journal in its field. Some of us have had the honour and good fortune to be published in it. I am one.

Anyone who meets Professor Kedourie as the result of submitting a manuscript to *Middle Eastern Studies*, can attest to the pleasure of receiving the two short sentences he writes (more quickly than other editors) to tell one that he has enjoyed reading one's work and will be pleased to publish it. What he says upon turning one down I am boastful enough to claim not to know. I sent to him the first article I wrote, a study of a British expedition to the Red Sea during the war of the Second Coalition. The moment he accepted the article, I became bold. Rose Louise Greaves, another of my favourite historians, had recently published a series of articles in the *Bulletin* of the School of Oriental and African Studies on Anglo-Iranian relations before the First World War. Dreaming of following her example, I sent Professor Kedourie three more parts of my article. To my delight, he accepted them. I drew the only reasonable conclusion: that the Great Game in Asia had been invented to keep me scribbling happily throughout my career.

A meeting with Professor Kedourie can be an ordeal, not always, but sometimes. I have met him on six occasions. About ten years ago, when we had not yet met, he accepted an invitation to lunch in a small, noisy Italian restaurant I was fond of at the bottom of Charing Cross Road – it does sound unlikely but once upon a time the food there was delicious. Nowhere less suitable for this meeting, however, could be imagined. He sat quietly, almost hesitantly, so effectively giving the impression that I was paying him the compliment in coming, rather than he me, that I became tongue-tied with fright. Going to his house for dinner for the first time while on leave in London last year was just as unnerving. I was the only guest and made so welcome that I stayed far too late. So where lurked the peril? Mrs. Kedourie, of course. Imagine oneself chattering away light-heartedly, between times chewing the walnuts she has cracked with a nut-cracker whose secret is known only to the family, when a word misplaced transforms one's smiling hostess before one's very eyes into the formidable intellect of Sylvia Haim. Foul, one wants to cry. Begin the conversation again. But I cannot have disgraced myself. They were kind enough to ask me back.

Just as Professor Kedourie gave me my first success, he gave me one of the most enjoyable moments of my career. An eminent (to be gracious) American historian, who shall here go nameless, was reviewing one of my books and evidently disliked the tone of it. But what else was to be expected, he asked, from a disciple of Elie Kedourie? Though technically not a disciple (to my regret, nobody sent me to see him while I was attending the London School of Economics), I am happy to be known as one. Professor Kedourie is, as I warned him at the time, now stuck with me, and will, I hope, therefore accept these essays as a token of the enjoyment his essays have always given to me.

Acknowledgements are due to the British Library, the Public Record Office, the Imperial War Museum, the Bundesarchiv and the Politisches Archiv des Auswärtigen Amts of the Federal Republic of Germany, the Israel State Archives, the United States' National Archives, Diş-Işleri Bakanliği Hazane-i Evrak, the National Library of Wales, the Hereford Record Office, King's College London, St. Antony's College, Oxford, the University of Durham Library, Cambridge University Library, the Bodleian Library, and the Royal Geographical Society, for the use of material from their collections.

Four friends and colleagues have given freely of their time and advice in helping to prepare this volume. William L. Cleveland atoned for his sinful delight in the fall of the British Empire by sharing his understanding of the modern Middle East. Ruth Baldwin and Terence J. Ollerhead of *The International History Review* have edited and proof-read, if not always with unfailing patience and goodwill, Ruth Baldwin has also drawn four of the delightful maps of which, like her jam tarts, she is rightly proud, and Jennifer Alexander has typed and corrected innumerable times. My thanks go to all of them. As it looks from the state of universities in this country as if we shall all be working together for a long time, how fortunate we are to enjoy one another's company so heartily.

E.R.I.E.
The Hotel Vancouver,
Epiphany, 1986

CONTRIBUTORS

MORDECAI ABIR is Professor of Middle Eastern and African Studies at the Hebrew University of Jerusalem. He is the author of, among other works, *The Contentious Horn of Africa* and *Oil, Power and Politics: Conflict in Arabia, the Red Sea and the Gulf*.

WILLIAM L. CLEVELAND is Professor of History at Simon Fraser University. He is the author of *The Making of an Arab Nationalist: Ottomanism and Arabism in the Life and Thought of Sati 'al-Husri* and *Islam against the West: Shakib Arslan and the Campaign for Islamic Nationalism*.

RODERIC H. DAVISON is Professor of History at the George Washington University. He is the author of *Reform in the Ottoman Empire, 1856-1876* and *Turkey*.

JOHN S. GALBRAITH is Professor of History at the University of California, San Diego. He is the author of, among other works, *The Hudson's Bay Company as an Imperial Factor, 1821-1869* and *Reluctant Empire: British Policy on the South African Frontier, 1834-1854*.

ROBERT A. HUTTENBACK is Professor of History at, and Chancellor of, the University of California, Santa Barbara. He is the author of, among other works, *British Relations with Sind, 1799-1843* and *Racism and Empire: White Settlers and Coloured Immigrants in the British Self-Governing Colonies, 1830-1910*.

JAMES JANKOWSKI is Professor of History and Chairman of the Department in the University of Colorado at Boulder. He is the author of *Egypt's Young Rebels: 'Young Egypt', 1933-1952* and co-author of *Egypt, Islam and the Arabs*.

MARIAN KENT is Reader in Social Sciences at Deakin University. She is the author of *Oil and Empire: British Policy and Mesopotamian Oil, 1900-1920* and editor of *The Great Powers and the End of the Ottoman Empire*.

JOSEPH KOSTINER is Lecturer in History at the Dayan Centre for Middle Eastern and African Studies at Tel Aviv University.

BERNARD LEWIS is Professor of Near Eastern Studies at Princeton University and a Fellow of the Institute for Advanced Study. He is the author of, among other works, *The Emergence of Modern Turkey* and *The Muslim Discovery of Europe*.

GORDON MARTEL is Associate Professor of History at Royal Roads Military College and an Editor of *The International History Review*. He is the author of *Imperial Diplomacy: Rosebery and the Failure of Foreign Policy* and editor of *The Origins of the Second World War Reconsidered: The A.J.P. Taylor Debate after Twenty-Five Years*.

FRANCIS R. NICOSIA is Associate Professor of History at St. Michael's College, Vermont, and the author of *The Third Reich and the Palestine Question*.

RUDOLPH PETERS is Senior Lecturer in Arabic and Islamic Studies in the University of Amsterdam and Director of the Netherlands Institute for Archaeology and Arabic Studies in Cairo. He is the author of *Jihad in Medieval and Modern Islam* and *Islam and Colonialism: The Doctrine of Jihad in Modern History*.

MARY C. WILSON is Assistant Professor of History at New York University. Her biography of King Abdullah of Jordan will be published shortly.

NOTES ON REFERENCES

ABBREVIATIONS

ADAP	*Akten zur deutschen auswärtigen Politik 1918-1945* (Baden-Baden, 1953)
Add. MSS	British Library, Additional Manuscripts
BA	Federal Republic of Germany, Bundesarchiv, Coblenz.
CAB	Public Record Office, Cabinet Records
CO	Public Record Office, Colonial Office Records
DBHE	Diş-Işleri Bakanliği Hazane-i Evrak, Istanbul (Ottoman Foreign Ministry Archives)
DUL	University of Durham Library
FO	Public Record Office, Foreign Office Records
IO	India Office Library, India Office Records
IWM	Imperial War Museum, London
ISA	Israel State Archives, Jerusalem
KC MSS	Hereford Record Office, Kentchurch Court Manuscripts
MSS EUR.	India Office Library, European Manuscripts
NLW	National Library of Wales, Aberystwyth
PA	Federal Republic of Germany, Politisches Archiv des Auswärtigen Amts, Bonn
POWE	Public Record Office, Petroleum Department Records
SAC	St. Antony's College, Oxford
USNA	United States' National Archives, Washington DC

SPELLING AND TRANSLITERATION

Turkish and Arabic words have here been rendered in English as simply as possible. None of the established systems of transliteration is followed in full. Thus the Arabic *'ayn* has been rendered (except in the names of the famous), the *hamza* omitted. More important, the English language has taken precedence over all other languages.

Any place, person, or term well enough known to be listed in *The Concise Oxford English Dictionary* or *The Oxford Dictionary for Writers and Editors* (formerly known as Collins) is spelled as it is spelled there. Thus, for example, Wahabi not Wahhabi, ulema not *'ulama*, Tartars not Tatars, Abdul Hamid not 'Abd al-Hamid, Shiites not Shi'i, and Coblenz not Koblenz. I have tried to make sure that if I have slightly offended all of the contributors, I have infuriated none of them. In return, I have brought into line with them my usually anglicized spellings of certain Middle Eastern names and have added the capital letters to Middle East in deference to Sylvia Haim.

INTRODUCTION:
SIX VARIATIONS ON A THEME

Edward Ingram

> Is it so easy, we are moved to wonder, in the flow of
> historical events to say which is 'root' and which is
> 'façade'? ... is it [the case] that what one clerk writes
> to another is ... as real as technological change or a
> change in economic relations?
>
> Elie Kedourie[1]

The answer to the first question asked here, given by Elie Kedourie himself and given correctly, is simple, much simpler than social and economic historians preoccupied with structures and the *longue durée* would have one believe. The answer is No, although they would answer Yes. The answer to the second question is equally simple. It is Yes, although they would answer No. They give the wrong answers and Professor Kedourie the correct ones because, unlike him, they underestimate the significance of events: they underestimate the men who sometimes cause events to happen and must live with what they have caused, more often inadvertently than by design. To anyone who died in the trenches, the events on the Western Front mattered more than the contradictions within the capitalist economy that had supposedly caused the war to break out. Similarly, they mattered more to the spinster school teacher in the English village, 'Miss Read''s Miss Clare perhaps, whose dead boyfriend was unlikely to be replaced owing to a nation-wide shortage within her rank in society. Telling her that had society been organized along different lines she might have been willing to marry a labourer would have been true, but hardly of comfort.

The significance of events will also be obvious to anyone who spent his childhood in Baghdad in the 1920s and 1930s, as Professor Kedourie did, or in Calcutta fifteen years later, as I did, and had to witness the English dying 'the slow white death reserved for privilege

in defeat':[2] losing the nerve for living up to their imperial re-
sponsibilities and calling it coming to terms with nationalism. His
world was destroyed while Sir Kinahan Cornwallis looked away
during the sack of Baghdad in 1941, mine as Earl Mountbatten of
Burma scuttled in New Delhi six years later with a stiff upper lip.[3]
How apt that Mountbatten should die at the hands of assassins from
the Irish Republican Army. In setting out to destroy by violence
what little remains of Great Britain, they follow his cause as they
follow his example.

Fond memories of the British Empire, of what it might and ought
to have been rather than what it was, and the knowledge that
whatever its faults it was a better place to live in than the states that
followed it, most obviously in the Middle East, cannot atone in the
eyes of Professor Kedourie for its failure to live up in the Middle East
to its predecessor, the Ottoman Empire. Much of his work on Middle
Eastern politics follows from the assumption that what the British
destroyed – the political framework of a stable, orderly, multinational community – they had a duty to replace. They had been
happy to pose as Moguls, why not as Ottomans? In the Middle East
and in India they should have recognized nationalism for what it was:
the vocabulary of an élite, borrowed from the West as the means of
oppressing fellow countrymen. National states are fictions, sometimes
necessary, sometimes viable fictions, but in the Middle East dangerous because unstable fictions. For stability, empires are needed, ruled
by governments capable of adjudicating fairly between groups with
varied interests often in conflict. In Canada the imperial government
is referred to, disparagingly, as 'Ottawa'. Nor dare one call Canada
an empire: confederation is the chosen euphemism. Canadians,
however, do have the good sense to forgo nationalism for bilingualism
and multiculturalism.

Professor Kedourie's lifetime interest in the relationship between
Western – particularly British – imperialism and political conditions
in the Middle East, how each affected and was affected by the other,
provides the theme running through and linking these essays written
in his honour. The theme is presented in six variations. How did
Islam and the West perceive one another? What, how much, and why
did Islam borrow from the West? What were the consequences of
borrowing, and how far did they cause a crisis in the Muslim world?
How did the British exploit the crisis and what techniques of
management did they employ? How did the international system

2

affect local politics in the Middle East? And how far did local politics, in turn, affect the working of the international system? Here is presented a world of clerks: travellers, ministers, ambassadors, proconsuls, generals, journalists, lawyers, and even an historian. What they wrote to one another was real enough to change a great many lives.

At different times, Islam and Christendom each reflected a mirror image of the other. For both, Europe first denoted a geographical area, only later turning into the symbol of a civilization. As Bernard Lewis explains in his survey of changing Islamic attitudes to the West, Islam as well as Christendom thought the other barbarous, insignificant, yet not to be ignored, as both shared a taste for the curious. Before Columbus, Muslims doubted whether Christians had anything to sell that they might wish to buy: in the nineteenth century, Christians looking towards the Ottoman Empire shared the same doubt. Such similarities, however, fail to disguise a dissimilar approach to conquest. Rudolph Peters asks whether war is not the normal relationship between Islam and outsiders who have not appealed for a truce. If this is so, the Camp David Agreement between Egypt and Israel cannot be justified, despite the ingenious pronouncements issued by religious scholars at the bidding of Anwar Sadat.

If Islam expects in theory to live at war, the Christian West expects in theory to live at peace, to justifiy its conquests to itself, if to nobody else, by its expectation of being appreciated. There are exceptions to this rule, of course. Francis R. Nicosia offers one in his study of the Middle Eastern policy of the Third Reich. Hitler, for whom race overrode everything, saw Arabs as inferior, because Semitic. No offers were to be made to them; no disappointments suffered on their behalf. The disappointment felt by the British, in contrast, was often acute. Consider Gordon Martel's portrait of the young Arnold Toynbee. Confident in the superiority of progressive Western civilization, he despises the Ottomans in the First World War for joining the wrong side in the crusade for democracy and nationality. A Wilsonian before Woodrow Wilson, certain that the panacea of self-determination will lead all other states to turn themselves into copies of a Great Britain in which wealth has been spread more fairly, he jumps into history wearing the clothes and carrying the intellectual baggage of one of Professor Kedourie's immortalized villains, the dreaded Stratford de Redcliffe.[4] The Ottomans must change. It will be good for them. It will be good for Great Britain to show them how to change.

The shift in power from Islam to the West during the violent rivalry that has constituted their relationship was first seen in the willingness of Muslim states to seek Western guidance about fighting. The first phase of modern Western imperialism came about, according to Lewis, by invitation, as it were, when the Ottomans, pricked on by their defeats by the Russians, turned to the West for models of military reform and later for support. In the nineteenth century they looked to Germany for their model, as who, eventually, did not. Von der Goltz and Liman von Sanders were symbols of an unbeaten and apparently invincible regime. For the Ottomans, however, the search for rejuvenation by victory in battle proved a failure. The search itself demanded changes in the education system which turned out to be far-reaching; the attempt to mitigate the failure led to almost as far-reaching changes in the style of government.

The Muslim states, having formerly been leaders in science, might naturally expect to import uninfected, as it were, any discoveries developed from their previous exports. How much else could they expect to import from the West without creating more problems than they solved? Roderic H. Davison demonstrates in his study of Ottoman diplomatic practice that by the end of the nineteenth century the Ottoman Empire had adopted most of the trappings and much of the substance of Western diplomacy. The advantage from doing so seemed obvious: the Concert of Europe, joined formally by the Ottomans in 1856, existed to preserve the existence of its members. The Ottomans, however, may have joined the Concert at the moment it fell apart. It did little to defend Austria against Sardinia or Prussia, nothing to prevent the revocation of the Black Sea Clauses in 1870, and when it acted at the Congress of Berlin in 1878, overturning the treaty of San Stefano seemingly on the Ottoman Empire's behalf, her ostensible friends, Austria-Hungary and Great Britain, soon proved a greater menace to her than Russia, her avowed enemy.

The Ottomans, like the rulers of all states best served by the *status quo*, regularly tried to apply the terms of treaties long after the circumstances the terms had once represented had disappeared. Nor did they always interpret the terms correctly. Whereas the Ottomans relished the Western principle of non-intervention, the Concert had, in fact, stood for the opposite principle: intervention by members in support of other members endangered by revolt. The Greek Rebellion, however, had taught the Ottomans that non-intervention was all they could hope for. The doctrine might at least ensure that they were-left alone to cope with disaffected groups such as the Armenians as best they could.

The most striking effects of the Ottoman Empire's membership of the Concert of Europe were to be seen in her redefinition of herself as a multinational secular state – rather than, as formerly, an Islamic state – and therefore as a state where, in a stridently nationalist age, no oppressed minorities were to be found. Whether or not any of the minorities who together made up the entire population of the state were oppressed, many of them called upon outsiders for support.[5] The Concert of Europe in theory buttressed the Ottoman Empire, but may in fact first have weakened her, then destroyed her. In giving its members the right of automatic interest in all its affairs, the Concert also expected the right to be exercised. The Ottomans lived up to their roles as both member of the Concert and Great Power when declaring war alongside Germany in 1914. Their choice of Germany may not have followed solely from the German predilections of the Young Turks. Germany, as Hitler would later prove, had both fewer substantive interests than the other Great Powers in the Middle East, while being able, as she had demonstrated at the congress of Berlin, to determine what went on in the region.

Paradoxically, at the moment in 1914 when the Ottoman Empire set out to play to the hilt the role of Great Power – for three years giving a remarkably good performance – she justified her role in Islamic terms and portrayed herself as an Islamic state as she had used to do. The vocabulary of Islam was used by both the Committee of Union and Progress and its Hashemite opponents, by the one to demand loyalty to, by the other revolt against, the sultan. As William L. Cleveland illustrates in his examination of the ideological role of Islam, each group offered parallel examples of its own achievements and the other's perfidy. The defeat of the British at Kut was portrayed by the CUP as the sort of success to be expected when all Islam fought side by side under the Ottoman banner. Who, then, asked the Hashemites, had been responsible for the disastrous losses in the Balkan Wars? When the CUP cited the loyalty of Indian Muslims to the caliphate to prove that the sultan was a legitimate ruler, the Hashemites merely rebels, the Hashemites replied that such

5

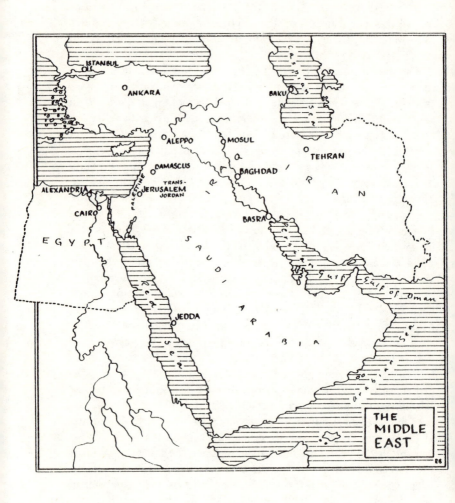

claims were undermined by the sultan's dependence on an infidel – a rash riposte for, if the sultan had become a German client, Husayn was making strenuous efforts to turn himself into a British one.

Finally, both the CUP and the Hashemites appealed to history. The hallmark of the power and unity of Islam was the Ottoman caliph, claimed one. Not so, replied the other: the Arabs had been disarrayed subject peoples until united by Muhammad, that is by an Arab. At this point the Hashemites had to concede what they appeared strenuously to deny: that their cause rested on a Western import. The CUP was accused of Turkish nationalism, of wishing to transform the Ottoman Empire into a Turkish state – rather as Prince Schwarzenburg had set out to turn the Austrian Empire into a German state after the débâcle of 1848-9. The one national group, however, entitled to claim the political leadership of Islam was the Arabs.

Cleveland suggests that such arguments tapped a deep well of Islamic sentiment, as significant as Arab or pan-Arab nationalism, which would resurface in the 1930s despite the triumph in the immediate aftermath of the First World War of groups bound up with the West. The sentiment was permanent, no doubt, but not all-embracing. As Peters explains in his analysis of jihad doctrine in Egypt under Anwar Sadat, the reappearance in politics of an Islamic vocabulary may partly depend upon a crisis developing out of too close relations with the West. Tension developed in Egypt after the reorientation to the West, accompanied by an open door economic policy, had flooded Egypt with Western consumer goods. The new bourgeoisie flaunted their wealth; the majority of the population, too poor to buy, derided what they could not afford as cultural imperialism.

The most interesting aspect for Peters of the tension leading eventually to the assassination of Sadat in 1981 is the relationship that had developed between foreign policy and revolution. If both the peace with Israel in 1979 and the inflow of consumer goods were proof of Western dominance, would the defence of Islam warrant the overthrow of the government as well as the denunciation of the illegitimate peace it had made? The doctrine of jihad, originally directed against the enemies of Islam, was reinterpreted by critics of Sadat in a manner echoing the claims made by the Hashemites against the Committee of Union and Progress. Sadat was accused of having betrayed Islam by turning himself into a lackey of western imperialism. Not all his critics necessarily wanted to remedy this development: those who gained most from his economic policy satisfied themselves by condemning the peace with Israel. Those who did seek a remedy, however, claimed that such apostasy transformed a duty normally borne by the whole community – to repel an invasion, for example – into one borne by every individual to rid the country of a ruler who has become an unbeliever.

The first, the most persistent, and according to Mordechai Abir in his study of Saudi Arabia, likely to be the most contentious variety of import into the Middle East from the West is education. What began in the Ottoman Empire as a remodelling of the curriculum to meet the demands of Western military training has developed in mid-century Saudia Arabia into two competing systems of higher education based on Islamic and Western principles. The Islamic universities are left under the control of the ulema in an attempt to alleviate the structural tension developing between Wahabi puritanism and Western-style modernization. The universities offering a so-called modern curriculum are staffed by foreigners who copy a foreign model, the British model until 1974, the American one thereafter.

Standards are kept low at Saudi universities for the reason that they are at Canadian ones, in an attempt to seem to provide opportunities for all. Jobs are even promised to all who graduate, but the jobs provided are deadening and lead nowhere. The best jobs go to graduates from United States universities or from the university operated by Aramco. This system perpetuates the class divisions it must seem to obliterate. Students from the country, for example, usually choose the Islamic universities, copying the behaviour of similar students in Egyptian universities who were easily attracted to the Islamic student groups suppressed by Sadat in 1979. According to Abir, the history of higher education in Saudi Arabia illustrates the transformation of the state into an American client. If declining oil revenues should compel the regime to cut the enormous education budget, a political crisis may arise out of the social tensions the expansion of the universities was intended to anticipate, if not resolve.

Until recently, that is until the Americans arrived, if one talked of Western imperialism in the Middle East, one meant the British. The French would dispute such a claim, of course, but never mind: they do not appear in these essays. The most remarkable aspect of

British imperialism is that by and large the British had developed no interests in the Middle East, substantive interests that is. The area was inhabited for them by symbols, and powerful symbols they turned out to be. As late as the Suez Crisis in 1956, when Great Britain destroyed her credibility as a Great Power, she did so in a failed quest for a victory in the Middle East. The choice of the Middle East as the site for British symbolic victories had been made as early as the war of the Second Coalition, in the hero's welcome given to Lord Nelson after his victory at the Nile and in the attempt to persuade Bonaparte in 1800 that the loss of Alexandria would undermine his victories over Austria at Marengo and Hohenlinden. The government of India, following the lead of London, tried to persuade the home government to take itself in with its own deception. The treaties made with Iran in 1801 were to seem to defend British India against made up enemies (the French, the Afghans, and the Russians) while in fact providing opportunities for expansion.

One of the most famous of such symbolic victories, as John S. Galbraith and Robert A. Huttenback explain in their study of British bureaucracy fighting – or rather not fighting – the First World War, was the plan to capture Baghdad that turned in April 1916 into the humiliating surrender of a British army to an Ottoman army at Kut. The capture of Baghdad was not thought to matter in itself. It would regild the armour tarnished so badly at Gallipoli, perhaps even stand in for, even if it could not actually bring about, a victory on the Western Front. Unfortunately a symbolic victory at Baghdad would demand a substantive sacrifice in India: the Indian Army would have to give up its heroic pose, the pose Englishmen in India had been required to take up as early as 1802. The Indian Army was not meant to fight: it was meant to give the appearance of being ready to fight. Seem ready enough and the Russians would not approach too close nor disaffected Indians seize the opportunity to rebel. In asking a pretend army to win a pretend victory, the British forgot that the Middle East happened to be inhabited by a formidable German ally.

One must not mock the British for the bureaucratic in-fighting and confusion in the Middle East that Galbraith and Huttenback describe so accurately. The conflicts between the government of India and the foreign office, between the Arab bureau and the political officer in Mesopotamia, and between the clients like Husayn, Ibn Saud, and the Idrisi, through whom they fought one another as vigorously as the enemy, represented long-standing differences between the two halves of a dual monarchy whose separate interests differed as radically as the interests of Hungary from those of Austria. Asking them to subordinate their separate interests to the common interest of winning the war would have been equivalent to surrendering the rewards of victory before victory was won. If everything one cherishes is to be given up for fighting, what will be left to fight for? The British, not used to fighting total war nor to fighting as a principal, had not prepared for such a role. Nor when it was forced upon them by 1917 did they learn the correct lesson from it. By their determination to defeat Hitler come what may, and to seek yet another symbolic victory in the Middle East, they bankrupted themselves without saving the Czechs or the Poles. They would march in the victory parades as United States mercenaries.

The British army officer in the Middle East in the First World War, bumbling around in a world he does not comprehend, is far to be preferred to know-alls like T.E. Lawrence and Ronald Storrs. A little ignorance and obstinacy is a much better guide in life than a little knowledge and enthusiasm. One need only read Martel's explanation of the origin of *The Chatham House Version* for proof of that. Arnold Toynbee took up the Arab cause from guilt. Martel sees the crucial moment in Toynbee's life to be his disappointment with the Versailles settlement. His guilt that he had escaped the trenches had been assuaged by the hope that his propaganda and later his work for the newly-established political intelligence department would help to create a Brave New World. An alliance with Islam had been needed to contain Germany and maybe to keep down the Greeks, whom Toynbee hated. When the Ottomans joined Germany instead of Great Britain, the mantle of Islam they had dropped was fitted on the Arabs in their place. At least Toynbee went into the war an honest racist imperialist, aware that the purpose of foreign policy is to better one's own country. In his disappointment with the Ottomans and guilt over the peace terms in the Middle East, he reformulated his position until doing as Arabs wanted took precedence over the interests of Great Britain – rather, as Elizabeth Monroe would have it, doing as the Arabs wanted was to be Great Britain's only interest in the Middle East.

Toynbee was not the only Englishman to feel guilt, but not everyone chose such malign forms of atonement. In the year following the First World War, the foreign office and the petroleum department were well aware – and occasionally remorseful – that they had done the Italians out of the spoils of victory in the Middle East promised to them for joining the allies instead of Germany. Not that they planned to make up the Italian loss; they resented every Italian suggestion that they should. Italian foreign policy in the twenties, especially under Mussolini, is usually treated as a joke; as the posturing of the greedily feckless, grabbing at everything and catching nothing. Marian Kent's amusing story of Anglo-Italian oil diplomacy in the Curzon era turns this picture upside down, however. One is left waiting in glee for the day the disdainful British will receive their come-uppance from Mussolini over Abyssinia.

The British demanded deference from the Italians, who were expected to go hand-in-hand with (as well as cap-in-hand to) the British in bargaining with the Turks for oil concessions, and whose requests for a reward for such good conduct was treated as blackmail – blackmail being anything sought by others that the British did not wish to give away. Italians were preferred to Turks and Bengalis: they were, after all, Europeans – but evidently only just. One senses that the British bullied the Italians every time they themselves had to give in to the Americans. The Italians were to be denied a share in the Turkish Petroleum Company just because the United States was powerful enough to insist on being granted one. The three British departments responsible had little difficulty agreeing to that.

The post-war negotiations with the Italians therefore provoked nothing remotely similar to the bureaucratic in-fighting between the British departments responsible for the war in the Middle East, which had led to some notoriously ill-planned expeditions to the Caucasus and Turkestan that tended, like Topsy, just to grow. They had been sent, however, in a good cause: to prepare for the loss of the war in Europe. The suddenness of Germany's collapse in 1918 took everyone by surprise. A moment earlier the Germans had been in the Ukraine and Ludendorff planning to ship submarines overland to the Caspian Sea in bits. Not all such expeditions were failures, nor were all men on the spot as irresponsible and difficult to control as Sir Percy Sykes, commander of the South Persia Rifles. The few officers sent instead of an army to cross the Jordan and deny to the French the area that became the Mandate of Transjordan, seem to have succeeded admirably. But as Mary C. Wilson shows in her study of Anglo-Transjordanian relations, the British found in the Amir Abdullah a collaborator of a type all too rare between the wars.

11

The Amir Abdullah made a success of his kingdom, rather less of a success of claiming the leadership of pan-Arab nationalism. One of his mistakes with the Arabs was to declare his support for Great Britain as soon as the Second World War had broken out. His rivals for leadership of the Arabs flirted with the Axis. None gained much for his trouble. Wilson shows that the British offered Abdullah no reward for his loyalty, or nothing he thought worth having. Ever since his bargain with Winston Churchill in 1921, by which he accepted Transjordan only, as he hoped, as a temporary halt on the road to Damascus, Abdullah had looked to the British to help him to realize his dreams of territorial aggrandizement. They looked to him, however, merely to keep order in a strategically important buffer zone, standing between Palestine and the Wahabi and helping to provide an all-Red aeroplane route from the Mediterranean to the Indian Ocean. Far from valuing Abdullah as a potential leader of the Arabs, they cherished him precisely because Transjordan was too poor, the structure of its society too traditional and tribal, to support the superstructure of a would-be nation state. Abdullah was to live contentedly on his subsidy from Great Britain.

That Abdullah had made a shrewder choice than some of his rivals, Rashid Ali and the mufti of Jerusalem, ought to have been clear long before 1939 from the tergiversations of German policy so clearly described by Nicosia in his account of the work of Fritz Grobba, the German minister at Baghdad. The Arabs who turned to Germany for support against Great Britain and France were attracted by Germany's traditional lack of interest in the Middle East. Arab nationalism, however, collided with Hitler's goals in two oddly complementary ways. The expulsion of the Jews from Germany easily overrode an interest in humouring Arab nationalism to embarrass the British. Even such small embarrassments as Hitler was willing to countenance – selling a few arms to the Iraqis and making a few inflammatory speeches – were intended to encourage the British to appease Germany in Europe rather than to signal a challenge to their paramount influence in the Middle East. Hitler looked East on the Continent. British dominance of most of the Middle East and British control over India – for Hitler held the Indian Congress Party at the same distance as the Arabs and for the same mixture of racial and geopolitical reasons – seemed a small price to pay for the conquest of *Lebensraum* in eastern Europe.

Even when Hitler quarrelled with the British, he did not take up with the Arabs. The territories they claimed for their national states were assigned to Mussolini or Vichy France. One of the few sensible aspects of the conduct of Europeans in the Middle East between the wars was their refusal to allow the Arabs to turn them against one another. Just as the Germans held back from trying to take advantage of the British in Iraq and Saudi Arabia, the Wafd party in Egypt failed in its attempt to obtain French and Italian support against the British in Egypt by withholding support for Arab nationalists in Syria and Tripoli. As James Jankowski explains, however, in his account of the transformation of the Wafd from a parochial Egyptian political party into the would-be leaders of a regional bloc, the extent of the transformation must not be exaggerated. The Wafd represented an imperialist's rather than a nationalist's dream. After the Wafd's disappointment with the Italians and the French, it moved far enough from its dismissal of the Peninsula Arabs as zeros to agree to co-operate with the other Arab states. Arabs should co-operate against Western imperialism, their common enemy. They should not expect the struggle to forge a common identity, but rather to strengthen individually the separate Arab states. The Wafd of course expected Egypt to be treated as *primus inter pares* by other Arabs. One of its spurs to action during the Second World War was a determination to prevent Nuri al-'Said from stepping into the pan-Arab shoes formerly worn by Faysal and coveted by Abdullah.

If the Arabs did not co-operate with one another – Abdullah because he was tied too firmly to the British, the Egyptians because, until the flow of oil turned the balance of power in the Arab world upside down, they despised the Saudis as greatly as they resented the British – and if the Western imperial powers, even if they did not co-operate, did not seek to take advantage of one another, why should the British have been expected to appease Arab nationalists? Wilson shows that Transjordan did not have the makings of a nationalist state, Jankowski that the Wafd, though nationalist, hardly saw itself as Arab and definitely not as pan-Arab, and Cleveland that the Arab revolt had not relied on nationalist rhetoric to legitimize itself. Was Arab nationalism bound to be recognized as the force of the future?

The limits to the nationalism of the Arab cause is most dramatically delineated here by Joseph Kostiner, who portrays Husayn's dream of an Arabic-Islamic empire as no more realistic than Abdullah's. Both needed and both failed to acquire Syria. The goal was unrealistic for Husayn for two complementary but entirely different reasons. Syria belonged to the French (in their eyes, anyway, and in British eyes). The Arab revolt was valued, by anyone who did value it, for helping to weaken the Central Powers, not for embarrassing the Allies. Husayn had to hope to be given Syria, because the structure of the Hashemite state and his longstanding feuds with his rivals in the Peninsula would prevent him from capturing it unaided. His own empire was merely an expanded version of the traditional tribal confederation, inherently incapable of concerting a sustained drive to reach a distant goal. Rivals such as Ibn Saud and the Idrisi would not help him, although neither would they try at that time to destroy him. The war provided all three of them with an opportunity to take advantage of the backing of their British patron to expand their local spheres of influence, without joining fully in the attack on their patron's enemy and their own suzerain. Why, therefore, take sides? The Ottomans had survived such crises too often, and too many other formerly outlying parts of the Ottoman Empire offered convincing proof that bids for independence led straight to the suffocating embrace of a European Power. Maybe the Hashemites were not making a bid for independence rather than autonomy. If they were making one, however, they deserved to follow the peshwa and the nizam of Hyderabad into the welcoming arms of the British. And, like their Indian predecessors, if they were given less than they expected – talk of the promises given in wartime would be irrelevant even if it were true – they were given more than they had earned.

Yet the British did appease Arab nationalism unduly, and one or two hints are given in these essays to explain why. In Egypt, for example, the Wafd borrowed the Western doctrine of self-determination – to which the British had agreed but had not meant to apply – and returned it to them in a form they found difficult to brush aside. Similarly, Husayn and Abdullah made hay with the notoriously meaningless so-called promises given to them by Sir Henry McMahon and Winston Churchill. The Germans made no such mistakes. Dr Grobba was forbidden to do anything for the Arabs that might offend the British beyond making them fulsome offers of sympathy. Nicosia makes plain that Grobba's suggestion that Ibd Saud could be turned into an effective German client was promptly rebuffed. Even discounting the Arabs' racial inferiority, they were thought by Hitler likely to prove a burden rather than an asset in the event of a war.

Here lies the oddity of the British. Having throughout the nineteenth century proclaimed their own liberalism to be a universal panacea, they abandoned it after the First World War, but nevertheless permitted their own puppets, parrotting their platitudes, to tie up their masters with their own strings. Such is the price of too eager a confidence in progress. Such a development ought to have been prevented in the interests of stability, order, and safe private life.[6] Preventing it would, of course, have required the courage to exercise control, to insist that private life must be placed ahead of political life – and by the 1920s such exertion proved beyond the capacity of the British. How fortunate to be able to reach this conclusion. One would not wish to blow a trumpet for pan-Arab nationalism in a volume of essays written in honour of Elie Kedourie. Would one ever wish to blow such a trumpet?

NOTES

1. Elie Kedourie, *Islam in the Modern World and Other Studies* (London, 1980), p. 299.
2. Michael Arlen, *The Green Hat* (London, 1924), ch. 1.
3. See Elie Kedourie, 'The Sack of Basra and the *Farhud* in Baghdad', in *Arabic Political Memoirs and Other Studies* (London, 1974), pp. 283-314; and 'Scuttling an Empire', *Commentary* (December 1985), 45-50.
4. See Elie Kedourie, *England and the Middle East: The Destruction of the Ottoman Empire, 1914-1921* (reprinted Hassocks, Sussex, 1978), pp. 9-19.
5. See Elie Kedourie, 'Minorities', in *The Chatham House Version and Other Middle Eastern Studies* (London, 1970), pp. 286-316.
6. See Elie Kedourie, 'Arabic Political Memoirs', in *Arabic Political Memoirs*, pp. 177-205.

II

ISLAM AND THE WEST

Bernard Lewis

> There was nothing unreasonable in believing that the Muslim
> world would attain the power and prosperity of Europe by
> the same methods Europe had used, and that this could be
> done without endangering any of the essential values of
> Islam.
>
> Elie Kedourie[1]

Until the nineteenth century, Muslims commonly spoke neither of
the West nor of Europe when they wished to designate the Western
or European world. The term West, when used in a cultural and
political sense, was applied inside and not outside the Islamic
oecumene. In the form *maghrib* – literally the land of the sunset – it
designated North Africa west of Egypt, that is the western part of
the Islamic world, contrasted with *mashriq*, the eastern half or land
of the sunrise. The term Europe occurs in a few places in early Arabic
geographical literature, then disappears. It entered through trans-
lations from the Greek, as part of the Greek geographical system of
continents, which was adopted in a fragmentary form by Muslim
geographical writers and dropped at an early date. Even when it was
used, the term Europe was purely geographical, and was never
injected with the cultural, historical, and latterly even political
content which the names of the continents acquired in European and
subsequently, under European influence, in universal usage.

For Muslims – as also for most medieval but few modern
Christians – the core of identity was religion, rather than nation,
country, or continent, and the basic divisions of mankind were
religiously determined.

In discussions of the inhabitants of the outside world in general,
the commonest designation until the nineteenth century, and in some
regions later, was *kuffar*, unbelievers. Where greater precision was
needed in distinguishing between different groups of unbelievers or

different political entities among them, Muslim historians tended to use ethnic rather than territorial terms. The peoples of Christian Europe are variously referred to as Romans (*Rum*), Slavs (*Saqaliba*), and, for the inhabitants of western Europe, Franks – a term which no doubt reached the Arabs via Byzantium, and was transmitted by the Arabs to the Persians, Turks, and other Muslim peoples. This practice of referring to the peoples of Christendom by ethnic names parallels the Western practice, until comparatively modern times, of denoting Muslims by such ethnic terms as Moors, Turks, and Tartars, in different parts of Europe.

The Muslim perception of these Western or European or Frankish lands passed through several phases. In the earliest Muslim accounts of Western Europe, mostly in geographical writings, these countries appear as remote and exotic, also as backward and unimportant. This perception was not greatly changed when the Westerners forced themselves on Muslim attention in Spain, Sicily, and Syria, and established direct contact in a number of ways.

In so far as there was a scholarly or scientific interest in the West, it was geographical. Muslim historians were not interested in the history of the outside world which, as they understood the value and purpose of history, lacked both value and purpose. Muslim theologians were little concerned with Christian doctrines – why after all should they be interested in an earlier and superseded form of God's revelation? And for the few that were interested, better information was more easily accessible among the many Christian communities living in the lands of Islam. There was no interest in the sciences and arts of Europe. They knew there was nothing of the one; they assumed there was nothing of the other. Only the geographers show some interest in the West, and even that a limited one. One geographical writer even apologizes for devoting some attention to these remote and uninteresting places. His excuse is the need for completeness.[2]

This indeed is the key to such interest as existed. Geography by definition should be universal, and a complete geographical survey must therefore include even the benighted and insignificant barbarians beyond the western limits. Some of these accounts include human as well as physical geography. Writers give some ethnological data, at times approaching almost an anthropology of the barbarian neighbours of Islam. Their sources of information were both written and oral. The written information came mainly from ancient Greek writings, from which Muslim scholars derived their first notions of the configuration of the European continent and islands. Oral information came from such few travellers as ventured from the Islamic world to Europe and back – pilgrims, merchants, and an occasional diplomatic envoy.

The scientific, geographical interest was supplemented by another motive, a liking for the strange and wonderful (al-'ajib wal-gharib). There was a general taste for curious and wonderful stories that found its apotheosis in the *Thousand and One Nights*. Travellers from the East to Europe, like travellers from Europe to the East in another age, had no difficulty in finding wonders and marvels and curious tales with which to regale their readers. This element continues into comparatively modern times. Thus, an Ottoman janizary officer who visited Vienna in the early eighteenth century adorns his otherwise factual, prosaic account of his trip with strange and wonderful stories of miracles performed during the Turkish siege and retreat some years previous to his visit.[3]

Practical and material interest in western Europe was for long very limited. Until the discovery of America, the colonization of south and south-east Asia and the consequent enrichment of the maritime powers, western Europe had very little to offer by way of exports. English wool and a few other small items are occasionally mentioned in Muslim sources, but they do not seem to have been of great significance. For most of the Middle Ages the most important export to the lands of Islam from Europe was, as from tropical Africa, slaves. They were imported in great numbers across both the northern and southern frontiers of Islam. Both north and south of the Islamic lands slaves were sometimes taken in war, sometimes seized by raiders, sometimes – with increasing frequency – offered for sale by African or European slave merchants. The supply of slaves from western Europe was eventually reduced to a mere trickle, acquired through the efforts of the Barbary corsairs; the supply of east Europeans continued for much longer, as a result of the Ottoman wars in south-eastern Europe and the raids of the Crimean Tartars among the Russians, Poles, and Ukrainians. There is little evidence, however, that these white slaves from Europe had any great effect on Muslim perceptions or ways, any more than did the much greater numbers of black slaves imported from tropical Africa.

Another important element in the Muslim perception of western Europe, from the Middle Ages onwards, was the military. Muslim visitors to Europe looked around them, as men do in hostile or potentially hostile territory, and noted information of military value, such as the location of roads, bridges, passes, and the like. The early triumphs of the Crusaders in the east impressed upon Muslim war departments that in some areas at least Frankish arms were superior, and the inference was quickly drawn and applied. European prisoners of war were set to work building fortifications; European mercenaries and adventurers were employed in some numbers, and a traffic in arms and other war materials began which has grown steadily in the course of the centuries. As early as 1174, Saladin wrote a letter to the caliph in Baghdad justifying his action in encouraging Christian commerce in the territories which he had reconquered from the Crusaders and in buying arms from the Christian states. 'Now', he says, 'there is not one of them that does not bring to our lands his weapons of war and battle, giving us the choicest of what they make and inherit...'[4] The result, he goes on to explain, was that these Christian merchants were supplying him with all kinds of armaments, to the advantage of Islam and the detriment of Christendom. The Christian church was of the same opinion, but all its efforts and denunciations failed to prevent the steady growth of this trade. Centuries later, when the Ottoman Turks were advancing into south-eastern Europe, they were always able to buy much needed equipment for their fleets and armies from the Protestant powers, and even obtain financial cover from Italian banks.

All this, however, had little or no influence on Muslim perceptions and attitudes, as long as Muslim armies continued to be victorious. The sultans bought war *matériel* and military expertise for cash, and saw in this no more than a business transaction. The Turks in particular adopted such European inventions as handguns and artillery and used them to great effect, without thereby modifying their view of the barbarians from whom they acquired these weapons. The real change in attitude began when the Ottoman and later other Muslim governments found it necessary to adopt not just European weapons, but European ways of using them. In the early eighteenth century the great French soldier Maurice de Saxe, observing battles between the Austrians and Ottomans in south-eastern Europe, put his finger on the main reason for the Ottoman lack of success: 'What they [the Turks] lack is not valor, not numbers, not riches; it is order, discipline, and the manner of fighting.'[5] The important thing was 'la manière de combattre', and it was this that gave the European enemies of the Ottomans their growing superiority in the battlefield. The Turkish commanders had certainly not read the *Rêveries* of Maurice de Saxe, but they had independently come to the same conclusion, and initiated a process of change which began as a limited military reform and culminated as a far-reaching social and cultural transformation.

Defeat in battle is the most perspicuous of arguments, and the lesson was driven home in a series of heavy blows. In the west, the Muslims were finally expelled from Spain and Portugal, and the triumphant Christians followed their former rulers into Africa and then into Asia. In the east, the Russians threw off the Tartar yoke and, like the Portuguese in the west but with far greater success, pursued their former masters into their homelands. With the conquest of Astrakhan in 1554, the Russians were on the shores of the Caspian; the following century they reached the northern shores of the Black Sea, thus beginning the long process of conquest and colonization which incorporated vast Muslim lands in the Russian Empire and brought the Russians as near neighbours to the heartlands of the Middle East. In central Europe the last great Ottoman attack failed before the walls of Vienna in 1683, and in the retreat that followed, the Ottomans lost Budapest, which they had held for a century and a half, and began their long rearguard action through the Balkan peninsula.

These changes gave a new importance to those elements in the Islamic world which were in one sense or another intermediaries between Islam and Christendom. They were of several kinds. The first group to achieve significance were the refugees who came from Spain and Portugal seeking asylum in North Africa and in the Ottoman lands of the eastern Mediterranean. These consisted of both Muslims and Jews, including some who had submitted under pain of death to enforced Christianization, and had then fled to more tolerant lands in order to declare their true religions. The Muslim Moriscos and the Jewish Marranos coming from Spain and Portugal to North Africa and the Ottoman lands brought skills, knowledge, and some wealth from what were then among the most advanced countries in Europe. Another group of newcomers from Europe, smaller but not unimportant, were those whom the Christians called renegades and whom the Muslims called *muhtedi*, one who has found the right path. Not all these adventurers found it necessary to adopt Islam. Some entered the Ottoman service while retaining their

previous religions. These newcomers – converts, adventurers, mercenaries, and others – helped to initiate what one may now begin to call
the Europeanization of Turkey.

By the seventeenth century the flow of newcomers from Europe,
whether renegades or refugees, was drying up. But if Europeans were
no longer coming to the Middle East, a new element was appearing
to take their place: Middle Easterners going to Europe. These were
from the Middle Eastern Christian communities who began to
establish contacts with western Europe in various ways, notably by
sending their sons to Italian and later other European colleges and
universities for education. The Greeks were the leaders in this
movement; other Christian communities followed. The Roman
Catholic Church had always been interested in the eastern Christians.
In the late sixteenth century the Vatican became increasingly active
among these communities, sending missionaries to work among them
in Lebanon and elsewhere, and founding colleges in Italy for the
study of their languages and the education of their clergy. Their
direct impact was in the main limited to the Uniate churches,
breakaway groups of the eastern churches that had entered into
communion with Rome and established close ecclesiastical and
educational links with the Vatican. The indirect influence of these
contacts spread to their orthodox co-religionists and even to their
Muslim neighbours. The school and order founded by the Catholic
Armenian Mekhitar became for a time the centre of Armenian
intellectual life; the Uniate Maronites of Lebanon, the first Arabic-
speaking community to communicate directly with the West, were
later to play a crucial role in opening the Arab world to Western
intellectual influence.

The Maronite impact on the Arab world did not become important
until the nineteenth century. Long before that, Greek and Armenian
Christians, for whom Turkish was a second or sometimes even a first
language, were filtering Western knowledge and ideas to the dominant Ottoman Turks.

Apart from these various Westernized or Westernizing Middle
Eastern Christians, there was, increasingly, a direct European presence which became more influential as the real power relationship
between Europe and the Islamic world changed to the disadvantage
of the latter. At first Westerners came mainly as traders or diplomats
(the latter were for long seen by the Ottomans as also being
concerned principally with trade). From the eighteenth century

onwards, another group of Europeans begin to appear – military and naval officers assisting in the training of the new style Ottoman forces. At first, these were hired on individual contracts; later they were serving officers seconded by their home governments.

All these changes made for increased contacts between Muslims and Europeans. Educated Greeks, Armenians, and Maronites, able to speak and write a Western language as well as having a good command of Turkish or Arabic, created a possibility for genuine cultural exchanges, beyond the limited political, military, and commercial interpreting of earlier times. European instructors in Muslim military academies made it necessary, for the first time, for young Muslim cadets to view Europeans as dispensers of useful knowledge and not merely as infidels and barbarians. And the steady advance of European power – penetration, encroachment, domination, in some areas even annexation – was finally bringing increasing numbers of Muslim statesmen and soldiers to the view that a better understanding of this Western world was essential to their survival.

One noticeable change is in the literature of travel to Europe. Until the seventeenth century we have almost no information about Muslim travellers to Europe. While European travellers to the East – soldiers, pilgrims, merchants, captives – had already produced a considerable literature, there was nothing comparable on the Muslim side. Few Muslims travelled voluntarily to the lands of the infidels. Even the involuntary travellers, the many captives taken in the endless wars by land and sea, had nothing to say after their ransom and return, and perhaps no one to listen. In this they differed markedly from their European counterparts, whose reports of their adventures seem to have been in some demand. An Arab prisoner of war in Rome in the ninth century, an Andalusian diplomatic visitor to France and Germany in the tenth, a princely Ottoman exile in France and Italy in the fifteenth, these and one or two others have left a few notes and fragments which constitute almost the whole of the Muslim travel literature in Europe.

The first sign of a change came in the far west of Islam, in Morocco. This was the first Muslim country to perceive, and indeed to feel, the rise and expansion of European power. The Moroccans had seen the loss of Spain, for many centuries a part of the Arab Muslim world, and had received Spanish Muslim exiles in their own land. They had undergone invasion by both Spaniards and Portuguese and had had difficulty maintaining themselves. Already in the seventeenth century, the Moroccans were facing problems which Turks, Egyptians, and Persians did not have to confront until centuries later. This experience, and the resulting awareness of danger, is reflected in a series of Moroccan reports written by ambassadors to Europe and more particularly to Spain.

The earliest of these Moroccan ambassadors to leave a detailed record of his travels and impressions was the vizier al-Ghassani, who was sent to Spain by the sultan of Morocco in 1690-1. His book, the first description of Spain by a Muslim visitor since the end of the Reconquest, is of quite remarkable interest. His comments on Spanish life and affairs reveal him as a man of intelligence and discernment, keenly interested in what he saw, and with considerable powers of observation and analysis. His discussion is not limited to the moment and place of his mission but extends outwards to cover other countries in western Europe, and backwards to embrace some centuries of European history. In addition to the political and military information which was presumably the primary concern of his government, he also devoted some attention to religious matters, including discussions of the confessional and the Inquisition; of social and economic matters, including some very revealing comments on Spanish customs and attitudes; and some perceptive remarks on the economic effects on Spain of the wealth of the Indies.[6] Al-Ghassani was followed by several other Moroccan ambassadors in the course of the eighteenth century. One of them, Muhammad ibn 'Uthman al-Miknasi, gives what is probably the first account in Arabic of the American revolution and the establishment of the United States.[7]

Ottoman travellers to Europe are, as one would expect, more numerous than Moroccans, but it was some time before their reports reached the level of interest and information that the Moroccan reports offer. Three examples may suffice, to illustrate successive phases in the Ottoman perception of the West and in the Ottoman manner of presenting their perceptions to their readers at home.

The first of the three was the famous traveller Evliya Çelebi, who went to Vienna in 1665 in the suite of a Turkish ambassador, Kara Mehmed Pasha. Evliya still represents an Islamic empire conscious of its unchallengeable superiority in religion and consequently also in wealth and power. In his comments he appears as amused, sometimes even playful, occasionally disdainful. But at the same time he offers something clearly different from the earlier tradition of unconcern and contempt. His description is very detailed and reveals to his Ottoman reader a society with many positive features – a well-disciplined army, a fair and efficient system of administration of justice, prosperous towns and countryside, and a thriving capital city. In general he avoids explicit comparisons between Ottoman and Austrian situations; the exceptions are for example his preference for European clocks and watches to those in use in Turkey, or his praise for the well-stocked and well-kept library of St. Stephen's Cathedral in Vienna, which he contrasts favourably with the mismanaged mosque libraries of Cairo and Istanbul.[8]

Evliya, even when he has something to praise, still reflects a society that is self-assured to the point of complacency. Yirmisekiz Mehmed Efendi, who went to Paris as ambassador in 1720-1, reflects a very different situation. Between Evliya's journey to Vienna and his own trip to Paris, much had happened. The Ottomans had withdrawn from Vienna and had lost Budapest, and their defeats at the hands of the Austrians had been sealed in the peace treaties of Carlowitz (1699) and Passarowitz (1718), in the second of which Mehmed Efendi himself had participated as Ottoman plenipotentiary. Even worse, the Ottomans were now acutely aware of a new and terrible danger, not yet perceived in Evliya's day – the threat of Russia from the north. Not surprisingly, therefore, Mehmed Efendi looked at France with a different eye, not that of a confident visitor from an unchallengeably superior power, but the anxious eye of an emissary from a state threatened on several sides. He came to Paris with a different purpose, seeking help and guidance and seeing for the first time in a west European country a possible model for reform, perhaps even, in a very limited sense, an ally against his sovereign's enemies.

Mehmed Efendi was interested in many things. He describes the observatory, the scientific instruments, the practice of medicine in France, industry and manufactures, the network of communications by road and canal, bridges and locks, and even says something about cultural activities, such as the theatre and the opera. In general, Mehmed Efendi does not make explicit comparisons, still less recommendations for change in a Westernizing direction. But these are implicit in some of his descriptions of French institutions, practices, and ways. His son, who accompanied him and later had a distinguished official career of his own, even learned French. This was a remarkable and for long a unique accomplishment.[9]

A document recently made known supplies an interesting addendum to Mehmed Efendi's account of his journey. On his return to

Istanbul, he appears to have distributed a number of gifts to his colleagues, family, and friends. The new appetites which these aroused can be gathered from the list of items which the grand vizier shortly afterwards asked a French dragoman, going to Paris on leave, to bring with him on his return to Istanbul. They include optical instruments, eyeglasses, binoculars, microscopes, burning mirrors, Gobelin tapestries, small repeating watches, pictures of fortresses, towns, and gardens, as well as many other items. There was also, according to the dragoman in question, a verbal request for a thousand bottles of champagne and nine hundred bottles of burgundy. The Frenchman complied with most of these requests and in particular brought a thousand prints of fortresses and other scenes.[10]

The third example is 'Azmi Efendi, who went to Berlin as Ottoman ambassador in 1790. Between Mehmed Efendi's trip to Paris and his own journey to Prussia, the Ottoman position had again deteriorated, this time very sharply. A disastrous war with Russia had ended in the treaty of Kutchuk-Kainardji of 1774, which gave the Russians immense territorial and other gains. This was followed by the Russian annexation of the Crimea and the rapid extension of Russian power in the Black Sea area. In 'Azmi's report, Europeans appear as powerful and advancing rivals, posing a major threat to the empire. In order to guard against them it was necessary to study them and perhaps even – so as to accomplish this purpose – to imitate some of their ways.

By this time the idea of imitation was no longer new or entirely strange in Ottoman circles, since several eighteenth-century writers had advanced it in various forms. 'Azmi's report, after the normal description of his travels and activities, contains a detailed account of the kingdom of Prussia under subject headings – the administration of the country, the inhabitants, the high government offices, the treasury, the population, the government food stores, the military, the arsenal, and the artillery magazines. 'Azmi speaks of the Prussian economic effort to foster trade and establish industry and to maintain a sound and healthy treasury. The most important passages are those in which he describes the structure of the Prussian army, with its system of training, and the efficiency of the Prussian state organization, with its hierarchy of established and competent officials. 'Azmi was not content, like some of his predecessors, to convey his recommendations by hints and suggestions. Instead, he ends his report with a series of specific recommendations for the improvement of the Ottoman governmental and military apparatus, by adopting some of the best features of the Prussian system. In time 'Azmi's report came to be an important text for Ottoman officers and officials pressing for urgently needed reforms. One of the interesting features of his report is his description of the Prussian system as what would now be called a meritocracy, and his recommendation that this be adopted in place of the traditional Ottoman system of patronage and clientage.[11]

From the late eighteenth century and during the nineteenth century – the date and pace differ from region to region – the Islamic world was subjected to the devastating impact of Western power, techniques, and ideas. Some regions were conquered and became part of the European empires of Great Britain, France, Holland, and Russia. Even the Ottoman Empire and Iran, though never formally conquered or occupied, found their independence in effect severely curtailed.

The first major change affecting Muslim perceptions of the West was in the channels and media of communication. Where previously Muslim visitors to Europe, even in the age of Ottoman retreat, had been few and far between, they now became frequent and numerous. From the end of the eighteenth century, the Ottomans and later other Muslim states established resident diplomatic missions in European capitals, thus bringing into being a whole group of government officials with direct knowledge of a European country and, increasingly, of a European language. This last was of special significance. Whereas previously Muslims had had to rely almost entirely on non-Muslims or new converts to Islam for interpretation and translation, there now emerged – at first slowly and reluctantly, then with rapidly gathering momentum – a new élite of native Muslims with a command of at least one European language. Such knowledge, previously despised, became tolerable, then useful, and finally indispensable. In the early years of the nineteenth century the first student missions were sent from Egypt, Turkey, and Iran to European schools – at first mainly military, then over the whole range of education. These few hundred students played an important role after their return to their own countries. They were the outriders of a vast army of eager young Muslims who lived for a while in a European city and, as is the way of students, learned more from their fellow-students than from their teachers. In the Europe of the 1830s and 1840s, there was much that was interesting to learn.

One result of the lessons learned was that after the mid-century, diplomats and students were followed by a third category of Muslim visitors to Europe – political exiles. Most important among these were the Young Ottomans, a group of liberal patriots who wished to bring their country the benefits of Western-style constitutional and parliamentary government, in which they saw the talisman of Western success and power. Before long groups of Muslim exiles, publishing manifestos, newspapers, pamphlets, and books, became a familiar feature of the European scene.

Perhaps the most important single development was education – not only of increasing numbers of Muslim students going to Europe but also, to an ever greater extent, by the establishment of Western schools and colleges in the Muslim lands and eventually even the partial Westernization of the schools established by the Muslim governments themselves. An important part of this process was the extension of military training through the modernization – which at that time meant the Westernization – of the armed forces. Western military advisers came from many quarters. Prussia, later Germany, maintained a series of military missions in Turkey from 1835 to 1919, with far-reaching effects on the Turkish army.[12] British and French military and naval officers also played a role, though a smaller one, in Turkey and a somewhat greater one in some of the Arab countries. The ending of a major war in the Western world often provided a supply of experienced military officers suddenly rendered supernumerary, and seeking an outlet for their talents. After the Napoleonic Wars, many French officers were available for service in Egypt. At the end of the American Civil War, retired American officers began to undertake the retraining and reorganization of the Egyptian army. Russian military lessons to the Muslim armies were for most of the eighteenth and nineteenth centuries administered on the battlefield rather than in the classroom. There were, however, some Russian officers training the Persian gendarmerie, and in more recent times Soviet military missions have begun to play a major role in several Muslim countries.

In this new phase the number of Muslim visitors to Europe increased greatly, and so too did the literature produced by them. For a long time the prevailing attitude towards Europe was one of respect, even of admiration. Muslim writers naturally enough did not regard the new masters of the world with any great affection, nor were they prepared to concede them any real merit in what was for them the most important aspect of all – the religious, a term which at that time, for them, included the cultural and intellectual. The old attitude of uninformed contempt, while still surviving no doubt among those who stayed at home, virtually disappeared among those who ventured abroad. The main stimulus was still the perception of their own weakness and poverty and the desire to emulate and if possible equal the wealth and power of the Western world. This desire became the more acute as events demonstrated with increasing urgency the dangers to which this inequality exposed the Muslim world – the dangers of domination, of exploitation, even of conquest.

There were, however, some differences of opinion as to the nature of the lessons to be learned; there were still some difficulties in making those lessons palatable among the largely unconvinced and unpersuaded public at home. Among the earlier writers in this period of growing European domination, two themes predominate, both of them developments of themes already perceptible in earlier writings. They are respectively the military and the political. The one began as a concern with Western weapons, then with Western methods of warfare. This in turn developed into a concern with Western technology and eventually industry, as the realization spread that it was to no small extent on these that the superiority of Western armies depended. In the course of the nineteenth century, Muslim awareness of economic inferiority began to equal their awareness of the more dramatic and more obvious political and military weakness of the Islamic world, and some Muslim rulers began to be concerned with economic development along Western lines, not just as a support for better armies and navies, but for its own sake.

The second change was a growing interest in Western methods of government. At first Muslim visitors showed no interest whatever in this topic. Apart from a few passing references in medieval texts, a first brief account was given in the mid-seventeenth century by the well-known Ottoman scholar and polymath, Kâtib Çelebi. His information is scattered and fragmentary, on some points remarkably detailed, on others strikingly inaccurate. The book was never printed and is little known. Other Ottoman writers of the period show little or no interest in European affairs, even just across their border. Thus, the extremely voluminous Ottoman chronicles of the seventeenth century pay only the slightest attention to the events of the Thirty Years War, and even less to its causes and consequences. A brief reference to European laws and forms of government occurs in a

Persian book written in 1732. The writer notes with regret that he had been unable to accept the suggestion of an English sea-captain whom he had met to visit Europe where, he implies, they order these things better. It is not until the mid-eighteenth century that we find the first factual acount of European governments and armies, written and printed by a Hungarian convert to Islam who rose high in the Ottoman service.[13]

The last years of the century saw a major reform effort. A new printing press was installed in Istanbul, from which a number of books, both original and translated, were published; foreign officers in greater numbers were appointed as instructors in the military and naval schools; permanent Ottoman embassies were opened in London, Paris, Berlin, Vienna, and St. Petersburg, and the French – first through their embassy in Istanbul, then through their newly acquired bases in Greece and Egypt – began to disseminate information and ideas about the recent revolution in France. By the beginning of the nineteenth century, an Ottoman historian speaks approvingly of parliamentary institutions in the states of Europe, for which he uses the striking euphemism 'certain well organized states',[14] and suggests in a very tentative way that similar consultative institutions would have a place in the Ottoman governmental and administrative tradition. The idea of consultative and deliberative procedures is deep rooted in Islamic theory and Ottoman practice. What was new was the idea, imported from Europe, of freedom as a political and not merely a juridical concept – freedom in the sense of the rights of the subject against the state, rights to be enshrined in a code of laws and protected by the law and the judiciary. It was these notions that gave rise to the Muslim constitutional movement which grew steadily during the nineteenth century and reached its climax in the Persian and Ottoman constitutional revolutions of 1905 and 1908.

Since then there have been great disappointments. Western military methods did not win the hoped-for victories; Western economic and political panaceas brought neither the prosperity nor the freedom for which they had been prescribed. In a mood of outrage and revulsion, there has been a return to older perceptions and responses, and to many the West again appears as something alien, pagan, and noxious, still hostile, but no longer terrifying. For the time being Western values in general, and Western political ways in particular, enjoy little esteem or respect. But it would be rash to say that they are dead in the Islamic world.

NOTES

1. Elie Kedourie, *Islam in the Modern World and Other Studies* (London, 1980), p.7.
2. 'Umari, ed. M. Amari, 'Al-'Umari, Condizioni degli stati Cristiani dell' Occidente secondo una relazione di Domenichino Doria da Genova', *Atti R. Acad Linc. Mem.*, xi (1883), text p. 15, trans. p. 87.
3. F. von Kraelitz-Greifenhorst, 'Bericht über den Zug des Gross-Botschafters Ibrahim Pascha nach Wien im Jahre 1719', *Akademie der Wiss. Wien: Phil. Hist. Kl. Sitzungsberichte*, clviii (1909), 26-77.
4. Abu Shama, *Kitab al-Rawdatayn fi akhbar al-dawlatayn*, 2nd edition, ed. M. Hilmi Ahmad (Cairo, 1962), i, pt. 2, 621-2.
5. Maurice de Saxe, *Mes Rêveries* (1757), i. 86-7, cited in *War, Technology and Society in the Middle East*, ed. V.J. Parry and M.E. Yapp (London, 1975), p. 256.
6. Muhammad b. 'Abd al-Wahhab, al-Wazir al-Ghassani, *Rihlat al-wazir fi iftikak al-asir*, ed. and Spanish translation by Alfredo Bustani (Tangier, 1940). Bustani's edition is somewhat abridged. For a full French translation from a manuscript, see H. Sauvaire, *Voyage en Espagne d'un Ambassadeur Marocain* (Paris, 1884). On these Moroccan travellers in general, see Henri Pérès, *L'Espagne vue par les voyageurs musulmans de 1610 [sic: recte 1690] à 1930* (Paris, 1937).
7. Muhammad ibn 'Uthman al-Miknasi, *al-Iksir fi fikak al-asir*, ed. Muh. al-Fasi (Rabat, 1965).
8. Evliya, *Seyahatname* (Istanbul, 1314 A.H.), vii; cf. German translation, R.F. Kreutel, *Im Reiche des Goldenen Apfels* (Graz, 1957).
9. There are several editions of the embassy report of Mehmed Said, in both the old and new Turkish scripts, with some variations in the text. The book was first published in Paris and Istanbul with a French translation as *Relation de l'embassade de Mehmet Effendi à la cour de France en 1721 écrite par lui même et traduit par Julien Galland* (Constantinople and Paris, 1757). A new edition of Galland's version, without the text but with many additional documents, was edited by Gilles Veinstein: Mehmet Efendi, *Le paradis des infidèles* (Paris, 1981). On these authors, see further B. Lewis, *The Muslim Discovery of Europe* (New York, 1982); and Faik Resit Unat, *Osmanli sefirleri ve sefaretnameleri* (Ankara, 1968).
10. Cited by Veinstein, pp. 48-9.
11. 'Azmi, *Sefaretname 1205 senesinde Prusya Kirali Ikinci Fredrik Guillaum in nezdine memur olan Ahmed 'Azmi Efendinin'dir* (Istanbul, 1303 A.H.), p. 52. German translation by Otto Müller-Kohlshorn, *Azmi Efendis Gesandtschaftsreise an den preussischen Hof* (Berlin, 1918) (not seen).
12. On the German military missions to Turkey, see Jehuda L. Wallach, *Anatomie einer Militärhilfe: die preussisch-deutschen Militärmissionen in der Türkei 1835-1919* (Tel Aviv-Düsseldorf, 1976).
13. Ibrahim Müteferrika, *Usul al-hikem fi nizam al-umem* (Istanbul, 1144 A.H.); idem, French version, *Traité de la Tactique* (Vienna, 1769).
14. Sanizade, *Tarih* (Istanbul, 1290-1 A.H.), iv. 2-3.

III

HOW AND HOW NOT TO NEGOTIATE WITH IRAN: POSTURES OF POWER IN 1802

Edward Ingram

> It was an ambitious policy, but it was ill-judged and
> reckless. Ill-judged because ... it was highly
> speculative whether the British would in any way
> benefit.
>
> Elie Kedourie[1]

Some of the most entertaining as well as most rewarding essays written by Elie Kedourie are cautionary tales, in which innocent Europeans, stumbling around the dream world they mistake for the Middle East, fall into traps usually of their own making. Who will forget the dire penalties paid by the British for Ronald Storrs' fondness for classical allusion and T.E. Lawrence's fondness for Faysal? And like other cautionary tales, the essays illustrate how small incidents often disclose important truths. Here therefore, in emulation, is the tale of a small incident in Anglo-Iranian relations that occurred in 1802. It concerns the death of an Iranian envoy in a brawl at Bombay. Hardly worth recounting? Perhaps. As a result of it, however, the British failed to turn Iran into a protectorate, and the careers of two of Great Britain's most eminent proconsuls suffered a setback. More important, the British in India are shown taking a step down the road towards the White Man's Burden: determined, above all, to maintain the correct posture, in the confidence that what they offer must be appreciated, that where they lead, others must follow. The lesson to be learned from the incident? That one should beware in diplomacy of sacrificing substance to style.

The Iranian envoy, Haji Muhammad Khalil, arrived at Bombay on 27 May 1802. Supposedly merely breaking his journey *en route* to Calcutta, he quickly revealed that his understanding of the purpose of his mission differed radically from the interpretation the British were anxious to place on it. At the time of his arrival, the governor of Bombay, Jonathan Duncan, was away at Surat. His absence ought not to have mattered. The envoy repeatedly urged him, however, either to return to Bombay or to arrange a meeting up the coast. Told by Duncan that the summer was the best time of year for a voyage to Bengal and that he ought not to waste it, he replied that, on the contrary, he had heard it described as the worst time.[2] When the real 'cause of the ambassador's long lingering at Bombay came to light' in early July, it turned out to be three personal financial claims he was pressing against the British. Duncan was expected to back him against a former business partner at Madras, against the British agent at Bushire over the ownership of some land, and most important, to pay 'a large indemnification and reward' for the help he had supposedly given the British four years earlier. They had then been pretending to urge the shah of Iran to support a rebellion in Afghanistan; pretending to hope that he would prevent the amir from invading British India.[3] 'Where is the reward of assistance and tribulation', Muhammad Khalil asked Duncan, 'or the gladdening fruits of labour?'[4]

Muhammad Khalil's mission had one purpose other than the pressing of these claims: to exchange ratifications of the two Anglo-Iranian treaties negotiated the year before by John Malcolm at the end of the mission to Tehran which made him famous.[5] For such a task the haji had seemed an obvious choice. One of the principal merchants of Fars who bore the honorary title of chief merchant of Iran, he had made his money from trading to India, was highly recommended by Malcolm,[6] and was the nephew of the shah's chief minister, Haji Ibrahim Shirazi. Unfortunately for Muhammad Khalil, however, in one of the reverses of fortune Professor Kedourie finds symptomatic of Middle Eastern politics, a source of patronage turned overnight into a source of danger when the shah, soon after Malcolm's departure, dismissed his chief minister and had him boiled in oil. Such a moment was not one in which Haji Ibrahim's dependants were wise to be out of the country, or to be consolidating the British connnection he had promoted to recoup his failing political fortunes.

Haji Muhammad Khalil, whose journey to India took him fourteen months, had left Tehran at the end of January 1801 in the company of Malcolm, who had travelled home to India by way of Baghdad. At Baghdad, however, the two men had parted. On learning of his uncle's disgrace, Muhammad Khalil hesitated to proceed without first obtaining fresh instructions from the new ministers.[7] Even when he received such instructions early in December, he delayed at Bushire, arguing with the British agent and Duncan about the suitability to a man of his rank of the vessel sent to transport him to India. He had claimed from the start that he had undertaken the mission against his will.[8] Given the risk he took going on with it – not that he had a choice: to have refused would have been more risky – he expected to be handsomely repaid by the British rather than the shah.

Undertaken apparently with reluctance, and continued with risk but in the hope of gain, the mission ended in the envoy's untimely death. On the evening of 20 July 1802, he was shot while trying to break up a fight between his sepoy bodyguard and his Iranian attendants, described by the British agent at Baghdad as 'a set of scamps as not easily to be matched'.[9] Four of them were killed, including the envoy's son-in-law; five others were wounded. Bombay recorded as the cause of the fight their 'gross indecencies and vicious pursuits', in a word pederasty.[10] Tired of the boys they had brought with them, supposedly they had propositioned the sons of their sepoy bodyguard who, two days before the fight broke out, had complained of them to Muhammad Khalil. He had done nothing.

Although the incident at Bombay was straightforward, the British response to it quickly turned into a production number worthy of ending a first act. Minute guns were fired from the ramparts of Fort William; all three governments of British India and all of the residents accredited to the Indian states went into mourning for forty days; the officers and sepoys of the guard were placed under close arrest; and in the most significant gesture of all, on 11 August the governor-general sent Malcolm to Bombay to manage the crisis, as the government of Bengal perceived it – 'to alleviate the sorrows of the King's slaves', Malcolm told the shah's chief minister[11] – and directed Duncan to receive him with the honours due to an ambassador.[12] That the incident would cause trouble was clear from the start. Although the survivors of the brawl were persuaded that it could be blamed only on the sepoys who began it, they expected them to be punished with a severity commonplace in Iran but outmoded even among the violent British.[13] The trouble would be caused less by Iranian expectations of the British, however, than by British conceptions of how they ought to be seen to conduct themselves. *Raison d'état* would bow before *noblesse oblige*.

Five days after Malcolm's arrival at Bombay on 10 October, he reported to Bengal that 'All's well – we are going on swimmingly'. He had soon put right the mistakes in handling the incident made by the government of Bombay. According to Malcolm, 'an over-desire to conciliate had led ... [Duncan] into error ... from timidity – the rascals bullied him'.[14] The accusation that Duncan would pay too dearly for the incident was partly based on a question he had put to the governor-general. In the autumn of 1801 the agent at Bushire had hired a boat from Muhammad Khalil's brother-in-law to send dispatches to Basra. The agent at Basra had sent the boat on to Bombay, and during the voyage it had been plundered by Arab pirates. Basra had recommended compensation of 12,000 rupees; Bushire had recommended only 5,000. At any other time Duncan would have paid the smaller sum. Should he pay the larger, he asked, owing to the death of the envoy? Certainly not, came the reply from Bengal: loss at sea and the loss of a brother-in-law were separate claims to be settled separately.[15]

Despite Malcolm's bragging, Bombay rather than Bengal followed the more determined line with the Iranians, perceiving that what matters most on such occasions is speed. Duncan, who had been appointed governor of Bombay in 1795, would remain there until his death in 1811, because just as he was planning to retire, most of the money he had saved was lost by his agent. In time, he would deserve the reputation he earned for indecision. There was nothing indecisive, however, in the steps he took to prevent the death of the envoy from causing a crisis in Anglo-Iranian relations. A week after he returned to Bombay from Surat on 5 August and on the same day Malcolm was appointed, Duncan told the British agent at Bushire to make to the government of Iran whatever explanations seemed necessary and enclosed letters to be forwarded to the shah and his ministers. Nor did Duncan countermand his instructions when he learned that Malcolm was on his way from Calcutta. Delaying while awaiting his arrival 'might be productive of serious ill-consequences'.[16]

Bombay did not expect the provincial government of Fars or the imperial government at Tehran to be upset by what had happened.

Duncan took steps to ensure that the letters written home by the survivors of the brawl were 'sufficiently favourable in tenour', and he warned the captain of the ship delivering them to Bushire not to let anybody ashore until the British agent had decided how best to break the news to the local authorities.[17] What most worried Bombay was the chance of a riot at Bushire. The inhabitants of Bushire, either enraged or pretending to be enraged at the killing of Muslims by infidels, might attack the British factory, destroying or looting the merchandise in store there. Such an event would upset Bombay more than it would have upset the governments of Bengal or Madras, because Bombay officials, unlike officials elsewhere in India, might still trade on their own account. Trade with Iran and the gulf had been declining in the late eighteenth century almost to extinction. The agent at Bushire had promised to revive it, importing to Bushire a large quantity of woollen goods to be sold on generous terms of credit. Disrupt trade with Iran and Bombay's private as well as official investments would suffer.[18]

To persuade the Iranian government to accept the British explanation that the brawl had been caused by 'the boisterous and intractable manner' of the envoy's retinue, Duncan authorized the agent at Bushire to make use of any 'means of favourable impression as you may have the means of applying'.[19] This careful circumlocution could be understood at Bushire only to refer to what are now called bribes, but were accepted in earlier times as presents or fees. When the boat bringing the news of the incident arrived at Bushire on 20 September, the British agent kept everybody on board for five days, putting it about that the boat had come from the Red Sea not Bombay while he wrote to the chief minister of Fars and to the minister's uncle, one of the shah's chief ministers, to explain the incident away. His letter contained the promise of 20,000 rupees, to be paid as soon as the shah had formally accepted the British explanation. 'Without money and presents', Bombay was reminded, 'nothing is to be done in this country.'[20]

The offer of presents was accompanied by an explanation of why the Iranian government need not take offence at the death of its envoy, also by a proposal. The explanation was not the one given by Duncan: the agent discarded that as unnecessarily detailed, substituting a new letter to the shah above Duncan's signature. The shah and his ministers were told that owing to Muhammad Khalil's long connection with the British, he could hardly be considered an

35

Iranian; that owing to the deceit he had practised on the British (in obtaining money from them in 1798 to help fund the rebellion in Afghanistan and, after pocketing most of it, claiming that it had not been paid to him), he ought not to have been chosen to be the ambassador. 'What disgrace would not such chicanery as this have brought on the Persian government, were such a representative to have reached ... the governor-general?'[21] The Iranians were left almost to draw the conclusion that the death of such a scoundrel was a cause for rejoicing.

The explanation was accompanied by a proposal that the shah prove his goodwill to the British by appointing one of Muhammad Khalil's retinue envoy, or by sending someone more suitable to Bombay to take his place. Until the end of October it seemed possible that the shah would agree: the British agent at Baghdad had been told that Iran's response was 'as favourable as could be wished'.[22] Although resentment had been caused by letters from the Iranians at Bombay written after, and contradicting, those written under British supervision, the agent at Bushire had managed to intercept most of them. The ministers at Fars seemed to be doing all they could to help the British and to be carrying their point against other ministers, such as the chief minister of Azerbaijan, who had been offered no inducement to help. Suddenly, however, at the beginning of November, success turned to failure. News reached Bushire of Malcolm's arrival at Bombay. 'No official answers have been received nor are we likely to have any', Bushire promptly warned Bombay, 'since the intelligence of Major Malcolm's coming has been known.'[23]

A small, if embarrassing, incident, which had looked like being settled reasonably quickly, at a reasonable cost, and by reasonable means, now blossomed into a misunderstanding between the governments of India and Iran that would set the tone of Anglo-Iranian relations until the revocation of the Anglo-Iranian treaties by Great Britain in 1838. An excellent example of the mutual disappointment felt by would-be paramount power and designated protectorate, it arose out of a typically faulty perception by each of the other's expectations. The British did do what the Iranians expected of them, if for entirely different reasons. They gained no credit by it. The Iranians did not do what the British expected, causing great resentment, although less of the Iranians than between the two groups of Anglo-Indians disputing about what could be expected of them.

'Malcolm returns to Persia', the British agent at Basra, Samuel Manesty told his colleague at Baghdad, Harford Jones, at the end of October.[24] How else was Malcolm's reception at Bombay with the honours due to an ambassador to be interpreted? That is how it was interpreted by the Iranians. From the moment of Malcolm's intervention, Bombay's attempt to persuade Iran to persevere with the mission to Bengal had no hope of success. Malcolm must first lead a second mission from the governor-general to the shah. Acceding to this demand would itself mislead the Iranians about the nature and extent of the government of India's interest in Iran. Bombay had been warned by Bushire before Malcolm's first mission to Iran, and the warning had been repeated in October, that the shah would interpret the arrival of a series of British missions at Tehran as evidence that the British needed his help against the French or the Afghans.[25] For this help he would expect them to pay dearly.

For all the shah cared, British missions to Iran need not lead anywhere: they had merely to take place. They were valued for themselves, and valuable they turned out to be. Their progress heightened the prestige of the Kajars in the eyes of the vassals they had not yet succeeded, and never would succeed, in completely overpowering: the presents and pensions distributed so lavishly turned eyes towards Tehran as the source of such extraordinary largesse. The cost to the Iranian government of the missions was negligible. The imperial government foisted the cost on to the provinces through which the envoy would travel (in by way of Fars and Isfahan, out by way of Hamadan and Kermanshah): they, in turn, foisted it out onto the impoverished villagers who were required to supply food. With luck, the British would demand to pay their own way; whereupon their payments naturally would not reach their suppliers.[26]

The Iranian perception that a new British mission was in the offing was confirmed by the arrival at Bushire on 2 December of Captain Charles Pasley, sent by Malcolm with letters from the governor-general to the shah and the governor of Fars. Pasley was Malcolm's cousin, had gone with him to Iran as his assistant, and was known to share his assumptions and to copy his style. Better yet for the Iranians, Pasley's arrival was followed by the recall of the agent at Bushire, who reported to the governor of Bombay, and his replacement on 10 January 1803 by a more senior official who was to report to the governor-general. The exchange appeared doubly important in

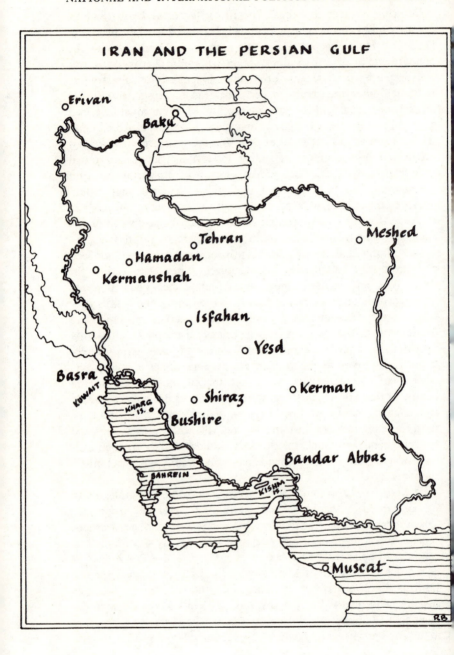

that an Englishman had been sent to replace an Indian. To the Iranian ministers, 'not men to interfere merely in the way of charity',[27] the return on a slow settlement of the incident now seemed likely to outdo the rewards they had been promised for a quick one. The Iranian mission at Bombay would not proceed to Calcutta until a fully-fledged British mission of apology had first been sent to Tehran.[28]

The first casualty of Malcolm's takeover at Bombay was the British agent at Bushire, 'turned out neck and heels'.[29] An Iranian who had lived for many years in India named Mehdi Ali Khan, he had been posted at Bushire since 1798 and was the last native to be employed by the government of India on diplomatic business. His appointment had caused an uproar in the Bombay civil service, who thought that a Muslim should not be given charge of the British flag, and had been criticized by the governor-general.[30] Mehdi Ali's most vehement critic had been his predecessor at Bushire, now, by chance, assigned to look after the dead envoy's retinue until Malcolm could settle with them. His greatest admirer, however, was Duncan, whom he had known for the fifteen years since Duncan had made his own reputation at Benares under Earl Cornwallis. Although Duncan agreed to recall Mehdi Ali Khan from Bushire, he softened the blow as much as he could; telling him that he wished to see him at Bombay in order to bestow in person the pension the East India Company had granted him, and telling the governor-general that the pension ought to be handsome, as Mehdi Ali was being recalled 'on general considerations of political expedience and not for misconduct'.[31]

That is not how Malcolm regarded the recall. He complained of the presents promised to the Iranian ministers, of the aspersions Mehdi Ali had cast on the character of Muhammad Khalil, of his inaccurate account of the brawl. His successor was told that, if expedient, he might publicly disavow him.[32] As Pasley, when he arrived at Bushire, could find no evidence of inaccuracy,[33] Malcolm's strictures were evidently directed against the government of Bombay as much as Mehdi Ali Khan. Or so Duncan understood them. He knew that Mehdi Ali was bound to have interpreted his instructions as he had, given the style in which the British had hitherto dealt with Indian and Middle Eastern states.[34] A year later Duncan planned to send Mehdi Ali Khan back to Iran. He died before he could go.[35]

Having recalled Mehdi Ali Khan from Bushire and sent Muhammad Khalil's corpse to Nejeff, to be escorted as far as Basra by Pasley, Malcolm turned early in November to reorganize the rump of the Iranian mission. As usual with Malcolm, activity involved expense, twice the sum the 'bullied' Duncan had planned to spend. 85,000 rupees were distributed as presents to the late envoy's relatives and attendants; another 45,000 were to be paid annually in pensions.[36] Never modest about his achievements, Malcolm was quick to imply that he deserved all the credit for preventing the incident from embarrassing Anglo-Iranian relations. 'The advantage I possessed in being personally known to the majority of the Persians had enabled me to conquer difficulties which to others would have been unsurmountable.'[37]

The rump of the mission were to remain at Bombay until the shah had replied to the letters written by Malcolm to the Iranian ministers on 16 November correcting the mistakes in Mehdi Ali Khan's account of the brawl – 'trifles but ... with us', the Iranians were told, 'any deviation from the truth is of magnitude'.[38] Malcolm assured the governor-general that his generosity and truthfulness was bound to 'perpetuate in the minds of the natives of Persia those favourable impressions which the whole of Your Lordship's proceedings are calculated to excite'.[39] How could they do otherwise when the shah was already 'very partial to the English'?[40] The answers to the letters, therefore, could be taken for granted. The Iranian envoy would be replaced; the mission continue on its way to Bengal.

The governor-general of India in 1802, on whom Malcolm fawned at the same time as he preened himself before everyone else, was the Marquis Wellesley, who had gone out to India in 1798 in search of the fame that had eluded him in England. As eager as Malcolm that the Iranian mission should continue its journey to Bengal as soon as possible, Wellesley had plans for it which would have surprised and alarmed the Iranians, had they possessed any inkling of them. To Wellesley, the postponement of the mission by the death of the envoy was 'the subject of the deepest public affliction'.[41] Afflictive that it had happened on British soil to a guest of the British, who could make amends only by demonstrating to the shah the government of India's embarrassment; more afflictive that it should happen when it did, just as Wellesley seemed in sight of the Indian Empire he had dreamed of since his arrival. Malcolm's settlement in November 1802 of the Iranian incident was followed in December by the treaty of Bassein with Peshwa Baji Rao II of Poona. One might realize

Wellesley's dream of Iran as a British protectorate, the other his dream of the Maratha Confederacy as one.

The Iranian mission must quickly continue its journey to Bengal to clear the way, by the ratification of Malcolm's treaties, for the two steps necessary to turn Iran into a British protectorate. The first step would be the surrender by Iran to the British of an island in the Persian Gulf – Kishm or, preferably, Kharg – on which they could set up a fortified base. The base was to tie Iran to British India in two complementary ways. As the trade of Iran and the gulf would be drawn to the base as if by a magnet, Iranian prosperity would depend upon friendly Anglo-Iranian relations. Similarly, stability in Iran would depend on the British, for, if crossed, they would be well placed to support the shah's rivals. Not that they intended to. They intended to support him against them. Exactly in the way Palmerston predicted that the treaty of Unkiar Skelessi would turn the sultan into a dependant of the tsar by teaching the sultan 'to look to the Russian army for the maintenance of his domestic authority',[42] Wellesley planned to turn Malcolm's treaties into a Middle Eastern version of an Indian subsidiary alliance. He would obtain in Iran what Palmerston was determined to prevent Russia from obtaining in the Ottoman Empire, 'the right of interference as a matter of course'.[43]

The second step was the appointment of a resident envoy at Tehran. Malcolm, naturally, saw himself as the ideal man for the post. He expected to be sent back to Tehran as soon as the treaties had been ratified and be given command of the troops at Kharg or Kishm. Imagine his disappointment at the death of Muhammad Khalil. 'I see in one moment the labour of three years gone to waste', he lamented, '... just when it was on the point of completion.'[44] If the shah could be pacified quickly, however, a new envoy might be sent from Iran to exchange the ratifications and cede the island in the gulf; Malcolm might yet be sent on a second mission to Tehran; and the crisis might yet 'terminate in the establishment of our influence in Persia on a firmer basis than it has ever yet rested'.[45]

Wellesley and his Kindergarten, of which Malcolm was a charter member, dreamed of an empire in India stretching from the tip of Cape Comorin to a frontier, yet to be devised, between the Russian and Iranian empires in the Caucasus. Iran was not needed to help to defend this empire against external threats – no fear of Bonaparte or Paul had ever moved Malcolm or Wellesley – rather to help to create the empire and stabilize it against threats from within. Of course, external threats would have to be used to persuade the East India Company and the board of control for India of the value of a protectorate over Iran, just as they would prove the need to forestall challenges in India from potential French allies, the peshwa and Sindhia. Persuade the board of control and the East India Company of the utility of an alliance with Iran, and they might be convinced more easily that British paramountcy in India was the only guarantee of stability there. With luck, the Iranian alliance would create a fear of the very enemy it was seemingly intended to dispose of.

In 1803, Wellesley's and Malcolm's luck ran out. The other members of the Maratha Confederacy went to war rather than accept Wellesley's claim that the treaty of Bassein turned all of them into dependants of the British. Despite a series of victories, the British, for the remainder of Wellesley's term in India, failed to overpower all the members of the confederacy at the same time. Similarly, Wellesley's and Malcolm's luck ran out in Iran when they failed, also for the remainder of Wellesley's term, to persuade the shah to revive the Iranian mission to India. Their hopes of Iran were anyway false, and their chances of realizing their hopes impaired by their inability to decide whether they wished to be influential or admired. The shah had no intention of handing over an island in the gulf. Malcolm had failed to persuade him to hand one over in 1801, nor had Muhammad Khalil been empowered to offer at Calcutta what had been refused at Tehran.[46] His mission was bound to have led to disappointment. His death led to greater disappointment than it need have done, only because Wellesley and Malcolm, dreaming of being influential *because* admired, followed Edmund Burke's rule that Englishmen abroad should behave at all times according to English standards of conduct.

To attempt to chart changes in attitude with precision is risky, perhaps foolish, leading to accusations of simplification and jarring over-confidence. Perhaps diplomatic historians are more willing than social or intellectual historians to be thus reckless, because significant questions of international relations are often represented by trivial symbols: one would be rash to suppose that the whirl of misunderstanding preceding the Crimean War, for example, concealed nothing of importance. Why join the school of English military historians, who are so eager to convey the smoke and confusion of battle that anybody reading their accounts knows no more than the combatants about what was taking place? Here, therefore, 1802 shall demarcate a boundary.

When F.G. Hutchins explained the steps by which the British argued themselves into assuming by the late nineteenth century that their rule over India would be permanent, emphasis was laid on the Mutiny of 1857 and the abolition of the East India Company which followed it as the moment when the English learned what Anglo-Indians already knew: that India could not be reformed on a European model with either the ease or at the speed evangelical and utilitarian reformers had supposed.[47] Indians must be held awestruck by soldiers and civil servants who effectively symbolized the power, as well as the claim to superior civilization, of Great Britain, by maintaining in all contacts with Indians an heroic posture eventually stereotyped in the heroes of G.A. Henty.

Although the rules of conduct for Anglo-Indians known as the Code of the Pukka Sahib may not have been finalized until the late nineteenth century, they had been implicit in the demand made by Burke. The willingness of Wellesley and Malcolm to meet the demand indicates that they belonged to a later generation than Duncan and Mehdi Ali Khan, to a generation that was to take a different approach to living amongst Indians and Iranians, because it had adopted a new method of government to reach its new political goal.

Duncan and Mehdi Ali Khan belonged to the last of the generation who, having begun their careers under Warren Hastings, had followed his example. It is not surprising, therefore, that a third such official, Colonel William Palmer, the British agent at Poona, had also run afoul of Wellesley and the Kindergarten and had been recalled a year earlier almost in disgrace. Their generation stood for government by management rather than example, recognizing that Asiatics had their own customs which suited them. Another echo of Burke, of course. But Burke was interested in England and Englishmen, mostly upper class Englishmen. Foreign customs might supply useful illustrations of the dangers of absolute power or too rapid reform: they were not to be cited by nabobs in defence of new methods of money making or power broking likely to disturb the balance of interests in the unreformed political system.

The nature of the change taking place in Great Britain at the turn of the eighteenth and nineteenth centuries is not to be misunderstood. Too much has been made of the Industrial Revolution: its impact has too often been pushed back into the mid-eighteenth century by historians showing the eagerness of undergraduates for whom enclosures turn peasants into factory workers overnight. The first phase of industrialization enriched men who already had money: landowners. The oligarchy was strengthened not weakened, becoming richer, more powerful, more conscious of its class interest. It also became more conscious of the badges of its class, despite its habit of referring to class as rank. The code of conduct eventually to point the way to improvement for Indians and Egyptians had been devised in an attempt to restrict and regulate change in Great Britain. In 1802 it was officially, as it were, designated the appropriate imperial posture of would-be successors to the Moguls.

Duncan, Palmer, and their generation stood for management rather than example because they also stood for diplomacy among equals rather than pretensions to paramount power. Until the arrival of Wellesley with the dream of empire which suited the needs of soldiers and civil servants who now depended on expansion for fortunes, the government of India had acted in foreign affairs as one Indian state manoeuvring among a number of states relatively equal in strength and had sought safety in the triple alliance of 1791 with Hyderabad and the Maratha Confederacy. Wellesley recognized no equals. Allies were to be turned into protectorates. As the Indian states learned to their cost, the only proof of goodwill acceptable to Wellesley was the surrender of their independence.

The replacement of balance of power politics by empire-building was accompanied by the replacement of management by example. The imperial posture was required to be self-satisfying, however, as well as admired. Wellesley and Malcolm showered apologies on the shah of Iran for the death of his envoy in a manner Duncan and Mehdi Ali Khan found unnecessary, therefore baffling and misguided. Separating style from goal, the latter had tried to make sure the envoy would be replaced, the mission continue on its way. As soon as Wellesley and Malcolm took control, a matter of business, however embarrassing – to be settled quickly and, if possible, to advantage – turned into a question of principle, a challenge to the government of India's self-image. One is reminded of Agatha Ramm's strictures on Gladstone for his habit of treating all questions as questions of principle, for being unable to tell as a result what mattered to Great Britain and what did not.[48] In 1802, the government of India, adopting the posture they and Burke thought appropriate to an imperial power addressing an associate, were confident of being admired for their condescension. Like Lady Catharine de Burgh addressing Miss Elizabeth Bennett, they let themselves in for a nasty surprise.

The death of the Iranian envoy, seemingly an embarrassment and challenge to British notions of good conduct, also offered an opportunity. Wellesley and Malcolm were given the chance to demonstrate the importance they attached to the mission in the hope of persuading the shah to treat it with a seriousness he had never intended. Their parade would leave him unmoved. It would unnerve, however, Mehdi Ali's successor, Jonathan Lovett, the newly appointed political agent, a good linguist who had been torn away from the compilation at Fort William of a Maratha dictionary for the government of Bombay, to be dumped in an outpost in the Persian Gulf and entrusted with duties for which he lacked both aptitude and inclination. He had taken Malcolm's parade over the brawl at face value – or, if he had not, he could not be contradicted when he later claimed that he had.

Having acted so properly by Iran, particularly in providing a British escort for Muhammad Khalil's corpse, 'which will... be considered a high compliment', Wellesley and Malcolm expected Lovett to have no difficulty in re-establishing the British reputation for good conduct.[49] Malcolm told Lovett that he might accompany Wellesley's letter to the shah as far as Shiraz or even, if the shah desired it, as far as Tehran. He was to travel quickly, however, and in the simple style befitting a messenger rather than an ambassador.[50] Such naïvety. Malcolm's own ostentation and extravagance had made travelling in Iran enormously expensive for Englishmen; the speed at which they travelled would be determined by the chamberlain sent to escort them. Trying to hurry merely aroused resentment and suspicion. If Wellesley wished to determine how his apology was received, he would now have to permit the Iranians to determine how it was to be presented. One week after Lovett reached Bushire on 10 January 1803, he repeated to Bengal the warning already given to Bombay: 'the question now is not who shall be sent ambassador, but shall any be sent at all, until the arrival of another on the part of the English Government'.[51]

The symbolic issue of the manner in which Wellesley's letter explaining the death of the Iranian ambassador should be delivered to the shah was debated throughout 1803, destroying Lovett's health. Sick when he arrived at Bushire, he lacked the stamina for standing up to Iranians and thought himself prohibited by his instructions from replying to them in the offensive manner they used to him. His journey was postponed by the government of Fars until the shah had returned from his summer camp, when Lovett was told that he would be expected to present himself in the style adopted three years earlier by Malcolm. Lovett tried to persuade the Iranians to permit Pasley to deliver Wellesley's letter. They refused, owing to Pasley's junior rank. Lovett even tried to flee to India, but his Iranian chamberlain arrived before the paquet boat from Bombay. 'A little schoolboy is fitter for an ambassador than you are', the chamberlain told Lovett.[52] Nothing Lovett could say would persuade the Iranians that he was not an ambassador. An ambassador they would have.

Frightened – or pretending to be – that any further delay in the delivery of Wellesley's letter might have 'the most serious consequences', in December 1803 Lovett appealed to the agent at Basra, Samuel Manesty, to exchange posts.[53] 'If you come everything is saved;' he told Manesty, 'if you do not the reverse is really too gloomy for me to think of.'[54] Manesty delightedly agreed. The doyen of British agents in the Middle East who had been stationed at Basra for almost twenty years, he had been angered when first Harford Jones, then Malcolm, and most recently Lovett had been entrusted with the political and diplomatic tasks for which he thought himself better fitted than all of them. He was right to feel slighted. Malcolm, in making his arrangements at Bombay, had done all he could to 'preserve the transaction from the *touch* of Mr. Manesty and Mr. Jones'.[55] Malcolm admitted that Manesty was an able man, but doubted whether he 'will answer in Persia. His firm boldness will remove the impressions which the *wearing* weakness of Mr. Lovett must have made but the style and expense which he will adopt will completely defeat one of the intentions of Mr. L[ovett]'s mission'.[56]

By the New Year of 1804, it was apparent that Wellesley and Malcolm, far from settling the incident arising from the death of the Iranian envoy, had compounded it. A new Iranian envoy had been named, but had not set out; the remaining members of his predecessor's retinue had given up waiting for him and gone home. They reached Bushire on 14 January. Frantic that the career he had planned for himself in Iran might elude him, Malcolm, echoed by Pasley, heaped abuse on Lovett in letters to Wellesley's private secretary. The thrust of their criticism: that Lovett had not stood forth as an English gentleman ought, telling the Iranians what was to be done. Consulting them was bound to lead to 'enormous and useless expense'. One hope remained for Malcolm, that the government of India would abandon the ratification of his treaties and start afresh. Let another British mission go to Tehran: 'the sooner an embassy goes ... to remedy all this bad work the better, but such ought to have credentials from the King'.[57] Malcolm, naturally, overlooked the tiresome facts that the bad work was his; that his new proposal would make it worse. Far from providing a quick method of turning Iran into a British protectorate, the new mission would convince the shah that the British, needing his help even more than he had supposed, would pay even more for it.

The British agent at Baghdad, Harford Jones, Malcolm's bitter rival for influence over British policy in the Middle East, doubted whether Lovett had 'had fair play at Bushire'.[58] Wellesley's and Malcolm's interest in the symbolic issue of how the British in India were to present themselves to Iranians and be perceived by them was preventing the settlement of two substantive issues about which decisions must be taken. The first was the fate of British trade with the Persian Gulf. Just as Lovett arrived at Bushire, two ships carrying British goods, including a valuable consignment of bullion, were plundered by pirates based in Iran. But for Wellesley's eagerness to use apologies to re-establish friendly Anglo-Iranian relations, Bombay would have taken steps to recover the plundered goods by force. Lovett, himself, hesitated to make strong demands on the government of Fars for help against the pirates, because his instructions seemed to place graciousness before bargaining. Malcolm and Wellesley hated to remember that they were employed by a trading company and that the British empire in India was intended to be profitable, despising anybody accustomed 'to the idea of having a stateroom and a shop in the same building'.[59] Where, one wonders, did they imagine that Great Britain's wealth had sprung from?

Although Lovett's failure to persuade the Iranians to help curb piracy in the gulf was one reason why he sent for Manesty, rather than handing over to Pasley, Manesty agreed so quickly to 'quit his station ... for the preservation of British credit in Persia', owing to his eagerness to affect the other issue awaiting a British response, the Russo-Iranian war.[60] Imminent since the Russian annexation of Georgia in 1801, the war eventually broke out in the summer of 1804

47

when a Russian army besieged Erivan, the fortress-town dominating north-west Azerbaijan. For the same reason, Malcolm was furious to learn in March of Manesty's arrival in Iran and did all he could to have him prohibited from 'interfering in politics...particularly those relating to Russia'.[61] Malcolm had good reason to be angry because, when Manesty reached Tehran in July 1804, he did exactly as Malcolm had feared: offered to convey to the foreign office an Iranian request for British mediation. At the time the shah declined the offer. In the autumn, however, after the extent of Iran's losses to Russia could no longer be hidden, messengers were sent after Manesty accepting it. In the next three years the Iranians were to turn their acceptance into a demand, on the ground that the terms of Malcolm's treaties required the British to protect them. They accompanied their demand by the threat that, disappointed by the British, they would seek help from Napoleon.[62]

When Wellesley heard that Manesty had gone to Iran, he was so angry that he disavowed him and refused to honour his bills. Only after Duncan had pointed out that such a step might endanger Manesty's life, did Wellesley relent, but he repeated his orders to Manesty to leave Iran immediately.[63] Wellesley resented the suggestion that Anglo-Iranian relations should be supervised by the foreign office, or by anybody except himself. He had already fought a bitter, if not altogether successful, battle with the board of control over its appointment of Jones, who had been allowed to act as if he were independent of the government of India. Wellesley needed control over British agents in the Middle East in order to disguise the imperialist policy he had formulated but dare not proclaim. The shah must not suppose that the government of India's interest in Iran now arose out of fear of Russian expansion – any more than Malcolm had implied that it arose out of fear of the French army in Egypt. Nor were Wellesley and Malcolm alarmed. The Kajars must be persuaded that they, rather than the British, would gain more from closer Anglo-Iranian relations. A stable frontier with Russia and protection from their subjects was to be reward enough for turning themselves into the most westerly of Wellesley's dependants.

Manesty, having rounded up as many Englishmen as he could lay hands on to puff up his consequence before setting out for Tehran, was bound to have misled the Iranians. But how else was he to manage when Lovett had persuaded the governor of Fars to accept the substitution only by stating that Manesty was much the higher in rank?[64] Malcolm, in an accurate prophecy of future Anglo-Iranian relations, warned Wellesley in March 1804 that the Iranians' 'great expectation of presents . . . will increase their demands in the hope of further concessions till you are obliged to break with them'.[65] Malcolm did not, however, as he ought to have done, hold himself responsible, nor did Manesty prove Malcolm's point. At the time Manesty left Tehran in July, his mission appeared a success. The shah had agreed to overlook the death of his envoy at Bombay, to punish the pirates who had plundered the British ships in the gulf, and to send a new envoy to Calcutta in place of Muhammad Khalil.[66] It all meant little, and it had cost much. Manesty had spent as much as Malcolm in 1800 – more than £100,000 – much more than Mehdi Ali Khan in 1799. He had followed Wellesley's personal rule that the representative of a rich and powerful state ought not to stint himself.

Even if Manesty's mission to Tehran followed from Wellesley's assumptions as well as Iranian expectations, it nevertheless took up valuable time. Wellesley and Malcolm spent 1804 and 1805 in exciting, but more and more frustrating because less and less decisive, war with the Maratha Confederacy. By the time Muhammad Khalil's successor (his brother-in-law, Aga Nabi Khan) arrived at Bombay in January 1806, having taken as long on the journey as his predecessor, Wellesley had left for England under a cloud. Malcolm was out of favour with Wellesley's successors, Lord Cornwallis and, after his death in August 1805, Sir George Barlow. Having been sent to ask for the help against Russia Manesty had offered and to tie Iran more closely to Great Britain, as the government of India seemed to have wished, Aga Nabi found himself rebuffed.[67] Cornwallis and Barlow were under orders to reverse Wellesley's bid for paramount power in India, to return to the government of India's former assumption that it would operate as one state among a number, with whom friendly relations would be maintained by helping to preserve rather than subvert their independence. Iran would be needed neither as the outpost of an empire, as a barrier to overland invasion, nor as a failing market worth reviving. All that remained was the post. Manesty was told in 1806 that his most important duty was to ensure the safety and quick transmission of the mail bag for London.[68]

So ended the first of the round dances in Iran of which the British became so fond they were still dancing them at the end of the First World War. Given the increasing interest of late eighteenth century

Englishmen in style and form as the hallmarks of gentlemen, one should not be surprised to find a demand in the colonies for a rigid adherence to what was thought to be proper. Keeping natives in their place was good practice for helping to keep the lower orders in theirs, and trade, investment, and successful careers in the colonies were merely one of the many forms of property the English assumed that all men of goodwill would do what they could to protect. Wellesley's posture was reasonable enough – and in Ireland he had trained in a good school – but can he really have expected to be appreciated by Iran? Maybe not, whatever Malcolm might say. Two communities, divided by belief and custom, may as well go their own ways, each accepting that the other is beyond understanding. So why pretend the opposite? For the benefit of everybody back home who insists that expansion is justified only by improvement.

If the British in India adopted their imperial posture partly to satisfy the tastes of both oligarchs and improvers back home, they paid a high price for it abroad. Until the denunciation of the Anglo-Iranian treaties by the British in 1838, the shah treated British willingness to spend as encouragement to ask. The more the British spent on him, the more he concluded that he must have something to offer for which they were willing to pay a high price. Similarly, British talk of the role Iran could play in helping to defend British India led the Kajars to suppose that the stability of Iran was a valuable asset in which they could trade. Not only the Kajars were misled. Their opportunities to take advantage of the British would increase during the Napoleonic Wars because the board of control and, at times, the foreign office seemed to share their supposition – or to assume that the government of India did.

The government of India did not believe, however, in the strategic value of Iranian goodwill, only in its political value. Wellesley and Malcolm talked of threats in an attempt to disguise their quest of opportunities for expansion. Iran was to become an outpost of empire, not an outpost of imperial defence. Asked why an outpost was needed when no threat was perceived, Wellesley would have answered – if he answered – that only if London could be convinced of the dangers from Afghanistan, France, and later Russia, would the quest for paramountcy in India be permitted. After 1802 it was temporarily forbidden. The implications of Malcolm's treaties had been as clear to the board of control as the implications of the treaty of Bassein. Not that this would have mattered, had Wellesley succeeded in defeating the Marathas and re-establishing the connection with Iran broken by the death of Haji Muhammad Khalil.

The death of Muhammad Khalil placed Wellesley and Malcolm in a dilemma. Dealing with the incident in the manner Bombay proposed would reveal Wellesley's purposes to the board of control and the East India Company. Keeping up the pose required to justify expansion and mislead his employers would hand over the initiative to the shah. Not that Wellesley and Malcolm understood their dilemma. They might not believe in improvement: they did believe themselves to be superior. They despised Iranians for their own customs while expecting them to admire British ones. They were right to demand admiration: British India was undoubtedly a better place to live in than early Kajar Iran. They were foolish to expect to receive it.

NOTES

1. Elie Kedourie, *Islam in the Modern World and Other Studies* (London, 1980), p. 242.
2. Muhammad Khalil to Duncan, June 1802, Duncan to Muhammad Khalil, 10 June, 2 July 1802, IO Bombay/SPP/381/35, pp. 4690, 4695, 4707.
3. Minute of Duncan, 5 Oct. 1802, *ibid.*, p. 4678. For the approach to Iran see Edward Ingram, *Commitment to Empire: Prophecies of the Great Game in Asia, 1797-1800* (Oxford, 1981), pp. 239-56.
4. Muhammad Khalil to Duncan, 8 July 1802, IO Bombay/SPP/381/35, p. 4711.
5. For Malcom's mission see Edward Ingram, *In Defence of British India: Great Britain in the Middle East, 1775-1842* (London, 1984), ch. 6; and M.E. Yapp, *Strategies of British India: Britain, Iran and Afghanistan, 1798-1850* (Oxford, 1980), ch. 1.
6. Malcolm to Duncan, 26 Sept. 1800, Royal Geographical Society, Melville MSS.
7. Encl. no. 4 in Jones to Duncan, 17 Dec. 1801, [Melville MSS] Add. MSS 41767, fo. 104.
8. Duncan to Wellesley, private, 6 April 1800, [Wellesley MSS] Add. MSS 13700, fo. 53; Muhammad Khalil to Malcolm, 26 March 1800, IO G/29/26, p. 193. See also K. Ekbal, 'Der politische Einfluss des persischen Kaufmannstandes in der frühen Kadscharenzeït, dargestellt am Beispiel von Haggi Halil Khan Qazwini Maliku't-Tuggar', *Der Islam*, lvii (1980), 9-35.
9. Jones to Malcolm, 6 Nov. 1802, KC MSS 9214.
10. 'Explanatory remarks upon Aga Muhammad to Duncan', 20 July 1802, IO Bombay/SPP/381/33, p. 3312.
11. Quoted in Sir J.W. Kaye, *The Life and Correspondence of Major-General Sir John Malcolm* (London, 1856), i. 192.
12. Wellesley to Cherry, 13 Aug. 1802, IO P/BEN/SEC/96, 30 Sept. 1802, no. 24.
13. Cherry to Wellesley, 21 July 1802, Duncan to Wellesley, 18 Aug. 1802, IO Bombay/SPP/381/33, pp. 2934, 3432.
14. Malcolm to Edmonstone, private, 15 Oct. 1802, Kaye, *Malcolm*, i. 191.
15. Duncan to Wellesley, 25 Sept. 1802, Wellesley to Duncan, 28 Oct. 1802, IO P/BEN/SEC/97, 11 Nov. 1802, nos. 16-17.
16. Duncan to Mehdi Ali Khan, 9 Sept. 1802, IO Bombay/SPP/381/34, p. 3900.
17. Duncan to Wellesley, 22 Aug. 1802, *ibid.*, 381/33, p. 3591.

18. For Bombay's trade see A.A. Amin, *British Interests in the Persian Gulf* (Leiden, 1967); Pamela Nightingale, *Trade and Empire in Western India, 1784-1800* (Cambridge, 1970); and J.B. Kelly, *Britain and the Persian Gulf, 1795-1880* (Oxford, 1968), chs. 1-3.
19. Duncan to Mehdi Ali Khan, 11 Aug. 1802, IO Bombay/SPP/381/33, p. 3321.
20. Bruce to Duncan, 12 Oct. 1802, *ibid.*, 381/37, p. 6151.
21. Mehdi Ali Khan to Duncan, with encls. nos. 1-4, 12 Oct. 1802, *ibid.*, pp. 6245, 6266, 6273, 6282.
22. Jones to Willis, 24 Nov. 1802, KC MSS 9214.
23. Bruce to Duncan, 3 Nov. 1802, IO Bombay/SPP/381/37, p. 6225; Lovett to Edmonstone, 19 Jan. 1803, IO G/29/29, no. 3.
24. Manesty to Jones, 28 Oct. 1802, KC MSS 6556.
25. Bruce to Duncan, 12 Oct. 1802, IO Bombay/SPP/381/37, p. 6151.
26. The best account of the treatment of a British mission is to be found in J.B. Fraser, *Narrative of a Journey in to Khorasan in the Years 1821 and 1822*, intro. Edward Ingram (reprinted New Delhi, 1984).
27. Mehdi Ali Khan to Duncan, 12 Oct. 1802, IO Bombay/SPP/381/37, p. 6232.
28. See Malcolm to Cherag Ali Khan, n.d., Kaye, *Malcolm*, i. 193.
29. Short to Jones, 28 Dec. 1802, KC MSS 8221.
30. Ingram, *Commitment to Empire*, p. 107.
31. Duncan to Wellesley, private, 22 March 1803, Add. MSS 13701, fo. 144.
32. Malcolm to Lovett, secret, 3 Nov. 1802, IO G/29/29, no. 1.
33. Pasley to Jones, 24 Dec. 1802, KC MSS 7995.
34. Duncan to Mehdi Ali Khan, 3 Nov. 1802, IO Bombay/SPP/381/37, p. 6317.
35. Duncan to court of directors, 10 Aug. 1804, IO L/PS/6/169, p. 79; same to Jones, 6 Aug. 1804, KC MSS 8263A.
36. Malcolm to Duncan, 2 Nov. 1802, to Wellesley, 11 Nov. 1802, IO Bombay/SPP/381/36, pp. 5362, 5670.
37. Malcolm to Shawe, private, 27 Oct. 1802, Add. MSS 13746, fo. 39.
38. Malcolm to Cherag Ali Khan, 16 Nov. 1802, IO Bombay/SPP/381/37, p. 6295.
39. Malcolm to Wellesley, 11 Nov. 1802, *ibid.*, 381/36, p. 5670.
40. Malcolm to Pasley, 18 April 1801, [Pasley MSS] Add. MSS 41961, fo. 140.
41. Wellesley to Clive, 11 Aug. 1802, IO P/BEN/SEC/96, 30 Sept. 1802, no. 17.
42. Palmerston to Bligh, 13 Oct. 1833, FO 65/206. See Edward Ingram, *The Beginning of the Great Game in Asia, 1828-1834* (Oxford, 1979), pp. 257-9.
43. Palmerston to Grey, 6 Aug. 1833, DUL Grey to Howick MSS.
44. Malcolm to Hobart, Aug. 1802, Kaye, *Malcolm*, i. 179.
45. Malcolm to Shawe, private, 19 Sept. 1803, Add. MSS 13746, fo. 291; Wellesley to Fath Ali Shah, 26 Aug. 1802, IO P/BEN/SEC/96, 30 Sept. 1802, no. 49A.
46. Mehdi Ali Khan to Duncan, 10 April 1802, IO Bombay/SPP/381/34, p. 3968.
47. F.G. Hutchins, *The Illusion of Permanence: British Rule in India* (Princeton, 1967).
48. Introduction to *The Political Correspondence of Mr. Gladstone and Lord Granville, 1876-1886*, ed. A. Ramm (Oxford, 1962).
49. Malcolm to Edmonstone, private, 13 Oct. 1802, Kaye, *Malcolm*, i. 189; same to Lovett, 16 Nov. 1802, IO G/29/29, no. 2.
50. Malcolm to Lovett, secret, 3 Nov. 1802, *ibid.*, no. 1.
51. Lovett to Edmonstone, 19 Jan. 1803, *ibid.*, no. 3.
52. 'General outline [by Charles Pasley]... of the political conduct of Jonathan Henry Lovett during his... residence at Bushire', 7 July 1805, IO G/29/28.
53. Lovett to Lumsden, 7 May 1804, IO G/29/29, no. 39.
54. Lovett to Manesty, private, 2 Dec. 1803, IO G/29/29.
55. Malcolm to Edmonstone, private, 13 Oct. 1802, Kaye, *Malcolm*, i. 189.

56. Malcolm to Shawe, most private and confidential, 25 Feb. 1804, Add. MSS 13747, fo. 85.
57. *Ibid.*
58. Jones to Adamson, 24 Nov. 1804, NLW MSS 4905E.
59. Malcolm to Shawe, private and confidential, 27 March 1804, Add. MSS 13747, fo. 176. For the attempts to deal with the pirates see Edward Ingram, 'From Trade to Empire in the Near East – II: The Repercussions of the Incident at Nakhilu in 1803', *Middle Eastern Studies*, xiv (1978), 182-204.
60. Manesty to Shawe, 30 Aug, 1804, Add. MSS 13704, fo. 66; encl. to Manesty, 30 Dec. 1803, in Lovett to Edmonstone, 30 Dec. 1803, IO G/29/29.
61. Malcolm to Shawe, private and confidential, 27 March 1804, Add. MSS 13747, fo. 176.
62. For the Iranian demands on Great Britain see Edward Ingram, 'An Aspiring Buffer State: Anglo-Persian Relations in the Third Coalition, 1804-1807', *Historical Journal*, xvi (1973), 514-20; for the Russo-Iranian war see Muriel Atkin, *Russia and Iran, 1780-1828* (Minneapolis, 1980), chs. 6-7.
63. Manesty to Wellesley, 10 Nov. 1804, IO G/29/28, no. 21.
64. Encl. no. 2 in Lovett to Edmonstone, 10 Dec. 1803, IO G/29/29.
65. Malcolm to Shawe, private and confidential, 27 March 1804, Add. MSS 13747, fo. 176.
66. Manesty to Wellesley, 18 July 1804, IO G/29/28, no. 15.
67. Ingram, 'Anglo-Persian Relations', pp. 521-2.
68. Ingram, 'Incident at Nakhilu', pp. 196-8.

IV

THE WESTERNIZATION OF OTTOMAN DIPLOMACY IN THE NINETEENTH CENTURY

Roderic H. Davison

> If the independence and integrity of the Ottoman Empire were to be preserved, it must begin immediately to reform on European lines.
>
> Elie Kedourie[1]

Such, in the judgement of Elie Kedourie, was the logic of the situation in which the Ottoman Empire found itself in the 1830s and 1840s. And such, he points out further, was the view of Stratford Canning when he returned in 1842 to enter upon a second ambassadorship at Istanbul. Such also was, in fact, the conviction of a small but growing number of Ottoman statesmen of the mid-nineteenth century. Among the Westernizing reforms they espoused was a restyling of Ottoman diplomacy.

For the nineteenth-century Ottoman Empire, diplomacy became more important than ever. To survive in a Europe ordered by five, then six, great powers, the empire needed all the diplomatic defence it could muster. Compared to those powers, the Ottoman Empire was weak. Its far-flung territories were hard to hold together. Minority nationalities, mostly Christian, within the empire came increasingly to seek autonomy and then independence by agitation and rebellion. The Ottoman armed forces were inferior to those of the European powers. Technologically the empire was far behind the West, and its economy was underdeveloped. The administrative structure based on Istanbul was inadequate to cope with the problems of the age. Throughout the century Ottoman sultans and statesmen moved spasmodically to introduce reforms of various sorts, to improve the administration, to create a polity that would bind all nationalities of the empire together, to foster economic development, and to build effective military and naval establishments. Progress was made along all these lines. Yet by the end of the century the *Devlet-i Aliye* (the 'Exalted State'), as the Ottomans called it, remained weak compared to the Western powers. The Sublime Porte still had to rely primarily on diplomacy for survival.

Survival meant warding off attacks by other powers and, if possible, preventing them from taking pieces of the Ottoman Empire for themselves. It meant, further, preventing other powers from interfering in domestic Ottoman affairs. Above all, it meant trying to fend off the intervention of one power or another in support of a rebellious nationality within the empire. The combination of Christian minority grievances and propaganda, an explosive nationalism, and diplomatic or military support from one or more of the great powers of Europe constituted, on repeated occasions, the major challenge to the survival of the multinational empire.

Under the pressure of events, the empire developed a diplomatic system that was increasingly Western in organization and style. The sultans had often, in the past, sent out negotiators and embassies when dealing with other powers, but these had been temporary. From the time of Sultan Mahmud II (reigned 1808-39) the Sublime Porte appointed permanent ambassadors and ministers to reside in the capitals of other major states, just as the European powers did. Also in Mahmud II's time, the title of *reis effendi*, the 'chief scribe' who had become responsible for the conduct of relations with foreign states, was changed to that of foreign minister. After 1836, a more European-style ministry developed slowly under the minister's direction. Likewise a new sort of personnel was attracted to the foreign ministry and to a considerable extent trained there, on the job; these were men who were more conversant with European outlooks and methods, who usually knew French, and who were more easily able to deal with diplomats from European countries.[2] These organizational aspects of the Westernization of Ottoman diplomacy are well known.

The manner in which the new diplomatic establishment operated is less well known. This is not the place to attempt a survey of the course of Ottoman diplomacy throughout the nineteenth century,[3] but it is instructive to identify and to describe briefly some of its characteristics in that period. They are here somewhat arbitrarily divided into principles and methods. The principles represent points

55

of view adopted by Ottoman statesmen, who referred to them constantly, based their representations to the European powers upon them, and saw in the sum of them the foundation of Ottoman foreign policy. Many methods served to carry out this policy; some of the more important will be included here. Methods merged into techniques, likewise more and more Westernized, some of which will also be mentioned.

The first principle which guided the actions of Ottoman statesmen and diplomats was, of course, that the independence and integrity of the Ottoman Empire must be preserved. Fuad Pasha, who was five times foreign minister, emphasized in instructions sent to all Ottoman representatives abroad in 1867 that 'the first and most important task of a Government is to look to its own preservation'.[4] In fact, a large part of the activity of these officials was in some way related to the struggle to prevent the loss of Ottoman territory, or the loss of governing authority over parts of Ottoman territory, either to minority peoples within the empire or to European powers. As one late-nineteenth-century analysis of Ottoman policy put it: 'It was necessary to preserve ourselves, to exist, not to let ourselves be violated or dismembered'.[5]

A second principle was that the Ottoman Empire was a state in which all people, of whatever religion, were equal; it should so be regarded by others. The Islamic character of the state was less mentioned as the century wore on, until the 1875-8 crisis. Formerly Islamic law was frequently referred to by Ottoman diplomats. In 1807, for example, the *reis effendi* explained that 'the very structure of the Imperial Government rests on the Muslim Sheriat'. The war against Russia (1806-12) occurred, he said, because 'in the face of Russia's tricks, the Imperial Government was forced by Muslim law to resist'.[6] This kind of reference to Muslim law as the basis for foreign policy tends to disappear from the vocabulary of Ottoman diplomats after the reform edict of Gülhane in 1839, and especially after the closer association with European powers in the Crimean War of 1854-6. Instead, more references appear to the equality of all Ottoman subjects. During the Crimean War, for instance, Mehmed Djemil Pasha, who was Ottoman ambassador in Paris, asked the French foreign minister not to address Sultan Abdulmedjid any more as 'Empereur des Musulmans', which was 'unfitting for a Sultan who had equal affection for all his subjects'. He should be addressed, said Djemil, as 'Empereur des Ottomans', or 'Empereur de Turquie', or

'Sa Majesté Impériale'.[7] In actuality, the Ottoman Empire was beginning to act in international relations more like a secular dynastic state, on the model of the major European powers.

A third principle was that the Ottoman Empire was a legitimate European power and, from 1856 on, a member of the Concert of Europe. The empire had in fact been an important European power since the fourteenth century, but it had never been a member of the 'club' of Christian monarchies. It had not been represented at the congress of Vienna in 1814-15, or at any of the meetings of great power monarchs or ministers that followed. But in 1840, after the reform edict of Gülhane, the Porte became an active participant in the European state system of the day as co-signer of the London Convention, which provided for action against Mehmed Ali. The empire was also a signatory of the Straits Convention of 1841, along with the five powers. Even more significant was the fact that the Ottoman Empire was represented at the congress of Paris in 1856, after the Crimean War, with all the great powers of Europe. The treaty of Paris, produced at that congress, confirmed that 'the Sublime Porte is admitted to participation in the advantages of the European public law and of the European concert' (Article 7). Thereafter Ottoman statesmen never let their Western counterparts forget that the empire was a legitimate European power, a member of the exclusive club of great powers. The Westerners usually acknowledged this. In 1868 the French foreign minister said to Djemil Pasha that 'Turkey, being one of the signatory Powers of the Treaty of Paris, is thus admitted to the European concert, while Greece does not have those advantages'. On that occasion, the meaning was that the Ottoman Empire would be invited to a conference of the great powers concerning the Cretan question and Greek-Turkish differences, while Greece would not be invited.[8]

Despite the insistence of the Ottoman statesmen on the principle of Ottoman membership in the Concert, however, the other members frequently failed to treat the empire as an equal. The most galling sign of inequality was the continuance of the capitulations, giving foreigners special rights on Ottoman soil. In such a situation the Ottoman statesmen used the Concert principle as vigorously as they could. 'By the treaty of Paris', says one Ottoman memorandum, 'the Sublime Porte was admitted to the bosom of the European family. This admission will be nothing but an expression so long as the capitulations in existence between the Sublime Porte and the

European Powers assure an exceptional position to foreigners living in Turkey.'[9]

A fourth principle was that existing legal regimes should be supported. In practice this meant that the principle of nationality, or of national self-determination, should not be allowed to subvert legitimate regimes. Because the Ottoman Empire was made up of nothing but national minorities – no single ethnic group or language group, not even the Turkish, constituted as much as fifty per cent – its very existence was threatened if the concept of national self-determination were admitted to be valid. Ali Pasha, many times foreign minister and grand vizier, opposed granting autonomy to this region or that because 'it would be impossible to prevent it from becoming rapidly and generally contagious'.[10] His colleague, Fuad Pasha, opposed the whole concept of creating homogeneous states based on nationality – the 'agglomeration of races', he called it.[11] A later foreign minister, Safvet Pasha, pointed out to the great powers of Europe that it was immoral to take provinces from one country just to make another country happy. He was arguing against the transfer of territory from Ottoman to Greek rule because of the principle of nationality.[12] The Ottoman statesmen were not using arguments from the past – they were not maintaining that Islamic rule was God-ordained. Instead, they were using modern secular arguments on the legitimacy of Ottoman rule, the legal authority of a government recognized by all the powers, and the right of a government to suppress rebellion. Rebellion was rebellion, even if nationalist; it was illegal, and was subversive of the law and order that all governments must uphold.[13]

A fifth principle on which the Ottoman statesmen based their actions was that international law must be observed by all governments. The Sublime Porte turned naturally to the Western law of nations because that law tended to support the *status quo*, which is what the Porte also was trying to do. When in the 1860s Crete was in rebellion and the rebels were receiving aid from Greece, and when at the same time other Greeks were conducting raids into Ottoman Thessaly, Fuad Pasha appealed to international law. Even if Greece is a free country and its citizens can act freely, he said, they still must observe international law. 'No country', he continued, 'is allowed to make its own laws superior to what is called the law of nations, which alone can serve as the common rule for international relations.'[14] In many other instances the Ottoman diplomats appealed to international law, as a kind of defensive insurance policy: it was an argument that other governments understood.

A corollary of the same principle, but so important to the Ottomans that it should be listed as a separate principle, a sixth one, is that treaties must be observed. After the Crimean War this principle of *pacta sunt servanda* became particularly important for the Porte, because the treaty of Paris (1856) gave the Ottomans a relatively favourable territorial settlement. Ali Pasha once referred to the settlement of 1856 as 'this treaty of Paris that Russia *detests* and that we must do everything possible to preserve'.[15] The treaty barred Russia from having a war fleet or naval arsenals on the Black Sea. In 1870, when the Russian government denounced this clause, the Porte appealed, though in vain, to the principle of sanctity of treaties. Other treaties also formed a basis for Ottoman policy. The Paris convention of 1858, which stipulated that Moldavia and Wallachia must be separate provinces although with some common institutions, was appealed to by the Porte on a number of occasions. When, in 1866, Karl of Hohenzollern was selected prince by the United Principalities of Moldavia and Wallachia, the Porte objected to the convening of a new conference of the powers at Paris unless they first agreed on respect for treaties – meaning the agreement of 1858.[16] After 1878, it was the treaty of Berlin to which the Porte most often appealed, even though it was not so favourable as the treaty of Paris of 1856 which it replaced in large part. Into the twentieth century, the Porte continued to hark back to the congress of Berlin, 'whose resolutions can be considered as the Magna Carta still today governing the relations of Turkey with the other Powers', as the legal counsellor of the Porte asserted.[17]

One provision of the treaty of Paris of 1856 provided a basis for Ottoman diplomacy that was so important that it also should be mentioned separately, as a seventh principle. This is the statement of the principle of non-intervention by other powers in Ottoman domestic affairs. Article 9 of the treaty stipulated that the communication of the Hatt-i Hümayun (a second major edict of reform) of 1856 to the powers 'cannot in any case, give to the said powers the right to interfere, either collectively or separately, in the relations of His Majesty the Sultan with his subjects or in the internal administration of his empire'.[18] The European powers had interfered on many occasions in the domestic affairs of the Ottoman Empire, often in favour of religious groups or individuals, as well as national minorities. After 1856 the Porte had a basis in treaty for its efforts to uphold the principle of the non-intervention by one state in the affairs of another. Article 9 of the 1856 treaty was thereafter often referred to by Ottoman diplomats in their communications to governments of the great powers of Europe. Djemil Pasha once even persuaded the French foreign minister to agree that 'the Ottoman Empire is a territory rendered sacred by the Treaty of Paris and on which no encroachment is allowed'.[19]

The seven principles that have been mentioned were all familiar to contemporary Europeans and were accepted by the European powers. The first one – preservation of the Ottoman Empire – was not a new principle, but it was as modern as it was traditional. The other six principles, or at least the form in which they were expressed, had been developed during the two middle quarters of the nineteenth century, a period of reform and Westernization known to Turks as the Tanzimat. Of these six – equality of Ottoman subjects, Ottoman membership in the Concert of Europe, the preservation of legitimate sovereign regimes and opposition to nationalist rebellion, the upholding of international law, respect for the sanctity of treaties, and non-intervention in Ottoman domestic affairs – only the last was not in theory accepted by all of the powers. Austria and Russia still believed that on occasion intervention might be not only a right, but a duty. This is not to say that all, or even any one, of the great powers of Europe lived up to professed principles in their international relations. Law and principle are less likely to guide the conduct of the strong than to be the recourse of the weak. But here the representatives of the weak, the Ottoman statesmen and diplomats, were speaking the same language and arguing from the same principles as the representatives of the other great powers. In principles, in attitudes, in modes of expression, Ottoman diplomacy was being Westernized.

The methods used by Ottoman statesmen and diplomats also accommodated themselves to the contemporary European situation. The most important method was not at all new – it was, simply, to win the support of whatever major powers would back up Ottoman interests. In the nineteenth century Russia was the most consistent opponent of, and threat to, the Ottoman Empire. Prussia – Germany after 1871 – was the least interested of all powers in the Eastern Question, until the very end of the century. Italy was the last and least of the powers. Therefore it was from Great Britain, France, and

Austria that the Porte sought assistance time and time again. These three had actually guaranteed the integrity and independence of the Ottoman Empire in 1856, but they often failed to live up to this promise. Nevertheless, the Ottoman records are full of appeals to these powers to support the interests of the empire in this question or that. These records also convey the distinct impression that Ottoman statesmen as a rule believed British help to be more likely and more efficacious than any other. From the 1830s onwards, the Porte was often successful in securing British backing, which of course Whitehall gave for its own reasons; British and Ottoman interests frequently coincided. The hope placed in British support was particularly urgent at the time of the defeat by Russia in 1877-8, a hope partly disappointed during the armistice and peace negotiations and the congress of Berlin.[20] Nevertheless, despite occasional disappointments, the usual attitude of Ottoman statesmen seemed to be: even if other support fails, Great Britain remains the best hope. This attitude began to change only in the late 1880s, when it became clear that Great Britain would not soon evacuate Egypt, which she had occupied in 1882.

A second method of Ottoman diplomacy was to avoid participation in international conferences, except in circumstances that were closely controlled. The Ottoman view of international conferences was born of experience. The great powers of Europe, when meeting in conference, tended to make demands of the Ottoman Empire, to interfere in its internal affairs with proposals of reform, or to plan for its partial dismemberment. In the days of Napoleon III and Cavour, between 1856 and 1870, conferences were doubly dangerous because the fertile imaginations of these two nationality-minded statesmen were full of map-changing schemes to remake Europe, almost always at Ottoman expense. Even if the Porte were not represented at a conference, what the other powers did might injure Ottoman interests, and so the Porte sometimes tried to discourage such meetings.[21] Only if the agenda were limited and if the results were determined by an *entente préalable*, was the Porte completely happy with an international conference. An example arises in 1864, when Ali Pasha himself proposed and convened a meeting of representatives of all of the powers. Here the agenda was limited to approving an agreement already reached by Ali with Prince Cuza of Moldavia-Wallachia; the conference met at Ali's house in Istanbul; and agreement was assured in advance.[22]

A third Ottoman method, common to all governments in modern times, was to seek to influence public opinion in other countries, especially through the press. In 1858, because of calumnies in the European newspapers, the Porte created a publicity bureau to furnish regular news bulletins on current questions to all Ottoman representatives abroad.[23] The bulletins had an irregular life, disappearing and being revived several times into the next century. The Ottoman diplomats also learned how to encourage European newspaper editors to publish stories favourable to their government, and how to place their own news stories with newspapers and press services. Musurus Pasha, for instance, as Ottoman envoy in London from 1851 to 1885, was able to furnish news bulletins to Reuters.[24] Perhaps the Porte was less effective in these efforts than the Western powers, but it learned rapidly and was competing on Europe's own terms.

A fourth and related method was to adopt the European tactic of maintaining, in rejoinder to some unfavourable proposal by another government, that public opinion in the Ottoman Empire would not accept it. The Porte's regard for public opinion seems to have developed only from the time of the Crimean War. Ottoman archives for some crisis periods thereafter contain batches of petitions signed by groups of Ottoman subjects expressing opposition to or support for one position or another; one suspects that on occasion these were encouraged and possibly orchestrated by Ottoman officials.[25] But the Porte could invoke public opinion without reliance on petitions. Sometimes in such cases a traditional element crept back into Ottoman diplomacy, and reference would be made not to general 'public' opinion but to 'Islamic' opinion. So, for example, when it was proposed after the congress of Berlin that much Ottoman territory, including Thessaly and the city of Yenishehir (Larissa) with its large Muslim population, be ceded to Greece, the Ottoman negotiators argued that it should not be done because Muslim public opinion would not accept it.[26] This exchange, of course, took place in the days of Sultan Abdul Hamid II (reigned 1876-1909), who made a point of cultivating Islamic opinion not only within his domains but abroad as well.

A fifth Ottoman method, employed only once, was to send the sultan on a goodwill visit to other powers. European monarchs of the nineteenth century were accustomed to visiting each other, doing business of state while they travelled for pleasure. Ottoman rulers traditionally had gone beyond the frontiers of their own empire only at the head of an army. In 1867, at the strong urging of his ministers, Sultan Abdul Aziz (reigned 1861-76) travelled to Paris, London, and Vienna, and made a stop in Germany as well. The trip was a success; the sultan evidently made a good impression. His foreign minister, Fuad, accompanied the sultan and was able to counteract influence that Russia was exerting in Paris.[27] But Abdul Aziz never developed the habit of European trips, as did his contemporaries, Shah Nasreddin of Iran and Khedive Ismail of Egypt. His successor, Abdul Hamid II, was probably too fearful for his own safety to travel abroad. Abdul Hamid did, however, play an active role in diplomacy, and was willing to write personal letters to other monarchs, as for example early in 1878 asking Queen Victoria for aid in the face of the Russian army's threat to Istanbul itself.[28]

There were many other methods used by Ottoman statesmen and diplomats in their conduct of the empire's foreign relations. A large number of them can be grouped together as exemplifying the adoption of European techniques. Ottoman foreign ministers and their representatives in foreign capitals soon became familiar with the ways in which Western diplomats operated, and adopted them, using the formal diplomatic note, the informal suggestion *à titre personnelle*, the *aide-mémoire*, the dispatch to be read to a foreign minister of which a copy might be left if desired, and the circular dispatch. They were at ease with the formalities of conference procedures, *compte rendus*, *procès-verbaux*, protocols, and the other minutiae of European diplomatic practice. Some of the Ottoman ministers and ambassadors excelled in using the best diplomatic French, and precise and polite phraseology. They became accustomed, especially in posts abroad, to the social amenities, quite non-Islamic in that both sexes were involved, that facilitate diplomatic intercourse: receptions, dinners, and balls.

After the telegraph system of Europe was extended to Istanbul in 1855, Ottoman diplomats quickly became used to employing that channel for urgent messages, and to using cyphers as well to keep their communications secret. In the foreign ministry in Istanbul, Western-style procedures gradually came into use for drafting documents, reviewing them, numbering them both in general series and in particular series by destination, writing précis of dispatches, registering incoming and outgoing communications, and filing. It is interesting to see in the foreign ministry the evolution of printed forms to make the work of the ministry, and the flow of paper within it, more regular and more efficient.[29] When documents were finally filed, they were at first apparently tied in bundles, and presumably then placed in *torbas*, large sacks, labelled by month, hung on pegs in the wall. But then the foreign ministry began using folders, and then cartons, in a Western fashion, leading to greater efficiency in the location of documents. Some of these techniques may seem like small matters. But, taken together they helped the Ottoman statesmen and diplomats to work as effectively as they could in the world of the European great powers.

These principles, methods, and techniques of Ottoman diplomacy, largely adopted or adapted from nineteenth-century European models, did not succeed in saving the Ottoman Empire in the long run. But they did help to prolong its life. They also made the empire a more comfortable participant in the international system dominated by the pentarchy of Europe, a system to which the Porte had by courtesy been admitted as a sixth member.

NOTES

1. Elie Kedourie, *England and the Middle East: The Destruction of the Ottoman Empire* (reprinted, Hassocks, Sussex, 1978), p. ll.
2. Carter V. Findley, *Bureaucratic Reform in the Ottoman Empire: The Sublime Porte, 1789-1922* (Princeton, 1980), ch. 4. Ercümend Kuran, *Avrupa'da Osmanli Ikamet Elçiliklerinin Kurulusu ve Ilk Elçilerin Faaliyetleri, 1793-1821* (Ankara, 1968), deals with an earlier attempt at permanent embassies.
3. There is no comprehensive study of Ottoman diplomatic history in the nineteenth century. The closest approximation is the cumulation of pertinent sections in Enver Ziya Karal, *Osmanli Tarihi* (vols. 5-8, Ankara, 1947-62). The present author is engaged in a study of Ottoman relations with the great powers in the post-Crimean period.
4. Circular, 20 June 1867, in Austria, Auswärtige Angelegenheiten: *Correspondenzen des Kaiserlichköniglichen Ministerium des Äussern* (2 vols., Vienna, 1868-74), i. 98.
5. Aali-Pacha, *Testament politique* (Coulommiers, 1910), p. 2. This is not by Ali Pasha, but is an apocryphal document composed in the 1870s or 1880s by someone in Ottoman employ, perhaps a Levantine or a European. Similar sentiments are in Ali Pasha's genuine memorandum of 3 shaban 1284/20 Nov. 1867, in Ali Fuad, *Ridjal-i Mühimme-i Siyasiye* (Istanbul, 1928), pp. 118-27.
6. 'Proceedings of a Conference with the British Ambassador, Sunday, 16 Zilkade 1221 (25 Jan. 1907)', Basbakanlik Arsivi (Istanbul), Hatt-i Hümayunlar no. 6971, translated by Halil Inalcik in *The Middle East and North Africa in World Politics: A Documentary Record*, ed. J.C. Hurewitz, (3 vols., New Haven, 1975-), i. 176.
7. Copy of Mehmed Djemil to foreign minister, 20 Nov. 1855, AE Mémoires et Documents, vol. 51, no. 16.
8. Djemil (Paris) to Safvet (Istanbul) no. 5291/593, 24 Dec. 1868, DBHE, S[iyasi Karton] 8, d[osya] 13 mükerrer.
9. Undated memorandum, probably 1890s, DBHE, S 47, d 1.
10. Ali to Musurus (London), tel., 16 Jan. 1867, DBHE, S 6, d 11.

11. Fuad to Ottoman ambassadors in Paris and London, no. 18523/15, 27 Feb. 1867, DBHE, S 6, d 11.

12. Safvet circular to Ottoman ambassadors, no. 52007/64, 8 Aug. 1878, DBHE, S 185, d D.

13. On Ottoman methods of dealing with nationalism, see Roderic H. Davison, 'Nationalism as an Ottoman Problem and the Ottoman Response', in *Nationalism in a Non-National State: The Dissolution of the Ottoman Empire*, ed. William W. Haddad and William Ochsenwald (Columbus, Ohio, 1977), pp. 25-56.

14. Fuad to Photiades (Athens), no. 18926/50, 24 April 1867, DBHE, S 37, d 13.

15. Ali to Safvet (Paris), conf. tel. no. 16951/299, 28 June 1868, DBHE, S 32, d 45. Ali underlined the word 'detests'.

16. Ali to Paris ambassador, no. 15962/87, 27 Feb. 1866, DBHE, S 30, d 44.

17. *Recueil d'actes internationaux de l'Empire ottoman*, ed. Gabriel Noradounghian (4 vols., Paris, 1897-1903), iii. IV.

18. Text of treaty, *ibid.*, p. 70.

19. Djemil (Paris) to Safvet (Istanbul), unnumbered, 31 Dec. 1868, DBHE, S 8, d 13 mükerrer.

20. DBHE, S 120 and S 185, with many documents on these events.

21. For example, the Porte argued against convening a five-power conference that was proposed in 1860: DBHE, S 46, d 5.

22. Ali circular to Ottoman representatives in Great Britain, France, and Italy, no. 10336/55, 29 June 1864, DBHE, S 30, d 36.

23. Fuad circular to Ottoman missions, no. 1910, 22 Dec. 1858, DBHE, S 126 mükerrer.

24. Musurus (London) to Safvet, tel., no. 7245/207, 25 April 1878, DBHE, S 121, d 60. See Roderic H. Davison, 'How the Ottoman Government Adjusted to a New Institution: The Newspaper Press', in *Proceedings of the First International Conference of Turkish Studies* (Bloomington, Indiana, forthcoming 1986?).

25. Evidence of this tactic at the time of the congress of Berlin, in June 1878, in DBHE, S 185, d B and Q.

26. Abdin Pasha to the powers, 26 July 1880, in *The Map of Europe by Treaty*, ed. Edward Hertslet (4 vols., 1875-91), iv. 2971.

27. Fuad (London) to Ali, tel. private and conf., unnumbered, 18 July 1867, DBHE, S 6, d 11.

28. Sultan Abdul Hamid's message was sent as a telegram to the queen: Server (Istanbul) to Musurus (London), no. 50069/12, 10 Jan. 1878, DBHE, S 120, d 58.

29. See, e.g., a single carton with documents extending over a quarter of a century, from 1861 to 1887, showing changes in forms: DBHE, S 531, on Bosnia.

V

THE ORIGINS OF THE
CHATHAM HOUSE VERSION

Gordon Martel

The road to hell ... is paved with good intentions ...
a piece of worldly wisdom which the agents of a great power
should cherish more than ambitions and attractive theories
about society or revolution.

Elie Kedourie[1]

Elie Kedourie has been a favourite historian of mine since I first came
across him as an undergraduate. I liked him before I read him. 'A
dangerous man', my teacher said, in a futile effort to encourage me
to read someone safer; 'pretends to be a scholar, but he's not really
objective'. Even then I cringed when people talked about objectivity;
those who were generally regarded as having achieved it seemed to
have done little beyond making a career out of tedium. Besides, when
one looked hard at these would-be social scientists, they rarely turned
out to be objective; most often one found the most commonplace
ideas encapsulated within an enormous scholarly apparatus. One
sharp blow to the shell would reveal a philosophy worthy of a butcher
or a hairdresser. The stories they told were convincing to the dull
and simple-minded because they seemed so straightforward. Only the
details of events were complicated – motives and ideas were quickly
passed over; bad men were rarely credited with having done good;
good men were rarely seen to have resorted to deception and tricks
out of honourable intentions. Irony and paradox were seemingly
unknown to 'objective' historians. I dashed eagerly to the library in
the hope of finding someone whose views of the past were not simple,
whose people were not straightforward, and whose own ideas leapt
from the page in a challenge to one's own assumptions. I was not
disappointed then. I have not been disappointed since.

One particularly vivid example of Professor Kedourie at his most stimulating is to be found in his treatment of Arnold Toynbee, first in 'The Chatham House Version' and later in *The Anglo-Arab Labyrinth*, two pieces that encourage me to plunge the knife a little deeper into that extraordinary mass of energy and ideas that made up the mind of Toynbee. I hope that this further dissection entertains Professor Kedourie. He inspired it.

According to Kedourie, the Chatham House Version is a particular interpretation of the recent history of the Middle East, propagated by the Royal Institute of International Affairs at a time when it was the only centre in the English-speaking world to devote steady and systematic attention to its affairs. Arnold Toynbee, who was the dominant influence of that institute, produced the Chatham House Version as a result of his idiosyncratic interpretation of history and his superficial view of society and politics. He encouraged others to follow his lead, to adopt his style: to argue by analogy, to believe that the Middle East could be understood by employing terms designed to describe Western society.

Above all, the Chatham House Version interpreted the affairs of the Middle East from a consistently pro-Arab point of view, leading its adherents to denounce the Ottoman Empire, the idea of a Jewish state, and supposed Western imperialism. Toynbee painted a picture of a naturally peaceful and innocent Arabic society, explaining away some extreme movements like Wahabism and pan-Arabism as mere responses to the oppression and fragmentation imposed upon the Arabs by others. The Turks, for instance, ruled their subjects as if they were cattle. But Westerners were proving themselves to be not much better: they were becoming the arch-aggressors of the world, a propensity that Toynbee traced back to the Jewish idea of a 'chosen people'. Thus the annual *Survey* of international affairs became a spokesman for the Arab cause, arguing from a radical anti-imperialist point of view – an interpretation directly connected with Toynbee's belief that the Balfour Declaration, which was incompatible with Great Britain's promises to the sherif of Mecca, was an exercise in imperialist double-dealing.

But where are the origins of the Version, so influential, so superficially persuasive, to be found? Many ideas of this kind have roots that are practically impossible to trace; we might guess at the influences of classical training, Edwardian liberalism, the First World War, but the connections will usually remain vague and difficult to document. Fortunately, in the case of Arnold Toynbee, we have an unexpected resource: he wrote frequent, conscientious, and thoughtful letters to his mother, letters that reveal his hopes and fears, his practical ambitions, his moral torments. When these letters are placed within the context of his writing and his official war-work, we have an unusual opportunity to gauge how these vague, general influences worked in practice; how, in fact, the Chatham House Version began.

Toynbee's early career ought to be of enormous interest to historians of the twentieth century; certainly no one believed more in the significance of Toynbee than Toynbee. In books like *Experiences* and *Acquaintances*, in numerous essays and lectures, he constantly referred to his own life as if it were of seminal importance. So eager was he to lay out the path of his movements and chart the progress of his ideas that he encouraged Hugh Trevor-Roper to conclude that he saw himself as a Christ-figure, providing a well-marked trail for his disciples to follow. Perhaps he marked the trail because he feared what might be found out about him if people strayed from it. Believing that he had discovered the true meaning of history, that he understood how the world's religions could be reconciled with one another, that he saw how the Cold War could be ended, he was eager to portray himself in a light that would encourage others to follow. The pre-Chatham House Toynbee, the Toynbee of the years before *A Study of History* is a rather different creature from the one that emerges from Toynbee's own pages. He is no less interesting for that; perhaps more so. The transformation of the young classical scholar and Oxford don into the super-historian and commentator on the contemporary world is a story full of significance for anyone concerned with the interaction of ideas and politics in the modern world.[2]

By all appearances Toynbee fitted smoothly into the well-worn groove of the young scholar. A brilliant student at Winchester, he followed the usual Wykehamist route to New College, where he quickly established a reputation as an undergraduate of exceptional promise. He showed so much promise that he was elected to a fellowship at Balliol immediately upon graduation. In the leisurely fashion of pre-war Oxford, he was then given the first year to travel in Greece. When he returned, he settled into the donnish life and was beginning to publish when war broke out.

Appearances can be deceiving. When war broke out Toynbee would have been hard pressed to decide which he loathed more,

Oxford or Greece. The images that he later contrived, of 'history' taking him and his generation 'by the throat' in 1914, of being suddenly struck by the parallels between the ancient and modern world, are misleading.[3] It would be closer to the truth to say that the outbreak of war gave him the opportunity to break free from the bonds of Oxford and traditional scholarship, to expound ideas that were rooted in Edwardian culture, and to find an audience receptive to these ideas.

Toynbee disliked Oxford because it seemed to him that it neither valued scholarship nor prepared students for practical life. The undergraduates were mostly concerned with athletics – 'Fancy rowing being the chief characteristic of an university' – while the dons were mainly devoted to food and drink: 'The whole business is piggish, in all the Colleges'.[4] He was a serious young man. He joined the Fabian Society, became involved in the Workers' Educational Association, and admired a young lecturer, Alfred Zimmern, who was applying the ideas of Graham Wallas to ancient Greece.[5] He wished to reform Oxford, making it both more idealistic and more practical. He wished to change the world and he resented the ease of the donnish life because he regarded it as a barrier to understanding and reform.[6] Toynbee was representative of an overlooked tendency among the 'generation of 1914': hard-working, serious-minded and worried not so much by the bourgeois decadence of materialistic culture, as by the failure to spread material benefits more widely and to integrate the various elements of society into a more cohesive national unit.[7] Like many others, he felt the strains that seemed to be pulling Edwardian Great Britain apart and sensed the impending challenge from Germany. He welcomed the challenge, hoping it would ease some of the strain.

The crisis of July 1914 came as no surprise. Seven years earlier, before leaving Winchester, Toynbee had argued that the *Entente Cordiale* had come about because of 'the Germans' ambition to attain world-dominion'.[8] His years at Oxford strengthened his conviction that a great war with Germany was inevitable, and that it would be a glorious struggle:[9]

it is no use . . . denying that war has magnificent human things in it – it does and always will stir one's blood – may there never be war again; but there will. Have you ever imagined what it would be like, to suddenly enrol oneself, and to go to slay and be slain? Yet it will probably happen to all of us comfortable civilized men – I think we shall be swept into some Titanic Weltkrieg before we have done, and become fodder for cannon and pabulum for history.

The pre-war Toynbee saw war as a dramatic test of a civilization, not a mark of its failure. In spite of the waste and the destruction involved, war was glorious because of the human effort and efficiency it called forth: 'it is the human effort and victory and advance to fresh undertakings that is the real unity, and real living spirit, of history: when it blazes forth from time to time, one rejoices, even though the fire is destructive'.[10] He wondered whether Great Britain could rise to the challenge; Germany had already proved that she could:[11]

a big war with Germany (which is surely coming) may do for us what the Revolution did for France – or it may shatter our nerves altogether, and cripple our industry, and exhaust all Europe into the bargain. We have lain luxuriously in bed since 1815, and now can't face getting up; the Boer war only made us poke a toe out, and we drew it under the bedclothes again. Germany, meanwhile, has had '48, '66, and '70.

When the war came Toynbee would regard it as a confrontation between ideas and ideals, not as a petty struggle of interests; he turned into a crusader without misgivings or hesitation.

A year in Greece (1911-12) had strengthened Toynbee's belief in the supremacy of British culture. He found the modern Greeks repulsive, lazy, and idle – 'dagos' – and saw a moral in the decline of Greece to the position of 'hanger-on' in Europe. Great Britain would find herself in the same position when the centre of civilization shifted to China: 'so let us meanwhile arm to the teeth and fight to the death in order to remain top dogs and the centre of the universe, and govern India and exploit W[est] Africa, and colonise Canada, as the Greeks exploited Thrace and colonised Sicily and governed Asia'.[12] The Toynbee habit of thinking in parallels and arguing by analogy, while keeping an eye on the grand design beneath events, was well entrenched before the crisis of the First World War. 'Ancient Greek politics were like modern – bribery and jobbery... Ancient Greek wars were like modern Balkan unrest: innocuous farce enlivened by occasional bloody massacres'.[13] Within a decade Toynbee would be appointed the first professor of Greek at the university of London; but he felt little sympathy for 'these half-baked, flabby-cheeked Greeks'. He had started out, he assured his mother, 'with the intention of seeing the best in them ... but it is no use'.[14]

When Toynbee left Greece he was not only interested in the contacts and conflicts between races, he was a racist. 'I think the greatest result of this year has been to make me appreciate the value of England', he reported, and also 'the soundness of race prejudice'.[15] He began to despise especially those cultures that seemed to be small remnants of a remote past, and those that seemed to imitate and depend upon those that were vigorous and independent. He wondered why the Europeans bothered to keep half a dozen warships to look after Crete, 'instead of hanging the whole population and having done with it'. Why not hang them? 'Their existence is utterly pointless: you feel that they will never get any further . . . there is no meaning in them, as there is in England, France, Germany, Russia, Japan'. He was anxious to see the Turks driven out of Europe – not because they were brutal oppressors, but because they were stupid and lazy. He proposed to replace them with a regime that would be 'more vigorous and brutal'.[16] He began to regret that the coming conflict between Great Britain and Germany might destroy them both: who would be left to shake the 'dagos' out of their lethargy, to civilize the world? 'Oh, how I sympathise with Anglo-Indians who want to kick babus'.[17]

These simple assumptions about national character, the virtues of Western civilization, and the nature of progress underlay Toynbee's wartime activities. Because he had contracted dysentery during his time in Greece, he was ruled unfit for military service when he tried to enlist a few months after war broke out. Quite spontaneously, he began to write articles and books in support of the war effort, receiving encouragement from his father-in-law, Gilbert Murray, Oxford's most famous classical scholar and a man eager to see that the war would be used to promote liberal causes. Toynbee fitted neatly into the liberal movement, seeing the war as a contest between British democracy and Prussian despotism, between progressive imperialism and militaristic exploitation. If the future progress of humanity depended upon a vigorous and healthy 'Western' civilization, then it was essential that the leadership of the West not be permitted to pass into the hands of militarists who would try to prevent continued development. Austria-Hungary was clearly a decaying, tottering structure whose hold over minority nationalities delayed their development; the decision of the Ottoman Empire to join forces with the Central Powers would make a stiffer job of the war, 'but it will be a simplification in the end: we shan't leave any bits of Turkey laying about, when we clear up the mess afterwards'.[18]

If Toynbee were at all uncertain where the responsibility for the war should be placed, the publication of the British White Book convinced him, the documents leaving 'no doubt whatsoever'.[19] He did not know quite what to believe when the stories of German atrocities began to circulate in Britain during the first month of the war; but he had no doubt that the war had to be fought to the finish: 'we go on to the very end of our strength: we can't live in a Europe where Prussia is top dog'.[20] From the beginning of the war the causes and atrocities were of less interest to Toynbee than the peace settlement. If Prussia won the war, Europe would be dominated by a militaristic despotism. The first concern of civilized men must be to prevent this possibility. 'I don't like the existence of people whose only chance in life comes through war: they are a disastrous breed, and the sooner we breed them out of civilised countries the better. All the Ostelbische Junkers are that sort'.[21] He wished to eradicate militarism without obliterating Germany – the war made sense to him only as a crusade on behalf of democracy and nationality.

Although he was still living in and teaching at Oxford, Toynbee immediately turned away from his classical studies and devoted his attention to the questions of nationality and the future peace settlement. With the real horrors of the war still to come, Toynbee was already wondering whether they were witnessing the beginning of a 'Decline and Fall', whether this was 'the Peloponnesian War of Europe'.[22] He comforted himself with the assurance that history did not repeat itself if men refused to let it, that men could make of the world whatever they wished. He resolved that he would be one of those who saw to it that the war would be taken as an opportunity for a new beginning. He disliked the screechiness of the Union of Democratic Control and considered their attacks on the government to be dangerous and disloyal, but he agreed with their programme: 'the veiled war of diplomacy is the root of all evil, and democracy all over Europe has got to conquer the domain of foreign policy as well as home affairs'.[23] Within three years Toynbee would be working within the foreign office and writing reports for the war cabinet.

The outlines of the views that Toynbee espoused once he began to work for the government were well-established beforehand; they acted as a kind of prism through which he viewed the events of the war and by which he tried to make sense of the masses of details that arrived on his desk. He was successful and persuasive because he was able to reduce the most complicated situations to a few simple generalizations: exactly the sort of thing that busy cabinet politicians liked to hear; and exactly the sort of thing that experts found repugnant.

In late October 1914, the Clarendon Press rejected Toynbee's manuscript on 'Nationality and the War', complaining that there was too much prophecy and suggestion in it and insisting that they could not endorse such definite policies as those he proposed.[24] He turned to a commercial publisher and the book appeared early in 1915, quickly followed by another, entitled *The New Europe*. Both books grappled with the question of nationality and how it ought to be taken into account when redrawing the map of Europe at the end of the war. Nationalism, as the most dynamic force in the modern world, must be understood and harnessed by the peacemakers in order to replace 'national competition' with 'national co-operation'.[25] The best way to achieve this was to destroy anachronistic forms of nationalism while promoting the right of national self-determination. The war had been caused by anachronistic Prussianism and the desperate attempt of the Habsburg and Ottoman Empires to forestall the demands of their subjects for national independence. Germany was a nation, but 'a menace to our civilisation' because she was united by authoritarian Prussia when the forces of the modern age were clearly moving in the direction of democratic self-government.[26] 'To us the state stands for "Co-operation"; to the German it still stands for "Power" . . . like the medieval despot, he regards human society as so much passive material to be bound or loosed, herded together or torn asunder'.

The 'new Europe' that the Allied Powers must create would be one that left Germany intact, but democratic; the Habsburg and Ottoman Empires must be dismantled and national states put in their place. Dismembering Germany would only create a tremendous grievance in the heart of Europe; impoverishing her would hinder the continued growth of Western civilization: 'you cannot destroy German wealth without paralysing German intellect and art, and European civilisation, if it is to go on growing, cannot do without them'.[27] Toynbee was a Wilsonian before Wilson. Although he had no doubt that 'it was the impossible point of view Germany has been getting herself into' that caused the war, the peace had to be constructed purely on the basis of 'what seemed the best arrangement for all of us in the future'.[28] Toynbee's role in the war, his participation in the propaganda effort, his disillusionment with the peace settlement, and his political activities between the wars cannot be understood apart from these growing hopes for a liberal peace founded upon the precepts of national self-determination and democratic politics.

These hopes grew as Toynbee's guilt increased and the horrors of war mounted. By November 1914 friends from Winchester and Oxford were being killed and he was wondering 'when there is all this going on, why am I not in it?'[29] He tried to assure himself that he was giving his best service by explaining Croats and Ruthenes to the English people. His familiarity with the horrors, although not first-hand, was not remote; friends returned to Oxford when on leave from the trenches and they described what was happening; early shell-shock victims were housed on the Woodstock Road. When one of his closest New College friends was killed he became distraught with grief and wished only to go out and get killed too.[30] Another friend had to persuade him that his desire for martyrdom may have been selfish and that he would have to resign himself to the 'soberer and harder' duty of 'a grey and inglorious life'.[31] Toynbee and others like him could justify staying safely at home only by believing that they were contributing to the creation of a new world. When the new world fell short of their ideal after 1919 their feelings of guilt returned, and they took it out on those they believed had betrayed them. But then Toynbee had believed from the start that there was 'a dash of the dago' in Lloyd George's blood.[32]

Many men thought they would discover their true selves under fire on the battlefield; Toynbee resigned himself to discovering what he could by working as a propagandist. In May 1915 he went down to London for the duration of the war to work in the newly-formed department of information, located at Wellington House. For almost two years he devoted his considerable energies to writing books and articles such as *The German Terror in Belgium*, *The German Terror in France*, *The Armenian Atrocities*, and 'The Death of Nurse Cavell'. He expected to learn from the experience: 'it will sober me and brace me – make more of a man of me, in fact. It gives me a chance of seeing what I can do in the life that lies beyond Winchester-plus–Oxford'.[33] The excitement of the war, the possibilities for the future that it opened up, and the restless guilt of being safely cloistered in Oxford intensified Toynbee's pre-war distaste for 'donism'.[34] By the end of the year he had decided to resign from Oxford to seek a career in the foreign office.[35]

It was not that Toynbee particularly enjoyed his work as propagandist; in fact he found it rather distasteful – 'no job for a gentle-man' – and was relieved when he moved on to proper intelligence work in 1917.[36] Then he felt he was doing useful work and enjoyed the sensation of power, of being part of a real drama: 'I hope I may be in at the death and somehow, through my present job, get a finger into the re-drawing of frontiers'.[37] But the war had first to be won, and the cost of winning was pressing down on Toynbee with ever-increasing pressure. When he saw war office films of the Somme in September 1916, he was almost overcome with shock and revulsion:[38]

the dead are not at all the worst. The more I learn about the war, the more it seems to me a comparatively simple, comfortable thing to be dead. What I shan't forget is the eyes of men filmed in trenches under fire or waiting to charge, or the prisoners and wounded and men with shell-shock coming in – broken men. The look on their faces isn't like anything one has seen ... Sometimes the men seemed one's own flesh and blood set down in hell, and sometimes they seemed little busy, swarming insects obeying some obscene corporate instinct – swarming in some place that was like photographs of the moon.

The horrors caused Toynbee to redefine his religious feelings and his understanding of history; they also helped to make him a fervent Wilsonian. He rejoiced at the news of Wilson's election victory in 1916, concluding that it represented the triumph of liberalism over reaction, and hoping that it would enable the American president to mediate between the warring parties.[39] After the Somme, Toynbee was willing to settle for a peace that was less than ideal, and, when Wilson announced his fourteen points, he thought he saw salvation at hand. There would be a compromise peace, but one based on nationality. He was even prepared to accept Wilson's attack on navalism: 'I can see no finer end to the British Navy than to become an International Institution'.[40] But a compromise peace arising from the stalemate on the western front was always a defective outcome in Toynbee's mind, to be resorted to only if there seemed to be no other means of bringing the horrors to an end. When Wilson brought the United States into the war Toynbee abandoned any idea of resorting to such a defective peace. Wilson was thus regarded as a saviour, 'as big a statesman as there ever has been', and a man whose political ability 'is astounding'.[41]

The entry of the United States coincided with Toynbee's move into 'Political Intelligence'.[42] When Lloyd George undertook to reorganize the chaotic profusion of propaganda services, his special commissioner, Sir John Buchan, concluded that the abilities of a small group of people at Wellington House, including Toynbee, were being wasted. Lesser talents could write propaganda for the masses. More useful would be to employ a select group of regional experts to sift incoming intelligence and write succinct weekly commentaries on developments for the war cabinet. Toynbee was to be responsible for Turkey and the Middle East.

Within two years Toynbee had thus been transformed from an isolated young scholar with no experience of practical politics into an 'expert' with a direct line of communication to the most important men in government: 'I sit there like a pundit and do enormously interesting work'.[43] He arrived in his new position with specific views concerning the nature of historical development, the rights of nationality, and the merits of British democracy; he was soon filtering information and summarizing events in light of these assumptions. Toynbee's great fear as a political intelligence officer was that the Muslim world would turn against Great Britain in the aftermath of war. Islam was a backward force, but one with great potential to do harm. Although it lagged half a millenium behind its Christian prototype, Islamic consciousness, like that of medieval Christianity, was 'the strongest bond of union between those who professed it'.[44] Previously, this had posed little danger to the West, because it had not been transformed into political consciousness, but pan-Turanianism and Bolshevism were now threatening to give a political impetus to Islam. The Turks were using the idea of national self-determination to justify the retention of all the territories of the old Ottoman Empire, and many Muslims were naturally inclined to view the only independent Muslim state as something that must be retained and strengthened. The Bolsheviks were doing everything they could to win the support of their Muslim population by encouraging the growth of congresses and supporting claims for national self-determination – under the umbrella of world revolution. 'The Islamic consciousness, hardly articulate and almost impotent hitherto, has now behind it the force of the Bolshevik Government'.[45] The Muslims of India, Toynbee darkly suggested, had much stronger claims to self-determination than those of Russia.

Great Britain's position in both Asia and Europe, according to Toynbee, depended upon an *entente* with revolutionary Russia and politically conscious Islam because, without their assistance, the whole land-bridge between Europe and the East was bound to come under some form of German control. Although he predicted that Russia was likely to remain Bolshevik, he was not responsible for analysing Russian policy or suggesting policies towards her.[46] He therefore concentrated on relations with Islam, where he saw two dangers confronting Great Britain: her championship of the Arab cause was regarded by other Muslims as a cynical device for the dismemberment of Turkey; and her secret agreements with Russia and France (recently exposed by the Bolsheviks) indicated that the Muslim world was to be divided among the Allied powers, 'the very contingency that Moslem opinion loathes and fears'.[47]

In a long and influential memorandum, which was enthusiastically endorsed by Buchan and Lord Milner, a member of the war cabinet, Toynbee anticipated the campaign to which he would devote most of his energy throughout 1918-19. Great Britain, he declared,[48] 'is incurring the full odium of the entente with Russia at the moment when the policy on which it was founded was broken down through the Russian Revolution and the repudiation of the Tsarist aims by the Bolsheviks. We are in danger of drawing upon our own heads the Tsardom's whole heritage of hatred in the Moslem world'.

He would soon be arguing that, as the revolution, together with the Arab revolt, had nullified the agreements with Russia, France, and Italy, the best possible solution to the dilemma would be to find a trustee to reconstruct the non-Turkish territories of the Ottoman Empire, Persia, and Afghanistan with the ultimate goal of allowing them self-determination. Toynbee became a crusader against the 'secret treaties', which he believed would deliver the peoples of the Middle East into the hands of the imperialists and forestall their development into progressive, self-reliant societies.

When Toynbee was given the task of defining British war aims in the Middle East he was accused by Lord Robert Cecil of ignoring the realities of Great Britain's situation. Toynbee, said Cecil, had ignored the claims of Greece and Italy and dealt with the treaty of London, the Sykes–Picot Agreement and the treaty of St. Jean de Maurienne as if they did not exist. He was especially critical of Toynbee's proposals for Iraq, Jezireh and Anazeh, which really represented 'the views of Colonel Lawrence and his school'.[49] He was right. Toynbee believed that Arab 'independence' under some form of British tutelage was the ideal solution for the Arabian peninsula. Great Britain would control the foreign relations of the new states, arbitrate disputes among them, and work towards the creation of an

Arab Confederation – aims, he said, that 'may be summed up as a British Monroe Doctrine for Arabia'. If France secured a protectorate for herself in Syria, she would be in a position to interfere in the tribal relations of the Arabian peninsula; therefore Great Britain must be given control of the relations between Syria and the independent Arab rulers in her hinterland. The British were also to act as tutor to a new Armenian state and build her up 'into an effective barrier against pan-Turanianism and also against German or Russian aggression in the direction of the Arab countries'.[50]

Toynbee's later reputation as an anti-imperialist is certainly misplaced when applied to his activities in the political intelligence department. He had no misgivings, no doubts, concerning both the right and the fitness of the British to maintain and expand the empire, although this was now to be justified on the basis of tutoring people to one day govern themselves. The French, the Germans, and the Italians were bad tutors: they ruled and exploited when they should have taught and developed (and the peoples of the Middle East knew this and would choose to come under the tutelage of Great Britain if they were given the choice). The record of the Italians in their colonies 'indicates that they would be oppressive and incompetent'; in Syria 'the French are not wanted by the Arabs . . . and the idea of French assistance is obnoxious to them'. Toynbee continued to argue that the disappearance of the old Russia nullified the secret treaties, but the entry of the United States into the war combined with Wilsonian rhetoric to give him a new and a more powerful argument with which to attack the treaties.

'The principles of nationality and democracy and the right of self-determination', Toynbee declared, were not merely one element in the aims of the Allies, 'but the essential aim and expression of their cause'.[51] He wished to see a situation whereby the peoples of the Middle East would form whatever political groupings they chose and which country, if any, should aid them. The inhabitants would undoubtedly want outside assistance, but 'the choice will be theirs, not ours'. The old agreements were to have no force:[52]

there should not only be freedom for the Arabs, Turks, Armenians, etc., to invite what Power they like, but . . . the various powers should be free towards each other to accept such invitations. Any private arrangements among the Powers by which some agreed to refuse invitations of assistance for the benefit of others, would obviously be simply a roundabout method of imposing those very restrictions on the liberties of the new States which we are professing to rule out.

He dismissed the Allied treaty provisions as a 'bizarre rearrangement' of boundaries redrawn 'according to the desiderata of the Powers'; provisions for the nationalities being fitted into this framework 'where they suited the Powers' convenience'.[53]

Subscribing to what critics were beginning to refer to as the 'Lawrence view' propelled Toynbee into a series of confrontations with other officers and departments that dealt with the Middle East. He fought with the political officer at Baghdad over the arrangements in Mesopotamia; with the India office over the value of the trucial system in the Arabian Peninsula; with the war office and the eastern department of the foreign office over the issue of co-operation with the United States.[54] These battles were not fought because of simple-minded idealism on Toynbee's part, although he was steadily becoming more convinced that he had succeeded in penetrating the mysteries of historical development and that this insight endowed him with a unique responsibility. He insisted that Great Britain had been handed an opportunity to secure permanent political advantages by supporting the Arab movement: 'the rise of the Arab movement has been a fortunate development for the British Empire at a crucial period of its history'.[55] Before the war Great Britain had been forced to conciliate and support the Ottoman Empire; now she could foster an anti-Turkish Muslim power by continuing to support the sherif of Mecca. And Husein's attitude to Great Britain and to Islam 'fits in admirably with our interests. He needs our financial and political support because he has broken with the Turks and cannot be self-sufficing; he will therefore look to us, and will let us have what we want in Mesopotamia'.[56]

Toynbee confidently believed, in spite of the horrors and chaos of the war, that a world redesigned according to liberal principles of self-determination and self-government would continue to work in the best interests of Great Britain, that the pursuit of British interests would benefit the world. He kept his eye on the big picture; small groups and minor interests must be rigorously subordinated to major ones. Proposing that the United States should act as trustee in some areas of the Middle East, he argued that 'there could be no arrangement better calculated to cement the Anglo-American Alliance', which, he claimed, 'is perhaps the one consideration in the War which is as important as the recovery of the goodwill of Islam'.[57] Uniting the Arab world, recovering the goodwill of Islam, cementing the alliance with the United States – these were Toynbee's ambitions, and next to them the Jews barely counted. He consistently treated the Jews as a minor pawn in the game of European diplomacy: Jewish opinion in Europe and the United States was worth conciliating, and a national home in Palestine was the best means of winning their favour – but Zionism must be carefully kept in check, and the connection with the movement must be subordinated to the greater need of winning the favour of the Muslim world.[58]

Besides, by the time the war ended, Toynbee was beginning to think his way towards a new interpretation of history, in which he would dismiss the interests of the small and the weak. 'Fossil' cultures like the Jewish must not be permitted to interfere with the progressive movement towards greater unity. Although he continued to champion the idea of national self-determination, he was becoming convinced that the important units were civilizations, not nations, and that national ambitions could be supported only in so far as they did not destroy the potential for greater unity. 'The war', he told his mother, 'seems to have put a meaning into all History'.[59] By 1918 he was thinking of writing a history of European civilization, 'treating it as a unity and not as a bundle of separate nations or states'.[60] His personal experience and the meaning of history were becoming fused together in his mind until they were inseparable; he was about to discover another crusade with which to fill the gap opened by the end of the war.

The experience of peacemaking at Paris was the final lesson in the education of Arnold Toynbee. Given his extreme and unrealistic hopes for a settlement based on national rights that would somehow overcome international competition, it is not surprising that this lesson was a study in disillusionment. For four years he had assured himself that only one thing could justify the carnage of the war: 'it feels as though everyone one had grown up with at Winchester or Oxford had just been fattened for slaughter . . . [but] if we did not make this sacrifice and gain what we mean to gain by making it, our civilisation would be bankrupt'.[61] The war represented the bankruptcy of the European state system, but 'a new order is coming'.[62] When the new order failed to come in Paris in the spring of 1919, Toynbee became ill and depressed. He spent most of the summer in bed, unable to settle to the work necessary in preparation for his new career at London University.

'The Conference has been a soul-destroying affair', he remarked.[63] He felt as if he were drifting aimlessly:[64]

I feel as if my roots were cut and I couldn't grow new ones [he told his mother] – though that is certainly an illusion, and I suppose it is really no more than the waves tossing when the wind has gone down. But that pathetic illusion of building something up, which we all cherished during the war, in self-defence, whatever we were doing, seems for the moment to have fallen flat . . . One had made believe during the war that one was building something up, and not merely assisting at a catastrophe, [he added to a friend][65] and now it has all fallen flat, and one sees the war for what it is – pure destruction. One had the pathetic delusion that because it wasn't one's fault one ought to be able to make some good come of it.

A Study of History and the Chatham House Version were the logical consequences of Toynbee's wartime experience, of his hopes and his despair. The politicians had lost the opportunity to save civilization because of their petty ambitions and senseless quarrels. Toynbee would save it for them. He could never return to Oxford, to life as a college don. The true story of history had to be told, could only be told, by one who had both been trained to tell it and taken a part in the making of it. Toynbee's work as a propagandist had trained him to write quickly and effectively for popular consumption; his work at the foreign office had given him an appetite for power, for participating in practical affairs; his classical training enabled him to see beyond and under the surface of events – or so he believed: 'I feel I am seeing deeper into history every day and have great things to write'.[66] There can be no doubt about the true meaning of the *Study*: 'I believe one can put one's experience of the War best in parables'.[67] 'I always come back to what I have been doing during the war – it is a plough I can't turn back from, and most of the field is still to do'.[68] His mission was to prevent a collision between Islam and the British Empire, 'to do something towards keeping a hand on the pulse and preventing the big catastrophe from occurring'.[69] After the war, history, propaganda, and the Middle East were woven together into a fascinating career, unique in the intellectual and political history of modern Great Britain. The consequences for scholarship and the state were equally disastrous.

NOTES

1. Elie Kedourie, *Arabic Political Memoirs and Other Studies* (London, 1970), p. 176.
2. H.R. Trevor-Roper, 'Arnold Toynbee's Millennium', *Encounters*, ed. Stephen Spender *et al.* (New York, 1963), pp. 131-51; John Barker, *The Super-Historians: Makers of Our Past* (New York, 1982), pp. 268-99.
3. Arnold J. Toynbee, *Civilization on Trial* (New York, 1948), p. 3.

4. To mother, 20 Oct. 1907, Bodleian Library, Toynbee MSS. These papers are still in a disorganized state, without a proper reference system.
5. To Robert Darbyshire, 17 Nov. 1909; to Alfred Zimmern, 9 Aug. 1930, Toynbee MSS.
6. To Darbyshire, 6 Nov. 1912, *ibid.*
7. See Robert Wohl, *The Generation of 1914* (Cambridge, 1980); and Roland Stromberg, *Redemption by War: The Intellectuals and 1914* (Lawrence, Kansas, 1982).
8. Arnold Toynbee, 'Entente Cordiale: Maximus' Dream', *c.*1905-7, Toynbee MSS.
9. To Darbyshire, 15 May 1911, *ibid.*
10. To mother, 26 Jan. 1912, *ibid.*
11. To mother, 8 March 1912, *ibid.*
12. To mother, 27 Nov. 1911, *ibid.*
13. To mother, 17 Dec. 1911, *ibid.*
14. *Ibid.*
15. *Ibid.*
16. To mother, 22 June 1912, *ibid.*
17. To mother, 17. Dec. 1911, *ibid.*
18. To mother, 31 Oct. 1914, *ibid.*
19. To mother, 16 Aug. 1914; to Darbyshire, 5 Sept. 1914, *ibid.*
20. To mother, 24 Aug. 1914, *ibid.*
21. To mother, undated [Oct. 1914], *ibid.*
22. To mother, 11 Oct. 1914, *ibid.*
23. To mother, 12 Nov. 1914, *ibid.*
24. To mother, 23 Oct. 1914, *ibid.*
25. Arnold J. Toynbee, *Nationality and the War* (London, 1915), p. 488.
26. Arnold J. Toynbee, *New Europe* (London, 1915), p. 18.
27. Arnold J. Toynbee, *Experiences* (Oxford, 1969), pp. 32-3.
28. To mother, 17 Nov. 1914, Toynbee MSS.
29. To mother, 12 Nov. 1914, *ibid.*
30. To mother, 11 Dec. 1914, *ibid.*; to Zimmern, 29 Dec. 1914, Bodleian Library, Zimmern MSS, Box 14, fos. 107-10.
31. From Herbert Paton, 14 Jan. 1915, Toynbee MSS.
32. To mother, 23 Sept. 1915, *ibid.*
33. To mother, 28 April 1915, *ibid.*
34. From Alan Wace, 10 Oct. 1915, *ibid.*
35. On wartime propaganda, see Michael Saunders and Philip M. Taylor, *British Propaganda during the First World War 1914-18* (London, 1983).
36. To Darbyshire, 16 Sept. 1917, Toynbee MSS.
37. To mother, 20 Sept. 1916, *ibid.*
38. To mother, 28 Sept. 1916, *ibid.*
39. To mother, 12 Nov. 1916, *ibid.*
40. To mother, 23 Jan. 1917, *ibid.*
41. To mother, 19 April 1917, *ibid.*
42. This was first established within the ministry of information as the intelligence bureau; at the beginning of 1918 the bureau was moved to the foreign office and became the department of political intelligence.
43. To Darbyshire, 5 May 1918, Toynbee MSS.
44. Unsigned memorandum [by Toynbee], 'The Formula of "The Self Determination of Peoples" and the Moslem World', secret, 10 Jan. 1918, FO 371/4353.
45. *Ibid.*
46. On the subject of Bolshevism, its possible success and the threat that it posed to Great Britain, Toynbee disagreed with the two members of Political Intelligence responsible for Russian matters, Professor J.Y. Simpson and Rex Leeper.

47. [Toynbee] 'Self-Determination of Peoples', FO 371/4353.
48. *Ibid.*
49. Minute on Toynbee's 'Memorandum for Mr. Hurst on Preparation of Draft Treaty with Turkey', n.d., FO 371/4363.
50. Unsigned memorandum [by Toynbee], 'The Settlement of Turkey and the Arabian Peninsula', secret, 13 Nov. 1918, FO 371/4352.
51. *Ibid.*
52. *Ibid.*
53. *Ibid.*
54. Unsigned memorandum [by Toynbee] on telegrams from the political officer at Baghdad, 28 Nov. 1918, FO 371/4353.
55. Unsigned memorandum [by Toynbee], 'French and Arab Claims in the Middle East in Relation to British Interests', 19 Dec. 1918, FO 371/4352.
56. *Ibid.*
57. Unsigned memorandum [by Toynbee], 10 Jan. 1918, FO 371/4353.
58. Minute by Toynbee, 14 Nov. 1918, FO 371/4369.
59. To mother, 1 April 1917, Toynbee MSS.
60. To Darbyshire, 5 May 1918, *ibid.*
61. To mother, 26 Oct. 1915, *ibid.*
62. To mother, undated [c. June 1917], *ibid.*
63. To Darbyshire, 21 May 1919, *ibid.*
64. To mother, 21 July 1919, *ibid.*
65. To Darbyshire, 21 July 1919, *ibid.*
66. To mother, 7 Jan. 1917, *ibid.*
67. To Darbyshire, 5 May 1918, *ibid.*
68. To mother, 21 July 1919, *ibid.*
69. To mother, 9 July 1919, *ibid.*

VI

THE ROLE OF ISLAM AS POLITICAL IDEOLOGY IN THE FIRST WORLD WAR

William L. Cleveland

> In Constantinople, as in the Arabic-speaking provinces, the mass of the population was quite offended and alienated by the Frankish ways of Young Turks and their contempt for Islam and its traditional way of life.
>
> Elie Kedourie[1]

No responsible commentator would now claim that Islam has lost its prominent role in Arab politics and society. There seems, however, to be some uncertainty about how it has survived the vicissitudes of the present century. During the 1920s, a small but dominant élite of relatively secular politicians rejected the notion that Islam could provide the principles for governing a modern, independent nation state. They embraced instead European-style constitutionalism beside which the Islamic order as represented by the defeated Ottoman Empire and the official religious establishment appeared ineffective and irrelevant. As Professor Kedourie has noted of the immediate post-war period: 'At that time it was fashionable to look upon "pan-Islamism" as nefarious, and upon the "national principle" as its efficacious antidote'.[2]

But the depreciation of Islam as a political ideology was short-lived. Mass alienation from imported political systems and secular politicians was reflected in the formation of Muslim organizations outside the formal political structure. In 1927, the Young Men's Muslim Association was founded in Egypt; it was followed a year later by the Muslim Brotherhood. Both organizations attempted to establish followings in Syria and Palestine. Popular disaffection led, in turn, to a change in élite attitudes which has been variously termed a crisis of orientation or a shift to Islam.[3]

This transition has been frequently studied and is most often treated as a new response to new circumstances. While there can be no denying the novelty of the existence of several Arab states under various forms of European control during the inter-war period, the assertion of Islamic values in the late 1920s should not be seen solely as a new development. As this essay shows, appeals to Islamic solidarity and to the defence of the Islamic order against the West dominated political discourse in the eastern Arab world during the First World War. The Arab spokesmen who voiced these appeals did not vanish with the Ottoman defeat. Throughout the 1920s they denounced Atatürk and the Egyptian secular liberals alike while continuing to assert that the subjugation of the Islamic community could only be ended by Muslims acting in harmony as Muslims. The emergence of Islamic activism towards the end of the 1920s represents a certain triumph for their position and must be understood, in part, as the persistence of sentiments and loyalties which were firmly grounded in the crisis of the First World War.

In March 1913, the Istanbul-based Arabic journal, *al-Hidaya*, published this invocation: 'Oh Islamic nations, leave aside your racial [*jinsiyya*] distinctions and let Islam serve as the bond among you. Become like a large family, a single, powerful bloc. This is a question of life or death'.[4] As tensions between the government of the Committee of Union and Progress (CUP) and the Arab provincial élite increased, pro-Ottoman Arabic publications stated the case for imperial unity, or Ottomanism, in unambiguous Islamic terms. With the outbreak of the Great War, these appeals intensified, and in November 1914 the Ottoman sultan-caliph proclaimed a jihad, demanding that Muslims the world over unite behind the Ottoman Empire in its confrontation with the Triple Entente. The call was directed primarily at the Arab subjects of the empire and warned them that if they failed to respond as a single community, both their faith and the state which protected it faced extinction: according to the proclamation, the Allied powers had, 'in the last century deprived the *Muslim* peoples in India, Asia, and most regions of Central Africa, of their sovereignty, their governments, and even their liberty'.[5] But the bond would not hold, and in June 1916, the Ottoman-appointed amir of Mecca, Sherif Husayn Ibn Ali, ordered his forces to attack the Ottoman garrisons in the Hejaz. And he, too, proclaimed a jihad and requested that the community of the faithful rally to his cause.

These two contending appeals to Islamic solidarity mark the transition from an Ottoman to a post-Ottoman Middle East, from a world that still honoured an Islamic caliph and an independent Islamic political and social order, to one that had to reconstitute itself under European occupation and European-inspired political systems without the presence of caliphal authority or imperial unity. Yet for all the political changes brought about by the First World War, the regional contest between Sherif Husayn and the Ottoman state was characterized by ideological continuity. Husayn's challenge to imperial authority was made on the grounds of Islamic legitimacy; the government, in turn, appealed to Arab loyalties by stressing the Islamic character of the Ottoman state and by linking the survival of the empire to the cause of the survival of Islam. As an examination of the content of Arab and Ottoman propaganda from the proclamation of the Arab revolt in 1916 to the end of the war will show, most justifications for the revolt presented it as an Islamic necessity, and most Ottoman appeals to their Arab subjects were based on the principle of Islamic solidarity.[6] The rebellion of Husayn did not prepare the Arab Middle East for secular politics or nationalist ideologies.

Before analysing the content of wartime propaganda, it will be useful to comment on the men who wrote it and the journals in which it appeared. The Arabic periodical press which flourished from the Young Turk revolt in 1908 to the outbreak of the war has been used profitably by historians to trace the development of Arab perspectives on the regional issues of the time. However, sources for the war years are more limited. The Ottoman government effectively silenced the public voices of Arab protest within the empire. Dissidents, and presumed dissidents, were arrested, exiled, in some cases executed, and their presses were shut down. Anybody who wishes to trace Arab opposition opinion during the war years must look for sources published outside Ottoman-controlled territories.

One such source is Sherif Husayn's newspaper, *al-Qibla*, published in Mecca from 1916 to 1924. *Al-Qibla* must be considered the organ of the Arab revolt and the most important forum for the justification of the revolt to Arab society. While Sherif Husayn's sponsorship of the paper determined its orientation, the opinions of its editor and frequent lead article writer, Muhibb al-Din al-Khatib, gave its bi-weekly issues their tone and content. A native of Damascus, al-Khatib (1886-1969) embodies all of the ideological complexities of the Ottoman-Arab Muslim élite of his generation. That this has made him difficult to categorize is evident from the differing scholarly interpretations of his achievements. To those determined to establish the Arab revolt as a model nationalist uprising, al-Khatib appears as 'one of the pioneers of the nationalist awakening'.[7] But to those who have focused on al-Khatib's full career, he was 'one of the most prominent figures of modern Islamic thought and a reformer who carried the banner of the Islamic mission for more than fifty years'.[8] Both assessments carry an element of truth, and al-Khatib's appointment to the editorship of *al-Qibla* provided him with a forum in which to express his views on the two social issues which most concerned him – Arab rights and Islamic order. They were inseparable components of the political whole.

An additional source of opinion on Arab-Ottoman affairs is Rashid Rida's influential Cairo journal, *al-Manar*. Although Rida, as the most prominent disciple of Muhammad 'Abduh, established his reputation primarily as a religious commentator in the *salafiyya* tradition, he was also involved in the politics of Syrian–Ottoman relations and was one of the founders of the Ottoman Decentralization Society. When Ottoman policies towards the Syrian provinces became entwined with the revolt of a descendant of the Prophet against the empire of the caliph, Rida became an active commentator on the unfolding drama.

There did exist Arabic language periodicals within the territory under Ottoman jurisdiction. The CUP founded Arabic journals which supported the Ottoman war effort and which sought to convince the Arab population to remain loyal to the Ottoman cause. One of them was *Jarida al-Sharq*, a newspaper published under Jamal Pasha's supervision in Damascus. Its editorial staff included some of the best-known Arab political journalists of the time, among them Shakib Arslan, Muhammad Kurd 'Ali, and 'Abd al-Qadir al-Maghribi. In a further effort to enhance the paper's credibility, prominent Syrian notables were listed on the masthead as holding responsible positions.[9]

Another Ottoman-sponsored journal was *al-'Alam al-Islami*, a handsome weekly magazine printed in Istanbul. It was edited by 'Abd al-'Aziz Jawish, an Egyptian known for his inflammatory pan-Islamic rhetoric and his strong CUP loyalties. He and Shakib Arslan were personal friends and ideological allies, and before the war Jawish and Muhibb al-Din al-Khatib had belonged to the same intellectual circles in Cairo. Given their shared hopes for the revitalization of Islamic society, it is not surprising that they sought to attract support to their wartime patrons by appealing to Islamic sentiments. But it is ironic that one was a rebel and the others loyalists even as they called for the same moral and social order.

The appearance of both *al-Sharq* and *al-'Alam al-Islami* in April 1916 may be taken as a concerted effort by the Ottoman government to appeal to Arab sensibilities. For the editors of the first issue of *al-'Alam al-Islami*, those sensibilities were most likely to be aroused by emphasizing the right of the Ottoman state to speak for the Islamic community at large: 'We call for the transmission of the order for jihad to all Muslims so they will rise up in defence of their faith, take vengeance on their enemies, liberate themselves, and make their religious community live again in its former glory ... That is why we are publishing this paper and placing it at the service of the interests of the Islamic world and the defence of its rights'.[10] 'Abd al-'Aziz Jawish's statement of purpose sharpened the Arab orientation of the journal, but left no doubt as to the appeal chosen by the Ottoman authorities: 'We wish to inform the Arab *ummas* of what has heretofore not been communicated to them concerning the deeds of their brother *mujahids* in the cause of protecting Islam and raising the beacon of the Muslims'.[11] Jawish wrote of the war as a God-given opportunity for Muslim redemption. In the crucible of combat, the weaknesses of the past would be transformed into a sense of purpose for the entire community of believers. Already, this had begun to occur. Referring to the Ottoman victory over the British at Kut, Jawish claimed that this was the kind of success to be expected when 'the swords of Islam are unsheathed'.[12] Those swords would be wielded by Muslims fighting together under the banner of the Ottoman-Islamic state.

In August 1916, *al-Qibla* appeared in Mecca to justify the Arab revolt. It made the same claims as Jawish had: that it was founded for the service of Islam and that the cause which it defended, the Arab awakening in the Hejaz, would achieve the liberation of all Muslims and lead Islam to the recovery of its past greatness. In competing with the established state for the same ideological ground, *al-Qibla* was led to stress the failures of the government in power and to equate those failures with a diminishing of Islam as a whole. Under the incompetent leadership of the CUP, the Ottoman Empire had retreated before petty Balkan kings, and the Ottoman flag had been lowered in Crete, in Bosnia and Hercegovina, and even in Salonika, 'the Qa'abah of the Unionists'.[13] This reversal in the fortunes of the once proud Ottoman Empire was also a diminution of the entire Islamic legacy; the state of Islam had lost territory to non-Muslims. The disaster was directly attributable to the CUP's neglect of the essence of the state's power: 'Without its Islamic religion and the throne of its Ottoman caliph, an Islamic community [*milla*] dies'.[14]

Here was the crisis addressed through an idiom familiar to both parties; the Islamic community was under attack and required active support from its members. The arena for the propaganda battle was defined as service to Islam – which party could most successfully portray its actions as dedicated to the advancement of the *umma* of Muhammad? Or, as the contest developed, which party could demonstrate most forcefully the Islamic unworthiness of the other; which party could show that the other had violated Islamic canons and no longer merited the support of the community?

For his part, Sherif Husayn was well aware that his revolt was directed against the state of the Islamic caliph. For all the attention given by historians to Husayn's care in covering his flanks, or failing to do so, in his negotiations with Great Britain, it might be argued that his greatest concern at the time was to justify his actions to a Muslim audience. As explained in the columns of *al-Qibla*, the amir of Mecca was motivated solely by a concern for the status of Islam; his movement was made necessary because the CUP leaders were ignorant of the faith and negligent in protecting it. They were portrayed as posing a threat to the very survival of Islam: 'The Ottoman Empire has been taken over by a reckless party which has launched an attack on Islam, an attack which is a *fitna* in every sense of the term . . . The leaders of the state do not care about religion or the *shari'a* . . . and have begun to live under the signs of apostasy and unbelief.'[15]

Evidence of the Unionists' betrayal of Islam was found in several aspects of their behaviour. One of the most consistently cited was their alleged attempt to Turkify Islam. This was a sensitive issue, for it raised the question of the role of nationalism within the universal religious community. As early as the turn of the century, Arab thinkers had concluded that if any national group was to be entrusted with the political leadership of Islam, it should be the Arabs. They, after all, had given birth to the faith through an Arabian prophet who received Allah's final message to mankind in the Arabic tongue. To deny this was to deny Islam. Thus *al-Qibla*'s claims that the CUP was engaged in a systematic effort to Turkify the Ottoman races was, in effect, an accusation that Islam was being eliminated from the consciousness of Ottoman subjects. By their policies, the Unionists were preparing the new generation of Turkish Muslims for the replacement of Islamic solidarity with Turkish nationalism; they were thus moving towards apostasy.[16]

This charge was supported by raising the delicate subject of the translation of the Koran. According to *al-Qibla*, the Unionists were telling the Turkish people that they did not have to learn the language of the Koran, for the Arabic words of God would soon be translated into Turkish. The paper reminded its readers of the seriousness of this act: 'A Koran not in Arabic is an imperfect Koran, and a copy of it remains *jahiliyya* [part of the pre-Islamic age of ignorance]'.[17]

Rashid Rida added his prestigious voice to this discussion. His litany of the wrongs committed by the Unionists mirrored, perhaps even inspired, the lists supplied by *al-Qibla*. He hurled accusations of heresy and apostasy at the CUP leaders, and was at pains to reveal that they personally ignored prescribed Islamic rituals.[18] Rida also insisted that the Turkification of the Koran and the commentaries on it amounted to the repudiation of Islam itself; such distortions of the faith were part of a long-term CUP programme of returning the Turkish people to paganism and replacing Islamic bonds with racial ones.[19] Yet in his support for the preservation of the Arab core of the universal community, Rida himself appeared to introduce a claim to racial distinctiveness. He was, however, careful to frame his arguments within the context of the well-being of the community as a whole. Claiming that from the moment it assumed power the CUP's main objective was the debasement of the Arabs, Rida drew the connection between Arab and Islamic greatness by frequently citing the *hadith* attributed to the Prophet: 'If the Arabs are diminished, so is Islam'.[20] From Rida's perspective, the Arab associations of Husayn's movement were less national than religious, and he congratulated the sherif for the great service he had rendered to all Muslims by placing the Hejaz under Islamic sovereignty and removing it from the rule of the 'enemies of Islam'.[21]

Both the CUP and the publicists for Sherif Husayn identified the question of the caliphate as a central subject in their debate and treated it with great care. For the most part, *al-Qibla* avoided any suggestion of exchanging a son of the Banu Hashim for a son of 'Uthman. Instead, the paper emphasized the crime committed by the Unionists against the sacred office; they had demeaned it by imprisoning its occupant. The CUP were accused of detaining Muhammad V in his palace, of scorning him by keeping him ignorant of affairs of state, and of ruling in his name without his consent. This was not portrayed as misgovernment, but as an offence against Islam: 'When the Unionists attack and scorn the religion, when they turn their wrath on its personnel and send the sheikhs and the ulema to prison, when they allow the palace of Yildiz, once the seat of the caliph of the Muslims, to become a pit of depravity, when all this takes place, then the whole world is able to compare the glorious past of Islam and its caliphate with their sorry present'.[22]

These actions, together with a list of defects in the personal characters of the CUP leaders, constituted sins against Islam. But did they justify revolt? Although *al-Qibla* published a long list of grievances against the CUP on behalf of the community of Islam, the imprisonment of the caliph appears to have been the most serious, for it could be presented as providing an Islamic necessity for revolt. By holding the caliph in captivity, the Unionists 'are exceeding the divine statutes of Allah, and he who transgresses the divine statutes is an oppressor'.[23] In these circumstances, the responsibility of dedicated Islamic leaders was clear, and Husayn's proclamations cited *hadiths* which justified action against the oppressor and claimed that Allah had chosen him to awaken his community and to remove the hands of the tyrants.[24]

It should be stressed, then, that in the early stages of the revolt the emphasis was on protecting and preserving Islam, not on extolling, or even identifying, Arab and Turkish national differences. *Al-Qibla* pointed to an Islamic ruler as the victim of wrong, not to the Arab nation.

If Islam demanded redress, if it needed to be rescued from the heretical hands of the CUP, what was the special role of the Arabs to be? Can one discover in *al-Qibla* a discussion of Arabism or national definitions that would promote a specifically Arab response to Unionist policies? Or that would provide foundations on which later nationalist theorists could build? The political vocabulary of the contributors to *al-Qibla* reflected a terminology in transition, a blurring of national and religious concepts and a reliance, in the end, on an Islamic ideology. There were no definitions of Arabism because neither the amir of Mecca nor his editor, Muhibb al-Din al-Khatib, were comfortable with them; nor were they certain that they constituted the most effective form of propaganda.

For example, the factor of unity of language, so important to inter-war pan-Arabists, was used to re-enforce religious, not national solidarity: 'It is the existence of the language of the Koran among the sons of Islam which makes possible Islamic unity, religious brotherhood, and the nationalist bonds which unify the *umma* of Muhammad and make it like one body . . . It is not easy to achieve mutual understanding among the Islamic peoples unless there is a common language among them, and that language is Arabic which cannot be considered exclusive to the Arab race just as Islam does not belong exclusively to the Arabs'.[25] In a similar vein, Muhibb al-Din al-Khatib linked Arab fortunes with those of the wider Islamic world: 'The Arabs were dependent on the power of Islam for their power. They have to strike at those who destroy Islam by neglecting it. This call to action includes all of the races of the *umma* of Islam, for the enemy of the *umma* is their enemy'.[26]

Perhaps the most striking example of this blending of the Arab and Islamic causes was provided by Fuad al-Khatib at the end of a passage condemning the Unionists for their ill-treatment of the caliph: 'Onward sons of Islam. Raise high your swords. On to death which is eternal life! You are fighting for the cause of the fatherland, for the cause of the Arabs, of the Turks, the Kurds, and the Circassians, in short, for the cause of all Muslims everywhere'.[27] This was not a clear call to Arabism. Rather, it was a justification of revolt on the grounds of Islamic solidarity.

It is true that the nationalist vocabulary of *al-Qibla* became more refined in the latter stages of the war. Instead of the Unionists as the sole enemy, the paper pointed to oppression by the Turanians, thus introducing an element of Arab–Turkish confrontation that had been lacking in 1916. In addition, the virtues of the Hashemite kingdom came to be more closely associated with its Arab characteristics.[28] But even as the Arab features of the emerging state were identified, its adherence to Islamic norms was presented as its principal source of strength. In an article entitled 'How We Can Serve Our Country', Muhibb al-Din al-Khatib issued a series of instructions built on

Islamic conceptions of justice and morality and in effect described an Islamic order whose guidance had been prescribed by Allah and His Prophet. By contrast, the Turanians were those who abused their custodianship of the community. If the advice which al-Khatib offered was followed, then Allah would grant victory to the Hashemite state because it would be organized, and its inhabitants would comport themselves, in a manner pleasing to Him.[29]

As Husayn's proclamation following the entry of his armies into Damascus revealed, his efforts to balance his Arab movement and his stated Islamic mission could provide some intriguing compromises. An earlier article in *al-Qibla* had criticized the Unionist regime for placing Christians in high administrative posts in the Syrian provinces.[30] Now, with the confessionally diverse Syrian capital in his hands, Husayn called for a non-sectarian regime. He did so on decidedly sectarian grounds, affirming that he would respect local custom (*'urf*) because it had status second only to the *shari'a*.[31] In the end, the revolt was justified as it had been in the beginning: 'Husayn defends his religion, and the Unionists violate it. He defends his *qawm* [nation, tribe] which the oppressors treat with contempt; he purifies Islam from the filth of the atheists, he brings together those whom the Unionists have divided, and he strengthens the *shari'a* which they have despised'.[32]

Al-'Alam al-Islami and *al-Sharq* presented a very different version of Husayn's ambitions and his relationship to the faith. In the same way that *al-Qibla* had employed Islamic terms and symbols to support the revolt, so did these Ottoman publications use religious propaganda to discredit Husayn and his movement. The separation of Arabs as Arabs was not treated nor were charges laid against Husayn as an Arab. In short, the Ottoman criticisms did not raise the subjects that are normally associated with two contending nationalist movements. But Ottomanism was not nationalism, and the Arab loyalists who wrote for the journals of the empire faced the difficult task of isolating Husayn and his family while placating Arab opinion at large. Thus, Husayn was accused of the same offences with which he had charged the CUP – he had betrayed Islam and its caliph at a time of crisis. His was the true discord, for he had 'divided the authority of the community and ignited the fire of *fitna* to aid the enemies of Islam'.[33] He was not just an adventurer, but a traitor and a heretic.

In launching their attack on Husayn's Islamic credentials, Ottoman journals were supported by official actions of the state. Following the proclamation of the Arab revolt, the CUP government stripped Husayn of his office, appointed Sherif 'Ali Haydar in his place, and provided the opportunity for the scornful designation by which Husayn was identified for the remainder of the war – 'the former amir of Mecca'. Among his alleged religious errors was his usurpation of the caliphate, his implementation of despotic laws which contradicted the *shari'a*, and his ruination of the house of Islam to achieve his selfish personal ambitions. These crimes, proclaimed one journal, 'generate anger in all whose hearts pulsate with love of religion'.[34]

Ottoman propaganda was careful to emphasize the legitimacy and authority of the reigning caliph and to portray Husayn's movement as religious treason. The sultan's full titles were asserted – he was the caliph of Islam, the commander of the faithful, the sovereign monarch, the *ghazi* who, in the full exercise of his rightful powers had proclaimed the jihad for the purpose of liberating all Muslims and restoring the glory of the religion. In this way, the Ottoman ruler was elevated beyond nationality, and the Turkishness of the Ottoman house was subsumed by its dedication to the larger cause of Islam. According to one author the sultans, throughout their centuries of rule, had observed the precepts of the religion, studied its doctrines, founded *madrasas* for its scholars, and consulted the opinions of its ulema. In short, 'the sultans of the House of 'Uthman had considered their most important function to serve the revealed law of Islam and to obey it'.[35] To serve this house was to honour the caliphate and the whole community of Islam. Thus was the pretender in Mecca isolated.

The Arab subjects of the empire were further reminded that the religious authority of the Ottoman caliph was recognized by Muslims elsewhere: 'The Muslims of India say that the Ottoman Empire can be proud of its defence of the faith and that its sultans can be proud of their service to the two holy cities and their defence of them; and they say that the Ottoman Empire is today the main prop of the *shari'a* . . . Those who secede are *kafir* [unbelievers], especially at a time when the empire is engaged in a general war for the liberation of Islamic communities'.[36]

In order to enhance its claim to be acting for the true liberation of Muslim lands, each party tried to suggest that the other's alliance with a foreign Christian power compromised its stated mission and circumscribed its freedom of action. *Al-Qibla* regretted that the Ottoman Empire had become a German province and that the decisions of the caliph were determined by Germany. The paper even claimed that by placing the armed forces of the state under German command, the CUP had effectively permitted the foreign occupation of the empire.[37] Similarly, Unionist attacks on Husayn's British connection pressed home to Muslim readers the awesome consequences of the former amir's impertinence: 'Sherif Husayn agreed with the enemy of the Hejaz to place the blessed house of Allah, the *qibla* of Islam, and the resting place of the Prophet under the protection of a Christian state at war with the Ottoman Empire . . . He does not serve the faith of Allah, of the messenger, or of the Islamic community'.[38]

Blinded by personal greed, Husayn had failed to consider the record of European imperialism when he entered into alliance with Great Britain. The full implications of Husayn's self-deception were drawn out by Shakib Arslan: Does not Great Britain prosper because of India, he asked? Is not the Red Sea the famous route to India; and does anyone think that the British will endanger their very existence by permitting the emergence of an independent Arab state on the shores of the Red Sea?[39] Another Arab commentator blackened Husayn's choice of allies with this stark warning to the community of believers: 'The goals of England and her allies are nothing less than to crush the Ottoman Empire, to extinguish the light of the Islamic caliphate, and to place shackles of captivity around the necks of 300 million Muslims'.[40] How, the Ottoman journals collectively asked, could Husayn be so deceived as to think that the powers which had stamped out the independence of Tunisia and Egypt, of Algeria and India, were friends of Arabs and Muslims?

Not only had Husayn entered into an agreement which would subject the holy places of Islam to Christian control, he had also permitted the Christian powers to select him as caliph. While this was not an entirely accurate interpretation of Husayn's public statements, it was an accusation likely to draw attention to his arrogance and to generate outrage among the Arab Muslims of the empire.[41]

In this regard, Husayn's weakness was contrasted with the power of the central Ottoman state. Was the pretender able to protect the religion, to found a government? Where were his experienced soldiers, his distinguished officers, his heavy war industries? Why, from such a tenuous position, did he aspire to the caliphate, an office which required power, intelligence, and independence?[42] *Al-Qibla* had a reply to these questions, one designed to touch a deep chord of Arab Islamic emotion. It was given by Fuad al-Khatib, who challenged his readers to recall that during the first Islamic awakening, the Arabs were no better off than they were today: Syria was controlled by Byzantium, Iraq ruled by Persia, and the Bedouin tribes divided amongst themselves. But the Arabs, guided by a Hashemite leader of vision, found unity in the Koranic revelations and vanquished both Byzantium and Persia. They are today guided by that leader's descendant, and 'the blood of the Prophet still courses in his veins'.[43]

But in the competition to establish historical claims to Islamic legitimacy, the echoes of the past were not the monopoly of one party. During the final months of the war, when Palestine had fallen to the British, *al-Sharq* pleaded for Islamic solidarity which could repeat in the present crisis its achievement throughout history. Enemies of the faith had taken Palestine from Islam before, but it had been recovered. Now, inspired by the spirit of 'Umar, Saladin, and Mehmet the Conqueror, Muslim commanders would surely recover it again.[44]

In these appeals, we see the selective use of Islamic history and an attempt to exploit it in a way that transcends the questions of national identification. The exchanges also reveal a longing for power, a sense of greatness interrupted. Although such desires were expressed in charges and countercharges, and although they were part of a bitter political struggle, they also reflected a wish for the same outcome – the restoration of the full independence and untarnished dignity of Islam. In mocking Husayn's weaknesses, the Ottoman journalists raised what they knew to be crucial questions about the central state as well. For that state to survive, for it to have any claim to sovereignty over Arab territories, the religious bond had to be paramount and accepted as such. From the Ottoman viewpoint, Husayn had broken the bond, and his rebellion had to be portrayed as an act against the faith. He was a traitor who sought to separate brother Muslims from one another and to aid the victory of the *kafir* over the believer. The duty of true believers in the face of such treachery was clear: 'Oh Muslims whose hearts are illuminated by the message of *tawhid*, beware of those faithless apostates who would lead you to the fires of hell. Renounce them and ignore their stupid words'.[45]

As with most political propagandists, the Ottoman supporters found it easier to vilify the opposition than to propose a positive programme of their own. Given the harsh realities of Jamal Pasha's policies in Greater Syria, how could Ottoman unity be made attractive to the Arabs? Just as *al-Qibla* had been reluctant to emphasize Arabism at the expense of Islamic solidarity, so did the Ottoman journalists find it necessary to link the Ottoman cause with the Islamic. They were, of course, more circumscribed than Husayn in their choice of symbols. By the very need to emphasize Ottomanism, they were prevented from employing the political vocabulary of nationalism. They produced a blend, weaving patriotism, Islam, and Ottomanism into a plea for communal solidarity which, in the end, was, like Husayn's, fundamentally Islamic. When referring to the sultan-caliph's subjects collectively, the government propagandists employed such phrases as 'we Ottomans', 'the people of religion', and 'people of the Islamic *umma*'. The state itself was portrayed in an assortment of patriotic/religious terms; it was at once *watan* (fatherland), *umma* (nation-state, Islamic community), and *milla*, a term originally used to designate the non-Muslim communities of the empire, but which came to be used to refer to the Ottoman state and the Islamic community.

In addition, the government publications always linked Ottoman and Islam. They formed integral parts of the same whole, so that one who served the Ottoman cause served also the Islamic one: 'Islamic valour and Ottoman heroism'; 'the Ottoman heroes and the Muslim *mujahidun*'; the British army confronted 'the Islamic armies'; 'the Ottoman Islamic soldiers' entered the battle.[46] And finally, it was, above all else, 'the brotherhood of believers' which bound the peoples of the empire together and which demanded that they never be separated.[47]

Despite the changing fortunes of the war and the development of a fledgling nationalist vocabulary by *al-Qibla*, the determination of both parties to compete for Arab loyalties primarily through the same Islamic ideology remained constant. *Al-Qibla* celebrated the start of its third year of publication by reaffirming its commitment to the advancement of Islam and invoking Allah's blessings on 'our great king', whose victory over the Turanians would make his office a haven for Islam and a buttress for the *shari'a*.[48] In much the same vein, *al-Sharq* marked its own second anniversary with the declaration that, 'above all else, *al-Sharq* desires the unity of the Muslims

97

in general and the Ottomans in particular, and [hopes for] the strengthening of their bonds with the throne of the caliphate'.[49] No matter what awareness of national differences might exist, neither party could give primacy to bonds other than Islamic. In their assessment of what would appeal to public opinion, and probably in the experience of their spokesmen, the struggle to preserve and strengthen Islam was the pre-eminent cause for the community of believers. To read *al-Qibla* and the Ottoman-sponsored Arabic publications together is to gain the impression that the preservation of the Islamic community was the central issue in the struggle.

One would have expected it to remain central once the war ended. But Islam lost its prominence in political discourse during most of the 1920s. Neither the Wafd in Egypt, the People's Party of Syria, nor the ex-Ottoman officers in Iraq – to say nothing of Atatürk – framed a political platform designed principally to appeal to popular Islamic sentiments. While these new political élites embraced European-inspired concepts of state and society, the propagandists who had defended the Islamic order during the war founded new journals in which they kept the Islamic political option alive. Their return to prominence towards the end of the 1920s coincided with a series of events which combined to resurrect powerful sentiments of Islamic solidarity.

During the Wailing Wall disturbances in Jerusalem in 1929, the front page of a Cairo weekly rang forth with the phrase 'Palestine is the Islamic world and the Islamic world is Palestine' as a reminder that the impulse to promote Islamic solidarity during periods of crisis was not dead.[50] The author of this declaration was the editor of the newspaper of the Muslim Brotherhood, the secretary of the Young Men's Muslim Association, the owner of the Salafiyya Press, and the publisher of the journal *al-Fath*; he was Muhibb al-Din al-Khatib, the former editor of *al-Qibla*. Two years later, the Islamic Congress of Jerusalem convened and inaugurated an intensive campaign to rouse Muslim public opinion by linking the cause of Palestine to the larger issue of Islam under attack. And when the French residency in Morocco passed the Berber *dahir* in 1930, Shakib Arslan, former member of the editorial staff of *al-Sharq*, launched an international Islamic crusade against the decree, warning, 'This issue is not confined to the attack on the Islam of the Berbers, but includes the entire world of Islam'.[51] The response to Arslan's appeal was widespread and marks the growing power of Islamic solidarity as an integrating force in the post-war era. To be sure, each Arab state faced its own set of political, economic, social, and imperial problems, and it would be foolish to suggest that Islam was received, utilized, or revived in the same way in each of them. But the growing interest in Palestine as an Islamic concern, Arslan's successful campaign against the *dahir* (the residency was forced to modify the decree in 1934), and the discovery of Islamic themes by Egyptian liberal politicians revealed the existence of a deep reservoir of Islamic sentiment.

Perhaps figures like Arslan and al-Khatib, with their appeal to Islamic bonds, more accurately reflected the sentiments of majority Arab opinion than the politicans of the period. As would-be moulders of public opinion during the war, they were able, when the time was right, to tap communal loyalties which had not been replaced by the post-war order. They may not have been sensitive to the social issues which attracted so many men to the Muslim Brotherhood, but they could argue that the very existence of the Islamic community continued to be threatened by the same forces which they had identified during the First World War. Theirs were the voices which provided an important link between pre-war, wartime, and post-war Arab ideology. They provided a continuous defence of Islam under attack; the campaign they waged is far from over.

NOTES

1. Elie Kedourie, *Arabic Political Memoirs and Other Studies* (London, 1974), pp. 147-8.
2. Elie Kedourie, *England and the Middle East: The Destruction of the Ottoman Empire, 1914-1921* (London, 1956), p. 150.
3. See, respectively, Nadav Safran, *Egypt in Search of Political Community* (Cambridge, Mass., 1961), and Charles D. Smith, *Islam and the Search for Social Order in Modern Egypt: A Biography of Muhammad Husayn Haykal* (Albany, 1983). The significance of the remoteness of leaders from masses is a persistent theme in Kedourie's work. See, for example, *Islam in the Modern World and Other Studies* (London, 1980), pp. 22-3, and *Arabic Political Memoirs*, ch. 1.
4. *Al-Hidaya*, iv, no. 4 (Rabi' al-Akhir), 1331, 177.
5. Geoffrey Lewis, 'The Ottoman Proclamation of Jihad in 1914', in *Arabic and Islamic Garland: Historical, Educational and Literary Papers Presented to Abdul-Latif Tibawi* (London, 1977), p. 102. Emphasis added.
6. One aspect of this question, based on the writings and proclamations of Sherif Husayn and his son, 'Abdullah, has been examined by C. Ernest Dawn, 'Ideological Influences in the Arab Revolt', in his *From Ottomanism to Arabism: Essays on the Origins of Arab Nationalism* (Urbana, 1973), pp. 69-86. My emphasis differs in that I am more interested in public propaganda than personal ideology, and I analyse material from Ottoman-sponsored publications.
7. Sulayman Musa, *Wujuh wa malamih* (Amman, 1980), p. 133.

8. Anwar al-Jundi, *A'lam al-qarn al-rabi' 'ashr al-hijri*, Vol. I. *A'lam al-da'wah wa al-fikr* (Cairo, 1981), p. 381.
9. Taj al-Din al-Hasani, later president of Syria, was designated as the publisher while Khalil al-Ayyubi was called associate publisher. A brief summary of *al-Sharq* is found in Adib Khaddur, *al-Sihafa al-suriyya* (Damascus, 1972), pp. 110-12.
10. *Al-'Alam al-Islami*, i, no. 1 (29 April 1916), 3.
11. *Ibid.*, p. 17.
12. *Ibid.*, no. 8 (22 June 1916), p. 4.
13. *Al-Qibla*, no. 1 (15 Shuwwal 1334), and no. 10 (17 Dhu al-Qa'ada 1334). Cf. Dawn, 'Ideological Influences', p. 82. The CUP movement began in Salonika; to call that city the Qa'aba of the Unionists was to brand the party with secularism.
14. *Al-Qibla*, no. 10 (17 Dhu al-Qa'ada 1334).
15. *Al-Qibla*, no. 1 (15 Shuwwal 1334). In this context, *fitna* means a civil war which threatens to create schism within the Islamic community; it thus connotes a doctrinal rebellion or heresy. See the article on the subject in *The Encyclopaedia of Islam* (new edition, Leiden, 1960-).
16. *Al-Qibla*, no. 40 (7 Rabi' al-Awwal 1335).
17. *Ibid.*, no. 3 (22 Shuwwal 1334); no. 6 (3 Dhu al-Qa'ada 1334).
18. Rashid Rida, 'Ara al-khawass fi al-masala al-'arabiyya', *al-Manar*, xix, no. 3 (29 Aug. 1916), 149.
19. *Ibid.*, pp. 159-60; and Rida, 'al-'Asabiyya al-jinsiyya al-turkiyya', *al-Manar*, xix, no. 2 (15 July 1916), 80.
20. Rida, 'Ara al-khawass', p. 167; and 'al-'Asabiyya al-jinsiyya', p. 81.
21. Rida, 'Ara al-khawass', pp. 166-7.
22. *Al-Qibla*, no. 10 (17 Dhu al-Qa'ada 1334).
23. *Ibid.*, no. 1 (15 Shuwwal 1334).
24. *Ibid.*, no. 31 (4 Safr 1335).
25. *Ibid.*, no. 3 (22 Shuwwal 1334).
26. *Ibid.*, no. 53 (19 Rabi' al-Thani 1335).
27. *Ibid.*, no. 3 (22 Shuwwal 1334). Fuad al-Khatib was the brother of Muhibb al-Din. He served as minister of foreign affairs in the Hejazi government and was a frequent contributor to *al-Qibla*.
28. See, for example, *ibid.*, no. 200 (17 Shuwwal 1336); no. 220 (4 Muharram 1337); no. 226 (25 Muharram 1337).
29. *Ibid.*, no. 53 (22 Rabi' al-Thani 1335).
30. *Ibid.*, no. 74 (9 Rajab 1335).
31. *Ibid.*, no. 220 (4 Muharram 1337).
32. *Ibid.*, no. 1 (15 Shuwwal 1334). Even the atrocities allegedly committed by the Ottoman garrison in Medina against the inhabitants of the city were described as 'religious sins' and as assaults against 'religious rights'. *Ibid.*, no. 56 (4 Jumada al-Ula 1335).
33. *Al-'Alam al-Islami*, i, no. 17 (24 Aug. 1916), 9. For further charges of *fitna*, see *ibid.*, no. 23 (5 Oct. 1916), 5; and *al-Sharq*, no. 688 (19 Shuwwal 1336).
34. *Al-'Alam al-Islami*, i, no. 22 (28 Sept. 1916), 4.
35. *Al-Sharq*, no. 667 (21 Ramadan 1336).
36. *Al-'Alam al-Islami*, i, no. 22 (28 Sept. 1916), 11.
37. *Al-Qibla*, no. 2 (18 Shuwwal 1334); no. 3 (22 Shuwwal 1334); no. 205 (5 Dhu al-Qa'ada 1336). Rashid Rida held similar views about the Ottoman–German alliance, even adding a dose of anti-Zionism to his attack. See 'Ara al-khawass', pp. 152-8.
38. *Al-'Alam al-Islami*, i, no. 18 (31 Aug. 1916), 9.
39. *Al-Sharq*, no. 609 (12 Rajab 1336).
40. *Ibid.*, no. 578 (5 Jumada al-Thani 1336).
41. *Ibid.*, no. 688 (19 Shuwwal 1336).

42. *Al-'Alam al-Islami*, i, no. 17 (24 Aug. 1916), 22.
43. *Al-Qibla*, no. 18 (19 Dhu al-Hijja 1334).
44. *Al-Sharq*, no. 574 (30 Jumada al-Ula 1336).
45. *Al-'Alam al-Islami*, i, no. 22 (28 Sept. 1916), 18.
46. See, for example, *al-Sharq*, no. 594 (24 Jumada al-Thani 1336); no. 689 (20 Shuwwal 1336); no. 578 (5 Jumada al-Thani 1336).
47. *Ibid.*, no. 609 (12 Rajab 1336).
48. *Al-Qibla*, no. 200 (17 Shuwwal 1336).
49. *Al-Sharq*, no. 612 (16 Rajab 1336).
50. *Al-Fath*, 12 Sept. 1929.
51. *Ibid.*, 17 Jumada al-Ula 1349. It is noteworthy that part of Arslan's crusade was played out in al-Khatib's journal; they were now, as in fact they had always been, defending the same cause. For Arslan's use of Islamic symbols and their effectiveness in the campaign against the *dahir*, see William Cleveland, *Islam Against the West: Shakib Arslan and the Campaign for Islamic Nationalism* (Austin, 1985), ch. 5.

VII

BUREAUCRACIES AT WAR: THE BRITISH IN THE MIDDLE EAST IN THE FIRST WORLD WAR

John S. Galbraith and Robert A. Huttenback

A veritable labyrinth in which officials and ministers were hopelessly lost.

Elie Kedourie[1]

In recent years bureaucracy has attracted the attention of many scholars, including Elie Kedourie in his study of the Anglo-Arab labyrinth. Much of what has been written reaches similar conclusions to those of early polemicists. Vincent de Gournay (1712-59), who allegedly gave bureaucracy its name, maintained that instead of its serving the public interest, it served only itself, and Balzac characterized it as 'a giant power wielded by pigmies'.[2]

Social scientists generally use less colourful language but are no less damning. Michel Crozier describes bureaucracy as 'a system of organization whose main characteristic is its rigidity, [it] will not adjust easily to change, and will tend to resist change as much as possible'. Robert K. Merton states that 'bureaucracy is administration which almost completely avoids public discussion of its techniques, although there may occur public discussion of its policies'.[3] Jacques Ellul contends that bureaucracy has made an illusion of the idea that the 'people' can control their government through the electoral process, as their elected representatives cannot control 'the behemoth under them – the bureaucracy'; Robert Khorasch's 'institutional imperative' holds that 'every action or decision of an institution must be intended to keep the institutional machinery working'; and Matthew Holden adds that the motto of the bureaucrat is 'my agency, right or wrong'.[4]

The mass of writings on bureaucracy produces not pessimism but despair – 'abandon hope all ye who enter here'. This essay will not relieve that bleak conclusion, indeed, it may reinforce it; but it will attempt to deal with one aspect of the phenomenon in more concrete terms than much of the recent writing on the subject, and to concentrate on a specific problem at a particular time – the British military and civilian establishments in the First World War, and the effect of inter-agency jealousies on the campaign in the Middle East.

The major offices of government at the time of the war had become much more professionalized than those of the nineteenth century. The old practice of appointment by influence and family connection had given way to a system of appointment by merit. Permanent under-secretaries were professionals whose tenure was not dependent on government changes, and their experience and expertise gave them considerable influence over their superiors. The numbers of staff were still small – Parkinson's Law had not yet been invented – but they constituted a bureaucracy in the sense that they were professionals whose careers were devoted to service to their offices. Their standards were the envy of the world; the system became a model for those of other countries. These characteristics, however, involved a narrowing of their perspectives through their identification of self with department. Their loyalties were to it and they jealously defended it against threats, real or imagined, from other departments. In the process the 'national interest' became almost indistinguishable from that of the department. But this characteristic was not a monopoly of the staff. It extended to the secretaries of state themselves who fought for their departments' interests. The consequences were disastrous to British fortunes in the Middle East, particularly during the early years of the First World War.

At the outset of the war top permanent officials had achieved considerable influence, no longer being the nearly anonymous aides of previous generations. Such names as Hankey, Eyre Crowe, and Vansittart represent powerful influences. But they reflected the policy positions of their ministerial supporters rather than the reverse. E.D. Morel considered Sir Edward Grey, the foreign secretary, to be 'a puppet of his permanent officials . . . a weak man',[5] but even if true the statement describes an exception. Asquith, Lloyd George, Balfour, Churchill, Milner, Curzon, and many others were powerful figures who frequently had as much experience in statecraft as their under-secretaries, and in some instances a great deal more. The decision-making process in this era does not reflect the impotence of the politician against the bureaucrat. What it does illustrate is the tendency of the minister to identify himself with the department which he led against the competing claims of other agencies, a phenomenon certainly not peculiar to the First World War. Churchill and subsequently Balfour, as first lords of the admiralty, were the champions of 'their' service, Kitchener of the war office and of the army. When Balfour replaced Churchill at the admiralty, he was called upon to respond to attacks on alleged mismanagement during the Gallipoli campaign. His response was that he was sure 'that the responsibility lay with the Army, not with the Navy', though he admitted that he had not inquired into the facts.[6] When he was translated into a new incarnation as foreign secretary, he blamed both the services and the ministers who presided over them for the mismanagement.[7]

Inter-service rivalries, of course, have existed as long as there have been professional military organizations. Officers have been bred to loyalty to their branch of service, and competitiveness with their 'sister' services. This could produce jealousies that might be detrimental to the national interest. Operating within their own compartments, senior officers had little to do with their counterparts in other services. Exchange of information on common problems was minimal. The Royal Navy and the army both maintained air arms using similar equipment but failed to exchange information which might be of value.

Neville Chamberlain, at the beginning of the First World War, when he was a member of Birmingham city council, heard that the Daimler factory was making airplane engines for both the admiralty and the war office. The admiralty had ordered the French Gnome engine but the war office had developed an improved engine designed at the Daimler factory, with a lifting power greater by a ratio of 12 to 7 over the Gnome and a life about four times as long. The war office had not communicated these facts to the admiralty; the existence of the superior engine was accidentally discovered by a navy inspector who happened to see it at the Daimler works and told Chamberlain on a social occasion. Neville then told his brother Austen, who was secretary of state for India, who in turn told

Balfour, first lord of the admiralty, who had not been told by the war office. This incident is a microcosm of a basic problem in communications between the armed services.[8]

Lack of co-ordination between the army and navy contributed to the failure of the Dardanelles campaign, but this deficiency did not apply to the armed forces alone. Every relevant branch of government involved in the hostilities against the Ottoman Empire in Mesopotamia and Arabia was culpable in greater or lesser degree for the disasters that befell the British forces during the first two years of the war. Each had tunnel vision; all of them acted in the classic bureaucratic fashion, subordinating policy decisions to department interests. Involved in the conduct of the war in the eastern theatre were the foreign office, the war office, the India office, the government of India, the Cairo agency, the sirdar of the Sudan, the Arab bureau, and the Levant consular service. Each of them viewed the others with suspicion or distrust, if not outright hostility. They guarded secrets from each other as zealously as they did from the Turks. In Mesopotamia (later known as Iraq) there were two British intelligence agencies. The home government and the government of India had agreed to a boundary between their respective jurisdictions along a line through Arabia to Basra. To the north of that line was the jurisdiction of Whitehall, and to the south, of Simla. Basra was assigned to India and the rest of Mesopotamia to the home government. Intelligence officers sent their reports to their superiors but these were not routinely turned over to the counterpart agency. Consequently, when Great Britain assigned to the government of India the management of the war in Mesopotamia as well as the occupation of Basra, India lacked essential intelligence of the area in which its forces had to fight.[9]

Before the war, the lines of authority for British officials involved with Persia and the Persian Gulf showed little evidence of coherent organization. The minister at Tehran was responsible to the foreign office, but the British consuls in various areas, particularly near the gulf, had a dual capacity. As consuls they reported to the foreign office, but they were also political agents drawn from the Indian political department, appointed by the government of India, and reporting to it on matters deemed political. On the Arab side of the gulf, the political agents were not consuls, except in Oman and Muscat. At Basra and Baghdad in Mesopotamia the consuls were members of the Levant consular service who, though appointed by the foreign office, depended on India for such services as protection.[10] This body traced its origins to the early years of the nineteenth century when British consuls appointed lesser consuls, consular agents, and vice-consuls – many of them unpaid and usually Jewish, Italian, Armenian or Greek – to act on their behalf. The establishment of the Dragomans' school at Constantinople in 1877 was an attempt to train British officials to replace the foreign appointees. And it was the graduates of this school, spread throughout the Ottoman dominions, who became the Levant consular service. Aden was treated as part of India. Its garrison was considered an Indian 'home service'. The general officer commanding, who was also the resident, reported to the government of India, which in turn received orders from the India office.[11]

These strange arrangements guaranteed confusion, contention, delay, and occasionally disaster. The consuls in south Persia often pursued their own foreign policy towards local chiefs without reference not only to the Persian government, which they treated as a cipher, but to the British minister at Tehran. Quarrels between the minister and these wayward insubordinates and between the foreign office and the political department in India were understandably frequent.[12] Outside Persia, some petty rulers were in effect clients of India and others, sometimes their rivals, clients of the foreign office or war office. This strange, irrational arrangement had continued because there had been no great emergency and because vested interests of the various jurisdictions wished it to continue.

The jumble of competing agencies had come into being over many years as the result of a series of *ad hoc* decisions relating more or less directly to British control of India. Prior to the First World War no effort had been made to systematize control. There seemed to be no need to do so. For most of the nineteenth century the main threat to India was seen as coming from Russia, and 'the Bear that walks like a man' would, it was thought, in the event of war try to reach India by land, probably through Afghanistan. The Indian military establishment was designed to keep the border areas as tranquil as possible; to exercise influence in Afghanistan and Persia to keep their regimes friendly to Great Britain. If Russia attacked, the Indian Army was charged with mounting a delaying action until troops from Great Britain could arrive. It was never conceived that it should have to take primary responsibility for fighting a war against a modern military power, such as in a sense the Ottoman Empire, particularly when backed by Germany, could be judged to be.

The capacity of the government of India to fight such a war was also greatly diminished by the heavy demands on it for troops to fight on the Western Front. During the winter of 1914-15, about one-third of the British army in France came from India. Three-fourths of the British troops in India and over half of the Indian troops had been sent off to France, Egypt, and East Africa.[13] These levies seriously weakened the strength of the Indian armed forces, which before the war had been subjected to drastic reductions in various branches as part of the reorganization initiated by Kitchener when he had been in command. The artillery was slashed, particularly in heavy guns, and other branches of the service were also affected, including the medical services. At the outbreak of the First World War, in consequence, the Indian Army was prepared to fight only a frontier war, but was called upon to take responsibility for the campaign against the Turks in Mesopotamia.[14]

The government of India was drawn into a conflict beyond its abilities to win as a result of a series of decisions, all of which seemed rational at the time to the authorities involved, but the combination of which produced one of the major disasters in British military history. The initial objective was the seizure of Basra at the head of the Persian Gulf, part of the government of India's sphere, and also important because of its proximity to the oil fields of Abadan. The town was occupied with little resistance, but instead of ordering the British troops to remain there in a defensive position, the government of India decided, on the basis of representations from the commercial community in Basra, to provide additional security by advancing further upstream to Al Qurna, at the junction of the Tigris and the Shatt al-Arab. Al Qurna was captured with little resistance.

The command in Mesopotamia then passed in March 1915 to Sir John Nixon, considered even by his critics to be 'a magnificent fighting soldier',[15] but known for his gallantry rather than his prudence, who selected Major General C.V.F. Townshend to command the 6th Division, which was to lead the offensive. Townshend, like his superior, was a thrusting general who would vigorously pursue a defeated enemy. These two came together at a time when the calibre of the adversary seemed to be low. The Turkish troops the British encountered had broken ranks and fled. The misleading ease of their early victories had led Sir Percy Cox, the political officer with the expeditionary force and a man with an awesome reputation as an expert on the Middle East, to suggest to the authorities in India and Great Britain in November 1914 that a lightning offensive to take Baghdad might be successful and would give an immense boost to British prestige.

Such advice was received with considerable interest by the British government, despondent at the failure of the Gallipoli campaign and the stalemate on the Western Front, and with some reservations, the government of India concurred. Townshend's apparently brilliant achievements produced a euphoria which led both the British and Indian authorities to authorize an advance on Baghdad. In reaching this decision they ignored the opposition of the military high command. General C.W. Robertson, the chief of the Imperial General Staff, guessing that Townshend would soon be facing 60,000 of the enemy, wrote: 'the combined staffs consider that an occupation of Baghdad cannot on military grounds be justified'.[16] The Turks whom the British had heretofore encountered were not first-line troops. They were ill-supplied because they were far from their home base and their transport was primitive. But as they were pushed back, the British transport was strained and the Turkish lines of communication shortened. Most important, as predicted by the general staff and admiralty war staff, fresh troops had been sent down the Tigris by the Turkish command. Townshend flung his tired division of about 10,000 against a well-entrenched enemy of 25,000, and the weary troops were forced to retreat into the village of Kut. There, after a long siege, they surrendered in April 1916.

In the last bloody phase of Townshend's offensive, and thereafter, all of the deficiencies in the Indian military system were exposed. The transport arrangements had been totally inadequate to supply the troops, and the wounded died by the thousands under conditions that were appalling because of the lack of medical facilities.[17]

Instead of taking action to deal with the breakdown of the system, responsible officers had made every effort to conceal it. Nixon, when the inability of the medical corps to cope with hundreds of casualties after the battle of Ctesiphon was already known to him, telegraphed to the government of India that 'the medical arrangements, under circumstances of considerable difficulty, worked splendidly'. An officer in charge of a hospital ship who protested over impure water and the lack of essential supplies was told that he was an 'interfering

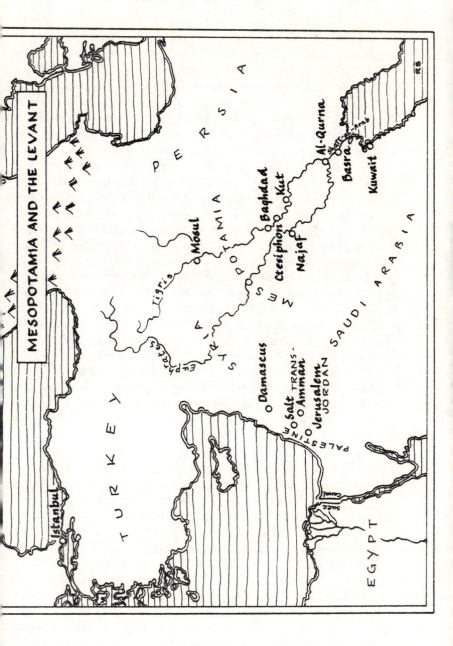

MESOPOTAMIA AND THE LEVANT

faddist'; that if he continued to complain he would be removed from his command.[18] This insistence on the code of loyalty to superiors produced a conspiracy of silence among the personnel of the various services. The viceroy, Lord Hardinge, before the casualties at Ctesiphon had overwhelmed the medical services, admitted that 'our hospitals in Mesopotamia leave much to be desired', but took no action to try to correct the deficiencies, relying instead on a quick and easy victory to eliminate the problem.[19] His commander in chief, Sir Beauchamp Duff, after Townshend was already besieged at Kut, continued to assert that in India itself and in the supply system to Basra, 'everything is right'.[20] But he admitted: 'when we do relieve Kut, there are various matters about which Townshend will have to explain'.[21]

The true state of affairs could not be kept secret. The facts of grave medical deficiencies, lack of transport, guns, and ammunition leaked to the press and produced a furore in Great Britain even more intense than that which had erupted after Gallipoli. The Asquith government was forced to appoint a parliamentary commission to investigate, and its report was devastating. As the attorney general, Sir F.E. Smith, told parliament: 'The Report is simply a cemetery of reputations'.[22]

Virtually every major figure who had participated directly or indirectly in decisions involving Mesopotamia was censured by the commission, some more severely than others. The surgeons-general who had served during the critical months before the surrender at Kut were condemned for gross incompetence and for attempts to conceal the facts. Hardinge, the viceroy, was credited with good intentions but castigated for not acting upon them. Austen Chamberlain, secretary of state for India, was chided for not knowing about the state of unreadiness in the medical services, and the war committee of the British cabinet, to which the Asquith government had assigned responsibility for co-ordinating the war effort, was faulted for its ineffectiveness. The list of the censured was a long one. But the commission determined the principal culprit to be General Nixon. They found that he had recklessly ordered the advance on Baghdad despite insufficient transport and the reports of large Turkish reinforcements.[23]

This indictment was unfair to Nixon. The decision to try to take Baghdad was made at the highest levels in Great Britain and India. It reflected the hopes of politicians that a brilliant victory would restore the prestige of Great Britain and its government, even though the capture of the city had little strategic significance. When the gamble failed the general, who had been hailed earlier for his brilliant victories, was branded incompetent. Many individuals were culpable, but a sacrificial victim was selected to expiate the sins of the guilty.

Assessments of guilt obscured the fact that the basic causes of the disaster were systemic. Ian Hamilton, who had been made the scapegoat in Gallipoli as Nixon was in Mesopotamia, commented that 'it takes a lot of brave fighting to make up for lack of imagination in the higher direction of the War'.[24] The validity of his observation can be documented. But the unimaginativeness which he condemned had far deeper roots. The British military establishment at the outbreak of the war was led by men whose experience in combat had been against the hill tribes on the borders of India or in the South African War, which after its first few months became a guerrilla campaign. Neither experience prepared them for the war they had to fight from 1914 to 1918, and decisions made in London did not transform the character of the officers who had to execute them.

The world perspective from Simla was utterly different from that of Whitehall. It continued to be so after the home government created the war council in November 1914. This body, renamed the war committee, was theoretically all-powerful, since it included the prime minister, the secretaries of state for war and foreign affairs, the chancellor of the exchequer, the first lord of the admiralty, and the heads of the military forces, but its conclusions were not always translated into action when transmitted to India. Its decision in February 1916 to assign to the war office command of all troops in Mesopotamia, although applauded by the Indian military,[25] did not automatically make unification of control a reality, nor was it achieved throughout the war or in the immediate post-war period. It was not until 1920 that the British government established a Middle East department to supervise the various areas conquered, and even this development did not end the jealousies which infected the men on the spot.

Resistance to homogenization affected every area of British authority in the Middle East. In Arabia three jurisdictions collided. Traditionally, the India office had regarded the Arabian peninsula as in the outer marches of its authority and important primarily in relation to the security of the Persian Gulf. Its policy was one of minimal interference in Arabian internal affairs as long as there was no threat to the gulf area.[26] After the British conquest of the Sudan, the sirdar involved himself in the affairs of the Red Sea littoral, but only on the Sudanese side, and the Cairo agency was concerned with the Suez Canal and adjacent areas. But until the outbreak of hostilities with the Ottoman Empire, India continued to claim Arabia as within its sphere. During the war the government of India retreated from these extensive claims, but still asserted its responsibility for affairs in Arabia south of the Hejaz.[27] The Cairo agency, which reported to the foreign office, extended its involvement into Arabia, but responsibility for military action was in the hands of the commander of the forces in Egypt, who took his orders from the Imperial General Staff.[28] Operations on both sides of the Red Sea were assumed by the sirdar of the Sudan, and command of naval forces was exercised by the admiral commanding the East India station.

This tangled skein of authority was further complicated by the formation of the Arab bureau as a special department in the Cairo agency under the command of Brigadier General Gilbert F. Clayton, the chief of Egyptian intelligence. Though he had military rank, Clayton was an appointee of the high commissioner, Sir Henry McMahon, and the personnel whom he selected were distinctly unmilitary types, recruited for their knowledge of Arabic and for their general intelligence, a strange collection indeed in the midst of the old-line officers who filled the numerous staff positions at Cairo. Jean Beraud Villars may have overstated the characteristics of the latter when he described them as 'caricatures of colonels and majors, old fighting cocks with bloodshot eyes who lived with the *Army Almanac* and the *Aldershot Regulations* on their tables',[29] but even more kindly critics conceded they were lacking in imagination.[30] Clayton's choice of personnel for his assistants predictably excited the ire of these traditional types. In addition to the celebrated T.E. Lawrence, they included George Lloyd, Aubrey Herbert, Leonard Woolley, and Colonel Newcomb, who prided themselves in such names as 'the five musketeers' and the 'Intrusives', the latter because they flaunted their contempt for military discipline and the lack of imagination of regular army officers.[31] In addition, Clayton had the temerity to appoint a woman, Gertrude Bell, to the bureau cadre.

The Cairo agency and its unruly creation, the Arab bureau, maintained an uneasy relationship but were united in their hostility to what they considered to be the benighted influence of the government of India with regard to the Middle East. Their superiors at London, the foreign office and the India office, also were in conflict with regard to Middle Eastern policy. The foreign office was concerned with the aspiration of Arab leaders for independence, the demand of the French for control of Syria, and the campaign of the Zionists for a Jewish homeland in Palestine.[32] The India office, on the other hand, viewing Arabia from the Persian Gulf, maintained its traditional contacts with Arab leaders in the east, including Ibn Saud, who ruled over the Nejd.[33] There were consequently two conflicting 'British foreign policies' with regard to Arabia. Cairo backed Husayn, the Hashemite ruler of Hejaz, as the leader of the Arab revolt, and the Indian authorities opposed granting him such status.

Indeed there was a third 'foreign policy', that of the zealots of the Arab bureau, in particular, Lawrence. Writing to a friend in 1915, Lawrence expressed the anti-Indian line with particular asperity: 'You know India used to be in control of Arabia – and used to do it pretty badly, for they hadn't a man who knew Syria or Turkey and they used to consider only the Gulf, and the preservation of peace in the Aden Hinterland . . . Then this war started, and India went on with the old game of balancing the little powers there'.[34]

At least in his own eyes, Lawrence became more Arab than the Arabs in the sense that he identified himself completely with their cause as he defined it. Husayn was 'his' Arab leader, and Lawrence fought for Husayn–Lawrence Arabia with great tenacity. Before Allenby's triumphal advance on Jerusalem, Lawrence expressed doubts as to the capability of the British army to defeat the Turks: 'I weighed the English army in my mind, and could not honestly assure myself of them. The men were often gallant fighters, but their generals as often gave away in stupidity what they had gained in ignorance'.[35] When the British failed to carry out what he considered to be their commitments to 'his Arabs', Lawrence felt personally betrayed. As the editor of his letters commented: 'He was anti-French because he wanted a purely Arab Government in Damascus, just as he was anti-Government of India because he wanted a purely Arab Government in Baghdad'.[36] But the Arabs he supported were strictly those with whom he himself was identified. Rival leaders such as Ibn Saud he treated as unworthy of support. In a memorandum to the British cabinet in 1918 he wrote erroneously: 'In the Nejd, the situation created by the indirect conflict of India and Egypt over Ibn Saud and the Idrisi presents no real difficulty. Both men are fortunately heretics in Islam, not much better than the Agha Khan in orthodox opinion'.[37]

Inter-agency conflicts also appeared in virulent form in Persia, where Great Britain was dedicated to maintaining the myth of Persian sovereignty while attempting to ensure that it was exercised only in the British interest. The Russian menace had been temporarily reduced for Great Britain by the Anglo-Russian agreement of 1907, under the terms of which the two powers agreed to divide Persia into three zones, Russian in the north and centre and British in the south-east, with an intermediate neutral zone. At the same time, they solemnly pledged themselves to respect Persian independence and territorial integrity. With the outbreak of war in 1914, the great menace became Germany and the Ottoman Empire, which were seen as a threat not only to India but to the oil fields of south Iran on which the Royal Navy increasingly depended.[38] Both Russia and Great Britain, while protesting their respect for Persian neutrality, organized Persian forces, which they controlled beneath the transparent façade of being under the command of the shah's government. This foreign intervention further weakened the authority of the government of Ahmed Shah. Power passed to various local chiefs whom the British and Russians sought to influence, with varying degrees of success.

The perceived gravity of the German menace did not result in the unification or even co-ordination of the competing British agencies. Indeed by the end of the war there were more groups operating independently of each other than there had been at the beginning. The government of India continued to resist any reduction in its control over its traditional areas of influence, in particular eastern and south-eastern Persia, and its stonewalling tactics frustrated the efforts of the home government to promote unification of policy control.

So far as the Indian establishment was concerned, military operations in south-east Persia were part of India's frontier defence and could not be detached from it. Attempts to change the chain of command compounded the problem. For example, the force stationed at Bushire was placed under the commander in Mesopotamia, who was under the war office, but also reported to the minister at Tehran. In other areas also the lines of authority were none too clear, with the result that the officer on the spot frequently made his own decisions without seeking authorization from higher authority.[39]

Sometimes confusion could paralyse action. For example, in

October 1915, the renowned German agent, Wilhelm Wassmuss, instigated an attack by tribal chiefs in the Shiraz area on the British consulate. In the process, they looted the Imperial Bank of Persia and captured the entire British community. The women were released but the men held prisoner.[40] The captors demanded that Great Britain release their followers who had been imprisoned, return the money and a consignment of tea that had been confiscated, reopen a road that had been blocked, and grant them a full pardon.[41] These demands presented the British minister and the government of India with a dilemma. Concession would encourage further hostilities, but there was disagreement among the various authorities as to what alternative course might be followed. The consul at Bushire pressed for the use of force. It was humiliating, he said, that three petty chiefs with only a few hundred adherents should successfully defy the British Empire when three British regiments were nearby at Bushire.[42] The government of India opposed military coercion, but refused to accept any terms that included full amnesty for the chiefs who had been involved not only in the Shiraz raid but in previous outrages, including the killing of two British officers.

Sir Percy Cox at Basra supported the Indian position. He considered it highly unlikely that the prisoners would be killed, and the risk to their health by their detention for some months further was of little moment in comparison with the devastating blow to British prestige from granting a full pardon: 'We shall be humiliated before our friends to an extent which will not be effaced during living memories'.[43] Sir Charles Marling, the minister at Tehran, backed by the foreign office, argued that if a full pardon were necessary to secure the release of the prisoners, it should be granted with the proviso that this immunity would be removed if the chiefs again 'misbehaved'.[44] Marling explained that even if Great Britain gave the assurance of pardon, the Farman Farma, the governor general of the province, could after the release make a claim for an indemnity as a pretext to punish the chiefs.[45] While this debate was going on, the commanding general of British forces in Mesopotamia entered the argument with the declaration that murderers should not escape punishment. Marling commented that 'it would be interesting to know why the GOC shoves his oar in. These matters concern him very remotely'.[46] Eventually, in August 1916, the prisoners were released without their captors being given amnesty but with all their other demands met. The release of the consul, however, was delayed because the military at Basra had sent the followers of the chiefs to Bombay rather than Bushire.[47] This controversy among agencies had resulted in the imprisonment of the consul and his associates for ten months.

The hostage crisis illustrated in microcosm the problems that conflicting jurisdictions produced for the execution of British policy in Persia. The grotesque array of agencies reflected the failure of the imperial government to impose its will on the various bureaucracies involved, and its acceptance of the continuation of rival sovereignties. The inability to create a clear line of authority resulted in part from the fact that the central government of Persia could not exercise effective control over powerful local chieftains. The writ of the shah's government did not extend a great distance beyond the capital, and even within that limited compass, Persian officials were perceived as puppets of the British. The British presence thus contributed to the weakness of the government.

The basic problem of Persian instability had engaged the attention of the various departments concerned at least since 1905, but the German threat gave the matter new urgency and led to the imperial government's decision at the beginning of 1916 to send a mission to south Persia.[48] What was at first to be a modest effort was increased in concept to 10,000 men when the Russians raised the size of the Cossack brigade in their sphere to these proportions. Those in the seats of power clearly had developed no great trust in Great Britain's new ally in Persia and had concluded that British prestige required parity when it came to non-Persian forces in the region.[49]

If unity of command is a sacred military principle, it was about to be violated again in Persia. But the blurring of lines of authority was the price bureaucrats in London and Calcutta were apparently willing to pay in order to deal with the conflicting and inflexible views of two vital governmental agencies. The foreign office argued that respect for Persian authority, sovereignty, and neutrality dictated that the British force in south Persia be nominally under Persian control; although real power would be vested in the British minister at Tehran, who would 'advise' the commanding officer on all matters considered political. To place the contingent under either the war office or the commander-in-chief, India, the foreign office maintained, would make a clear sham of Great Britain's purported respect for Persia's independence and her neutrality in the war – an admission that might encourage the Germans and Turks to treat Persia as a belligerent. The government of India, for its part, continued obdurately to insist that the defence of Persia was inseparable from that of India itself.[50]

Inevitably, a compromise was forged, under the terms of which the India office was made responsible for personnel and *matériel* as well as budgetary allocations, while all other matters were placed under the jurisdiction of the British legation at Tehran.[51] By this inexplicit and vague arrangement, the British attempted to maintain the fiction that the British force, now called the South Persia Rifles, was really subject to the authority of the shah's minister of war; with political decisions (actually made by Sir Charles Marling, the British minister at Tehran) being formulated by the Persian cabinet.[52]

The South Persia Rifles assumed the task of maintaining order that had previously been performed by the Persian gendarmerie officered by Swedes.[53] British intelligence agents alleged that at least some of these officers were pro–German, and they were all discharged, but the rank and file were offered employment in the new unit. A complication developed when an impotent Persian cabinet, fearful of popular reaction, insisted that the force be placed under the titular authority of the Farman Farma. As it was understood that the action was purely symbolic, Marling did not press the issue.[54] The operational authority of the South Persia Rifles did not extend to the British force at Bushire, however, which remained under the commander-in-chief, Mesopotamia, himself subject to the orders of the war office.

All that was needed further to poison this murky brew was the unhappy choice of Brigadier Percy M. Sykes as commander of the South Persia Rifles. Sykes had been selected because as an officer of the Indian Army he had had considerable experience in Persia and as consul at Kerman in the 1890s had purportedly developed a cordial relationship with the Farman Farma.[55] The government of India judged him the officer 'obviously the best qualified' for the job.[56] But Sykes craved power, and was vainglorious in pursuing it. The legation at Tehran soon nicknamed him 'Pomposity',[57] and Lord Hardinge, who as viceroy has strongly recommended him, a few months later drastically altered his opinion. In October 1916, he wrote of Sykes: 'We always thought that Persia was the most suitable sphere of activity for him, but I confess that I am now beginning to have my doubts as the combination of a swollen head, bluster and incompetence is bad and not conducive to harmony'.[58]

For a commander of Sykes's character, the lack of a traditional line of authority provided a golden opportunity for self-assertion and brought on a fiasco bordering on disaster. Within a few months of his appointment he was clashing with consular officers at Fars and Kerman over his insistence that they be under his authority 'except as regarding office routines'. He defended this position by insisting that continuity of policy could be maintained amidst 'intricate and constantly changing problems' only by vesting authority to make major political decisions in a single individual – himself.[59] He was rebuked by both the government of India and the minister at Tehran, who reminded him that his responsibility was confined to the South Persia Rifles, but these admonitions did not chasten him.[60] Rebuffed in one area, he tried again in another.

Sykes conceived of his South Persia Rifles as an army, not merely a military police contingent his superiors had authorized. The unit was not impressive in numbers or in their success as a peace-keeping force, but it had an impact upon the general population in the areas through which it passed. An Indian official described the troops' passage along the Bandar Abbas-Kerman road as leaving in their train 'a welter of disorder'.[61] As the duke of Wellington reputedly said of some new recruits: 'They may not frighten the enemy, but they certainly frighten me'.

In the summer of 1916, when 800 Russian troops at Isfahan were threatened by Bakhtiaris with some Turkish support, the foreign office decided to offer the assistance of Sykes's force, stationed at Yezd about 200 miles to the south-east, as a means of 'maintaining the influence and prestige of the allies in that province'.[62] Sykes's unit had by this time achieved a total strength of only 450, including 340 infantry and 60 cavalry, two mountain guns and two machine guns.[63] The Russians, however, accepted the offer and Sykes proceeded with alacrity to Isfahan. Once arrived, he was reluctant to leave. He explained to Marling that the Russian military authorities regarded his column as part of General Baratoff's army and that the Russians would consider his departure 'almost in the light of desertion'. Under these conditions he did not wish to leave Isfahan without Russian consent, even though his assistance had been provided temporarily during an emergency which had apparently ended.[64] Marling found Sykes's assertion incredible. If Sykes was indeed under Russian orders, he remarked, 'the only force we have in Persia will be employed for Russian as apart from British or even joint interests'.[65] General Gough, whose troops had been temporarily diverted from

Bushire to Shiraz pending Sykes's arrival from Isfahan, warned that any delay would probably mean 'complete anarchy' in the province.[66]

Sykes, however, pressed his case. He stated that Baratoff had informed him that General Chernozuboff, the overall Russian commander in the area, had issued orders for combined operations intended to 'solve finally' the Turkish problem in Persia and that he needed Sykes's column as the garrison of Isfahan in order to release Russian troops for the offensive.[67] This report was received with incredulity. Not only was it ludicrous that a great Russian offensive should depend for its success on 450 men, but Chernozuboff's command and Baratoff's were independent of each other. Beyond that, no Russian commander would conscript Sykes's assistance without at least informing the British authorities. Marling noted: 'He doesn't want to leave Esfahan on any little adventures'.[68]

When Sykes was asked to document his assertion that the Russian command in Persia continued to need his presence, he replied that he was 'unable to disclose more of the Russian plans as they were confided to me somewhat unwillingly and under promise of secrecy'.[69] Marling reminded him that he was a British officer and that no pledge of confidentiality could absolve him from communicating information to his own superior authorities,[70] but this chastisement did not elicit a satisfactory reply.

By the beginning of 1917, the British authorities in Persia, India, and Great Britain, with the exception of Lord Curzon, had all lost confidence in Sykes, yet he was not recalled until December 1918 – a monument to what could be achieved by even an ineffectual 'man on the spot' when the government which supposedly guided his actions was equivocating, vacillating, and divided. As Robertson wrote to General C.C. Munro, the new commander-in-chief, India:

The present situation is quite ridiculous. The stumbling block seems to be Sykes himself of whom Lord Curzon has a great opinion. The central point as to whether one commander is required or not was overlooked in talking about the difficulties for providing for Sykes. And so we have got no forwarder in the matter.[71]

Concentration on the deficiencies of Sykes can obscure the fact that not even a paragon could have been effective in his position. He was called upon to achieve great ends with small means. His force attained a maximum strength of less than 11,000 men, predominantly mercenaries, recruited from the defunct Persian gendarmerie, with little discipline and less ardour for the fight. Tangled lines of authority between the Tehran legation and the government of India and between the political and military officers – consul and the commander of the troops – would have produced serious problems for the most fastidious of officers. Throughout Sykes's tenure, rival departments of government condemned lack of unity of command, each demanding to be placed in charge. Month after month, year after year, officials at London and in the Middle East bemoaned the lack of system, but little was done.

In part, this perpetuation of disunity resulted from efforts to achieve cohesiveness through decisions at the highest level. Responsibility for co-ordination was vested in the Eastern Committee, created in 1915 after several incarnations under other names.[72] The personnel of this committee included the secretaries of state for war and foreign affairs, the chancellor of the exchequer, and the heads of the military forces. In theory, it was virtually omnipotent; in practice it frequently appeared the opposite. There were two basic reasons for the committee's weakness. First, every member represented a department, and frequently was a spokesman for his constituency. In addition, the heavy load of responsibility which each of the members had to bear made scheduling of committee meetings difficult, and when the meetings were held the members often came unprepared, having failed to read the mass of documents which staff members had prepared.[73] Even when they did try to digest this material, their understanding of the actual state of affairs could be limited. Lord Robert Cecil, who as deputy to Balfour at the foreign office assiduously studied the reports placed before him, confessed in September 1918 his puzzlement as to precisely what was going on in the Middle Eastern theatre, in particular in Persia and Transcaucasia. There was a Colonel Haig, an Indian officer at Isfahan. Did he have any direct military authority? Sykes, also an Indian officer, commanded the South Persia Rifles, but who commanded the Indian troops? Then there were troops at Bandar Abbas and a small expedition under General Douglas proceeding from Shiraz to Bushire. Under whose command was he? Most complicated of all were the operations in the north involving two generals and a naval captain, each acting independently of the other and, perhaps, of any other authority.[74] Robertson was not unaware of these difficulties. He feared also that members of the committee would force parochial considerations on the whole cabinet. 'If no trained minds are brought to bear on many questions which may arise', he wrote, 'the Cabinet will inevitably be influenced by those members who are most persistent in pushing their views. These members may not be the best qualified to express an opinion.'[75]

Cecil's puzzlement was understandable, particularly when the men on the spot were none too clear themselves as to the chain of command. This uncertainty was particularly evident in north Persia and the Caucasus, where the British government had made *ad hoc* arrangements in an attempt to establish control over the border areas in which Russian influence and authority had evaporated. There were three commands involved in this British effort to bolster their authority. Major-General L.C. Dunsterville, in youth the model for Stalky in Kipling's *Stalky and Company*, was now in his chronological maturity a charming personality with somewhat uncertain credentials as a military commander. Gertrude Bell found him 'a truly delightful creature, generous, enthusiastic, entertaining'.[76] Dunsterville had been selected in January 1918 to lead a cadre of commissioned and non-commissioned officers to recruit an army in Georgia and Armenia and take control of the Caucasus and the Baku oil fields.

Major-General Sir Wilfrid Malleson was assigned in June 1918 to a mission to Meshed in the Persian province of Khorasan. He was given free rein to hold up any Turco-German advance along the railway on the frontier between Persia and Russia. Like Dunsterville, he was assigned too small a detachment and too little money to carry out so large a task.[77] One writer has written with some hyperbole that in accordance with the tradition of the British army, the proverbial two men and a boy 'were sent out to meet a possible concentration of 200,000'.[78]

The third member of the triumvirate, Captain Norris, was directed by the admiralty to seek to establish British naval control of at least the southern section of the Caspian Sea. The missions of these three overlapped, but they were under different authorities, whose instructions they did not always obey, and had little or no contact with each other. Norris had remarkable success for a time in the Caspian, but all of the missions were eventual failures. The hoped-for army of Armenians and Georgians did not materialize, and the forces arrayed against the tiny British forces were too powerful for them to withstand. Dunsterville, committed to fighting the good fight, sought to persuade the commander of the British army at Baghdad, his titular superior, to provide two divisions to repel the Turks in the Caucasus, and he gained the support of Sir Charles Marling and eventually of the Eastern Committee to carry out what Sir William Marshall, the general officer commanding in Mesopotamia, considered to be 'this mad enterprise'.[79]

Though the expedition was assigned to Marshall's command, he had no part in its planning and considered that the scheme violated all the rules of military strategy. Marshall maintained that if the objective was to knock the Ottoman Empire out of the war, it could best be achieved by striking at its vitals. Diversion of troops to the periphery with 700 miles of communications to defend, mostly in mountainous country, he considered not just irrational but lunatic. He used the excuse of bad weather to defer the departure of the mission as long as possible, but his delaying tactics ended when he received peremptory orders to send it on its way. He stated later that he had written a letter of resignation but was deterred from sending it by his senior officers.[80]

Marshall's recollections are supported by General Thomson, who succeeded Dunsterville. Thomson wrote that 'the whole force of Mesopotamia had been immobilized to provide a weak demonstration at a non-vital point'. The British, said Thomson, had a weakness for sending out military missions with inadequate resources, which then made appeals for more men and money, not enough to achieve their objects but depriving other forces more vital to the campaign. The Germans, he said, seemed to use military missions more cleverly than did the British. With minimal resources and maximum use of diplomacy supported by judicious bribery, they had achieved much greater success. All the British missions, said Thomson, started as a small contingent, ended as an army, and none except that led by Lawrence achieved any significant objective.[81]

In all sectors of the Middle East, efforts to promote unity of command were delayed, and to a considerable extent frustrated by resistance from the various departments involved and from officers serving under their jurisdiction.[82] Each of the 'men on the spot' involved in the Middle East campaign saw the war from his own perspective and sought to guard the interests he was appointed to protect. His superiors at London, while they sought to co-ordinate the war effort, were affected by the same consideration. There was nothing unique in these cross-currents, which were endemic to the nature of agencies generally. In addition, the fiascos that occurred in the Middle East, although compelling in themselves, were no more disastrous than many of the miscalculations on the Western Front.

Military organizations, like others, all suffer from labouring under the burden of various degrees of disorganization. Some British officers in the First World War were impressed with what they considered to be the superior organization of the German high command. Perhaps their German counterparts, seeing the British high command at a distance, made similar comments about the British.

NOTES

1. Elie Kedourie, *Islam in the Modern World and Other Studies* (London, 1980), p. 311.
2. Quoted in Martin Albrow, *Bureaucracy* (New York, 1970), pp. 16, 18.
3. Michel Crozier, *The Bureaucratic Phenomenon* (Chicago, 1964), p. 195.
4. Robert K. Merton, 'Bureaucratic Structure and Personality', in *The National Administrative System*, ed. Dean L. Yarwood (New York, 1971), p. 380; Jacques Ellul, *The Political Illusion* (New York, 1967), p. ix.
5. Robert Khorasch, *The Institutional Imperative* (New York, 1973), p. 24; Matthew Holden, Jr., 'Imperialism in Bureaucracy', ed. Yarwood, p. 69.
6. A.J.P. Taylor, *The Troublemakers* (Bloomington, 1958), p. 97.
7. Balfour to Chamberlain, private, 18 Feb. 1916, [Balfour MSS] Add. MSS 49736.
8. Balfour to Cecil, 12 Sept. 1917, Add. MSS 49738. The identification by executives with institutions over which they preside to the extent that they consider these organizations the extension of themselves is a common phenomenon, as both of the writers of this article can attest.
9. A. Chamberlain to Balfour, secret, 15 June 1915, Add. MSS 49736.
10. 'Causes Contributing to Errors in Judgment', Mesopotamia Commission, CAB 19/26.
11. John Marlowe, *Late Victorian* (London, 1967) p. 40.
12. Memorandum, 'Aden', secret, by A. Chamberlain, 29 June 1917, CAB 24/18 (GT 1237). See also R.J. Gavin, *Aden under British Rule, 1839-1967* (New York, 1975).
13. Marlowe, pp. 41-2.
14. India office memorandum on Military Assistance Given by India in Prosecution of the War, secret, for imperial war cabinet, 11 March 1917 CAB 19/28.
15. Edmund Dane, *British Campaigns in the Nearer East, 1914-1918, I: The Days of Adversity* (London, 1919), p. 106.
16. George Buchanan, *The Tragedy of Mesopotamia* (Edinburgh, 1938), p. 69. Buchanan was one of the critics.
17. 'Secret: The Present and Prospective Situation in Syria and Mesopotamia, a Paper Designed by the General Staff in Consultation with the Admiralty War Staff', 19 Oct. 1913, Robertson MSS I/9/9, [Liddell Hart Centre for Military Archives, King's College London].
18. See John S. Galbraith, 'No Man's Child: The Campaign in Mesopotamia, 1914-1916', *International History Review*, vi (1984), 358-83.
19. Buchanan, pp. 30, 45.
20. Hardinge to W.R. Laurence, private, 26 Nov. 1915, MSS EUR F 143, fo. 73.
21. Duff to Hardinge, 30 Dec. 1915, [Cambridge University Library,] Hardinge MSS 67.
22. Duff to Robertson, 28 March 1916, Robertson MSS I/32/17.
23. *Parliamentary Debates*, 5th Series, 1917, XCV, 12 July 1917, 2162.

24. Mesopotamia Commission, 'Findings and Conclusions', CAB 19/26. Also Cd. 8610, 1917.
25. Hamilton to Wedgwood, 24 Oct. 1916, IWM Wedgwood MSS.
26. Duff to Robertson, 28 March 1916, Robertson MSS I/23/17.
27. H. St. John Philby, *Arabian Jubilee* (London, 1954), p. 33.
28. Basil Liddell Hart, *T.E. Lawrence* (London, 1935).
29. Until 1916 there were three separate commands in Egypt: Sir Archibald Murray headed the Mediterranean Expeditionary Force; Sir John Maxwell was in charge of the troops in the Egyptian delta and Western desert; and Major General Altham was commander of the Levant Base, which was created as a supply pool for the Gallipoli, Salonika, and Egyptian theatres. Archibald P. Wavell, *The Palestine Campaigns* (Freeport, N.Y., 1972, first publication, 1931), p. 41.
30. Jean Beraud Villars, *T.E. Lawrence* (New York, 1959), p. 70.
31. See David Kelly, *The Ruling Few* (London, 1952).
32. Introduction by editor, Robert O. Collins, to Gilbert F. Clayton, *An Arabian Diary* (Berkeley, 1969), p. 61. For the results see Elie Kedourie, *In the Anglo-Arab Labyrinth: The McMahon–Husayn Correspondence and its Interpretations, 1914-1939* (Cambridge, 1976).
33. Marlowe, p. 123.
34. R.O. Collins, in Clayton, p. 57.
35. Lawrence to Hogarth, 22 March 1915, in *The Letters of T.E. Lawrence*, ed. D. Garnett (London, 1938), p. 195.
36. Liddell Hart, pp. 240-1.
37. Garnett, pp. 182-3.
38. Lawrence, 'Memorandum for Information of Cabinet', 4 Nov. 1918, Garnett, p. 267.
39. The menace was not illusory. See Otto Victor Karl Liman von Sanders, *Five Years in Turkey* (Annapolis, 1927), p. 134.
40. Chamberlain to Chelmsford, 21 Sept. 1916, private, [Chelmsford MSS] MSS EUR E264/2.
41. F.A. Hamilton, 'Wassamuss', *Journal of the Royal United Service Institution*, lxxx (1935), 141-2. Wassmuss has been called 'the German Lawrence'. The identification is appropriate to the extent that they were both men of imagination and energy.
42. Trevor, Bushire, to minister, Tehran, 18 June 1916, FO 248/146.
43. Trevor to minister, Tehran, 25 June 1916, *ibid.*
44. Telegram, Cox to India, 27 June 1916, *ibid.*
45. Grey to Marling, 16 June 1916, *ibid.*
46. Marling to Bushire, 22 June 1916, *ibid.*
47. Note by Marling on government of India to India office, 25 July 1916, *ibid.*
48. India to Bushire, repeated to Basra, Tehran, Bombay, 12 Aug. 1916, *ibid.*
49. F. Safire, 'The South Persian Rifles' (Ph.D., Edinburgh, 1976), pp. 1-2. (The title of Farman Farma means 'The Issuer of Commands'.)
50. India to Sykes, 20 April 1917, FO 248/1185.
51. Marling to Sykes, 12 Oct. 1916, *ibid.*
52. See, e.g., Chamberlain to Chelmsford, private, 21 Sept. 1916, MSS EUR E264/2.
53. Marling to Hardinge, private, 23 April 1917, FO 248/1185.
54. *London Times*, 30 Nov. 1915. The officers were not under the orders of the Swedish government.
55. Marling to Hardinge, private, 20 June 1917, FO 248/1185.
56. Firuz Kazemzadeh, *Russia and Britain in Persia, 1864-1914* (New Haven, 1968).
57. India to FO, 19 Jan. 1916, FO 248/1143.
58. Note in Sykes to Tehran, 20 Nov. 1916, *ibid.*
59. Hardinge to Grant, private, 4 Oct. 1916, MSS EUR D660/11.
60. Sykes to India, 10 July 1916, FO 248/1153.

61. Marling to India, 11 July 1916; India to Sykes, 14 July 1916, *ibid*.
62. Grant to Hardinge, 30 Aug. 1916, Hardinge MSS 24.
63. FO to Marling, 19 Aug. 1916, FO 248/1154.
64. Marling to Gough, confidential, 20 Sept. 1916, FO 248/1143. This was the core element of what became the South Persia Rifles.
65. Sykes to Marling, 16 Sept. 1916, FO 248/1154.
66. Marling to FO, 16 Sept. 1916, *ibid*.
67. Gough to India, 16 Sept. 1916, *ibid*.
68. Sykes to India, secret, 30 Sept. 1916, *ibid*.
69. Note, n.d., *ibid*.
70. Sykes to India, 11 Oct. 1916, FO 248/1154.
71. Sykes to Tehran, 10 Oct., 12 Nov. 1916, *ibid*.
72. Robertson to Munro, 13 Feb. 1917, Robertson MSS I/22/55.
73. The committee was first called the war council, established in November 1914. In June 1915, it became the Dardanelles Committee and later in the year its name was changed to the Eastern Committee.
74. Memo, secret, for war cabinet, by E.S. Macdonough, 'The War in the East', July 1918, CAB 27/28.
75. Cecil to Balfour, 15 Sept. 1918, CAB 27/24.
76. Notes by Robertson, 30 June 1913, Robertson MSS, I/9/4a.
77. Elizabeth Burgoyne, *Gertrude Bell* (2 vols., London, 1958, 1961), i. 94.
78. C.H. Ellis, *The Transcaspian Episode, 1918-1919* (London, 1963), p. 176.
79. L.V.S. Blocker, *On Secret Patrol in High Asia* (London, 1922), p. 6.
80. William Marshall, *Memories of Four Fronts* (London, 1929), p. 287.
81. *Ibid*., p. 308.
82. Thomson to Pipsqueak, 19 Dec. 1937, IWM Lyndon Bell MSS.

VIII

THE HASHEMITE 'TRIBAL CONFEDERACY' OF THE ARAB REVOLT, 1916-1917

Joseph Kostiner

> It is inappropriate to demand that political settlements
> should be 'natural' or 'logical'. Politics is neither like
> a geometrical theorem, nor like a mating instinct.
>
> Elie Kedourie[1]

The nature of the Hashemite state which emerged during the formative phase of the Arab Revolt (1916-17) is worthy of study for two reasons. First, in comparison with the relatively well-known diplomatic and military aspects of the revolt, this aspect of it has been relatively ignored. Second, to investigate the nature of the state that developed during the Arab Revolt is to focus upon the revolt's tribal infrastructures; thus shedding new light on its dynamics, successes, and failures.

There is no evidence to suggest that the Hashemites either developed a concrete, pre-designed vision of state prior to the revolt, or tried to realize such a vision after the revolt began. Rather, their notions of statehood derived from their *Weltanschauung* and their aims in the revolt. The paramount idea in Hashemite political thought, which stands out both in Sherif Husayn's writings and in those of his son, Abdullah, is the Hashemites' adherence to the values of traditional *sunni* Islam, and specifically to the tenure of the incumbent (Ottoman) Muslim state, as long as it remained devoted to these values.[2] Thus, Husayn's appointment in 1908 as keeper of the holy places in the Hejaz had been accepted and perceived by him as a manifestation of loyalty to the state, and notably to its head, Sultan Abdul Hamid. Accordingly, the Hashemites stressed that their resort to rebellion was only a means of protecting the holy law (*shari'a*) and the traditional ways of the empire, after the new Ottoman élite, the Committee of Union and Progress, had blatantly violated them.[3]

The other ideas ostensibly motivating the Hashemites are not easy to discern, mainly because the scarcity of their writings makes it difficult to judge whether a specific idea was merely being made use of, or was a deep-rooted conviction, and at what point, if at all, it was dominant in Hashemite thought. Thus, writers such as George Antonius, C. Ernest Dawn, and Elie Kedourie differ in their views of the Hashemites' motives. Antonius stressed their Arab nationalist inclinations, Dawn their dynastic and religious ambitions, and Professor Kedourie pointed out Husayn's aspirations to become a caliph (*khalifa*) over an Arab-Muslim state. In fact, these motives complemented rather than contradicted each other in forming the Hashemite state of mind, each exerting its own impact according to the moment of its appearance.

One of their most important goals was independence for the Hejaz under the hereditary leadership of Husayn's family. This grew out of a continuous Hashemite effort to weaken the Ottoman grip on the province, and from Husayn's own ambition to prevent a rival Hashemite clan (the Dhawu Zayd) from gaining ascendancy over his own clan (the Dhawu 'Awn). After 1914, as the Committee of Union and Progress made greater efforts to tighten its grip on the Hejaz (and other provinces), and particularly after Husayn discovered a Unionist plot to depose him in January 1915, independence became an acknowledged goal of the anti-Ottoman revolt. At the same time, however, an additional goal evolved in the minds of Husayn and his sons: the formation of an independent Islamic-Arab empire controlling a large territory in the Middle East. This goal emerged from two developments: first, British officials in Cairo, in exchanges with Abdullah, encouraged Husayn to aspire to a 'caliphate', in return for Hashemite support during the war. Second, the contacts maintained by Husayn's other son, Faysal, with Arab nationalist groups in Syria (commencing in March 1915), led the Hashemites to believe that they were accepted as leaders of the whole 'Arab Movement'.[4] The two goals were complementary: the 'liberation' of the Hejaz was only to be the first stage in the acquisition of additional Arab territories within which a large Islamic-Arab state would eventually be formed.

One must therefore challenge Dawn's claims, first that the revolt was mainly a means to attain Hashemite supremacy in the Hejaz, overpowering regional rivals such as Ibn Saud of Nejd and Muhammad al-Idrisi of Asir, and second, that Husayn might have viewed the Hejaz as the core of his aspirations.[5] The skirmishes between the forces of Husayn and Idrisi in 1911, and the tension caused by a force led by Abdullah, which came to tax 'Utayba tribesmen on the Nejd–Hejaz border area in 1915, should be regarded as no more than 'frontier' incidents.[6] There is no evidence, prior to late 1917, to suggest the existence of a conflict in the Peninsula of a magnitude to have motivated Husayn to launch an operation, such as the Arab Revolt, merely to overpower a regional rival.[7] The Hashemites' aims in the revolt cannot be considered to be merely regional and dynastic, nor can the independence of the Hejaz be considered in isolation.

The revolt, then, had wider nationalist aims. Even if Husayn and his sons did not fully adopt Arab nationalist secular and ethnic notions, they did back the Arab nationalist 'case' as religiously valid and as a political platform.[8] This is evident from various sources. It was the territorial scheme, formulated by the Syrian nationalists and Faysal in the Damascus Protocol of April 1915, which was the basis of demands for the future caliphate that Husayn presented to the British high commissioner in Egypt, Sir Henry McMahon, in July of that year. Executions, arrests, and other persecutions committed in early 1916 by the Unionist government against Arab nationalists (in both Syria and the Hejaz) were issues high on the Hashemite agenda, as Husayn's first proclamation of revolt demonstrates.[9] Moreover, the Hashemite intention of focusing on Syria further indicated their inclination to follow the prevalent trend of Arab nationalism. Thus, in February and April 1916, Husayn told the British that he would send Faysal to Syria in order to co-ordinate the tribal and urban uprisings expected there. 'This is the beginning of the principal movement', he stressed.[10] In February 1916, the new high commissioner in Egypt, Sir Reginald Wingate, noted that Husayn's 'desire to strengthen his position in the Syrian hinterland is intimately connected with his aspirations to the Caliphate';[11] and T.E. Lawrence noted that Husayn's objection in the summer of 1916 to the appointment of a nationalist Arab officer, Ja'far al-'Askari, to lead the revolt's regular forces followed from Husayn's wish that 'Mecca must deliver Damascus' and not vice versa.[12]

That the two main ideas that motivated the Hashemites – adherence to the traditional Muslim order and the making of a large independent Arab state – were in fact complementary is borne out by Abdullah's memoirs, and to a somewhat lesser extent by Husayn's few writings, wherein the Arabs constitute a distinct nation (*al-Umma al-'Arabiyya*) and possess a particular culture and language, which qualify them for a leading role. However, the Arabs' excellent qualities were notably Muslim in nature: they were the 'heart' of Islam, carriers of its culture, and executors of its laws. Their superiority would flourish best in a traditional Muslim state, which they would lead according to the *shari'a*.[13] As Dawn noted, this is in fact the classic theory of the universal caliphate with a special emphasis on the Arab elements' leading role, underlined by theologians such as Muhammad 'Abduh, Rashid Rida, and 'Abd al-Rahman al-Kawakibi, whose ideas probably influenced men like Abdullah.[14]

This theory implied, first, that the future Hashemite state was to be an imperial state, spreading over a number of provinces and including a variety of rulers and populations. Second, the Hashemites as *ashraf* (the Prophet's descendants) were to be leaders of the state, with Husayn as its head. This is evident both from the promises high-ranking British officials made to Husayn, and from his own promise in the first proclamation of revolt, that in the light of the Unionists' offences against the caliphate 'they [the Muslims] deserve by law an *imam khalifa* who would be independent, able to execute the holy law and elevate the level of justice'.[15] Being the leader of a revolt against the Unionists, there is little doubt whom Husayn had in mind for this role, although he did not claim the title officially. Third, as this citation indicates, the law and values of the empire were to be traditionally Islamic, based on the *shari'a*. Fourth, the Hashemite state was to be a fighting and expanding entity, intent mainly on conquering Syria and establishing it as the empire's centre. This was not merely an ideological aim which prevailed prior to the outbreak of the revolt, but a practical military goal which set the revolt's strategy and course. Thus, even the initial conquests in the Hejaz were regarded by Husayn and his sons as a step towards Syria.[16] Moreover, in November 1916, when Lawrence succeeded in persuading both the commander of the British forces in Egypt, General Edmund Allenby, and then Husayn himself, to allow the Arab forces under Faysal to become Allenby's 'eastern flank' during his advance into Palestine and Syria, the Arabs readily accepted this task.[17]

However, several aspects of the prospective state were left

undefined, particularly the relations between tribes and rulers and the type of government. The state's exact borders and the method of expansion into Arab territories adjacent to the Hejaz were also not delineated. In May 1915, Ronald Storrs, then MacMahon's secretary, commented that it would be impossible 'to elaborate any theory as to the precise nature of this adumbrated body'.[18] The vagueness of the design pointed towards complications in the future.

In addition, the British authorities, who supported and financed the revolt, themselves did not carry out a uniform policy in the Peninsula. Thus, Aden conducted negotiations with Idrisi in Asir, signing a treaty with him on 30 April 1915, with the aim of starting another anti-Ottoman revolt. British officials in the Persian Gulf (answerable to the India office) led by the British resident, Sir Percy Cox, focused on improving relations with Ibn Saud, with whom a treaty of friendship was concluded on 26 December 1915, practically acknowledging his independence. Generally speaking, India office officials sought tranquillity both around the Gulf and in India, and therefore feared the destabilizing influence of the Arab Revolt. Attempts by Cairo, the Gulf, Aden, London, and India to co-ordinate policy in Arabia were made in the early months of 1915 and again in November 1916 but to no avail.[19] Such division among British departments had a decisive impact on the Hashemite state-in-the-making.

The Hashemites' relations with neighbouring rulers determined certain characteristics of the emerging state. First, they affected the Hashemites' ability to annex large territories, a goal which in itself was overly ambitious, as some of the territories were dominated by the powerful and quasi-independent tribes and rulers of central and southern Arabia. Second, they affected the new empire's ability to establish an internal order that would both define the authority of Husayn and each of the other rulers in the state, and regulate their mutual relationships. This was, in the best of circumstances, an immensely difficult issue: only a wise, imaginative, sensitive yet firm policy could alter the Peninsula's system of quasi-independent and separate tribal states, which quarrelled continuously over unmarked and disputed frontier areas as well as claims to suzerainty over certain tribes.

Inter-state relations, too, were complicated by quarrels, such as that between the Hashemites and the Saudis of Nejd. This quarrel had begun with the short-lived Saudi occupation of the Hejaz in the early years of the nineteenth century, and was aggravated by the religious antagonism between the Wahabi inhabitants of Nejd, followers of the *tawhid* (oneness of God) and the more regularly orthodox *shafi'i* Hejazis. Hashemite attempts to tax Saudi tribes in 1910, and as late as November 1915, further exacerbated relations. Moreover, Husayn's growing political and financial power, boosted by the British, was construed by other local rulers as strengthening his ability to act against them, thus compounding their resentment of him.[20] Finally, the fact that rulers such as Idrisi and Ibn Saud had their own treaties with the British, encouraged them to view themselves as equal to Husayn, and to resist any concessions in his favour. In the face of these difficulties, Husayn displayed an attitude of superiority and contempt towards his regional rivals. However, as regional supremacy was not the Hashemites' main objective in the revolt, Husayn did not develop a comprehensive strategy for dealing with them. The consequences were manifested in the early stages of the revolt.

Husayn's relations with Idrisi came to a showdown during the summer of 1916. On 18 June, with the aid of a British naval bombardment, Idrisi's forces captured the important port of Qunfida on the Yemeni coast from the Ottomans. This operation should have been regarded by Husayn as a step towards the realization of both Arab nationalist and British aims, fully congruent with the Arab Revolt. Instead, Husayn focused on his own short-term benefits. Exploiting old contacts with clans in this and other towns of Asir, he demanded to take over the town on behalf of 'local wishes', and even deployed forces in the area, thereby threatening to precipitate a clash between two Arab nationalist forces. The British, under the influence of Arab bureau officials, and more fearful of a possible crisis in their relations with Husayn than with Idrisi – whose relatively small forces left him no option but to remain pro-British – sided with the former.[21] On 23 August, Idrisi reluctantly waived his claim to Qunfida in favour of the Hashemites. But he also stopped his 'active help against the Turks' and demanded that Husayn 'not interfere with him in his own region and not trespass on his limits'.[22] Husayn had missed an opportunity to extend his realm to the south, to maintain order among its rulers through an agreed settlement, and a territorial boundary was thus set for the Hashemite state which it could not breach. Ironically, on 27 September Qunfida was reoccupied by the Ottomans, under whom it remained until 1919.

A similar relationship developed with Ibn Saud. After the Hashemite occupation of Mecca in July 1916, Husayn suggested to Ibn Saud that he join the Arab Revolt. Ibn Saud replied favourably, promising to help 'with all his powers', predicating his assistance 'on Husayn's written undertaking [to] abstain from trespassing on his territory or interfering with his subjects'.[23] In fact, we know from Ibn Saud's other communications to the British during this period that he valued the revolt only inasmuch as it would distract the Ottomans from Iraq, on Nejd's northern frontier. He therefore refrained from co-operating with the Ottoman contender to the sherifate, Ali Haydar, just as he rejected Husayn's pretensions to speak for Arab unity. Ibn Saud was obviously not inclined to surrender to the Hashemites any of his territories or sovereignty. Husayn's acceptance of Ibn Saud's conditions was therefore essential, if there was to be any co-ordination between the two.

On 5 September Husayn replied, describing the Saudi demands as coming 'from a man either bereft of his reason or intoxicated'.[24] In Saudi eyes, this was an open provocation, foreshadowing future conflict over territory. Ibn Saud passed on Husayn's communication to Cox, explaining his fears. On 19 October, Cox reassured Ibn Saud of Nejd's frontiers and of the latter's independent status, as acknowledged by the British in their treaty of friendship – 'and the Sharif must recognize the full import of the treaty'. In addition, Cox agreed that Ibn Saud should start a campaign, separate from the revolt, against the Rashidi pro-Ottoman state of Jabal Shammar,[25] thus further prohibiting co-operation between Nejd and the Hejaz. The importance of these developments lies, once more, in the limits they placed – this time sealed by British guarantees – on the Hashemites' ability to integrate into their kingdom territories lying east of the Hejaz.

Husayn's designation of himself as 'King of the Arab Countries' on 5 November 1916, marked the culmination of his thoughtlessness in relation to his regional counterparts. Apparently, the declaration was made by Abdullah, in his capacity as Hashemite 'foreign minister', to impress the British and other Arab chiefs, but was made without prior consultation with any of them. Abdullah's explanation of the event further attested to the declarations' incoherence and inconsistency: although Ibn Saud was respected as 'chief of Arabs', Ibn Rashid was a 'traitor', and Idrisi was not recognized 'to be

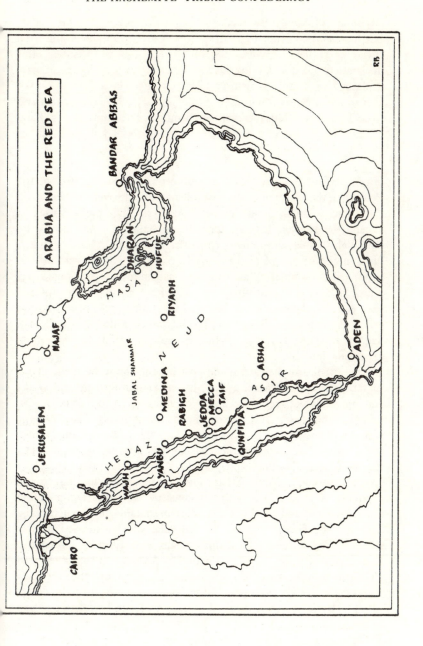

ARABIA AND THE RED SEA

anything'. Husayn must therefore be the 'only King of the Arabs', but his claims did not touch the other leaders' individual and local sovereignty: 'let everyone rule his part'.[26] Not surprisingly, this declaration did not develop into a viable regional policy; moreover, it clashed with other British and French interests and only aroused British and French resentment. On 3 January 1917, the British and French informed Husayn that they would regard him only as 'King of the Hejaz', thereby reinforcing the territorial and political restrictions on the new state.

Unable to expand towards the southern and eastern parts of the Peninsula, the Hashemite state established its rule over the Hejaz and the Transjordanian desert approaching Syria. The method used to expand the Hashemites' territory and to stabilize it was termed by Abdullah 'tribal groupings' (*ijtima'at 'ashiriyya*).[27] Accordingly, Husayn and/or one of his sons would make an alliance with several major tribes dominating an area the Hashemites sought to conquer. These tribes then constituted the bulk of the forces which captured the region and became the basis of Hashemite rule over it. Each group constituted a link, or what Lawrence called a 'step', in a 'ladder' of tribes that was ultimately meant to facilitate Hashemite expansion into Syria.[28]

The initial group which made possible the conquest of the Hejaz (notably the cities of Mecca, Taif, Jedda, Yanbu, Rabigh, and Wajh) and operated between July and November 1916, consisted of the 'Utayba, the 'Awf, and, during the battle of Rabigh, the Zubayd sections of the Harb, the Juhayna, Hudhayl, Subay', Bani Harith, and Buqum.[29] A second group was formed approximately between the months of February and July 1917 to facilitate the Hashemite advance through Wadi Sirhan into Transjordan, leading to the conquest of Aqaba on 6 July. It consisted of tribes living in the northern Hejaz and southern Transjordan (notably Jawf), such as the Billi and the Huwaytat; and the Ruwalla, which extended passive support. The formation of a third group was begun by Faysal and Lawrence just prior to the occupation of Aqaba, and continued into 1918. It was again made up of the Ruwalla, the Huwaytat, the Bani 'Atiyya, Bani Sakhr, and part of the Shararat, dominating the desert south of Syria. Contacts were also made with the Druze population in the Huran, who assisted in fighting in the battles of Ma'an and Tafila and in cutting Ottoman supply lines over the Yarmuk river.[30]

The relations between the Hashemites and the tribes were complicated. The initial recruitment was based on extended bargaining, which took place over a period of weeks before each group was formed.[31] For a tribe's consent to join a Hashemite alliance, it was paid a large sum, rather than being fully integrated into the new alliance or being required to reform its basic values or structure. The main form of payment was monetary. It was effective owing to the economic difficulties which Peninsula tribes faced in the wake of the naval blockade the British imposed in order to disrupt Ottoman supplies on both Red Sea ports and the port of Kuwait, and from the difficulty the tribes experienced in maintaining trade routes with the Ottoman-dominated Syrian and Iraqi markets.[32] The subsidy of approximately £125,000 per month in gold which Husayn received from Great Britain was mostly distributed to the tribes by Husayn's sons, and became a major source of economic relief for them. In addition they received a constant flow of rifles and ammunition which enabled them to loot Ottoman convoys and military posts.[33]

The recruitment of a tribe was often prompted by incentives as well as threats exerted by the advancing Hashemites. For example, the Billi Sheikh Sulayman bin Rifada, who had remained pro-Ottoman when the revolt broke out, reluctantly joined the Hashemites after Wajh in his tribe's grazing zone had been captured on 25 January 1917.[34] The northern tribes also joined as the Hashemites advanced. Another means of arousing pro-Hashemite loyalty was mediation of quarrels among tribal sections, as in January–February 1917, when Abdullah succeeded in mediating a feud among sections of the 'Anaza and the Faqun which helped him to establish a friendly group in Wadi 'Ays and to lay siege to Medina.[35] Faysal and Lawrence acted similarly among the northern tribes.

The Hashemites failed, however, to co-operate fully with the tribes. Thus, a large tribe like the Ruwalla, which was dependent on the markets of Damascus and could not be helped by Hashemite subventions, did not fully join the Hashemite alliance until May 1918, although its leader had accepted money from Faysal.[36] Delays in payment to the tribes which had supported Abdullah in laying siege to Taif resulted in defections. Husayn ceased paying tribes whose active participation in the fighting was not required, and this policy prompted sections of the Harb to attack the forces of Husayn's son, Ali, in the last quarter of 1917. Finally, the disappearance of Hashemite forces from a tribe's grazing zone occasionally led to its becoming pro-Ottoman, as in the case of the Billi after Faysal's forces had moved further north.[37]

One major factor missing from the Hashemite tribal system was Arab nationalist ideology. In the opinion of many observers, if these tribes were at all affected by ideological motives, their feelings were usually against central government, not for unity and state-building. 'They were fighting to get rid of an empire, not to win it', wrote Lawrence.[38] Apparently, the Hashemites did not expect to encounter nationalist ideals or to encourage them; Faysal usually inspired tribes to win a battle by emphasizing victories and booty,[39] and it was only in May 1918 that he delivered a speech to the Ruwalla hailing Arab unity.[40] The various Arab officers who helped to lead the revolt (defectors and former prisoners from the Ottoman army) and who held nationalist views, usually stuck to operational and training tasks; even the representative of the Syrian nationalists at Faysal's camp, Nasib al-Bakri, exerted little if any influence.

The bond between the Hashemites and the tribes was personal. It was usually instigated through contact with the tribal chief alone. In the contacts made with Nuri Sha'lan of the Ruwalla and 'Awda Abu-Taya of the Huwaytat, the chief received money for distribution to the tribe, after which his personal pledge of loyalty guaranteed the tribe's co-operation.[41] Only once, when Husayn declared himself king, was a wider pledge of loyalty (*bay'a*) required from the notables of the Hejaz.[42]

The Hashemite military force was originally tribal, but included thousands of Arab prisoners, captured by Abdullah in Taif and by the British on various fronts. As early as December 1916, an Egyptian officer, 'Aziz 'Ali, was training about 4,000 soldiers in Rabigh, and Faysal tried to turn his forces in Yanbu into a standing army.[43] After the occupation of Wajh the regular army was divided into three 'commands': the northern command under Faysal, led by a Baghdadi former Ottoman officer, Ja'far al-'Askari; the eastern under Abdullah in Wadi 'Ays; and the southern command under Ali in Yanbu and Rabigh. There were infantry and cavalry units, supported by British training officers and engineers, and by Egyptian artillery units. Altogether, the force numbered about 10,000 regulars.[44]

The rate of regular to tribal forces in the different Hashemite battles is not known, but tribal forces were definitely more numerous, and tribal values dominated the strategy of the revolt, particularly with respect to the breakthrough into Syria. Only during the initial weeks of the revolt did the combined Arab forces function both as a small scale 'hit and run' capability and as a prime strategic tool deciding major battles. Once the Arab armies had become Allenby's 'eastern flank', they functioned as guerrillas. According to Lawrence, whose ideas lay behind this step, the Arab forces should not try to destroy the Ottoman enemy, but carry out small scale operations, disrupting the enemies supplies, harassing him in the desert, and thereby distracting Ottoman units from hindering Allenby's progress in Palestine. In Lawrence's view, this strategy suited tribal traditions: the Arab forces were marked by their lack of an *esprit de corps* and regimental discipline, but each tribesman had an 'individual excellence', best manifested in guerrilla warfare.[45]

The making of the Hashemite state had negative effects on the urban population of the Hejaz for several reasons. The fighting and the blockade imposed on the Red Sea ports undermined the trade of local townsmen; the growing importance of nomadic tribes threatened the safety of towns and trade routes; and the rise of Husayn to power was viewed with dismay by urban notables, many of whom were supporters of both the Dhawu Zayd and the Ottomans. Only in the second half of 1917, after the fighting had moved northwards and the blockade had been lifted, did the situation of the townsmen improve.[46] Consequently, Husayn's support grew among them, mostly, however, in Jedda, whose population was profoundly pro-British.

The state's framework for law and order was minimal. The Ottoman civil code was abandoned and replaced by the *shari'a*, which was applicable only to townsmen, for tribal practices governed tribes. However, even the *shari'a* was reported unsuitable for dealing with modern aspects of life and in need of additions. Internal taxation was reported 'in abeyance', taxes being only occasionally collected. Taking into account a drastic decrease in pilgrimage because of the war, the state's revenues from customs and estates amounted to no more than £8,000; the Hashemite state was thus heavily dependent on British assistance. Husayn did recruit police units, mostly from his old bodyguards, but their usefulness was limited to the towns.[47]

The system of government was patrimonial. In addition to the official sheikhs who ruled the towns, the Hashemites appointed their own agents to carry out their policies. Husayn did so in the Hejazi towns, and Faysal maintained order in this way in Transjordan as late as November 1917, when he appointed a young dignitary from among his aides, 'Ali al-Harithi, to co-ordinate his policies in Azraq. Several of these agents were *ashraf*, sometimes related to Husayn's family; a network of some 800-900 of them was dispersed among the tribes.[48]

Executive power was officially held by a council of ministers (*majlis al-wukala*) which was established some time prior to Husayn's coronation. It was led by Husayn's son Ali as grand vizier, and included Abdullah as foreign minister, Faysal as minister of the interior, 'Aziz 'Ali as minister of war, and five Meccan notables as ministers of justice, public works, *awqaf* and holy places, education, and finance. There was also an 'advisory assembly' (*majlis al-shura*) led by Abdullah and eleven other notables, five of whom were *ashraf*.[49] The sources do not specify what authority was actually vested in these bodies, but it is clear that they enjoyed no real power; they took no important decisions regarding the war, and the absence of Abdullah and Faysal from their respective ministries – they were away at the front – attests to their marginality. Apparently, institutions representing law, order, and the towns were considerably less important than those in command of the fighting, which were also in charge of distributing money and recruiting the tribes.[50] Thus the staff of each of the Hashemites, who had such authority, formed centres of power. Abdullah's staff in Wadi 'Ays, including the sherifs Shakir and Nasir, known as remarkable military leaders, constituted one such centre. However, the most formidable centre grew around Faysal after the occupation of Wajh and on the march to Syria. It included the Arab officers Ja'far al-'Askari, Nuri al-Sa'id (of Baghdad), and Mawlud Mukhlis (of Tripoli) who commanded the regular army; the Syrian nationalist Nasib al-Bakri; 'Awda Abu-Taya of the Huwaytat; 'Ali of the Bani Harith tribe; and Lawrence.[51]

The interesting point about these centres of power and particularly Faysal's, was their detachment from Husayn. Apparently, after his reluctant permission in November 1916 for Faysal's forces to move northwards on the eastern flank of Allenby's army, Husayn remained in the position of an 'elder statesman', notified about events either for formal confirmation (for example, the decision to move Abdullah to Wadi 'Ays, which was taken after the fall of Wajh by a forum of Faysal's and Abdullah's staffs and several British officials), or after the fact. Only in June 1918 was he consulted on a serious issue, being asked to permit Abdullah's and Ali's armies to join Faysal's forces in the north, which he vetoed. In any event, a gap developed between

Husayn in the Hejaz and Faysal, who effectively became the leader in the area north of Wajh.[52]

Several conclusions may be drawn from this description of the Hashemite state. First, the variety of tribal and urban groups incorporated into the state did not transform it into a cohesive 'political community', whose diverse segments actively supported the new state. Tribal values, focused on narrow primordial ambitions rather than on state interests, prevailed among the population and often characterized the Hashemites' own attitude towards both tribes and the state's neighbouring rulers. Moreover, the traditional divisions among the tribes, and between them and the townsmen, were not narrowed. No social or political super-tribal organization, either a political party or a movement, was developed. Second, the basic form of political bond was an *ad hoc* one, maintained only through subsidies and personal connections. The state failed to establish either nation-wide institutions or an effective administration. Law and order were maintained only by the *shari'a*, which was at best partly applicable and was decadent in comparison with the Ottoman law. No economic development took place, the economy remaining totally dependent on foreign aid. Third, the governing bodies that constituted the 'centre' of the new state failed to control its 'periphery', namely, the remote and newly captured territories. Real power was vested in regional headquarters which had the actual financial resources, and the political and military control.

These qualities are characteristic not of a developing empire, but rather of a typical 'tribal confederacy'. Briefly, this term refers to a type of confederate state based on a power and duty-sharing relationship between a ruler, usually governing an urban centre, and tribes dwelling on its periphery. The ruler usually possessed religious authority and held the right to wage war, but had to offer the tribes trade and religious facilities, and to provide a minimal administration for the state. The tribes acknowledged his authority, fought for the state, and sometimes paid tribute to its government; in return, they enjoyed full autonomy. Obviously, the rules governing such states were flexible, highly personalized, and only slightly institutionalized. As several analysts have shown, this was the prevalent type of state in various parts of the Arabian Peninsula from the inception of Islam until the twentieth century.[53] The Hashemite state which developed during 1916-17 appears to have been a variation of the type.

One reason why the Hashemite state did not develop beyond a kind of tribal confederacy was circumstantial pressure. During the crucial period of no more than one and a half years, the leaders were busy fighting, while the state's demography and territories were constantly changing. These were not favourable conditions for state building. On the other hand, the Hashemites made virtually no attempt – indeed, were not even reported to harbour designs – to develop a unified and coherent state.

Another reason why the Hashemite state did not develop was the Hashemite perception of statehood – their belief in maintaining the framework of a Sunni-based empire, but without a practical design for an internal regime. This attitude expressed itself in two ways. First, Husayn never sought to bring about major social changes or to reform tribal values. The only substantial re-organization he introduced was the implementation of the *shari'a* as the exclusive law, with himself as leader. Apparently, he viewed the application of proper Islamic law and the ascendancy of an Arab-Islamic leader of the Prophet's clan as epitomizing the Sunni character of the state. Otherwise, society remained unchanged. Lawrence noted that 'there was never any pan-Arab secret society in Mecca because the sherif has always been the Arab government'.[54]

Second, probably because of their growing co-operation with the tribes since 1908, Husayn and his sons had great faith in the tribal life style and favoured it. After their arrival in the Hejaz, Husayn made his sons acquire tribal manners. Lawrence noted that Husayn's 'tastes and sympathies had been always tribal', and that the 'the revolt was a tribal movement and the Shareef a tribal chief who has thrown in his lot quite definitely with the tribesmen'.[55] He praised Faysal's ability to organize each tribe under its tribal leader and to know how to recruit and mediate their feuds.[56] In spite of the territorial growth of the Hashemite state, it remained essentially a tribal confederacy and therefore could hardly form the foundation of an empire.

The various British authorities dealing with Peninsula affairs encouraged the formation of different tribal confederacies, partly owing to their (notably those at the India office) disillusionment with the Arab Revolt. They were probably irritated by the Hashemites' feuds with their neighbours, the new state's ultimate dependence on British military and financial assistance, its modest military achievements, and most of all, the minimal response the revolt generated among the Arab provinces which seemed to them to attest to the weakness of the 'Arab movement' altogether.[57] Consequently, during 1917 British officials in Baghdad and Aden sought to encourage new formations, outside the framework of an Arab empire, which would complement British interests in a way more suitable to the realities and divisive characteristics of the Peninsula. In April 1917, Cox suggested forming a pro-British confederacy based on the Saudi state, Kuwait, a pro-British section of the Shammar tribe, and tribes dwelling in the Iraqi Muntafik area. Cox thought that this alliance would capture the Rashidi state and thereby establish pro-British domination as far as Syria.[58] However, this scheme did not materialize. At the same time, and until 1918, the Aden authorities negotiated a confederacy among the Hashid and Bakil tribes in northern Yemen under Idrisi.[59]

Thus, by the end of the First World War, the Hashemite state had become no more than another important confederacy in the region rather than the hub of an empire. As such it competed with its neighbouring tribal states. After 1918 their feuds escalated, finally precipitating the Hashemite state's demise. Characteristically, its northern headquarters, led by Faysal, broke off from the main body of the state, becoming the head of the new Arab kingdoms of Syria and Iraq.

NOTES

1. Elie Kedourie, *The Chatham House Version and Other Middle Eastern Studies* (London, 1970), pp. 387-8.
2. 'Abdullah ibn al-Husayn, *Mudhakkirati* (1st ed., Jerusalem, 1945), pp. 27-8.
3. Amin Sa'id, *al-Thawra al-'Arabiyya al-Kubra* (Vol. I: Cairo, 1934), pp. 104-14; Husayn Ibn 'Ali, 'Manshur al-Thawra al-Awwal 26 Haziran 1916', in *al-Thawra al-'Arabiyya al-Kubra, Wathaiq wa-Asanid*, ed. Sulayman Musa (Amman, 1966), pp. 27-76.
4. These motives are best summarized by C. Ernest Dawn, 'The Amir of Mecca al-Husayn ibn 'Ali and the Origin of the Arab Revolt', in *From Ottomanism to Arabism*, ed. C.E. Dawn (Urbana, 1973), pp. 1-53, and Elie Kedourie, *In the Anglo-Arab Labyrinth* (Cambridge, 1976), pp. 5-65.
5. Dawn, 'Husayn ibn Ali'; and also C.E. Dawn, 'Ideological Influences in the Arab Revolt', in *From Ottomanism to Arabism*, pp. 69-86.
6. Note by Cornwallis, 10 Jan. 1918, FO 882/7, HRB/18/1, and Memorandum by A.T. Wilson, Relations with the Ibn Sa'ud, No. 2, 12 Jan. 1917, SAC Philby MSS Box XV.2.
7. I believe that Husayn directed his main effort against Ibn Saud only after H.B. St. John Philby first visited the arena in November-December 1917.
8. See George Antonius, *The Arab Awakening* (fifth impression, New York, 1965), pp. 156-9.

9. Husayn, 'Manshur al-Thawra'.
10. Husayn to McMahon, 18 Feb. 1916, IO L/PS/10/387, P3655.
11. Wingate to Clayton, private, 23 April 1916, DUL Wingate MSS file 130/S.
12. T.E. Lawrence, *Seven Pillars of Wisdom* (reprint, Harmondsworth, 1978), p. 172.
13. 'Abdullah, *Mudhakkirati*, pp. 237-49; Husayn, 'Manshur al-Thawra', *passim*.
14. Dawn, 'Ideological Influences', *passim*.
15. Husayn, 'Manshur al-Thawra', p. 69.
16. For Abdullah's attitude see *Mudhakkirati*, p. 143.
17. Lawrence, *Seven Pillars*, pp. 332-6; also Soleiman Musa, *T.E. Lawrence: An Arab View* (London, 1966), pp. 80-2.
18. Quoted by Kedourie, *Labyrinth*, p. 25.
19. Arab Revolt: Sir M. Sykes's Report, 13 Dec. 1916, IO L/PS/10/586, P5263, No. XXL.
20. Wingate to secretary of state, 23 Dec. 1917, FO 371/19117/3056.
21. Sykes's Reports, 16 and 23 Aug. 1916, IO L/PS/10/586, P3311 and 3484, Nos. 5 and 6; and Ronald Leslie Colman, 'Revolt in Arabia 1916-1919: Conflict and Coalition in a Tribal System' (Ph.D., Columbia, 1976).
22. *Arab Bulletin*, 15 Nov. 1916, No. 30.
23. *Ibid.*, 14 Dec. 1916, No. 33.
24. *Ibid.*; and Salah al-Din al-Mukhtar, *Tarikh al-Mamlaka al-'Arabiyya al-Sa'udiyya fi Madiha wa-Hadiriha* (Vol. I: Beirut, 1958), pp. 181-3.
25. Memo by Wilson, 12 Jan. 1917, SAC Philby MSS Box XV/2.
26. *Arab Bulletin*, 8 Nov. 1916, No. 29, and 26 Nov. 1916, No. 32.
27. 'Abdullah, *Mudhakkirati*, pp. 108-25.
28. Lawrence, *Seven Pillars*, p. 345.
29. 'Abdullah, *Mudhakkirati*, pp. 145-6; *Arab Bulletin*, 6 Feb. 1917, No. 41.
30. *Ibid.*; and Lawrence, *Seven Pillars*, pp. 155, 164, 345-8.
31. *Arab Bulletin*, 16 Jan. 1916, No. 13, and 28 Feb. 1917, No. 43.
32. Colman, 'Revolt in Arabia', pp. 96-101; and Appendix K of the 'Summary of the Hejaz Revolt', by the general staff, war office, 31 Aug. 1918, IO L/PS/18/B287.
33. Colman, 'Revolt in Arabia', pp. 67-90.
34. Lawrence, *Seven Pillars*, p. 164.
35. 'Abdullah, *Mudhakkirati*, pp. 136-7.
36. Summary of Hejaz Revolt, Appendix L, IO L/PS/18/B287.
37. *Arab Bulletin*, 6 Feb. 1917, No. 41.
38. Lawrence, *Seven Pillars*, p. 103.
39. *Ibid.*, p. 136.
40. *Ibid.*, pp. 363-4.
41. H.B. Liddel-Hart, *T.E. Lawrence in Arabia and After* (London, 1934), pp. 183, 189.
42. Sa'id, *al-Thawra*, p. 293; 'Abdullah, *Mudhakkirati*, p. 130.
43. Sa'id, *al-Thawra*, pp. 219-20; Liddel-Hart, *Lawrence*, pp. 125-6.
44. *Ibid.*, p. 291; Sa'id, *al-Thawra*, pp. 222-4.
45. Lawrence, *Seven Pillars*, pp. 193-202, 346-8.
46. *Arab Bulletin*, 6 Feb. 1917, No. 41; Colman, 'Revolt in Arabia', pp. 208-10.
47. T.E. Lawrence, 'The Sherifs', 27 Oct. 1916, FO 882/5, HRG/16/57.
48. Lawrence, *Seven Pillars*, pp. 102-3.
49. *Arab Bulletin*, 26 Oct. 1916, No. 27, and 26 Nov. 1916, No. 32.
50. *Ibid.*
51. Information about these persons can be found in all the above listed sources.
52. Musa, *An Arab View*, pp. 177-8.
53. This is evident from Kister's discussion of the Tamim, and Sergeant's and Rosenfeld's analysis of the Hadramawt and the Rashidi states respectively. See Talal Asad, 'The Beduin as a Military Force: Notes on Some Aspects of Power Relations between Nomads and Sedentaries in Historical Perspective', in *The Desert and the Sown*, ed. Cynthia Nelson (Berkeley, 1973), pp. 61-73.

54. Lawrence, 'The Sherifs', FO 882/5, HRG/16/57.
55. Lawrence to Wingate, 'Report on the Hejaz', 22 Nov. 1916, FO 882/6, HRG/16/85.
56. Lawrence, 'Emir Feisal, Creator of the Arab Army', in *Evolution of a Revolt*, ed. S. and R. Weintraub (London, 1967), p. 84.
57. Gertrude Bell, Comments on paragraph 3 of Sir M. Sykes's memorandum to Mr Picot, FO 882/3, Ap/17/14.
58. Cox to foreign department, government of India, 15 Jan. 1917, FO 371/3046/13924.
59. See IO L/PS/10/609, file 3280, part one.

IX

GUARDING THE BANDWAGON: GREAT BRITAIN, ITALY, AND MIDDLE EASTERN OIL, 1920-1923

Marian Kent

In the years following the First World War, when a Middle Eastern peace settlement was being negotiated, Italy was particularly anxious to secure the gains promised to her by her allies in return for entering the war on the allied side. Increasingly she felt that these gains were being denied to her, while her allies, Great Britain and France, collected their substantial winnings in the Middle East. Continually she tried to climb on the bandwagon, where she had been promised a place, only to have her knuckles rapped by its British driver. By the time she had worn down British resistance to her claims, she was herself losing interest in them, and the reluctant offer to her, when finally made, never led to anything.

By 1920, having failed to make the gains in the Middle East promised under the treaty of London in 1915 and the Saint-Jean de Maurienne Agreement in 1917, Italy's hopes were based on the Tripartite Agreement.[1] Signed on 10 August 1920, the same day as the treaty of Sèvres, the agreement was destined to have a similarly unsuccessful outcome. By this agreement Italy's territorial ambitions in Southern Anatolia took the form of an Italian sphere of influence, while her newly developing economic ambitions were to be partly realized through a monopoly of coal mining in the Heraclea basin. Arrangements were set out also for joint participation in the Anatolian and Baghdad railways. By a self-denying clause in Article 2 of the agreement the three signatory powers, Great Britain, France, and Italy, undertook not to apply for, nor to support applications by their nationals for, industrial or commercial concessions in any area where the special interests of one of the other signatories had been recognized. Under Article 6 the mandatory powers were given the same rights and privileges within their mandated territories as were powers with recognized spheres of influence. As Italy never took formal possession of her sphere of influence, however, whereas the mandatories did take possession of their mandated territories (with their important oil and other economic potential), Italy was to feel increasingly discriminated against.

This minor agreement was to provide the mounting block for Italy's efforts to climb aboard the Anglo-French oil bandwagon between 1920 and 1923. Although her attempts to make economic gains were directed at more than oil concessions (for in the series of agreements she had made between 1915 and 1920 oil had not been mentioned), as soon as she became aware of the potential of the Mesopotamian oil concession, promised to the Turkish Petroleum Company (TPC) by the Turkish government but never granted owing to the outbreak of the First World War,[2] and with a potentially fluid share participation, she sensed an excellent opportunity both of obtaining recompense for her lost wartime gains and of ensuring her own economic future.

Italy's pursuit of economic gains in the Middle East following the signing of the Tripartite Agreement can be divided into three phases. The first, purely oil, phase lasted from August 1920 until early 1922. Parallel with this were Italian efforts to obtain a broader range of economic concessions through direct negotiation with the Turks. Italy also sought to persuade Great Britain and France to give substance to the virtually meaningless Tripartite Agreement. The second phase consisted of Italian pressure at the Genoa Conference of April–May 1922 on the British delegation led by the prime minister, David Lloyd George, and the repercussions of these discussions at the foreign office. The discussions continued, after a short break, with the visit to London in June and July 1922 of the Italian foreign minister, Carlo Schanzer, in pursuit of a broad agreement on a number of still unsettled wartime claims, including Middle Eastern concessions and, especially, oil.

By late 1922, the Fascists were in power in Italy, riding on popular dissatisfaction with a government patently unsuccessful in its foreign policy of resurrecting Italian national pride. The third phase of the Italian pursuit, therefore, lasted from November to December 1922, with Italian pressure on the British negotiators during the preliminary stages of the Lausanne Conference. By the end of that year the chief British negotiator, Lord Curzon, formerly the most formidable obstacle to Italian pretensions, had retreated before the continual Italian wearing-away tactics and – especially – owing to the need to find a solution to Turkish intransigence over Mosul. Consequently, on 16 December 1922, Curzon told the Italians that they might be awarded a participation in the oil company concessionnaire, provided a solution to the Mosul problem were reached. Such a solution, as it turned out, was not found for some years, by which time Italian interest had waned and the British found it both undesirable and unnecessary to keep their bargain.

The first phase of Italy's efforts to share in the Anglo-French arrangements for exploiting oil in Asiatic Turkey saw an exchange of letters from 16 August 1920 to 22 July 1921 between the Italian ambassador at London, first Imperiali then de Martino, and Lord Curzon, the British foreign secretary, arguing the case for and against an Italian share. The first salvo in the campaign was fired by Italy only six days after the signing of the treaty of Sèvres and the Tripartite Agreement.[3] It expressed Italy's surprise and dismay at having learnt of the San Remo Agreement of the previous April. Such an arrangement, Italy felt (doubly offensive in having been made on Italian soil), was clearly intended to ensure for Great Britain and France a monopoly of most of the world's oil supply. Not only did the agreement contravene the Covenant of the League of Nations, Italy declared, but it was a 'grave menace' to her own supply of fuel.

The ambassador's second and third letters, of 23 October and 22 November, repeated and expanded his arguments,[4] while his fourth, of 16 March 1921, advanced the further, and key, proposition that the Italians should be able to enjoy all the benefits of the San Remo Agreement – which they had previously so strongly condemned.[5]

The foreign office, in reply, expressed its own surprise at the Italians.[6] It could not believe, at first, that the Italians could 'possibly have read' the text of the San Remo Agreement, published though it was, for its terms could not 'in the remotest degree' support the Italian interpretation. The British simply felt, as Lord Hardinge minuted, that 'the Italians have no oil anywhere and I see no reason why we should have any negotiations with them on the subject. The French gave a "quid pro quo". The Italians have none to offer.'[7] The British therefore replied that the San Remo Agreement governed

Anglo-French co-operation and reciprocity in countries where the two states already had considerable oil interests; in no way did they seek to establish a monopoly.[8] In Mesopotamia the agreement recognized 'long-standing French interests' and was a practical arrangement to ensure French co-operation over the transport of oil to the Mediterranean through French mandated territory. In return the French would receive a share of the output or in the TPC. The agreement, argued Curzon, would facilitate not hinder the oil from reaching European markets and thus increase rather than diminish the oil supply for Italy. Privately, the foreign office believed that American oil interests, seeking their own share in Mesopotamia, had put the Italians up to making their demands.[9]

The foreign office replies to the other Italian notes took a similar line, though hitting rather harder.[10] In January 1921 Curzon wrote that the British were 'unable at first sight to understand on what basis Italy could be included in an arrangement founded on an exchange of reciprocal advantages ... unless she were in a position to contribute herself thereto', and he invited the Italians to submit concrete proposals for co-operation. At that point opinion in the foreign office was still divided over whether or not to defend the San Remo Agreement by pointing out that Italy's gains under the Tripartite Agreement were just as 'monopolistic'. D.G. Osborne, for instance, opposed taking such a line, feeling that his government's case against the Italians was poor.[11] By July, however, patience had worn thin over 'the familiar wail' of the Italians and their 'barefaced suggestion' of Italian participation without reciprocity. This time there was no quibbling over the niceties of pointing out Italy's 'practical monopoly in the future development of the Heraclea coal basin'. Furthermore, the Italian suggestion that the British government should undertake, in effect, to subordinate British interests to Italian groups seeking oil concessions, oil purchases, or the direction and administration of oil companies in the regions covered by the San Remo Agreement, was described in foreign office minutes as 'a most outrageous demand' and 'quite absurd'.[12]

In 'the conviction that they will share our view as to the totally inadmissible nature of these pretensions', the foreign office consulted the petroleum department. The latter suggested one sop to the Italians (which, the foreign office minutes observed happily, 'does not mean very much'):[13] a reminder that nothing in the San Remo Agreement prevented British and Italian groups from making joint arrangements and receiving the support of their governments where it had not already been given to other interests. The French, too, were consulted, with Italian permission, about this reply,[14] which is why it took de Martino from 16 March till 22 July to receive it. One point in the last Italian note, however, was seized on delightedly by the foreign office. This was the voluntary exclusion by the Italians of the mandated territories from the areas in which equal economic privileges were sought. This meant, of course, Iraq and its Mesopotamian oil. The excluded territories, excluded possibly by mistake, were not allowed to be reinstated until the abortive London negotiations of June and July 1922, and were to provide a valuable argument against the Italians.

After such a long wait, the British letter of 22 July could only be a great disappointment for the Italians, as the foreign office had fully expected.[15] Indeed, considering the number and nature of the advantages the Italians had sought in their note of 16 March, the foreign office felt that the surprise was not in their disappointment at the reply received, but in their optimism that any of the demands made could have been granted.[16] The petroleum department had even received a visit from Dr Giannini of the Italian embassy, the object of which, the foreign office felt, 'was doubtless to try and frighten us with the spectre of an Italian–U.S. combination in the oil question. This spectre does not seem very alarming for the U.S. can scarcely be sufficiently hard up to accept or relish Italian assistance in their oil schemes'.[17]

The British message was clear, and there for the moment the matter rested. The bandwagon was only for those with instruments and expertise to offer, neither of which the Italians possessed, only a grievance about their lost wartime gains, which the British, try as they would, could not deny. Much better equipped with offerings – and the muscle to back them up – were American oil interests, especially Standard Oil. They were supported by their government through growing American pressure for an 'open door' for economic development in the Middle East or, alternatively, for American participation in the exploitation of Mesopotamian oil.

Discussion at this time of American participation in the TPC exposed the British dilemma over the Italian claims. Although by January 1922 American participation had been accepted in principle, the discussions that month about how the principle might be implemented were overshadowed by the parallel discussions about

Italy. Both the colonial office and the foreign office felt that the Italian claims should be considered at the same time as the American ones.[18] Only the petroleum department disagreed. Its director, Sir Philip Lloyd Greame, thinking the Italian claims 'less important', wanted to ignore them until the outcome of the American negotiations was known.[19] He argued that making Italy a party to such an agreement would increase the difficulty of resisting demands by other interests. Second, he felt that including Italian interests would 'jeopardise and probably destroy' British control of the TPC. If it were decided, Sir Philip continued, that the Italians should be included, they could be offered a proportion of the oil produced rather than a share in the operating company. One important advantage of admitting the Americans first, the foreign office saw, was that as the British government generally conceded that the TPC's claim rested on a diplomatic rather than a legal foundation (a view the company disputed), early American participation would undoutedly strengthen a shaky claim.[20] There were, nonetheless, some misgivings at the foreign office about excluding the Italians from direct participation in the company. As D.G. Osborne commented: 'I wish we could give the Italians a share too. I suppose we should if they had as big a stick as the Americans'.[21]

At the same time as Italy was pursuing her oil aspirations she was also keeping up pressure on the British over her broader Middle Eastern economic aims. She did this both through exchanges with the British embassy in Rome[22] and at the various conferences on Middle Eastern questions. The best example (and most important result) of this pressure was the 'Accord Particulier' signed at Paris on 25 March 1922 during a series of meetings of foreign ministers.[23] Italy wanted this small annex added to the Tripartite Agreement as a guarantee that it would be fulfilled despite changing circumstances.

The Italians also opened negotiations with the Turks – both at Istanbul and Ankara – in their pursuit of economic concessions, much to the indignation of the British. Having failed in their efforts to extract economic advantages from the Kemalist delegates to the London Conference in March 1921,[24] the Italians, following the signing of the Franklin–Bouillon agreement of 20 October between the French and the Ankara Turks, immediately sent their own emissary to Ankara. That this effort was also unproductive did little to assuage foreign office annoyance at it.[25]

What upset the foreign office far more, and caused serious

dissension between the prime minister and the foreign secretary, was the next attempt of the Italians to secure economic concessions from the Turks in the spring of 1922.[26] This time they dealt with the Istanbul government. The Italian excuse, when confronted with British displeasure at this further breach in allied unity in negotiations with the Turks, seemed lame.[27] Curzon declared it 'ridiculous. We are dealing with Oriental diplomatists not with children who are given sugar plums in the nursery'.[28] He denied vehemently Schanzer's claim in April to have told him 'all about the agreement' and to have kept the British ambassador at Istanbul fully apprised of the negotiations. Schanzer, he declared, had merely mentioned to him that the Turks had made certain offers and he had warned the Italians several times against taking them up. Curzon protested formally to the Italian ambassador: 'In spite of past disappointments', he wrote to de Martino on 27 April, 'I had hoped that on the basis of the Paris terms the three allies would thenceforward present a united front to Turkey; that they would renounce petty and selfish gains in order to secure the common good', and he continued in an even stronger vein.[29]

Hardly surprisingly, a public and diplomatic furore arose over the matter. Schanzer declared himself 'deeply hurt' by Curzon's 'violent' note,[30] the British and Italian press took up the matter, and questions were asked in parliament.[31] The Italian foreign ministry complained to the British ambassador and to the foreign office about the 'deplorable' effects British press attacks were having on the current international negotiations at Genoa. To calm the heated debate, early in May the foreign office issued a formal statement to the press, in most carefully chosen words.[32]

For a time, the Italians had the support of the British prime minister. Lloyd George, who was at Genoa and had had to listen to a bitter protest from Schanzer at the meeting of 4 May,[33] took Schanzer's part and telegraphed stiffly the same day to Curzon via the lord privy seal, Austen Chamberlain.[34] The perspective in Whitehall on the Italian–Turkish agreement was, however, very different from that at Genoa, and Chamberlain made clear to Lloyd George his complete support of Curzon's stance.[35] Curzon's foreign office colleagues felt the same, and their minutes on Schanzer's formal reply on 8 May to Curzon's protest were colourful about its 'false claims and assumptions'; in the end it was intentionally left unanswered.[36] Curzon wrote both formally and privately to the prime minister about Schanzer's protest, which he declared to be 'the most disgraceful piece of diplomacy I have ever known . . . It only shows what loose ideas of honesty these foreign statesmen have'.[37] He greatly regretted any embarrassment to the prime minister, 'but the source of the mischief is at your elbow, that is, Schanzer himself, not here'.

As a final gesture the foreign office sorted out, through Sir Horace Rumbold at Istanbul[38] and Sir Ronald Graham at Rome,[39] that the Italians had never, as Schanzer claimed, told the British of their negotiations with the Turks. Any last doubts on the matter were dispelled by Contarini, the secretary-general of the Italian ministry of foreign affairs, whose position was comparable with that of permanent under-secretary at the British foreign office. Contarini told the British ambassador that in his personal opinion the Italian government had made a serious mistake in signing the agreement with the Turks without keeping the British government fully informed; the whole matter had been put through during his absence, and had he known about it, he would have advised against it.

The fuss over the Italian–Turkish agreement aside, the Italians were mainly concerned at the Genoa Conference of April–May 1922 to try to turn to their own advantage the discussions on the resumption of Russia's international trading relations and to press their oil claims on the British. The question in the negotiations with Russia of reopening Russian oilfields to the world was used by the Italians as a route back into the San Remo Agreement. They aimed, in fact, to reopen the discussion closed by Curzon's letter of 22 July 1921, as their draft note of 16 April submitted to the British delegation made quite clear.[40] It finished up, indeed, declaring that if Great Britain were not prepared to make the required statement on Italian participation in the TPC, then Italy would, in effect, wreck the Genoa Conference. The Italians kept up the pressure on the British delegation throughout April and early May, Schanzer and Giannini making repeated visits to Lloyd Greame.[41] They ascribed their renewed importunities to the demands of Italian public opinion, which strongly criticized the San Remo Agreement. The Italian parliament was due to reopen early in May and MPs were lobbying the foreign minister, warning him that the question would be raised in the chamber in discussion of the results of the Genoa Conference.[42]

There was growing discontent in Italy, owing to the belief that Italian interests were being sacrificed at Genoa, and the British delegation to the conference fully realized that with the Italian government's present position being 'none too steady', it could easily be toppled.[43] The British delegation, especially Lloyd Greame, were anxious, therefore, that their colleagues in the petroleum department and the foreign office should suggest a formula about oil participation to the Italians that, 'while safeguarding our essential interests and our engagements with the French, will adequately save their face'.[44] Close Italian co-operation was essential at Genoa, especially by early May, and this made the Italian pressure more effective. Pressure, too, was coming from outside, for on 11 May even the special correspondent at Genoa of *The Times* had a letter in that day's issue to the effect that 'there is joy this morning in some Italian journals over a report that Italy will receive a share in the San Remo Petroleum Agreement'.[45]

But if the Italians were simply reiterating their demands of 16 March 1921, adding the threat to wreck the conference if they were not fulfilled,[46] the British were equally unable to improve on their letter of 22 July. To the foreign office the Italians' problem lay not in the formula to be devised but in the facts themselves.[47] In any case, there was considerable resentment at what the British regularly described as Italian 'blackmail'. 'I do hope that we shall resist this incessant blackmail', minuted Curzon. 'Do the Italians ever support anybody without trying to extract a consideration?'[48] Despite the resentment, as the Genoa Conference was about to adjourn Lloyd George sent Schanzer on 17 May a bland restatement of British views, drawn from the British letter of 22 July 1921, and offered verbally a general reconsideration of all still unsettled Anglo-Italian interests.[49] The foreign office, which had approved this step beforehand, hoped fervently that it would end the matter.[50]

Perhaps the fact that Lloyd George himself had sent the letter temporarily gave the hoped-for respite to the foreign office. Lloyd George, after all, had clearly developed a good relationship with Schanzer during the Genoa Conference. In his support of Schanzer over Curzon's 'violent' letter, Lloyd George had remarked that he 'thought perhaps he went further than the foreign office' in always believing 'that Italy alone could develop the part of Asia Minor which fell within her zone'; indeed, 'he was very pro-Italian'.[51] When the Italian parliament came to debate the Genoa Conference, therefore, the British escaped surprisingly lightly. True, 'Perfidious Albion' was mentioned by more than one speaker in the debate, which lasted from

3 to 8 June, but Schanzer himself, speaking on 7 June, spoke warmly of Lloyd George's attitude towards Italy's 'legitimate aspirations', and declared that the close *rapprochement* between the two of them at Genoa had led to the offer to examine jointly all questions of interest to the two countries.[52] The British ambassador reported that the foreign minister's speech was received 'well, if not enthusiastically' by the chamber, and it was much the same with the Italian press.[53] The foreign office, however, observed that 'M. Schanzer appears to regard H.M.G. as more closely and irretrievably bound to Italy than the foreign office are at present aware'.[54]

A broad Anglo-Italian understanding was, nonetheless, now on the programme for the foreign office, and throughout June and early July it was given detailed study, with Schanzer visiting London for discussions.[55] The foreign office, not surprisingly, was never as keen as the Italians on reaching such an agreement, feeling that Great Britain had far less to gain from it than Italy. As has already been obvious, the foreign office had little time for the Italians. Curzon described them as 'abounding in excellent professions while steadily pursuing clandestine and tortuous acts. I have never known them take up what was ostensibly a friendly attitude without demanding a price for it'. Nothing was to be gained from closer ties with Italy, 'except annoyance to the French', nor would Italy ever help Great Britain 'with either spontaneity or efficacy – except at a price which it would be unwise to pay'.[56]

The permanent under-secretary, Sir Eyre Crowe, held similar views.[57] When, at the request of the prime minister, the foreign office prepared on 22 June a memorandum of its views on an Anglo-Italian agreement, it came out strongly against such an understanding.[58] Before Schanzer's visit to London, the *Mondo* had published on 11 June an article on the proposed agreement and Lloyd George's purportedly favourable attitude towards it.[59] The format of the agreement and the terms to be agreed on, especially over oil, were described, also Italy's claim to participate in the supply of oil from Romania, Asia Minor, and the Caucasus. The article, commented Crowe, showed 'how widely the Italians are opening their mouths. It will be noted that the alleged arrangement consists entirely of one-sided concessions to Italy'.[60]

Despite the foreign office's distaste for an Anglo-Italian agreement, Schanzer did come to London and a series of formal discussions on a number of topics was held between 26 June and 7 July. During the discussions Italy continued to press her claim for concessions in Asia Minor, and especially for joint Anglo-Italian oil projects, indicating her misunderstanding of the seriousness of Lloyd George's letter of 17 May 1922.[61] In reply to an Italian draft agreement of 1 July, the British presented their own version four days later.[62] Over oil the British counter-draft stated that Great Britain would support the Italian search for oil concessions, but only in Northern Anatolia outside the French zone, the area the Italians had mentioned. Privately, however, the British suspected that the Italians were also thinking of Iraqi oil; their insistence in the discussions on the withdrawal of the self-denying portions (especially Article 6) of the Tripartite Agreement seemed to suggest it. The British also undertook in their counter-draft to support the Italians diplomatically with the Turks in 'any reasonable claim' for economic concessions in their zone under the Tripartite Agreement, provided that nothing infringed on the interests of British nationals or British firms and that the Italian government agreed 'to take into friendly consideration' the interests of the Smyrna–Aidin Railway Company.

This less-than-enthusiastic British support for Italian claims for economic and oil concessions in Asiatic Turkey naturally did not satisfy Italy. After pointing out the counter-draft's many deficiencies, Schanzer could only accept Lloyd George's suggestion that the talks should be regarded as purely exploratory, a preparation for more formal discussions later on.[63] A joint communiqué stating this in the blandest of terms was drawn up on 7 July, and thereupon Schanzer returned to Rome, in a state, Graham reported, of considerable bitterness and depression and amid Italian press attacks on Great Britain.[64]

Schanzer had, presumably, long foreseen his likely fate if he could not bring off a foreign policy *coup* over the Middle East, hence his energetic efforts. Now he returned to considerable criticism, especially from the leader of the rapidly rising Fascist party, Benito Mussolini. Within weeks, the Fascists had taken power and Schanzer had lost his position. A *post mortem* on the failure of the negotiations held between Graham and Contarini concluded that, while the Italians undoubtedly blamed much of the failure on British intransigence, it ought really to be attributed in large part to Schanzer's exaggerated expectations (shared by the Italian press and public) that British gratitude for Italian co-operation at Genoa would overcome all obstacles to Italy's receiving her rightful post-war inheritance.[65]

A final blow to Schanzer's reputation at both the foreign office and the consulta came with the British discovery of the Maissa mission to Ankara, at the very moment of the government's fall from power.[66] Despite the official explanation, yet again it appeared that the Italians were engaged in clandestine negotiations with the Turks, and on the eve of the Lausanne Conference. A British protest to Mussolini had the mission stopped, and Graham ascertained from a very disillusioned Contarini that he had disagreed with Schanzer on this matter as on so many others. Contarini described Schanzer as weak, undecided, and distressingly shortsighted, adding that the consulta generally had regarded him as the most unsatisfactory minister they had ever had.[67]

Was the new Italian regime likely to suit the British any better than the old? This question naturally interested the foreign office, witnessing the Fascist leader taking over the foreign ministry as well as the premiership. Mussolini himself was anxious to appear conciliatory to the British, telling Graham that 'Signor Schanzer had gone to London with a large basket under his arm which he hoped to fill with plums without the trouble of picking them. Such was not his own method of doing business'.[68] And he reiterated his desire for good relations and co-operation with Great Britain, although predicting difficulties until 'the deep sense of injustice' felt by the Italians since the war was removed. The Italian foreign ministry clearly felt enthusiastic about the decisiveness, strength, and apparent reasonableness of its new political head.[69] The foreign office, however, was more guarded. The apparently new-look Mussolini seemed a great improvement over the bombastic and chauvinistic Fascist leader in opposition. But, as Harold Nicolson noted: 'It may well be that he will prove to be the Venizelos of Italy: on the other hand he may turn out to have no more political acumen than Garibaldi or Gambetta'. All Great Britain could do, he felt, was 'wait and see'.[70]

It was Mussolini himself who initiated the third phase in the Anglo-Italian discussions over oil and economic concessions in the Middle East, but his tactics turned out to be little different from his predecessor's. At the Territet meeting, *en route* to Lausanne on 19 November, Mussolini tried unsuccessfully to persuade the British and French to sign in a private session a formula stating the equality of Italian, British, and French interests, duties, and rights in the Middle East. They refused to sign, as Italy was patently not their equal, and instead drew up a harmless, face-saving formula.[71] Two days later at Lausanne, however, Mussolini claimed, or had his ambassador at London claim on his behalf, that Curzon had agreed to the principle of Italian participation in the British mandates in the Middle East.[72] When the ambassador mentioned that Mussolini had declared that his co-operation with the allies in the Middle East depended on an immediate exchange of notes, and spoke of Italy's need to derive something tangible from her co-operation with the allies, the British knew they were on familiar ground.

The British formal reply of 4 December, that Mussolini 'had been under a complete misapprehension as to what Lord Curzon had said on the occasion',[73] was merely diplomatic flannel; Curzon's aggrieved denial of the supposed agreement,[74] his record of the conversation,[75] and his later minutes on the documentation, where he described the episode as 'this impudent attempt at blackmail',[76] all called the Italian bluff.

Italian attempts to obtain commercial advantages persisted at Lausanne. Curzon telegraphed to the foreign office on 1 December in great exasperation that he had 'had to speak plainly' to the Italian delegates 'about this shameless attempt at blackmail which seems to be inseparable from Italian conceptions of policy and renders any dealings with them very difficult'.[77] 'I should not be surprised', he continued, 'if they are all the while seeking to negotiate some private agreement with the Turks'. What the Italians were doing, in fact, was attempting in the autumn of 1922 to form with the British and French a tripartite syndicate to share the pre-war German railway interests in Turkey, and various other concessions. When neither of the two allies took up the suggestion, it was dropped, until in early 1923 the Italians proposed a similar scheme to the French, which did lead to an agreement.[78] It had been intended to include the British but, although the foreign office considered the scheme to be 'in substance innocuous', its agreement was so hedged about that in the end nothing more was heard of the matter.[79]

Despite Curzon's impatience with activities which divided the attention and potentially the loyalties of the allies in the hard bargaining at Lausanne over the Turkish peace, he was not immune to Italy's oil claims. Indeed, he informed the foreign office on the same day that he had complained so strongly about the Italian behaviour, on 1 December 1922, that 'Italy's claim is indeed difficult to resist'.[80] Italy had, he considered, legitimate claims under Article 9 of the treaty of London, which the Tripartite Agreement had been designed to satisfy. Now that the treaty of Sèvres was inoperable, those portions of the Tripartite Agreeement were no longer applicable. It seemed to him, therefore, 'of greatest importance in order to liquidate Italy's general claim upon us, which Signor Mussolini is obviously determined to press, that every endeavour should be made, however great the technical difficulties, to give Italy some percentage of shares in the Turkish Petroleum Company, even if that percentage be not as great as those of France and America'. The 'political importance' of such a settlement to the British, Iraqi, Italian, and Turkish governments 'cannot be over-estimated', he stressed, and the 'Company must be made to realize that the value of their rights is entirely dependent on diplomatic and political support'. High politics aside, however, Curzon personally considered that 'the whole matter is intensely sordid and distasteful'.[81]

In response to Curzon's forceful telegram, the foreign office, the petroleum department, and the colonial office attempted to speed up the long on-going negotiations over American participation in the TPC, for this question had to be settled before the settlement of Italian claims. The Americans were to receive a 20 per cent participation on condition that the state department accepted this as a full settlement of American claims and undertook not to question the TPC's right to the concession. All parties were to accept Curzon's decision regarding Turkish and Italian participation and to share *pro rata* in providing it.[82] It took some arm twisting by the government on Shell,[83] but on 12 December the two oil companies (Shell and the Anglo-Persian Oil Company) agreed to accept the government's offer of arbitration over American entry into the TPC.[84] Although the agreement contained no reference to either Italian or Turkish participation, the companies were well aware of the claims of those states, and were expected strongly to oppose any further reduction in their shareholdings.[85] The petroleum department felt, nonetheless, that it would be possible 'to deal more effectively with the Turkish and Italian claims once the question of American participation had been satisfactorily settled'.

Thus armed, Curzon took the initiative and on 16 December 1922 informed the Italians that when the question of Mosul had been definitely settled (and Great Britain had no intention of surrendering the vilayet), Italy would be given a share of the oil. The Italians, he wrote, thereupon 'expressed the most unbounded gratification'.[86] An attempt by Mussolini to turn this concession into a foreign office guarantee of Italian participation in Mesopotamian oil, and to tie it to an undertaking that the government of Iraq would provide Italy with land suitable for Italian emigration was, however, not successful. As Curzon commented, 'I imagine this to be fantastic . . . Mussolini is no statesman'.[87]

The British debated the question of exactly how the Italian participation would be arranged throughout 1923. Opinion differed as to whether this should be done by a shareholding participation or by a guarantee of oil supply on preferential terms.[88] There was difference of views, too, over whether the Italian share participation would have to come out of the 20 per cent entitlement of the government of Iraq or out of the other shareholdings.[89] The foreign office, the petroleum department, and the colonial office were all involved in these discussions, held despite the protests of the TPC.[90] As long as there seemed an urgent need to reach an agreement with the Turks at Lausanne – for the Italian claim was usually considered in tandem with the Turkish one – the discussions were intense. But once the Lausanne Conference was over, leaving the Mosul dispute still not settled (it was eventually referred for arbitration to the League of Nations), the intensity evaporated, along with the possibility of Turkish participation. In fact, the Lausanne agreement, made in July 1923, did not mention oil concessions or the TPC. By late in the year, the company's arrangements with American and French interests were, in spite of earlier hopes, still not completed. In December, the three departments were still discussing the need to plan for Italian participation.[91]

It was anyway too late. As the arrangements for the TPC's concession were held up pending the Mosul frontier settlement – not settled until June 1926 – so the Italian pressure for compensation through participation in the oil concession also abated. Italy still continued her search for other economic concessions,[92] but by late 1925 the *New York Herald Tribune* was reporting a semi-official statement from Rome that Italy had no interest, directly or potentially, in Mosul oil and that she had not been offered a concession or any arrangements there, a report which gave the foreign office considerable satisfaction.[93] Mussolini himself was to give the *coup de grâce* to Italy's hopes of Mesopotamian oil. The serious war scare in Turkey which he stimulated in April 1926 was one reason why the Turks became more amenable to reaching in June a settlement with Great Britain over Mosul.[94] And once Mosul was legally and irretrievably within Iraq, Italy's oil pretensions could be forgotten forever.

The irony of this final phase of the pursuit of the oil bandwagon was that when Italian fingers had, by the end of 1922, nearly pulled Italy aboard, the prolonged waiting for the final arrangements saw the grip relax and the fingers slip away, even without British help. For most of the time between August 1920 and December 1922 the foreign office, demonstrating considerable anti-Italian feeling, and not entirely without reason, took every opportunity to rap the Italians' knuckles. It changed its policy over Italy's oil pretensions in December 1922 because the change seemed necessary to help break the deadlock at Lausanne. There was, nonetheless, from time to time a glimmer of guilt within the foreign office over its prejudice, which was summed up in 1926 by one of Italy's formerly most vehement critics, Sir William Tyrrell. Under the influence of Italian press invective over allied betrayal of Italy's post-war gains, Tyrrell admitted privately to his colleagues: 'The treatment of Italy by the allies with regard to Asia Minor was I believe neither wise nor "quite nice"'.[95] Great Britain did treat Italy badly, but Italy did bring much of it on herself by her blatant opportunism. Italy's policy towards Middle Eastern oil was thus both the result of and the encouragement for Great Britain's policy of guarding the bandwagon.

NOTES

1. Cmd 963: Treaty Series No. 12 (1920), *Tripartite Agreement between the British Empire, France and Italy respecting Anatolia. Signed at Sèvres August 10, 1920.*
2. See Marian Kent, *Oil and Empire: British Policy and Mesopotamian Oil 1900-1920* (London, 1976), *passim*, but especially pp. 109-10, 155-7.
3. Imperiali to FO, memorandum (trans.), 16 Aug. 1920, FO 371/5085, no. E10130. Also included in D[ocuments on] B[ritish] F[oreign] P[olicy], ed. E.L. Woodward, *et al.* (London, 1947-83), First Series, [vol.] xiii, [no.] 313, p. 342, with a different date, but 16 August is the formal date. Curzon's view on the change in Italian ambassadors from Imperiali to de Martino (a change for the worse for Great Britain, he felt) are in Curzon to Lloyd George, 29 Oct. 1920, private, Lloyd George MSS F/13/1/30 [House of Lords Library].
4. Imperiali to Curzon, note (trans.) no. 2202, 23 Oct. 1920, FO 371/5086, no. E13385; also *DBFP*, xiii. 329, pp. 363-5; and Imperiali to Curzon, note (trans.) no. 2394, 22 Nov. 1920, FO 371/5086, no. E14896.
5. De Martino to Curzon, note (trans.), 16 March 1921, FO 371/6360, no. E3650. See also minute by Crowe, 9 March 1921, *ibid.*, no. E3182.
6. Minute of Weakley, FO 371/5085, no. E10130; Curzon to Imperiali, 17 Sept. 1920, *DBFP*, xiii. 318, pp. 346-7.
7. Minute of Hardinge, 28 Aug. 1920, FO 371/5085, no. E10130.
8. Curzon to Imperiali, 17 Sept. 1920, *ibid.*, no. E11058; also *DBFP*, xiii. 318, pp. 346-7. On the agreement see Kent, *Oil and Empire*, Ch. 8 and App. IV.

9. Minute of Weakley, FO 371/5085, no. E10130.
10. Curzon to de Martino, 18 Jan. 1921, FO 371/6360, no. E3650 (successive drafts are in FO 371/5086, nos. E15464 and E16273, and FO 371/6360, no. E571); and 22 July 1921, FO 371/6361, no. E8153.
11. Minutes in FO 371/5086, nos. E14896, E16273.
12. Minute of Weakley, 9 April 1921, FO 371/6360, no. E3650.
13. Minute of Oliphant, 11 April 1921, and his letter to the petroleum department, 21 April, *ibid.*, no. E3650, and minute of Forbes-Adam, 5 May, *ibid.*, no. E5173.
14. Briand to Hardinge, 15 July 1921, FO 371/6361, no. E8153.
15. See, e.g., minute of Lindsay, 18 May 1921, FO 371/6360, no. E5562, and Clarke to Osborne, S.541, 3 Aug. 1921, FO 371/6361, no. E8954.
16. Minute of Weakley, 10 Aug. 1921, *ibid.*, no. E8954.
17. Forbes-Adam to Clarke, 17 Aug. 1921, *ibid.*, no. E8954.
18. Shuckburgh to Crowe, 3 Jan. 1922, secret, no. CO 63088/1921, FO 371/7782, no. E132; minute of Weakley, 5 Jan. 1922, and Curzon to Churchill, 10 Jan. 1922, *ibid.*, no. E132; CO minute, 12 Jan. 1922, CO 730/27, no. CO 169532.
19. Clarke to Crowe, 3 Jan. 1922, S.559, FO 371/7782, no. E156.
20. Minute of Weakley, 13 Feb. 1922, FO 371/7783, no. 1590.
21. Minute of Osborne, 24 Jan. 1922, FO 371/7782, no. E782.
22. See correspondence in FO 371/7853, no. E316.
23. FO 371/7859, nos. E3508 and E3509; repeated in *DBFP*, xvii. 565, pp. 721-8, and 566, pp. 729-38; see also Graham to FO, 18 March 1922, tel. 145R, FO 371/7857, no. E3005.
24. See correspondence in *DBFP*, xvii. 60, 69, 75, 81, 107, 108, 114, 120, 177 n. 4.
25. FO memorandum, 'Italian Aspirations in Asia Minor', 14 Dec. 1923, FO 371/9140, no. E11946; Rumbold to FO, 6 Jan. 1922, tel. no. 13, FO 371/7853, no. E320. See also *DBFP*, xvii. 433, 435, 436, 441, 443, 457.
26. Hardinge to Curzon, 12 April 1922, desp. 935 urgent, and Curzon to de Martino, 17 April 1922, FO 371/7861, no. E3935; and further correspondence in FO 371/7862-5. The actual agreement is in FO 371/7865, no. E5201. The concessions included coal, electricity, irrigation, and silver-lead mining.
27. Schanzer to Italian embassy in London, 21 April 1922, 'very urgent', passed on unofficially as a note verbale to FO, 24 April 1922, FO 371/7862, no. E4314 (registry date is 26 April, but from the following memorandum it was clearly 24 April. The version in *DBFP*, xvii, 610 n. 3, pp. 797-8 gives only the date of 21 April 1922). 'Memorandum by Mr. Lindsay of a discussion with the Italian ambassador', 24 April 1922, *ibid.*, no. E4371.
28. Minutes of Curzon on Lindsay's memorandum of 24 April 1922, *ibid.*, no. E4371.
29. Curzon to de Martino, 27 April 1922, *DBFP*, xvii. 611, pp. 798-800.
30. Gregory to Chamberlain, 4 May 1922, tel. 152, *DBFP*, xvii. 621, p. 808.
31. FO minutes on parliamentary questions of 3-5 May, FO 371/7863, nos. E4619, E4620, FO 371/7864, no. E4760.
32. It appeared in the *Morning Post* on Monday, 8 May 1922. This unilateral British statement also served to cut the ground away from the Italians' insistence on a joint communiqué: see *DBFP*, xvii. 625 n. 2, pp. 811-12.
33. 'Note of a conversation held at the Villa D'Albertis, Genoa, on Thursday May 4, 1922, at 10.45 a.m.', secret, S.G.-24, Lloyd George MSS F/13/3/21; also *DBFP*, xix. 110, pp. 726-9.
34. See n. 30 above.
35. Curzon to the British delegation, Genoa, 5 May 1922, *DBFP*, xvii. 622, p. 809.
36. Schanzer to Curzon, 8 May 1922, trans., and FO minutes, 12-14 May 1922, FO 371/7864, no. E4951; further FO minutes, 24 May 1922, in FO 371/7865, no. E5201.
37. Curzon to Lloyd George, 6 May 1922, private, and 8 May 1922, Lloyd George MSS F/13/3/20 and F/13/3/22. This quotation is included in C.J. Lowe and M.L. Dockrill,

The Mirage of Power (London, 1972), ii. 369, where it is ascribed to Hardinge and the Hardinge MSS.

38. Curzon to Rumbold, 6 May 1922, tel. 200D, FO 371/7863, no. E4489; Rumbold to Curzon, 7 May 1922, tel. 238, *DBFP*, xvii. 626, pp. 812-13.

39. Graham to Curzon, 4 May 1922, desp. 390, FO 371/7864, no. E4755; Graham to Curzon, 8 May 1922, tel. 182D. *ibid.*, no. E4768.

40. Note by the Italian government, Genoa, 16 April 1922, FO 371/7783, no. E4291.

41. Lloyd Greame to Clarke, 29 April 1922, memorandum, 'Italy and the San Remo Agreement', *ibid.*, no. E4536.

42. Lloyd Greame to Clarke, 20 and 26 April 1922, secret, *ibid.*, no. E4291. For background see Carole Fink, 'Italy and the Genoa Conference of 1922', *International History Review*, viii (1986), 41-55.

43. Gregory to FO, 5 May 1922, tel. 156, very urgent, *ibid.*, no. E4635.

44. Lloyd Greame to Tyrrell, 13 May 1922, very urgent, *ibid.*, no. E5055.

45. Reported in minute of Weakley, 11 May 1922, *ibid.*, no. E4883.

46. Italian note included in Lloyd Greame to Tyrrell, 13 May 1922, very urgent, *ibid.*, no. E5055. See also n. 40 above.

47. Minute of Weakley, 18 May 1922, *ibid.*, no. E5055.

48. Minutes, 18 May 1922, *ibid.*, no. E5055.

49. Lloyd George to Schanzer, 17 May 1922, in Maxe to Curzon, 18 May, *DBFP*, xxiv. 1 n. 30, pp. 8-9.

50. Gregory to FO, 11 May 1922, tel. 177, very urgent, FO to Gregory, 11 May 1922, tel. 101, urgent, and minute of Lindsay, 15 May 1922 (marked as seen and approved by Crowe and Curzon), FO 371/7783, no. E4883. Minute of Weakley, 20 May 1922, *ibid.*, no. E5156.

51. See n. 33 above.

52. Graham to Balfour, 8 June 1922, reports in desps. 517, 518, and 519, FO 371/7658, nos. C8408, C8409, and C8410.

53. Graham to Balfour, 9 June 1922, desp. 527 encl. 'Summary of the Italian press, June 9, 1922', *ibid.*, no. C8413.

54. Minute of Nicolson, 14 June 1922, *ibid.*, no. C8410.

55. Documentation on the subject is included in a major confidential print (11988) entitled 'Anglo-Italian Agreement, May to June 1922', FO 371/7673, no. C12744. Most of the original documents included in the print are to be found in FO 371/7672 and some in FO 371/7671.

56. Minute of Curzon, 24 May 1922, FO 371/7673, no. C12744, p. 2.

57. Minute of Crowe, 9 June 1922, *DBFP*, xxiv. 1 n. 1, p. 1.

58. Memorandum respecting the Anglo-Italian 'entente', prepared in the Foreign Office, on Signor Schanzer's Formula, on June 22, 1922, *DBFP*, xxiv. 1, pp. 1-10.

59. Graham to Balfour, 12 June 1922, desp. 542, and 16 June 1922, desp. 557, FO 371/7671, nos. C8770, C8777.

60. Minute of Crowe, 21 June 1922, *ibid.*, no. C8770.

61. The Italian oil position is set out in Schanzer's note to the FO of 27 June 1922, FO 371/7800, no. E7219, the Italian delegation's proposed draft agreement of 1 July 1922, FO 371/7672, no. C9636, and in the records of the conversations. See, for instance, that of 28 June 1922, ICP 249-E, *DBFP*, xxiv. 4, pp. 49-50. See also, for FO criticism, minute of Weakley, 29 June 1922, FO 371/7800, no. E7219.

62. 'British Counter-Draft. (Third Revise, July 5, 1922);', *DBFP*, xxiv. 9 Appendix, pp. 111-17.

63. 'Notes of a Conversation held in the Prime Minister's Room, House of Commons, on Thursday, July 6, 1922, at 5.30 p.m.', secret, ICP 249-I, *DBFP*, xxiv. 9, pp. 101-11; 'Note of a Conversation held at 10 Downing Street, on Friday, July 7, 1922, at 5 p.m.', secret, ICP 249-J, *ibid.*, 10, pp. 117-26.

64. Graham to Balfour, 11 July 1922, tel. 219R, and 12 July 1922, tel. 222R, FO 371/7672, no. C10008; Graham to Balfour, 13 July 1922, desp. 650, and 14 July 1922, desp. 651, *ibid.*, nos. C10159, C10160.

65. See, i.e., Graham to Curzon, 2 Nov. 1922, desp. 1014, FO 371/7659, no. C15149.

66. Correspondence on this abortive mission is included in FO 371/7908, nos. E11970, E12003, E12083, E12084; FO 371/7911, no. E12406; FO 371/7673, no. E14980.

67. Graham to Curzon, 8 Nov. 1922, desp. 1034 confidential, FO 371/7911, no. E12550; also Graham to Curzon, 5 Oct. 1922, desp. 905, FO 371/7659, no. C13993. On the Italian foreign ministry – the consulta – at this time and on Contarini see Alan Cassels's excellent book, *Mussolini's Early Diplomacy* (Princeton, 1970), pp. 3-9, and on Contarini and Schanzer, see H. Stuart Hughes, 'The Early Diplomacy of Italian Fascism: 1922-1932', in *The Diplomats 1919-1939, Vol. I: The Twenties*, ed. Gordon A. Craig and Felix Gilbert (New York, 1965), pp. 213-17.

68. Graham to Curzon, 2 Nov. 1922, desp. 1014, FO 371/7659, no. C15149.

69. See n. 67 above.

70. Minute of Nicolson, 6 Nov. 1922, FO 371/7908, no. E12084.

71. Curzon to FO, 20 Nov. 1922 (drafted on 19 Nov.), *DBFP*, xviii. 206 n. 3, pp. 309-10; 'British Secretary's Notes of . . . [the meeting] held at the Grand Hôtel des Alpes at Territet, at 7.30 p.m. on November 19, 1922'; *ibid.*, 206, pp. 308-17, show very clearly the secondary and uninformed role of Mussolini in the public discussion. See also accounts in Cassels, *Mussolini's Early Diplomacy*, pp. 15-16, 25-7, and Harold Nicolson, *Curzon: The Last Phase 1919-1925* (London, 1934), pp. 288-9. The interpretation in C.J. Lowe and F. Marzari, *Italian Foreign Policy 1870-1940* (London, 1975), p. 190, that Curzon's policy was 'deliberately ambiguous' is debatable.

72. Memorandum by Crowe, 27 Nov. 1922, FO 371/7916, no. E13333; two short passages are quoted in *DBFP*, xviii. 253 n. 2, p. 363.

73. 'Record by Sir E. Crowe of a conversation with Italian ambassador', 4 Dec. 1922, *DBFP*, xviii. 253, pp. 362-5.

74. Curzon to Crowe, 29 Nov. 1922, FO 371/7965, no. 13737; see also memorandum of 4 Dec. 1922, *DBFP*, xviii. 253 n. 3, pp. 363-4.

75. Curzon to Crowe, 22 Nov. 1922, tel. 13, E13063/27/44, *ibid.*, 213, pp. 323-4.

76. Cassels, *Mussolini's Early Diplomacy*, pp. 27-9, examines both possibilities, of Mussolini's misunderstanding of Curzon, and of an attempt to bluff. The latter would, on form, and on the evidence, appear to be more likely.

77. Curzon to FO, 1 Dec. 1922, tel. 62, *DBFP*, xviii. 244, pp. 352-3.

78. Documentation on the scheme is to be found in FO 371/9140, file E1045/44; see especially, minute of Waley, 'The Position of Italy in regard to Turkish Concessions', 25 Jan. 1923, *ibid*, no. E1170. See also Curzon to Graham, 15 Feb. 1923, desp. 256, FO 371/9066, no. E1904.

79. Curzon to secretary, board of trade, 6 March 1923, FO 371/9140, no. E2055. A fuller account of this episode, drawn from Italian sources, is to be found in Cassels, *Mussolini's Early Diplomacy*, pp. 33-6.

80. Curzon to FO (for colonial secretary and president of the board of trade), 1 Dec. 1922, tel. 63 (by bag), FO 371/7785, no. E13523; POWE 33/98, fos. 102-3.

81. Minute by Curzon, 6 Dec. 1922, FO 371/7785, no. E13523.

82. FO to Curzon, 7 Dec. 1922, tel. 55 (by bag), *ibid.*, no. E13523.

83. FO (for president, board of trade) to Curzon, 9 Dec. 1922, tel. 62 (by bag), *ibid.*, no. E14007.

84. Clarke to Crowe (for Curzon), 13 Dec. 1922, S.610, POWE 33/98, fos. 73-5; also FO 371/7785, no. E14034 (in peace conference files, FO 839/10, no. 535).

85. Turkish Petroleum Company to director, petroleum department, 13 Dec. 1922, no. T.2, in Clarke to Crowe (for Curzon), 19 Dec. 1922, S.611, POWE 33/98, fos. 73-5, 90-2; also FO 371/7785, no. E14256.

86. Curzon to Crowe, 17 Dec. 1922, desp. 44, *ibid.*, no. E14205 (FO 839/10, no. 535).
87. Memorandum by Crowe, 19 Dec. 1922, and minute of Curzon, 21 Dec. 1922, FO 371/7919, no. E14422.
88. See, e.g., 'Note supplied to Lord Curzon and approved by the Prime Minister and Lord Curzon', encl. in Clarke to Weakley, 2 Jan. 1923, S.611, also minute of Weakley, 2 Jan. 1923, FO 371/8994, no. E125; Clarke to president, board of trade, 3 Jan. 1923, POWE 33/98, fos. 44-5.
89. See, e.g., Clarke to Osborne, 22 June 1923, FO 371/8995, no. E6157; Vernon to Clarke, 26 June 1923, CO 730/51, no. CO 30749; Clarke to FO, 24 Dec. 1923, no. 319/23; and Oliphant to Clarke, 5 Jan. 1924, FO 371/8996, no. E12097.
90. Turkish Petroleum Company to director, petroleum department, 24 Jan. 1923, no. T20 confidential, POWE 33/201, fos. 95-7; also FO 371/8994, no. E1399.
91. Oliphant to Shuckburgh, 4 Dec. 1923, FO 371/8996, no. E10969; Clarke to FO, 24 Dec. 1923, no. 319/23, and Oliphant to Clarke, 5 Jan. 1924, *ibid.*, no. E12097.
92. There was, especially, the long-running rivalry from late 1923 with a British group to gain control of the Anatolian railway system. Documentation on this competition covers several years. For a short summary of the early stages see FO 371/9140, no. E11946.
93. *New York Herald Tribune*, 30 Sept. 1925, extract included and discussed in FO 371/10828, no. E6419; also Graham to Chamberlain, 30 Oct. 1925, desp. 925, and FO minutes, *ibid.*, no. E6704.
94. See, e.g., FO 371/11554, nos. E2460/2460/44, E2291/2291/44. See also Cassels, *Mussolini's Early Diplomacy*, pp. 308-9.
95. Minute of Tyrrell on FO 371/11533, no. E3925/226/44.

X

THE EGYPTIAN WAFD
AND ARAB NATIONALISM,
1918-1944

James Jankowski

At its inception at the close of the First World War, when it emerged in an effort to send a 'delegation' [*wafd*] to the Paris Peace Conference, the movement known thereafter as the Wafd was a specifically Egyptian nationalist movement dedicated exclusively to the cause of Egyptian independence. A quarter of a century later, in the closing years of the Second World War, the same Wafd initiated and led the inter-Arab negotiations which by 1945 resulted in the formation of the League of Arab States. On the surface, it would seem that an appreciable evolution in the regional orientation of the Wafd had occurred; from an initial concentration on Egyptian nationalism and a corresponding avoidance of involvement in Arab or Muslim affairs, to the promotion of Egyptian leadership of the Arab world. But was such actually the case?

The subject of this study is the attitude of Egypt's premier political party of the inter-war period to the neighbouring Arab world in the period between the end of the First and the end of the Second World Wars. The regional orientation of the Wafd in this period has been discussed by Elie Kedourie, among others, in his usual provocative manner:[1] therefore, the following is less an explication of Wafdist attitudes and policies than an exploration of the motivation and the content of the movement's emerging 'Arabism'. In brief, our focus is upon why the Wafd gradually came to espouse Arabist policies, and what those policies appear to have meant to its leaders.

The initial Egyptianist orientation of the Wafd during the revolution of 1919 is indisputable. The meeting of 13 November 1918 between the high commissioner, Sir Reginald Wingate, and three Egyptian leaders, which in the nationalist imagination has always been regarded as the start of the revolutionary sequence, was characterized by demands relating to Egyptian – and only Egyptian – independence from Great Britain.[2] The charter of the new organization of the Wafd, drafted a few weeks later, made this exclusively Egyptian orientation explicit: in it, the movement pledged itself to work for 'the complete independence of Egypt', making no mention of possible external affiliations for an independent Egyptian state.[3] The first extended theoretical statement of the Wafdist position came in a manifesto drafted in January 1919 for presentation at the Paris Peace Conference: it similarly omitted any reference to possible external affiliations for Egypt, emphasizing instead that the people of Egypt formed 'une seule et unique race parfaitement homogène au physique comme dans sa mentalité et ses moeurs'.[4]

Rather than asserting any Egyptian affiliation with its neighbours, the Wafd initially emphasized Egypt's lack of regional ties. In the aftermath of the First World War, the object of such disclaimers was the Ottoman Empire of which Egypt had until 1914 been a part. In its post-war statements discussing the issue of Egypt's relationship to the Ottoman Empire, the Wafd consistently took the position that the First World War had ended any Egyptian connection with the Ottomans. On the one hand, Egyptian independence was justified on Wilsonian grounds because Egypt was a well-defined, homogeneous nation and 'because independence is the natural right of nations'.[5] The movement also based its demands for independence on the historical argument that Egypt had been striving to free itself from alien Ottoman domination since the nineteenth century, only to be prevented from attaining independence by the action of the European powers in 1840-1.[6] In the Wafdist view, Egypt had been definitively separated from the Ottoman Empire when made a British protectorate in 1914 and, since the new Wilsonian principle of national self-determination prohibited the imposition of foreign rule over a people against their will, neither the Ottoman Empire nor Great Britain had any legitimate basis for continued domination over Egypt.[7]

The actions of the new nationalist movement were consistent with its words. Although apprehensive British reports during the spring of 1919 sometimes claimed Ottoman instigation of anti-British activity,[8] there is no positive evidence to corroborate the claim. Similarly, in 1920 Lord Allenby was unable to confirm reports of a financial connection between the Turkish nationalist movement and the Wafd, and in 1922 a visit to Ankara by the Wafdist delegation to the peace conference at Lausanne was coldly received by the new Turkish government, which refused to support the Egyptian demand for admission to the talks.[9]

As the leaders of the Wafd viewed Egypt as totally separate from the old Ottoman Empire, they also perceived no direct connection between their activities and the new Arab nationalist movement developing in western Asia. On the programmatic level, the official manifestos of the Wafd ignored any possible link between Egyptian and Arab nationalism. Again, deeds were congruent with words: there is no indication that Egyptian and Arab nationalists co-operated in the immediate post-war era, and the Wafdist delegation at Paris in 1919 is reported to have refused to collaborate with an embryonic 'Society of Eastern Nations', on the grounds that its mandate from the Egyptian people related only to the independence of Egypt.[10]

Rather than perceiving any link between the two nationalist movements, the leaders of the Wafd definitely felt superior to their fellow-Arabs, and resented what they viewed as unjustified Allied preference for Arab over Egyptian nationalism. This was apparent at the meeting of 13 November 1918, when one of the Egyptians present acidly noted that Egyptians 'consider themselves far more capable of conducting a well-ordered government than the Arabs, Syrians, and Mesopotamians to whom the Anglo-French Governments have granted self-determination'.[11] The complaint was repeated the following year, when Arabs were allowed to participate in the peace conference but Egyptians were not: in the eyes of the Wafd, the presence of a delegation from the remote and backward Hejaz was a clear justification for an 'infinitely more developed' Egypt to be represented at the conference.[12] Eventually, the Wafd argued that the preference accorded to Arab nationalism was one of the causes generating the post-war nationalist uprising in Egypt:

Another cause of encouragement to us was the recognition of the independence of our brothers of the Hedjaz, who speak the same language as ourselves and are of the same religion as most of us. The Arabs of the Hedjaz did not before have a separate political existence like ourselves. In fact, within a century they were under our political control . . . Was it illogical for us to expect from the British government, in view of the oft-repeated assertions of its members, treatment as least as generous as that accorded to the Arabs of the Hedjaz?[13]

Despite the surface recognition of the Hejazis as 'brothers', the thrust of the argument is clearly one of Egyptian superiority to the Arabs of the Hejaz and of Egyptian pique at the favouritism granted to the more primitive over the more advanced.

This position of aloofness from regional ties in general and Arab nationalism in particular characterized the Wafd throughout its early history. Two incidents of the mid-1920s may serve to illustrate the movement's original avoidance of involvement in regional affairs. The first concerned the struggle for ascendancy in the Arabian Peninsula between Ibn Saud of Nejd and King Husayn of the Hejaz. As Ibn Saud's forces were overrunning the Hejaz in the autumn of 1924, the beleaguered Hejazis put out feelers for Egyptian intervention to stop the conflict.[14] When the approach became public knowledge, it was vehemently rejected by most of the native Egyptian press, including those journals associated with the Wafd. The more regionally-inclined and pro-Wafdist newspaper, *Kawkab al-Sharq*, had earlier expressed the view that 'events in the Hejaz can be considered as local Egyptian events' because of the religious significance of the area: but its animosity to the former rebel King Husayn kept it from advocating Egyptian intervention on his behalf.[15] To *al-Balagh*, the closest thing to an official Wafdist journal in the 1920s, the idea of Egyptian intervention in the Hejaz was ridiculous; an Egypt which had yet to liberate itself fully from British domination was in no position to assume such an external burden.[16] At any rate, Egyptian intervention in this instance would amount to pulling British chestnuts out of the fire through rescuing its Sherifian client-state: what happened in the Arabian Peninsula was simply of 'no concern' to Egypt, and involvement in peninsular affairs would bring 'no benefit' to Egypt itself.[17] This dismissal of the notion of an active Egyptian policy in Arabia was fully shared by the Wafdist ministry in office in 1924. Within a few days of the suggestion of Egyptian intervention, the Egyptian government effectively anticipated the possibility by publicly announcing that it would remain neutral during the war.[18] Nor were Arabian affairs in general viewed as particularly important by the Wafd later in the decade: as late as 1930, Sa'd Zaghlul's successor as leader of the party, the then prime minister Mustafa al-Nahhas, responded to a British inquiry concerning the possibility of Egyptian recognition of Saudi Arabia with the admission that 'he was not very familiar with the situation in the Peninsula'.[19]

A second occasion for Wafdist action in regard to Arab nationalism in the mid-1920s came in the following year, when rebellion against the French Mandate in Syria led to brutal French repression, including the bombardment of Damascus. The Wafd was out of office at the time and so could make no official response on behalf of Egypt. But it could and did involve itself by offering moral and financial support to the Syrian nationalists. Wafdist journals such as *Kawkab al-Sharq* called on Egyptians to give aid to Syrian victims of French oppression.[20] By far the most prominent Egyptian to speak out publicly in support of the Syrian rebels in the wake of the French bombardment of Damascus was Sa'd Zaghlul, who on 5 November 1925 issued a 'declaration to the nation' expressing Egyptian 'sympathy for our suffering brothers'.[21] Zaghlul added his voice to those calling for Egyptians to contribute to Syrian relief, making a personal donation of £100. Other prominent Wafdists soon followed his lead.[22]

But Wafdist sympathy for the Syrian Revolt of 1925 needs to be set in context. Zaghlul's statement of 5 November, while justifying Egyptian concern with events in Syria on the grounds of 'the firm bonds of history, language, religion, customs, and geographical propinquity' which linked Egypt to Syria, nonetheless emphasized the universalist rather than nationalist reasons for aiding the Syrians: 'we think that this [financial aid] is the least that a neighbour must do for a neighbour, the least of what a man can give to his fellow man'.[23] In a response to a group of Syrians who visited him a few days later to thank him for his support, Zaghlul similarly asserted that he felt about the events in Syria what 'every Egyptian, every Easterner, indeed every human being', should feel.[24] Perhaps most revealing about the Wafdist leader's attitude towards Arab affairs in the mid-1920s is what he was saying privately. According to his Wafdist colleague 'Abd al-Rahman 'Azzam, Zaghlul's declaration of 5 November had been made only at the prompting of 'Azzam, and even then he had at first resisted the idea of involving himself. It was in his initial rejection of 'Azzam's request that Zaghlul developed the famous equation concerning the Arabs and their nationalist movement which has often been used to characterize the attitude of the Egyptian élite towards Arab nationalism at the time: 'If you add a zero and a zero and a zero, what is the result?'[25] Both Zaghlul's initial disparagement of the Arabs as well as his later expression of sympathy for the suffering Syrians need to be taken into account in evaluating the Wafdist position on Arab nationalism in the 1920s.

The first signs of a shift in the position of the Wafd towards Arab nationalism appeared in the early 1930s. The shift was undoubtedly conditioned by the internal and external circumstances of the period.

Internally, the Wafd experienced severe repression by the autocratic and palace-linked regime of Isma'il Sidqi. Locked in a bitter struggle with Sidqi and the palace and lacking domestic levers for asserting itself owing to rigid government controls over publication and assembly, the Wafd's first steps towards involvement in Arab affairs in the early 1930s may have been part of an effort to gain popularity through the use of an external issue.[26] In the regional arena, the early 1930s witnessed a renewed trend towards Arab co-operation. After the conclusion of the Anglo-Iraqi Treaty of Alliance of 1930 which formally conferred independence upon Iraq, King Faysal mounted a low-key but real campaign to achieve a greater measure of collaboration among the states of the Arab East. Iraqi efforts to forge an 'Arab alliance', to unite Syria with Iraq, and to promote an 'Arab congress' to discuss the prospects for Arab unity, all provided new stimuli to Egyptian involvement in Arab affairs.[27]

The Wafd's new interest in Arab affairs manifested itself in various ways. In 1931, Baha al-Din Barakat and Makram 'Ubayd paid separate visits to the Fertile Crescent, during which both of them spoke favourably about the renewed movement towards Arab political co-operation being fostered by Iraq and stated that Egypt would benefit from involvement.[28] Late in 1931, the Wafd gave its support to the Islamic congress being organized in Jerusalem. The idea of the congress had been received with hostility by the Sidqi regime and the Egyptian palace, and it is not surprising to find the Wafd, then in opposition, attempting to use the event to make political capital.[29] A year later, two prominent Wafdists known for their sympathy to Arab nationalism, 'Abd al-Rahman 'Azzam and Hamid al-Basil, were made members of the preparatory committee by the Arab nationalist leaders then attempting to organize a popular Arab congress. But a split in the Wafd itself nullified this attempt to involve the party in the Arab nationalist movement: both 'Azzam and Basil were among a group of Wafdists who broke with Nahhas in late 1932, and their putative involvement in the congress led to the party declining to take part in it when it should occur (it never did).[30] By 1933, the Wafdist leadership was involving itself in what was becoming the transcendent issue of Arab politics, that of Palestine. Unlike the party's response to violence in Palestine in the late 1920s, when it had not come out in support of the Palestinian Arab cause and when it had rejected Palestinian appeals for assistance,[31] its reaction to Arab demonstrations in Palestine in late 1933 was more positive, Nahhas sending a telegram to the Palestinian leader Musa Qazim al-Husayni offering his condolences to those injured in the protests and praising the Palestinian struggle against imperialism.[32]

Our concern here is primarily with the causes of this change in the Wafd's attitude to Arab affairs. A full explanation of Wafdist policy must await the examination of the relevant Egyptian archives. But data in the public record of the day, as well as in the available British materials, do indicate the way the thought of Wafdist leaders was developing by the middle of the inter-war period.

One indication comes from a consideration of the views during his trip to the Fertile Crescent in 1931 of the figure who was becoming the Wafd's second most important leader in the 1930s, Makram 'Ubayd. Some of Makram's public remarks at receptions in Lebanon and Palestine were devoted to the subject of inter-Arab co-operation, and presented a coherent and consistent explanation of why he now viewed Egyptian involvement in the movement towards Arab unity as desirable. Makram devoted much of a speech delivered in Sofar, Lebanon, to the subject of 'Arab brotherhood'.[33] While acknowledging the bonds of blood, language, history, and religion which united the Arabs, the main thrust of his presentation was that another link existed 'more powerful than these; it is the bond of suffering'. In his view, all Arabs were students in the same 'school of suffering', his euphemism for contemporary Western imperialism. Since imperialism had treated all Arabs in a similar fashion, the Arabs ought to 'exploit this unity for the sake of buttressing our sovereignty and our independence'. Although Makram explicitly rejected the idea of Arab unity in the sense of the creation of one state uniting all Arabs, he did enjoin his audience to strive for what he termed 'political-economic unity': practical collaboration in the political and economic spheres which would strengthen each Arab country. His concept of Arab unity thus meant the adoption of 'one aim and one goal' by all Arabs, rather than their fusion in one political unit. Despite his opening references to racial, historical, and cultural bonds, Makram's sense of Arab unity as manifested in this address was a highly contingent one deriving primarily from the specific circumstances of the modern era of imperialist domination.

In a speech at Jaffa a few days later,[34] Makram reiterated many of the points. He again defined Arab brotherhood in distinctly contemporary terms: the fact that all Arabs were 'brothers studying in one school, the school of suffering, indeed the school of revolution against

170

suffering'. Addressing most of his remarks to the global theme of the struggle of colonized peoples for liberty and justice, he linked Arab, eastern, and human 'patriotism' as three complementary movements working to defend the 'dignity' of the oppressed.

Makram 'Ubayd did not restrict his advocacy of Arab political co-operation to Fertile Crescent audiences. In an interview with the *Kawkab al-Sharq* upon his return to Egypt in September 1931,[35] he spoke of the 'patriotic' and 'political' bonds linking Egypt with its Arab neighbours. Repeating that 'the bond of shared suffering' united all Arabs, he declared that 'the best way to achieve our patriotic aspirations is [through] solidarity and mutual aid between Egypt and all Arabic-speaking peoples'. Possibly anticipating more Egyptian resistance to the idea of Arab political collaboration than had marked opinion in the Fertile Crescent, he also hastened to assure his countrymen that there was no incompatibility between such a 'political bond' based on the common needs of all Arab peoples and their individual patriotic movements.

Makram's advocacy of Egyptian involvement in Arab politics in 1931 was far different from the Wafdist disdain for Arab nationalism in 1919 or Sa'd Zaghlul's addition of Arab zeros in 1925. It is also necessary to emphasize that the basis of his advocacy of an Arab policy for Egypt was a practical and instrumental one: the necessity of solidarity and co-operation between all peoples – Arab, eastern, world-wide – who had been forcibly enrolled in the 'school of suffering' by Western imperialism.

This contingent sense of Egypt's need to involve itself in Arab politics for the sake of its own nationalist aspirations was paralleled in the testimony of a (former) Wafdist leader, 'Abd al-Rahman 'Azzam, a few years later. 'Azzam had left the Wafd in 1932, and his strongly pro-Arabist public statements of the mid-1930s could no longer be considered indicative of Wafdist opinion.[36] But a private letter concerning 'the Arab unity movement' which he wrote to a British associate in late 1933, sheds some light on both the previous Wafdist aloofness from Arab politics and its recent adoption of a more sympathetic attitude.[37]

'Azzam began his account by emphasizing how 'the strength of the local patriotism' prevalent in Egypt in the 1920s had succeeded in 'isolating Egypt from its co-religionists and its brothers beyond its frontiers'. The bulk of his presentation centred, however, upon how this exclusive Egyptian nationalism was beginning to fade and to be replaced by a greater openness to involvement in regional affairs. As evidence of the shift, he cited Makram's evolving position as seen in his trip of 1931 and a current press controversy over the Egyptian versus the Arab nature of Egypt, in which the bulk of opinion had spoken in favour of Egyptian affiliation with the Arab world.[38] What is most instructive are the reasons he offered for this recent movement towards involvement in Arab affairs on the part of Egyptian politicians, both Wafdist and otherwise. In his view, the earlier abstention from Arab affairs had in large part been due to the Egyptians' desire to win the support of the French and Italians for Egypt's national aspirations by not antagonizing them over colonial issues; since such support had not manifested itself, Egyptian politicians were now coming to believe that 'it was a mistake to give up their Arab friends for the sake of not offending certain European powers'. In terms of the Wafd in particular, it was 'Azzam's opinion that the party now desired 'popular support' in the Arab world (by implication because of domestic political imperatives), and that its recent steps in the direction of the Arabs derived in good part from that partisan consideration. In view of these changing perceptions on the part of Egyptian leaders, 'Azzam concluded that 'Arab Unity' was 'the ideal of the future', based as it was on both 'a very strong sentiment and a true practical interest'.

The weight which can be given to Makram's speeches of 1931 and 'Azzam's letter of 1933 is reinforced by the similarity in their explanation of the Wafd's drift towards an Arab policy. Both tie that development to the requirements of Egypt's own struggle against imperialism; both portray it in primarily political and pragmatic, rather than philosophical and ideological, terms; and both present it as a complement, rather than an alternative, to the Wafd's fundamental Egyptian nationalism. Incomplete as this evidence of the early 1930s may be, it is also not inconsistent with the later and fuller evidence about the Wafd's changing position on Arab nationalism available from the later 1930s and early 1940s, when the shift in the party's position accelerated and took on practical significance.

After several years in the political wilderness, the Wafd returned to office in May 1936, remaining there until the end of 1937. These two years were not lacking in stimuli to an active regional policy on the part of the Egyptian state. On the one hand, the Anglo-Egyptian Treaty of Alliance of August 1936 provided the opportunity for the

Egyptian government to operate with greater freedom in foreign affairs; on the other, renewed initiatives by the government of Iraq towards Arab political co-operation, as well as the intensifying crisis in Palestine, furnished the occasion for it to do so.

The Wafdist ministry's approach to Arab politics in 1936-7 contained elements of both the party's traditional Egyptianist orientation as well as signs of a new outlook regarding the Arabs. The ministry of Mustafa al-Nahhas did more to promote official Egyptian involvement in Arab affairs than had any of its predecessors, Wafdist or other. Administratively, new sections for Arab affairs were established in the ministry of foreign affairs and the publications department in late 1936, and a committee was created in the ministry of commerce in 1937 to explore possibilities of improving economic relations between Egypt and its Arab neighbours.[39] Practical efforts in 1937 to foster economic interaction included an agreement with Iraq reducing tariff rates, a new commercial agreement with Palestine, and the appointment of a commercial attaché in Jerusalem.[40] At least one leading Wafdist figure played a public role in promoting an Arab orientation in Egypt in 1936: the speaker of the Egyptian senate, Mahmud Basyuni, was the president of a new 'Arab Union Society' established in the summer of 1936.[41] It was Basyuni and the Arab Union which in late 1936 inaugurated discussions of an international Arab congress to meet in Cairo to discuss Arab co-operation.[42] Most significant was the ministry's political involvement in the Palestine issue in 1936-7: Nahhas's initial confidential intimations to the British that 'we also are Arabs' and so concerned with the crisis developing in the Mandate; his repeated efforts in 1936 to serve as a mediator between Great Britain and the Palestinian Arabs; the ministry's public and private support (in parliament; in Nahhas's conversations with the British ambassador, Sir Miles Lampson; in the League of Nations) of the Palestinian Arab cause in the wake of the Peel Commission Report of July 1937.[43]

But there were also severe limitations to the 'Arabism' of the Wafd in 1936-7. The support of Wafdists for the idea of an Arab congress in 1936-7 was limited to that of a congress which would discuss non-political subjects: parallel Palestinian Arab efforts to promote a congress which would address political issues as well met with a negative response.[44] The question of a political versus a non-political Arab congress produced a split in the Arab Union Society between Basyuni, who is reported to have wished to avoid becoming 'associated with activities likely to acquire a political complexion', and other members of the group.[45] In the end, no such congress materialized. The overtly political activities of the Wafdist ministry of 1936-7 also demonstrated a considerable residue of its traditional Egyptianist outlook. The ministry drew public Arab criticism for its efforts to restrict pro-Arab demonstrations within Egypt during the Palestinian general strike of 1936,[46] and Nahhas's own views on the Palestine question in 1936 had a definitely Egyptianist tone. Terming himself 'the chief Arab leader', he declined collaborative intervention with other Arab governments on the grounds that it would be better to leave 'Egypt as a card to be played later'.[47] When Nahhas spoke against the Peel Report to Lampson in July 1937, the thrust of his remarks was upon the potential effects of partition upon Egypt itself: the possible territorial threat to Egypt of a Jewish state, and the problems such a state might cause Egypt's own Jewish community.[48]

Perhaps the best indication of the still basically Egyptianist outlook of the Wafd in the late 1930s comes from the response of the Nahhas ministry to Iraqi suggestions for closer co-operation between the two states. The ministry firmly refused to consider the idea of an Egyptian–Iraqi treaty for cultural and military co-operation when the Iraqis suggested one in late 1936 and early 1937. As Nahhas explained his position to the British when queried about the idea in March 1937, he was simply 'too busy with other things' to become 'involved in general complications'; rather, he preferred 'first to consolidate Egypt's own position' before considering its regional role.[49] Thus, while the Wafd's flagon may have contained a more Arabist brew by 1936-7, it was still a weak blend.

The Wafd was dismissed from office in December 1937, and remained in opposition until restored to power, through the good offices and tanks of the British, in February 1942. Even out of power it continued to demonstrate a partly Arab orientation, particularly in its use of the Palestine issue as a club with which to beat its ministerial successors for their insufficient and ineffective efforts in regard to the problem.[50] But it was only upon its assumption of ministerial office in February 1942 that its gradual movement towards a more Arabist position took tangible form and had significant results.

From its first months in office, the language and actions of the Wafdist ministry of 1942-4 indicate an acceptance of closer Egyptian interaction with the neighbouring Arab world. The ministry's first

Speech from the Throne in March 1942 declared its intention of a 'raffermissement des rapports de fraternité, d'amitié, et de coopér-ation entre l'Egypte et les nations soeurs de l'Orient, auxquelles elle est unie par les liens indéfectibles de la religion, de la langue, du voisinage et [in terms reminiscent of Makram 'Ubayd's speeches a decade earlier] la communauté de souffrances et d'aspirations'.[51] Practical measures aimed at promoting Arab interaction in the cultural field were soon undertaken. From the spring of 1942, the Egyptian ministry of education conducted discussions with the Iraqi legation in Egypt for the establishment of a joint bureau to co-ordinate educational and cultural co-operation between the two countries.[52] Such an agency was established by the end of 1942: consisting of representatives from Egypt and Iraq but theoretically open to participation by any Arab state which wished to affiliate, it was charged with such matters as curriculum co-ordination, student and teacher exchanges, and the organization of Arab cultural events.[53] In the political sphere, the Nahhas ministry in 1942 pursued an active policy in relation to both Syria–Lebanon and Palestine. Action concerning the French position in Mandatory Syria in 1942 included Nahhas approaching the Free French authorities to call for the establishment of representative government in Syria and Lebanon and a well-publicized meeting with Syrian and Lebanese leaders where he endorsed their demands for free elections.[54] In regard to Palestine, Nahhas met a group of Palestinian journalists in January 1943 and followed the meeting by dispatching memoranda to the government of the United States protesting against American policy towards Palestine.[55]

At first, the new Wafdist ministry does not appear to have had any plans for promoting institutionalized Arab political co-operation among the Arab states. One Wafdist leader explicitly denied such a desire on the part of the ministry in its early months in office, when Nahhas's intermediary with the British, Amin 'Uthman, informed Lampson in May 1942 that Nahhas had 'no intention of raising issues of Arab Federation'.[56] A report that Nahhas had brought up 'a project of Arab Federation in which Egypt would play the predomi-nant part' in his talks with Syrian and Lebanese leaders in June 1942 could not be verified by British inquiries.[57] But there is evidence to suggest that the idea of Egyptian, and Wafdist, leadership of the movement towards Arab political co-operation was gradually taking hold among Wafdist leaders by the end of 1942. Thus in an address on the anniversary of the revolution of 1919 given on 13 November 1942, Nahhas declared Egypt's determination to work for the national aspirations of the Arabs and went on to call for 'Arab and Eastern' countries to form 'a strong and cohesive bloc', led by Egypt, which could play a positive role in the post-war international order.[58] A few days later, Nahhas privately told Lampson of his government's desire for Egyptian ' "leadership" of the neighbouring Arab states who would certainly be looking to Egypt to lead a solid Arab block in [post-war] peace discussions'.[59] These references to the desirability of the creation of some sort of Egyptian-led regional organization in the Middle East would seem to reflect both longstanding Wafdist ideas of the utility of Arab co-operation *vis-à-vis* imperialism, and the newer, wartime-inspired concept of a post-war world dominated by regional coalitions of states.[60] Egypt's leadership of her neighbours was thus the key both to the perennial struggle against the British and to the assumption of a larger role in the post-war world.

But vague aspirations for regional co-operation and leadership do not comprise a positive policy designed to achieve such aspirations. Three developments in early 1943 appear to have prompted the Wafdist ministry to take tangible steps to promote Arab political co-operation. The first took place in Iraq. It was in late 1942–early 1943 that Nuri al-Sa'id of Iraq formulated and circulated his ideas for a new Arab League among the states of the Fertile Crescent and excluding Egypt.[61] Given Nahhas's evolving concept of Egyptian regional leadership, Nuri's plan was an obvious threat. In addition, Nahhas reportedly had been angered by the Iraqi declaration of war on the Axis in January 1943, which he apparently interpreted as an effort to win Allied support for Iraq's bid for regional leadership.[62] An Egyptian riposte was clearly in order.

The second stimulus was also an external one. On 24 February 1943, Sir Anthony Eden made a public statement in support of Arab co-operation but noting that any steps towards federation would have to be taken by 'the Arabs themselves'.[63] Eden's remarks – the second statement in support of Arab federation made by him during the war – were immediately read by Arabs as an encouragement to undertake discussion of closer political co-operation.

Eden's speech was the spark for the third and possibly the most vital development which prodded the Wafd into an active Arab policy in 1943. This was a purely domestic event: the efforts of the Wafd's internal opponents to seize the initiative on the subject of Arab unity. Immediately after Eden's statement, the veteran Egyptian Arabist 'Abd al-Rahman 'Azzam published an article in *al-Ahram* in which he called on the Arabs to respond to Eden's encouragement by convening a 'free Arab conference' to discuss Arab unity.[64] 'Azzam's summons to an international conference which would have included both official representatives and leading proponents of an Arab policy in Egypt was soon endorsed by other prominent non-Wafdists.[65] Perhaps most important, the idea of an Arab conference at which there was a good prospect of the Wafdist ministry being over-shadowed by their more historically Arab-inclined rivals appears to have had the support of the Egyptian palace in early 1943.[66] Opposition agitation for an international conference was soon rein-forced by an Iraqi manoeuvre pointing in the same direction: on 17 March 1943, Nuri al-Sa'id wrote to Nahhas suggesting the convening of an Arab conference, official or unofficial, to discuss the question of Arab unity.[67]

Faced with these pressures from the British, the Iraqis, and the Egyptian opposition, the Wafdist ministry was not slow in formu-lating a positive policy concerning Arab political co-operation. At the end of March, the Egyptian government entered into formal nego-tiations with Iraqi representatives sent to Egypt to explore the question of an Arab conference: these failed when the Iraqis favoured a conference which both official and unofficial representatives would attend, while Nahhas would countenance only a meeting of Arab government representatives.[68] At that point, Nahhas boldly imposed a *fait accompli* on both his internal and external rivals: speaking on behalf of the ministry before the Egyptian senate on 30 March 1943, the minister of justice, Sabri Abu 'Alam, announced the Egyptian government's intention to begin individual consultations with the other Arab governments with a view to arranging a future conference of Arab states to discuss the question of Arab federation.[69] With this public declaration, the Wafdist ministry not only effectively pre-vented the possibility of an unofficial conference on Arab unity at which its rivals might be represented as well, but also neatly moved to ensure that Egypt would be responsible for any future negotiations concerning Arab unity.

Contemporary interpretations of the Wafdist initiative of 1943 presented it as being motivated by purely political considerations. In the British view, it was a short-term manoeuvre by Nahhas designed to 'maintain for himself the leading role as against Nuri Pasha and at the same time to obviate any danger that the Opposition and the Palace would steal his thunder at a conference run on a non-official basis'.[70] To Sir Walter Smart, oriental secretary at the embassy in Cairo, the initiative was merely a 'political stunt' undertaken by the ministry 'to gain internal prestige, to make up for weaknesses in its internal position'.[71] Nuri al-Sa'id is reported to have attributed Nahhas's initiative to 'personal reasons',[72] and another major Arab leader who was soon to become involved in Egyptian-led negotiations, Amir Abdullah of Transjordan, later termed the initiative 'a game organized by Nahhas Pasha for his own ends'.[73]

But to see the Wafd's new policy as no more than a 'political stunt' may be to take too narrow and too cynical a view. The idea that tangible benefits were to be had for Egypt and the Egyptian national cause from increased Arab solidarity had been developing within Wafdist circles since the early 1930s, and by the early 1940s were being reinforced by the idea that the post-war world would be dominated by regional power groupings. There is no particular reason to suspect that Nahhas did not mean what he said in 1942 about the promotion of Arab 'brotherhood, friendship, and cooperation' in order to create 'a strong and cohesive bloc' led by Egypt. The timing of the Wafd's adoption of an Arab policy in March 1943 was unquestionably determined by short-term political considerations; but the motive behind the new policy also represented a gradual shift in the general outlook of the movement from assuming that Egypt had little or nothing to gain from regional political co-operation to assuming that a great deal of advantage was to be gained from it.

The statement of 30 March 1943 marked the beginning of Wafdist leadership of the wartime movement towards Arab federation. Over the next year and half, the Egyptian government undertook a series of bilateral negotiations with each of the then-independent Arab states. These discussions culminated in the convening of an official inter-Arab conference in Alexandria in September–October 1944, a meeting which drew up the preliminary blueprint for the League of Arab States. The minutes of Nahhas's meetings with the representatives of the Arab governments and of the Alexandria Conference, conveniently provided to the British by the Egyptians and thus accessible in the British archives, provide the best indication of the Wafdist position on Arab nationalism as it had evolved by the mid-1940s.[74]

The dominant Egyptian figure in the inter-Arab negotiations of 1943-4 remained the prime minister and foreign minister, Mustafa al-Nahhas. It was he who conducted face-to-face negotiations with the representatives of Iraq, Transjordan, Syria, Lebanon, and the Yemen; it was he who corresponded with King Ibn Saud to solicit his opinions; and it was he who represented Egypt at the Alexandria Conference. As a later British evaluation of the negotiations put it: 'Nahhas was the unchallenged master of the Wafd and of his Government. He could therefore decide upon a policy and execute it'.[75] Given this personal primacy of Nahhas among the Egyptians during the negotiations, his personality and diplomatic approach are a matter of some interest.

Coarse but authentic in style, forceful but erratic in behaviour, Nahhas's great strength was his apparent embodiment of Egyptian peasant characteristics; his weaknesses, on the other hand, included an often-impulsive approach to political action and traits of egotism and self-aggrandizement which frequently alienated others and made him more imperious as the years passed.[76] Much of this was reflected in his conduct of the inter-Arab negotiations of 1943-4. His verbosity was proverbial: the Iraqis came away from their first discussions with him in March 1943 complaining that, despite his lack of knowledge of Arab affairs, he had 'perorated at them without allowing them to get a word in edgewise'.[77] Both the Syrians and the Iraqis went out of their way to cater to his vanity, the former reportedly expounding on how 'the name of Nahas [*sic*] would be inscribed in the annals of all Arab countries', the latter publicly acclaiming him as the 'Leader of the leaders of the Arabs' while privately commenting 'flatter an Egyptian and you fuddle his brain'.[78]

Nahhas's conduct of negotiations left something to be desired. In his face-to-face discussions with Arab representatives as well as in his correspondence with King Ibn Saud, Nahhas's official posture was always apparently open-minded. He would initially avoid offering his own opinions while presenting each Arab leader with what was in effect a questionnaire soliciting his views on the forms of Arab political co-operation he thought possible and/or desirable. But Nahhas's personal penchant for unilateral action repeatedly irritated the other Arabs and occasionally hindered progress in the negotiations. Thus his ministry's declaration of 30 March 1943, made without prior notice to other Arab governments including the Iraqis with whom he had just met, upset the Iraqis and drew an irate response from the proud Ibn Saud.[79] Similarly, Nahhas's incomplete public summary of his correspondence with Ibn Saud, a summary which presented Nahhas in a more and the king in a less favourable light, outraged Ibn Saud and seems to have substantially delayed agreement on the terms of an Arab conference.[80] In 1944, Nahhas's invitation to other Arab governments to attend a conference in Alexandria was dispatched without prior consultations with the Saudis, which again angered them.[81] Nahhas's most extreme use of the *fait accompli* occurred at the Alexandria Conference in October 1944, when he publicly released the preliminary text of the Alexandria Protocol to the press in order to prevent possible changes in the text agreed upon by the delegates present, but not yet approved by all of their governments.[82] Against these vagaries must be set the indisputable facts that Nahhas was successful in arranging an international conference of seven disparate and often-opposed states, and that the conference did result in a formal agreement providing for the establishment of a new international organization.[83] But whether this result came about because of, or in spite of, his diplomatic abilities is problematic.

Of greater moment than Nahhas's skill as a negotiator are the substantive positions taken by the Egyptian government in the negotiations of 1943-4. In brief, the Egyptian government repeatedly disavowed any interest in Arab political union. The most it was willing to consider was some form of institutionalized consultation and co-operation between existing Arab regimes. Even that position was not always consistently maintained, Nahhas occasionally questioning whether Egypt would participate in an Arab federation, should one be created.

Already in the Egyptian-Iraqi discussions of July 1943, it was the position of both governments that 'Union under a central Government was ruled out as unrealizable owing to external difficulties and internal differences and disagreements'.[84] The Egyptian position was substantially the same during the negotiations with the Transjordanians and the Lebanese; in those with the Syrians, the question of the form of Arab political interaction was left to be decided in the future.[85] Nahhas's envoy to the Saudis in the fall of 1943 presented an even more reserved position on Arab unity, telling the British that an 'Arab Federation as such could never assume a strong political character and that Nahas [sic] was not in favour of it so doing. He added that he could not see Egypt or any other Arab country surrendering any of its prerogatives in favour of a political Arab Federation. He thought that the question could never pass beyond the bounds of cultural, social, and perhaps economic collaboration and that certainly Nahas [sic] Pasha had no ideas beyond these three forms'.[86]

Nor did the Egyptian government always see Egypt as part of even a loose Arab federation. The questionnaire Nahhas presented to other Arab governments initially left the matter of Egyptian participation in any federation for their decision. In the negotiations with Iraq in July 1943, the Egyptian position was that Egyptian participation in an Arab organization was not assured and that there was still 'the possibility that Egypt may not adhere to the Arab Union'.[87] Nahhas expressed stronger reservations to the Lebanese in January 1944, reportedly taking the position that Egypt did not wish to be 'drawn into the orbit of a Pan-Arab consortium of Asiatic states' but rather envisaged herself playing a role in the Arab world analogous to that of the United States in relation to Latin America: 'that is to say, Egypt might participate in a yearly conference of Arab states (on the lines of the Pan-American Conference) to exchange ideas on subjects of mutual interest, but would not form part of any Arab Federation or Confederation even if one eventually came about'.[88] Other Wafdist leaders were even more sceptical of the prospects of Arab unity than Nahhas, Amin 'Uthman at one point calling the inter-Arab discussions 'considerable nonsense'.[89]

In positive terms, the Wafdist ministry appears to have had no definite concept of the form of Arab political co-operation it desired at the start of the discussions. It took until nearly the end of the long negotiating process to formulate and expound a definite concept of Arab federation. That position emerged only at the Alexandria Conference in the fall of 1944, where Nahhas proposed a formula for Arab political co-operation which postulated a league of independent and equal states, and which rejected the concept of a league council having the power to make decisions binding on its members: only when two members of the league should refer a dispute between them to the council should that body's decisions be 'effective and binding' on the members involved.[90]

The Wafdist ministry was more certain about what it did not want.

At the head of that list stood the rival projects for Fertile Crescent unity which had been proposed by the governments of Iraq and Transjordan in the early 1940s, or any political combination which might threaten Egyptian primacy in the Arab world. In late 1943 a 'reliable source' informed the British that Nahhas was 'strongly opposed to the idea of any union between Iraq and Syria, lesser or greater, because he thinks that such a state might take the place of Egypt as the predominant local power in the Levant'.[91] Nahhas himself told the Syrians in October 1943 that he was extremely sceptical concerning the possibility of uniting the Fertile Crescent in view of the differences in local conditions among the regions involved.[92] Almost a year later, on the eve of the Alexandria Conference, Nahhas demonstrated great concern over the possibility of an Iraqi–Syrian–Lebanese diplomatic combination which might challenge Egypt's pre-eminent position in the current inter-Arab negotiations.[93]

The final element of the Wafdist position in the negotiations of 1943-4 is the assumption of Egyptian leadership and primacy apparent in the words and deeds of the Egyptians who took part in the discussions. Much of the material already cited reflects such an Egypt-centred outlook on the part of Nahhas and the Wafd. The form imposed by the Egyptian government on the negotiations is a case in point; its seizure of the initiative from the Iraqis in March 1943, its request that Arab representatives come to Egypt to talk, and Nahhas's determination to persuade the other Arab governments to authorize Egypt to conduct bilateral negotiations.[94] A similar insistence on Egypt's leadership was manifested in late 1943, when the Egyptians demanded that Cairo should be the site of any conference, denying a Saudi claim that Mecca would be the most appropriate place to hold it.[95] Most indicative in this respect was the consistent Egyptian disavowal of any form of integral Arab unity, which might have threatened the existing Egyptian primacy in the Arab world as well as its image of the role of Egypt in the Arab world as analogous to that of the United States in the Americas.

A microcosm of the barriers still separating the Egyptian Wafd from the Arabs and Arab nationalism in the early 1940s is provided by a brief consideration of a visit of Nahhas to Palestine in June 1943. While the trip had a purely Egyptian dimension (an effort by the prime minister to persuade the queen mother, Nazli, then estranged from her son, to return to Egypt), Nahhas also used it to promote his claims to Arab leadership. Prior to Nahhas's departure, the Wafdist journalist Mahmud Abu al-Fath arranged for Palestinian Arab presentations to Nahhas which expounded on his pre-eminent position in the Arab world.[96] The trip itself was the occasion for fulsome welcomes and praise of Nahhas's leadership by Palestinian Arabs,[97] and Nahhas's replies are reported to have 'invariably expressed the idea that here is a leader of a great Arab nation and the potential leader of the united Arabs'.[98] At home the Wafdist press used the event to characterize the prime minister as 'the leader of the Orient and of Pan-Arabism'.[99] Yet Nahhas could not escape his own basic Egyptianism. Apparently the only tense moment in the trip came at a luncheon in Jaffa when Nahhas refused to eat the food prepared by his Palestinian hosts, instead preferring to eat an Egyptian meal prepared by his own cook. While part of the reason for this *gaucherie* may have been his 'exaggerated idea of the severity of food control in [wartime] Palestine',[100] it is not unreasonable to see the incident as an indication of the limitations of Nahhas as an international emissary as well as the degree to which the 'Leader of the leaders of the Arabs' remained an Egyptian at heart.

NOTES

1. One of Professor Kedourie's studies which deals in part with the Wafd in relation to Arab nationalism is 'Pan-Arabism and British Policy', in *The Chatham House Version and Other Middle Eastern Studies* (London, 1970), pp. 213-35. Recent studies which *inter alia* explore the Arab policies of pre-revolutionary Egyptian governments and political parties in some detail include Ahmad M. Gomaa, *The Foundation of the League of Arab States: Wartime Diplomacy and Inter-Arab Politics, 1941 to 1945* (London, 1977); James Jankowski, 'Egyptian Responses to the Palestine Problem in the Interwar Period', *International Journal of Middle East Studies*, xii (1980), 1-38; *idem*, 'The Government of Egypt and the Palestine Question, 1936-1939', *Middle Eastern Studies*, xvii (1981), 427-53; Ralph M. Coury, 'Who "Invented" Egyptian Arab Nationalism?', *International Journal of Middle East Studies*, xiv (1982), 249-81, 459-79; Thomas Mayer, 'Egypt and the General Islamic Conference of Jerusalem in 1931', *Middle Eastern Studies*, xviii (1982), 311-22; *idem*, *Egypt and the Palestine Question, 1936-1945* (Berlin, 1983); *idem*, 'Egypt and the 1936 Arab Revolt in Palestine', *Journal of Contemporary History*, xix (1984), 275-87.
2. Wingate to Hardinge, 14 Nov. 1918, FO 141/773, 7819/3; for later accounts of the meeting see 'Abd al-'Aziz Fahmi, *Hadhihi Hayati* (Cairo, 1963), pp. 76-89; 'Abd al-Rahman al-Rafi'i, *Thawrat Sanat 1919* (Cairo, 1946), i. 57-60. The formation and early activities of the Wafd are explored in detail in Elie Kedourie, 'Sa'd Zaghlul and the British', in *The Chatham House Version*, pp. 82-159.
3. Text in Ahmad Shafiq, *Hawliyyat Misr al-Siyasiyya* (10 vols., Cairo, 1926-32), *tamhid* i. 154-6.
4. 'Les Revendications Nationales Egyptiennes. Mémoire présenté par la Délégation Egyptienne chargée de défendre la cause de l'indépendance de l'Egypte', FO 407/184, no. 66, and DUL Abbas Hilmi II MSS, file 35.

5. From a Wafdist manifesto of early 1919 addressed to the representatives of the foreign powers in Egypt, in Rafi'i, *Thawrat*, i. 106-7.

6. *Ibid.*

7. Memorandum of Sa'd Zaghlul, 6 March 1920, FO 371/5019, E1641/1641/16; cf. 'Abd al-'Azim Muhammad Ramadan, *Tatawwur al-Haraka al-Wataniyya fi Misr min Sanat 1919 ila Sanat 1936* (Cairo, 1968), p. 405.

8. For one example see the 'Memorandum by Sir R. Graham on the Unrest in Egypt', 9 April 1919, FO 407/184, no. 152.

9. For the former see Allenby to Curzon, 5 Aug. 1920, FO 141/433, 10770/47; the latter is discussed in a memorandum on 'Turco-Egyptian Relations', 29 Dec. 1922, FO 141/514, 12390/53, and in Ramadan, *Tatawwur*, p. 409.

10. Mahmud Abu al-Fath, *al-Masala al-Misriyya wa al-Wafd* (Cairo, n. d.), p. 199; see also FO 407/187, no. 279.

11. Wingate to Hardinge, 14 Nov. 1918, FO 141/773, 7819/3.

12. 'Les Revendications Nationales Egyptiennes', FO 407/184, no. 66.

13. Manifesto 'To the Members of the House of Commons' from the Egyptian delegation in Paris, 13 July 1919, DUL Abbas Hilmi II MSS, file 35.

14. See *al-Ahram*, 4 Oct. 1924, p. 1; *al-Siyasa*, 6 Oct. 1924, p. 2.

15. *Kawkab al-Sharq*, 28 Sept. 1924, p. 1; *ibid.*, 29 Sept. 1924, p. 4 (quotation from the latter).

16. *al-Balagh*, 7 Oct. 1924, p. 2.

17. *Ibid.*, 19 Oct. 1924, p. 1.

18. *al-Ahram*, 7 Oct. 1924, and *al-Balagh*, 9 Oct. 1924, p. 2.

19. Memorandum on 'Recognition of Ibn Saud by Egypt', 12 Feb. 1930, FO 141/501, 583/1/30.

20. Egyptian press reaction to events in Syria is surveyed in Lloyd to Chamberlain, 23 Nov. 1925, FO 407/201, no. 54.

21. Published in *Kawkab al Sharq*, 6 Nov. 1925, p. 4.

22. Lloyd to Chamberlain, 23 Nov. 1925, FO 407/201, no. 54; Coury, 'Egyptian Arab Nationalism', p. 252.

23. *Kawkab al-Sharq*, 6 Nov. 1925, p. 5.

24. *Ibid.*, 9 Nov. 1925, p. 5.

25. See 'Azzam's later recollections of the incident as published in *al-Usbu' al-'Arabi*, 17 Jan. 1972, p. 43. While 'Azzam did not date the conversation in this memoir, he mentioned it and set it in its proper temporal context in a private letter to a British official in 1933. See FO 141/711, 834/2/33.

26. Mayer, *Egypt*, p. 28.

27. See Khaldun S. Husry, 'King Faisal I and Arab Unity, 1930-1933', *Journal of Contemporary History*, x (1975), 323-40.

28. For Barakat's views on his trip see *Filastin*, 26 April 1931; *ibid.*, 3 May 1931; *Mirat al-Sharq*, 29 April 1931. Makram's views are discussed below.

29. See Mayer, 'General Islamic Conference', pp. 312-14, 317-19.

30. 'Memorandum on the Proposed Arab Congress', 30 Dec. 1932, FO 141/768, 1190/2/32; Loraine to Oliphant, 20 Jan. 1933, FO 141/756, 137/2/33; Humphrys to Simon, 2 Feb. 1933, FO 141/756, 137/4/33.

31. See Mayer, *Egypt*, pp. 21-3; Jankowski, 'Egyptian Responses', pp. 5-6.

32. Reported in FO 371/17003, J2570/11/16.

33. As reported in *Filastin*, 3 Sept. 1931.

34. As reported in *ibid.*, 12 Sept. 1931, p. 4.

35. As reported in *ibid.*, 18 Sept. 1931, pp. 1, 4.

36. For one example of his Arabist views in the early 1930s, see his 'al-Imbiraturiyya al-'Arabiyya wa Hal An an Tatahaqqaqu', *al-Hilal*, Feb. 1934, pp. 385-9.

37. Letter from 'Azzam to Hamilton, 10 Oct. 1933, enclosed in FO 141/744, 834/2/33.

38. Numerous articles on the subject appeared in *al-Balagh* in Aug. to Oct. 1933. Excerpts from many of these are republished in Anwar al-Jundi, *al Ma'arik al-Adabiyya fi al-Shi'r wa al-Nashr wa al-Thaqafa wa al-Lugha al Qawmiyya al-'Arabiyya* (Cairo, 1961), pp. 17ff.
39. Kelly to Eden, 4 Sept. 1936, FO 371/19980, E5831/381/65; *al-Rabita al-'Arabiyya*, 9 Dec. 1936, pp. 105-6; *ibid.*, 16 Dec. 1936, p. 154; Gomaa, *League of Arab States*, p. 36.
40. Lampson to Eden, 28 May 1937, FO 371/20801, E3080/698/93; report on the Egyptian–Palestinian commercial agreement in FO 141/644, 138/14/37; Mayer, *Egypt*, p. 65.
41. For his selection see *al-Rabita al-'Arabiyya*, 22 July 1936, pp. 20-1.
42. See the reports compiled in FO 141/537, 403/251/36.
43. See Mayer, *Egypt*, pp. 48-53, 64-82; *idem*, 'Egypt and the 1936 Arab Revolt', *passim*; Jankowski, 'The Government of Egypt', pp. 428-33, 442-6.
44. Lampson to Eden, 17 Dec. 1936, FO 371/19980, E8028/381/65; material on the Arab congress is contained in FO 141/675, 52/1/37.
45. Quotation from Lampson to Eden, 9 Jan. 1937, FO 371/20786, E351/351/65; also FO 371/20786, E577/351/65; Mayer, *Egypt*, pp. 60-1.
46. See Jankowski, 'The Government of Egypt', p. 429.
47. *Ibid.*, pp. 430-1.
48. *Ibid.*, p. 432.
49. As reported by Lampson to Eden, 26 March 1937, FO 141/481, 181/3/37; see also Mayer, *Egypt*, pp. 61-3; Coury, 'Egyptian Arab Nationalism', pp. 273-4.
50. Mayer, *Egypt*, pp. 85, 89-90, 94, 99; Jankowski, 'The Government of Egypt', p. 434.
51. Text contained in FO 371/31571, J1946/38/16.
52. Dispatch from Lampson, 16 Dec. 1942, FO 371/35528, J125/2/16.
53. Statute in *al-Rabita al-'Arabiyya*, 2 Jan. 1943, p. 7; see also Lampson to Eden, 2 Jan. 1943, FO 371/35528, J490/2/16; telegram from Lampson, 4 April 1943, FO 371/35531, J1519/2/16.
54. See Gomaa, *League of Arab States*, pp. 153-4; Mayer, *Egypt*, pp. 166-8.
55. *Ibid.*, pp. 173-6.
56. Telegram from Lampson, 10 May 1942, FO 371/31337, E2986/49/65.
57. Memorandum, 'Egypt and the Arab World', 29 June 1942, FO 141/840, 356/13/42; see also Mayer, *Egypt*, pp. 167-8.
58. Text in *al-Rabita al-'Arabiyya*, 21 Nov. 1942, pp. 10-11; summary in FO 371/31575, J4665/38/16; see also Mayer, *Egypt*, pp. 169-70.
59. Telegram from Lampson, 16 Nov. 1942, FO 371/31575, J4692/38/16.
60. See the discussion in Evan Lerman, 'The Egyptian Question, 1942-1947: The Deterioration of Britain's Postwar Position in Egypt, Al-Alamein to the U.N. Debate of 1947' (Ph.D., London, 1982), pp. 152-7.
61. For its initial formulation see Gomaa, *League of Arab States*, pp. 69-70.
62. See Mayer, *Egypt*, p. 172.
63. Quoted in George Kirk, *The Middle East in the War*, vol. ii of the *Survey of International Affairs, 1939-46* (London, 1952), p. 336.
64. *al-Ahram*, 28 Feb. 1943, p. 3; see also 'Material for a History of the Arab Union, 1939 to 1945', FO 371/45241, E9471/3/65.
65. See *al-Ahram*, 1 March 1943; *ibid.*, 2 March 1943; 'Weekly Political and Economic Report', 25 Feb.-3 March 1943, FO 371/35530, J1322/2/16.
66. Telegram from Lampson, 13 March 1943, FO 371/35530, J1203/2/16; 'Weekly Political and Economic Report', 4-10 March 1943, FO 371/35530, J1366/2/16; telegram from Lampson, 31 March 1943, FO 371/34956, E1919/506/65.
67. Copy enclosed in FO 371/34956, E2027/506/65; see also Y. Porath, 'Nuri al-Sa'id's Arab Unity Programme', *Middle Eastern Studies*, xx (1984), 91-2.

68. Telegram from Lampson, 4 April 1943, FO 371/35531, J1519/2/16; 'Political and Economic Weekly Report', 25-31 March 1943, FO 371/35531, J1615/2/16; Lampson to Eden, 16 June 1943, FO 371/35536, J2855/2/16; Mayer, *Egypt*, pp. 183-4; Porath, 'Arab Unity', pp. 92-3.

69. Text in *al-Ahram*, 31 March 1943, p. 3; copy in dispatch from Lampson, 1 April 1943, FO 371/34957, E2096/506/65.

70. 'Political and Economic Weekly Report', 25-31 March 1943, FO 371/35531, J1615/2/16.

71. 'Memorandum: Egypt and the Arab World', 3 May 1943, FO 141/866, 149/2/43; same judgement by Smart in 149/142/43.

72. Memo by Clayton, 7 Aug. 1943, FO 141/866, 149/90/43.

73. Quoted in Patrick Seale, *The Struggle for Syria: A Study in Postwar Arab Politics, 1945-1958* (Oxford, 1965), p. 13; see also Y. Porath, 'Abdullah's Greater Syria Programme', *Middle Eastern Studies*, xx (1984), 183-4.

74. The negotiations of 1943-4 have been analysed in depth in Gomaa, *League of Arab States*, pp. 165-231.

75. 'Note on the Present Stage of the Arab Unity Conversations', 11 March 1945, FO 141/1010, 32/77/45.

76. See the portraits of Nahhas presented in Jacques Berque, *Egypt: Imperialism and Revolution*, trans. Jean Stewart (London, 1972), pp. 520-1; and in Afaf Lutfi al-Sayyid-Marsot, *Egypt's Liberal Experiment, 1922-1936* (Berkeley, 1977), p. 105.

77. Reported by Lampson to Eden, 16 June 1943, FO 371/35536, J2855/2/16.

78. The former is from the minutes of the Syrian–Egyptian discussions of Oct. 1943 as transmitted in FO 371/34963, E7981/506,65; the latter is cited in Seale, *Struggle for Syria*, pp. 22-3.

79. For the Iraqi response see the telegram from Lampson, 4 April 1943, FO 371/35531, J1519/2/16, and Porath, 'Arab Unity', 93; Ibn Saud's response is discussed in FO 371/34959, E3595/506/65.

80. Shone to Eden, 14 Sept. 1943, FO 371/34962, E5770/506/65, and Jordan to Eden, 11 Sept. 1943, FO 371/34962, E5822/506/65.

81. See Gomaa, *League of Arab States*, pp. 205-11.

82. *Ibid.*, p. 225.

83. See *ibid.*, pp. 190, 216, for a defence of Nahhas's diplomacy.

84. Minutes of the discussions as transmitted in FO 371/34961, E5376/506/65.

85. FO 371/34962, E6291/506/65; FO 371/34963, E7981/506/65; FO 371/39987, E1349/41/65.

86. Dispatch from Jordan, 2 Oct. 1943, FO 371/34962, E6264/506/65.

87. Minutes of the discussions as transmitted in FO 371/34961, E5376/506/65.

88. From an account of the negotiations relayed by the Lebanese foreign minister, Salim Taqla, to the British, in FO 371/39987, E871/41/65.

89. Note by Lampson, 28 July 1943, FO 141/866, 149/81/43.

90. From the minutes of the Alexandria Conference in FO 371/45235, E455/3/65.

91. Reported in a telegram from Shone, 5 Sept. 1943, FO 371/34961, E5352/506/65.

92. Minutes of the discussions as transmitted in FO 371/34963, E7981/506/65.

93. Telegram from Lampson, 26 July 1944, FO 371/39989, E4478/41/65.

94. For an example see the minutes of his discussions with Nuri al-Sa'id as contained in FO 371/34961, E5376/506/65.

95. Dispatch from Shone, 28 Oct. 1943, FO 371/34963, E6706/506/65.

96. Telegram from Lampson to Eden, 8 June 1943, FO 371/35535, J2530/2/16.

97. Examples of Palestinian praise for Nahhas are contained in FO 141/906, 149/58/43.

98. From a report on the trip in FO 141/906, 855/10/43.

99. See the press reports in FO 371/35535, J2693/2/16 and FO 371/35535, J2786/2/16.

100. The incident is discussed in FO 141/906, 855/10/43.

XI

A PASSAGE TO INDEPENDENCE: KING ABDULLAH AND TRANSJORDAN, 1920-1951

Mary C. Wilson

> In Transjordan, as in the Middle East generally, it is
> power which attracts popularity, not the other way around.
> Abdullah's career is a case in point.
>
> Elie Kedourie[1]

Transjordan was the Arab state most identified with British interests until Great Britain's withdrawal from the Middle East after the Second World War. Although its ruler, King Abdullah, was considered an Arab nationalist when he arrived in Transjordan in 1920, his reputation was later tarred by accusations of collusion with Great Britain and of seeking to profit from this collusion to the detriment of Arab interests at large.[2] He was the only Arab leader publicly to accept the Peel Commission's report advocating the partition of Palestine in 1937.[3] And, when the Second World War broke out, he was the only Arab head of state who immediately and unequivocally announced his support of Great Britain.[4] Yet Transjordan received its independence in 1946, and when King Abdullah was assassinated in 1951 his dynasty survived.

Abdullah used the rhetoric of Arab nationalism to legitimize his position within Transjordan and to justify his ambitions beyond his borders. But he failed to distance himself sufficiently from Great Britain to give his rhetorical position reality. He was unable to build an independent position for himself within Transjordan and unsuccessful in identifying his interests with those of the Arab nationalist movement at large. Of course, he was beholden to Great Britain for his throne and for the financial support that kept Transjordan solvent. But others in the Middle East had similarly benefited from

Great Britain's patronage. For example, Abdullah's brother, Faysal, was equally beholden to Great Britain for his throne in Iraq. Yet Faysal, although he was not above criticism on nationalist grounds, nevertheless managed to retain his position as symbolic head of the pan-Arab nationalist movement and to follow a consciously nationalist policy in Iraq.[5] When Faysal died in 1933, the aegis of pan-Arabism passed to his own young and untried son Ghazi, rather than to the older and more experienced Abdullah.

Even this brief glance in Faysal's direction gives rise to questions of a comparative nature. Without implying that Faysal set a standard for behaviour, one must consider in what ways Abdullah and Transjordan differed from Faysal and the circumstances of Iraq. How did Abdullah come to be widely accused of being a British puppet while Faysal was able to maintain his identification with Arab nationalism?

Looking beyond familial and personal comparisons, other questions arise. How was Transjordan different from the other Arab states under mandate and from Egypt? Why was there no obvious nationalist struggle there? No Wafd party and no 1919 revolution as in Egypt? No massive tribal uprising as in Iraq in 1920? And no countrywide revolt as in Syria and Palestine in the 1920s and 1930s respectively? Why did Abdullah parade his loyalty to Great Britain at the outbreak of the Second World War when other Arab regimes flirted with the idea that an Axis victory would have the virtue, at least for them, of ridding the Middle East of British and French control?

These questions are often answered in terms of Abdullah's personality, in terms of his political commitment (or lack thereof), and in terms of the comparative benignity of British administration in Transjordan. For historians, however, a more meaningful analysis of Abdullah's position can be found in examining Transjordan's social and economic structure. And, quite apart from any personal proclivities on Abdullah's part, this structure simply did not permit him to resist Great Britain to the degree necessary to maintain his credibility as a nationalist. Nor did it provide the material base for the development of an organized nationalist movement in Transjordan.

But, if Transjordan's socio-economic structure helps to explain Abdullah's political actions and his dependency on Great Britain, it begs one final question: how did Transjordan manage to survive the ebb of Great Britain's power in the Middle East after the Second World War?

Transjordan in 1920

In 1920, when Great Britain first established a rudimentary presence in Transjordan, it was the least desirable part of greater Syria (Transjordan, Palestine, Syria, and Lebanon) which Great Britain and France had divided between them. Transjordan was in Great Britain's sphere of influence as drawn by Mark Sykes and François Georges-Picot in 1916, but since the end of the First World War, it had been ruled from Damascus as a province of Faysal's kingdom of Syria. Great Britain was content with this arrangement because she favoured Arab rule in the interior and Faysal was, after all, a British protégé. But France was not content. After France was awarded the mandates for Syria and Lebanon at the San Remo conference in April 1920, French troops occupied Damascus and ousted Faysal and his government.

It was not until the French occupied Damascus that Great Britain was forced to turn her attention to Transjordan. It suddenly became important to know exactly, 'what is the "Syria" for which the French received a mandate at San Remo?' and 'does it include Trans-jordania?'.[6] The British foreign secretary, Lord Curzon, decided that it did not and that Great Britain would regard the area as independent, but in the 'closest relation' with Palestine.[7] Fearful that France might push her occupation southwards despite Curzon's opinion, a very tentative British presence was established there by sending some political officers from Palestine, where Great Britain was already ensconced, across the Jordan river to the villages of Irbid, 'Ajlun, Salt, Amman, and Karak.

Although Great Britain may not have wanted France in Trans-jordan, the territory's strategic uses were few. It provided the land link between the British mandates of Iraq and Palestine, so that pipelines to the Mediterranean might be built through territory controlled by Great Britain from end to end, and so that aeroplanes, capable of only short hops in those days, would have a place to refuel in British-held territory in mid-desert. But these advantages were slight, certainly too slight to warrant the use of British troops at a time when the British public was clamouring for demobilization and when the troops in the region were already occupied with a massive tribal uprising in Iraq, a revolution in Egypt, and communal strife in Palestine. And so, the British political officers dispatched across the Jordan river to establish a presence in Transjordan were sent without any plans for sustained military support. Their instructions were to foster local self-government through tactful advice and kindness, and to encourage trade and other ties with British Palestine. If they got into trouble, it had already been decided in London that 'it was better to lose a few officers than to involve an Army'.[8]

To the Arabs, and specifically to the Arab nationalists who had supported Faysal in Damascus, Transjordan was a province of Faysal's kingdom of Syria.[9] After the French occupied Damascus in July 1920, Transjordan became the logical jumping-off point for the diplomatic or military reconquest of Syria. Although it was in Great Britain's sphere of influence, she had yet to establish a solid presence there. Arab nationalists therefore hoped to have some say in its fate. Great Britain had always been more accommodating to Arab nationalism than had France, and Arab nationalists continued to hope that Anglo-French rivalry might help them to overthrow, or at least to weaken, French rule in Damascus. And so, as Great Britain was casting about for a policy for Transjordan in the wake of France's occupation of Damascus, Arab nationalists regrouped in Amman. From there, they hoped to keep alive the struggle for Syria and they invited Faysal's older brother Abdullah to lead the movement.

Abdullah, at that time, was considered an Arab nationalist. His support of and participation in the Arab revolt had guaranteed him that status. Although some Arab intellectuals criticized the revolt and Sherif Husayn's alliance with Great Britain at the expense of the Ottoman Empire, the clock of history could not be turned back and, for better or worse, the family of Sherif Husayn of Mecca who had first forged that alliance remained the focal point for the Arab nationalist movement. Nationalists found the sherifians useful symbols, giving the Arab nationalist movement an appearance of unity and stressing the continuity of nationalist demands with the unfulfilled promises made by Great Britain to Husayn during the war.[10] Responsive to nationalist urgings which coincided with his own ambitions, Abdullah left Mecca and marched northwards at the head of some 500–1,000 tribal levies in the fall of 1920.[11]

The timing of Abdullah's arrival in Amman in March 1921, on the eve of the Cairo conference which was to lay down the lines of post-war British policy in the Middle East, was planned by his nationalist advisers. Likewise, the bargain he struck with Winston

Churchill in Jerusalem during the conference proceedings was deemed necessary by most nationalists. They recognized that with France in control of Syria and totally opposed to any dealings with Arab nationalists whatsoever, a compromise with Great Britain was needed in order to retain an organizational base anywhere near Damascus. Although Abdullah had marched northwards from the Hejaz vowing to reconquer Damascus, he reached, in good conscience, an agreement with Churchill to stay in Amman for a period of six months and to keep the territory clear of anti-French and anti-Zionist agitation to the best of his ability during that time. In return, he was given a stipend of £5,000 a month and the vague undertaking that the British would do what they could to smooth his way to Damascus.[12] (Years later this 'promise' became a subject of controversy. At the outbreak of the Second World War, Abdullah wrote to Churchill to remind him that he had kept his part of the bargain and was waiting for Great Britain to fulfil hers.[13] The British administration, of course, denied that any such promise had been made, although George Antonius believed that Churchill had 'trick[ed] Abdullah into remaining in Amman as ruler of Transjordan on the promise of a real settlement which was never realized'.)[14]

Abdullah's first council of ministers in Transjordan reflected his ambitions and his ties with the Arab nationalist movement. Composed entirely of nationalists who had previously served Faysal in Syria, it looked like a government in exile. At its head was Rashid Tali'a, a Druze from the Shuf region of Lebanon who had served Faysal as *mutasarrif* and military governor of Hama, acting minister of the interior, and finally military governor of Aleppo. At the time of his appointment he was under sentence of death *in absentia* in French Syria. Under him were Amin Tamimi from Nablus, formerly an adviser to Faysal; Mazhar Raslan of Homs, who under Faysal had been the *mutasarrif* of Salt; Hasan al-Hakim, a Damascene who had served Faysal as financial adviser; and 'Ali Khulqi al-Sharairi from 'Aljun (the only Transjordanian on the council), who had served as the military governor of his home province under Faysal.[15]

This council lasted barely six months. It was ousted after a tax rebellion in Kura in the Irbid district which the chief British adviser fancifully attributed to the disgust of the Transjordanians at being ruled by Syrians.[16] It was succeeded by a council under Mazhar Raslan who was viewed as a lukewarm nationalist by many of his peers. Raslan in turn was succeeded by 'Ali Rida Pasha al-Rikabi, a political chameleon from Damascus who had adroitly switched his allegiance from the Turks to Faysal in 1918 and from Faysal to the French in 1920. Although the British knew that local opinion condemned Rikabi as 'corrupt and possibly bought by the French', whose 'best friends feel themselves obliged to express the most complete reservations as to the integrity of his moral character', he was nonetheless welcomed as a useful and co-operative chief minister.[17] The composition of these councils also changed from the urbane and active Arab nationalists of the first council to the Hejazi cronies of Abdullah, local nonentities, and co-operative Palestinian functionaries of later ones.

Transjordan and Arab Nationalism

The complexion of Abdullah's ministerial councils altered over time because nationalism was, in a sense, an ideology alien to Transjordan. This does not mean that the inhabitants of Transjordan were not attached to their homes or their ways of life, or that they were not prepared to defend them from perceived threats. They were. What it means is that Transjordan was on the periphery of the mainly urban centres of nationalist activity and thought, and that owing to demography and to socio-economic structure, organized nationalist expression was not easily achieved there.

When Abdullah first marched into the area, he had two distinct groups to contend with: traditional leaders and nationalists.[18] Most of the former were from the area of Transjordan and were sheikhs of nomadic and semi-sedentary tribes or communal leaders whose positions of leadership were based on a combination of inherited familial prestige and personal merit. Few had been formally educated and none belonged to any nationalist organization prior to 1920. The latter were from the towns of Syria, Palestine, and the north-west corner of Transjordan, and came from respectable middle class families. They were educated, generally in secular institutions, and most were professionals – lawyers, military officers, or bureaucrats. The most important characteristic of this group, however, was that all its members were, to some degree, ideologically motivated. Many belonged to nationalist organizations and most had been politically active, either with Faysal in Damascus or against Zionism in Palestine.

Both groups had a distinct function for Abdullah. The nationalists had organizational skills and experience and familiarity with British and French goals, military power, and political susceptibilities. More important, they had an ideology which could legitimize Abdullah's ambitions in Transjordan and beyond, and attract followers across regional, confessional, and class lines. The traditional leaders were in control of Transjordan south of Amman and they could either facilitate Abdullah's passage northwards and justify his political usefulness to Great Britain, or they could withhold crucial support.

The story of Abdullah's first five years in Transjordan is largely the story of the struggle between these two groups for local hegemony. Given the territory's socio-economic background and Great Britain's ultimate financial and military control, Arab nationalist concerns gradually lost out to local concerns manipulated by Great Britain for her own ends. For example, the issue of 'Transjordan for the Transjordanians', raised in the early 1920s against 'rule by Syrians', was fostered by British officials among the tribal leaders and petty notables of the Transjordanian villages in order to turn nationalists, who were generally from outside the borders of Transjordan, out of office. It had nothing to do with Arab nationalism, but naturally appealed to local dignitaries jealous of their own local positions and lacking in vision and any ideological commitment to Arab nationalism. Significantly, it was not a slogan that lived on into the 1930s when the Transjordan administration came to be dominated by co-operative Palestinians.

After the first period of excitement in Amman in 1920 and 1921, the climate there grew inexorably more inhospitable to Arab nationalists. Abdullah's support was not constant since, to establish his own position, he was forced to bow to British and local concerns. Although Churchill had instructed Herbert Samuel, the high commissioner of Palestine, that 'the same latitude must be given to Abdullah in speeches that he makes as would be given to any Member supporting Government, but with a shaky seat',[19] little latitude was allowed him in his actions. For political reasons he was allowed to speak the language of Arab nationalism (within bounds), but for the same reasons he was not allowed to back up his rhetoric with action. More important, the tools available to resist British dictates were few, as there did not exist in the social and economic structure of the country any pockets of independent influence on which he could draw to resist the British magnet. When conflicts of interest arose between Great Britain and himself or between Great Britain and the nationalists during this period, he either shifted responsibility onto his nationalist advisers for being too extreme in their demands, giving Great Britain further cause to encourage their expulsion from the country, or he simply failed to carry out British wishes, cultivating an appearance of 'languidity' and a lack of interest in day-to-day affairs. He was so successful at seeming to stay aloof from the political battleground that when H. St. John Philby first arrived as chief British representative in Amman in November 1921, he characterized Abdullah as an ideal constitutional monarch.[20] (His appreciation changed drastically a year later in the face of Abdullah's obvious reluctance to establish actual institutions of constitutional rule.)

At the same time, tribal unrest in Transjordan and Wahabi attacks from the south made Abdullah more than ever conscious of his dependence on Great Britain and pushed him ever deeper into her embrace. In 1922 and 1924, Ikhwan raids struck within ten miles of Amman and in 1923 the Transjordanian 'Adwan tribe rebelled against Abdullah. British troops protected him and Jordanian territory during all three incidents. After the 'Adwan rebellion, Philby judged that 'the Amir and his Government have been driven by the Adwan rebellion into a sense of dependence on British help and I feel confident that they will now be less inclined to disregard well-meant counsels'.[21] Philby used the occasion advantageously to remove from office and expel six men belonging to the pan-Arab Istiqlal party. These included three Arab Legion officers and one member of the council of ministers. The 1924 Ikhwan raid helped to guarantee Abdullah's acceptance of a British ultimatum which demanded strict scrutiny and control of the Transjordanian budget by a British financial adviser and British control of the Arab Legion.[22]

The deepening freeze on nationalist activities in Amman and the granting of general amnesties in Syria, Lebanon, and Iraq combined to encourage Arab nationalists to return to their home countries where they might engage in nationalist struggles on their own turf. In the process, however, pan-Arab ideals were inevitably sacrificed to small state interests. This occurred in all the Arab mandated states and Egypt, but while the other Arab states maintained viable nationalist movements on their own, Transjordan did not.

Once Faysal's former supporters left Amman, the town lost its temporary importance and reverted to being a political backwater. Transjordan was never very important to Arab nationalist movements thereafter, except when the situation in neighbouring countries was disturbed. This occurred during the 1925-7 revolt in Syria and the 1936-9 rebellion in Palestine. The importance of Transjordan during these periods of struggle was mainly owing to its geography rather than to its political climate. Abdullah gave no support to the rebels other than asylum and passage through the country. His lack of engagement called attention to the growing distance between his position of dependence on Great Britain and his claims to leadership in the Arab world based on an identification with Arab nationalist goals.

Although Abdullah's tactics and interests gradually diverged from those of the Arab nationalist movement, this does not mean that he alone of all Arab leaders co-operated with the mandatory powers. Certainly King Faysal of Iraq, the National Bloc leaders of Syria and Lebanon, Hajj Amin al-Husayni in Palestine, and the Wafd in Egypt were not averse to striking deals with European powers. But these leaders dealt with Europe from a certain position of strength, from their position as leaders who, using nationalist ideology, could mobilize popular support to make things difficult for Great Britain or France. The concessions they gained were won in a complex process of manifesting political strength and leadership through strikes and demonstrations on the one hand, and negotiating with the mandatory power on the other. Concessions gained by Abdullah were most often rewards for good behaviour. As he opposed the conventional benchmarks of increasing independence, like elections and constitutions, what he won was often more personal than public and did not necessarily serve to enhance his prestige. As one observer noted in 1943: 'The people were less grateful than they would otherwise be for the increases in internal autonomy . . . since every advance in self-government increases the absolute power of the Amir'.[23]

Abdullah, from the confines of Transjordan, could not mount any effective resistance to Great Britain. Transjordan did not afford the sort of raw material to create and sustain a nationalist movement necessary to temper Great Britain's ultimate control. Under the Ottoman Empire it had been important chiefly as the territory through which the *hajj* caravan passed between Damascus and Medina. It did not form a province of its own, but was included at different times under the *vilayet* of Damascus or as part of the *sanjak* of Jerusalem. There did not exist in Transjordan that class of Ottoman civil servants and local notables which had first begun to feel uneasy as power was centralized in Istanbul after the Young Turk revolution of 1908. There was no class of large merchants or ex-Ottoman bureaucrats and other professionals which might have formed the nucleus of a national bourgeoisie. During the inter-war period when cities were the primary focus and location of nationalist politics, Transjordan had no major city. There was no natural centre which, through its trade with the countryside as well as its governmental functions, could attract the attention or mould the political consciousness of the entire territory. In 1920 the largest town was Salt, with a population of around 10,000. Amman at the time was a village with somewhere between 2,000 and 5,000 inhabitants. Indeed, Transjordan's population in general was low and sparse.[24] It did not provide the interplay of varied interests which might have formed a base for organized political action. There were no centres of religious learning, for example, nor was there a corps of popular religious leaders which might have provided the focus and means of political mobilization. Tribal sheikhs, and following them their tribesmen, were rapidly assimilated into the state structure. On the one hand fearful of Wahabi aggression and on the other attracted by the possibilities of land ownership, they accepted the new British order, or at least they did not actively oppose it. Finally, Transjordan had no natural resources and few taxable assets, leaving Abdullah dependent on his British subsidy.

Under the British mandate no new structures of political organization or mobilization were created. Transjordan's security force, the Arab Legion, was firmly controlled by Great Britain. It did not become a path to political power as did the armies of Iraq, Egypt, and Syria. Education available in Transjordan by 1940 was still rudimentary and had not yet created an indigenous intelligentsia of any weight. The pupils of all schools – elementary and secondary, government and private, male and female – numbered 13,854 in 1938-9 and the number of students educated outside Transjordan was minuscule.[25] While in other Arab countries lawyers formed the backbone of local administration and nationalist parties, in Transjordan native ministers had at most a secondary school education until the 1950s (except for one prime minister who had trained to be a veterinary surgeon at Edinburgh University).[26] Moreover, the formal institutions of national government – the council of ministers and the chamber of deputies – lacked political independence and power. Industrial establishments were few and tiny and there was no

196

concentrated or easily mobilized working class.[27] Population and urbanization increased during the mandate, but by 1940 Amman and Salt still had a population of only 20,000 each. Transjordan gained little economic and demographic importance until the 1948 war.

Owing to the structural inability of Transjordan to support nationalist politics, Abdullah increasingly took on the aspect of a British puppet. He was not unaware of his position, and it was for reasons of political necessity as well as of personal vanity that he tried constantly to extend his power and influence beyond the borders of Transjordan. Thus, while other Arab leaders in the inter-war period concentrated mainly on gaining a monopoly of political power within their own borders by using the appeal of nationalism, Abdullah's political energies were directed mainly towards expanding his boundaries. The realm of real political action for him was outside Transjordan, where he hoped to escape the structural constraints of his arid country in order to build a position for himself which could command the respect not only of the Arab world but of Great Britain as well.

Abdullah's ambitions ranged from reconquering his familial base in the Hejaz which had been taken over by the Saudis in 1925-6, to uniting Hashemite Iraq with Hashemite Transjordan under himself, to establishing a greater Syrian state with himself on the throne in Damascus. The major problem he faced in realizing any of his extraterritorial ambitions was that he was so closely identified with British interests inside Transjordan that outside he was easily discredited by neighbouring rulers and nationalist élites who in no way wanted to play second fiddle to him or to anyone else. And he was not powerful enough and had too little to offer to be an attractive or useful ally.

The Evolution of British Policy

Although Great Britain had at first been reluctant to move into Transjordan, once there she found reasons to stay. The reason for her initial involvement was simply to keep France out. Great Britain did not want France in occupation of more territory in the Middle East than was strictly necessary, she wanted to protect her rear in Palestine, and Transjordan was too close to the Suez Canal for Great Britain to regard a French presence there with total peace of mind. A second reason, readily at hand for Great Britain to justify taking any trouble at all in Transjordan, was communications. Transjordan provided a land link between the coast of the Mediterranean and the Iraqi oil fields. Pipelines, roads, and telegraph lines (at one time Great Britain even projected a railroad) could be built entirely through British-held territory from Baghdad and the oil fields of northern Iraq to the coast of British Palestine. Transjordan also lay astride the alternate route to British India – the chief route ran through the Suez Canal. And it added one more section to the huge swath of territory in the Middle East dominated by Great Britain in one way or another; it was one more ball which Great Britain could juggle to the advantage of her overall position in the region. By divvying up favour and punishment in varied patterns throughout the region, Great Britain was able to check the pace and intensity of regional discontent.

The agreement struck between Churchill and Abdullah at the Cairo conference was short-term because Great Britain's chief concern at the time lay in getting Faysal safely on the throne of Iraq and in firming up her administration in Palestine. Once those two important issues were settled there would be time enough to turn to Transjordan. In the meantime Great Britain wanted to keep her options open. As for Abdullah, the six-month term had suited him, too, as he hoped to move on to Damascus. The very impermanence of the agreement seemed to suggest that bigger and better things awaited him, and he did not want to over-commit himself to Great Britain at the risk, possibly, of losing a better prize. T.E. Lawrence believed that the French might invite Abdullah to rule Syria and impressed Churchill with his belief.[28] The French, however, quickly made it clear that they entertained no such notion.[29] Abdullah's original six months in Transjordan stretched into a lifetime.

Great Britain was not, at first, committed to maintaining Transjordan separately from Palestine. Some British officials, notably the first high commissioner of Palestine, Sir Herbert Samuel, wanted it to be brought under the Palestine administration directly, without the blind of native government. In this, Samuel was influenced by his sympathy for Zionism and his desire to add to the territory that would be available for Jewish settlement. Samuel was consequently disappointed when Great Britain decided not to send troops to Transjordan.[30] Although he adhered loyally to London's directives, which were at variance with his own views, he repeatedly urged that troops be dispatched to Jordan with direct administration to follow.[31] Churchill expressed the general feeling in the Middle East department that such direct rule would ultimately be desirable when he put off making any binding statements about Transjordan's future, 'at any rate until the Constitution of Palestine is definitely promulgated'.[32]

The Palestinians did not accept the constitution offered by Great Britain, however, and they successfully boycotted the elections of 1923, because participating in either would have implied their acceptance of the terms of British rule in Palestine, including the undertaking to foster there the creation of a Jewish national home. As it became increasingly obvious that Palestine would not settle easily or quickly under the yoke of the British mandate, the idea that Transjordan might come directly under the government of Palestine grew less and less attractive.

The political separation of the two states helped to protect Palestine from the spread from Arabia of Wahabism, a creed and an ideology inimical to European intervention in Muslim lands. Just as Great Britain was discovering the depth of Palestinian opposition to the mandate, she became acutely sensitive to the extent to which Wahabism might magnify and galvanize anti-British sentiment. Given that Abdullah was already an enemy of Ibn Saud, and as long as Transjordan did not come under the same pressure of Zionist colonization as Palestine, the tribes of Transjordan with occasional help from the Royal Air Force would be an effective barrier to the spread of Wahabism, whether by conquest or by propaganda.[33] This strategic utility, although crucial to the continued independence of Transjordan from Palestine, did not immediately result in the adoption of a positive policy towards state-building in Transjordan. Until the end of the 1920s, Great Britain regarded Transjordan 'more as a buffer to Palestine than as a country capable of development in itself'.[34]

Gradually, however, Transjordan took on the outward political trappings of a state. The first step was the 1923 'assurance' that Great Britain would 'recognize an independent government in Trans-Jordan under His Highness the Amir Abdullah ibn Husain', provided that the government was constitutional and a treaty with Great Britain was signed. The second was the fulfilment of these two conditions by the 1928 organic law and Anglo-Transjordanian agreement.[35] But it was not until the end of the decade, when Great Britain undertook a fiscal survey and the settlement and rectification of individual claims on Transjordan's lands, that the foundation of a national economy and tax structure was laid.[36] Even so, agricultural development was slow and investment in anything other than land was almost non-existent until the peculiar supply patterns of the Second World War allowed some in Transjordan to make fortunes which they then turned to agriculture, trade, and, in a very limited sense, manufacturing and the extraction of raw materials.

Until 1937, Transjordan's needs were most often subordinated to those of the far more important and more troubled land of Palestine. However, with the admission by the Peel Commission that British policy in Palestine was contradictory and its finding that the only way to resolve the contradiction was to partition Palestine between Arab and Jew, Transjordan suddenly came into a position of prominence. For, concomitant with the partition of Palestine, it was suggested that Transjordan should rule those parts of Palestine left to the Arabs and that a transfer of population might be entailed.[37] Hence the tables were turned in the Palestine–Transjordan relationship. Rather than Transjordan's being threatened with inclusion in Palestine as in the early 1920s, it now stood to be one of the heirs to Palestine's destruction. The 1937 proposition, however, was dropped in the face of Arab resistance; with the Second World War clearly on the horizon Great Britain was anxious to have a secure Middle East in her corner.

The Second World War and the End of the Mandate

Abdullah's fate, having been divorced from nationalist politics by his position in Transjordan, was still in British hands by the time the Second World War created new possibilities for independence and unity in the Arab world. Indeed, in his attempts to further his candidacy as king of greater Syria during the war, the only arguments he could muster in his favour predated his partnership with Great Britain in Transjordan: that as the eldest living son of Sherif Husayn, the leader of the Arab Revolt, he deserved to inherit the rewards of that revolt however delayed they might be in coming, and that once Syria was free from French control, it should revert to a Hashemite monarchy, as in 1920, with himself Faysal's heir.[38] But these claims held little appeal in the light of the nationalist struggles since the Arab Revolt in which Abdullah had played little part. There were other men now less tainted by contact with Europe, who served as better foci for pan-Arab sentiments. And, in any case, twenty years of separate existence and separate development had caused the original ardour for Arab unity to cool.

Abdullah aspired in the Second World War to play a role similiar to that of his father, Sherif Husayn, in the First World War. He wanted to be the chief Arab ally of Great Britain and, by dint of that position, to be recognized as the most important Arab leader east of Egypt. He hoped to trade on his utility to Great Britain in order to establish with British help an Arab kingdom, either greater Syria or a united kingdom of Transjordan and Iraq, that would be more successful than Faysal's short-lived kingdom of Syria. But, in the twenty years since the First World War, Great Britain had developed too many interests in the Middle East and courted too many allies to be obliged to rely on one alone. Even though there were British statesmen who were also twenty years out of date in thinking of one supreme Arab leader, their thoughts did not turn to Abdullah. Winston Churchill, for example, felt Ibn Saud to be the 'greatest living Arab' and would not have objected to the extension of Saudi dominion over Iraq and Transjordan, provided that Ibn Saud agreed to a settlement in Palestine.[39] Thus, while London surely appreciated Abdullah's loyalty and his contribution to the campaigns in Iraq and Syria in 1941, he was not likely to be rewarded in the coin of his own choosing.

Given Abdullah's ultimate reliance on Great Britain, perhaps one of his greatest disappointments occurred when the British reconquered Syria for the allies in 1941 and handed it back to the Free French, rather than putting Abdullah on the throne in Damascus in fulfilment of Churchill's 'promise' of 1921. But the truth was that although Abdullah was Great Britain's man inside Transjordan, his ambitions simply did not fit British policy outside. In anticipation of Syria's independence, Great Britain made friends with the leader of the National Bloc in Syria, Shukri al-Quwwatli,[40] and had no need to impose the unpopular Abdullah on Syria in order to safeguard Great Britain's position. Likewise, there would be no benefit for Great Britain from uniting Transjordan with Iraq or from having Abdullah replace Ibn Saud in the Hejaz.

When Transjordan was given its independence in 1946 its relationship with Great Britain changed little. The treaty that superseded the mandate guaranteed British interests and Great Britain's ongoing involvement in Transjordan's affairs: the British resident's title changed, but his functions remained the same.[41] Prior to the negotiations with London, Abdullah had secured Iraq's promise of financial support should British aid be cut off with the granting of independence, but he was distinctly relieved when Great Britain agreed to maintain her financial support at its established level.[42] He preferred to be beholden to a distant power than to his nephew in Iraq. In 1948 the treaty was revised to erase some of its more obvious signs of continued subordination to Great Britain. But the offending passages were simply put into secret codicils.[43]

Nonetheless, 1948 did mark the beginning of a change in Abdullah's relationship with Great Britain. For in that year Abdullah's ambitions outside Transjordan and British policy finally came together. When Great Britain decided to give up her mandate in Palestine, she supported the extension of Abdullah's rule to the portion of Palestine left to the Arabs. She did so because she feared that an independent Palestinian state 'would be a hotbed of ineffectual Arab fanaticism and after causing maximum disturbance to our relations with the Arabs would . . . be finally absorbed by the Jewish state',[44] and because she hoped to reintroduce her influence into at least part of Palestine through her client and ally Transjordan. This final coincidence of interests between Great Britain and Abdullah sealed Abdullah's reputation, in the eyes of all Arabs but the most loyal Transjordanians, as Great Britain's tool in the Middle East. But this estimation does not mean that Abdullah failed to achieve some of his objectives. Indeed, the extension of Transjordanian rule to the west bank allowed two things to happen which created a future, if not for Abdullah personally, for his descendants.

With the withdrawal of Great Britain from the Middle East after the war, one might have expected Transjordan, so dependent on British support, to wither away. But the partition of Palestine and the emergence of Israel, which resulted in the addition of the west bank and of large numbers of Palestinian refugees to Transjordan, created an entirely new situation which, far from weakening Transjordan's position, strengthened it. A new balance of forces emerged in the region. This balance, which included the United States, the United Nations, the Arab states, and Israel in addition to Great Britain, supported the continued existence of an independent Jordan, as the newly enlarged state was called, in recognition of its valuable role in satisfying at least the immediate social and economic needs of the Palestinians. In particular Jordan, by providing a home and nationality for the great concentration of refugees, allowed Arab regimes to engage in Arab nationalist and anti-Israeli rhetoric at will, without being called to back up their rhetoric with action. Because

Jordan was useful in pacifying the Palestinians, Israel was also a part of this balance of forces. As Jordan now served the interests of more than one state, it was finally able to diversify its sources of political and financial support to avoid being dependent on any one of these states as it had formerly been on Great Britain.

The addition of Palestinian refugees to Jordan also transformed the social and economic structure of the country. The Palestinians came to Jordan with some capital, they attracted more capital, and they were better educated and had stronger contacts with the Arab world and with Europe than had the relatively isolated Transjordanians. Thus, besides the new regional balance of power which gave added outside support to Jordan, the internal nature of the state was changed by the international aid that Jordan attracted through the Palestinians, the political and administrative skills of the Palestinians themselves, and the remittances from the Palestinian diaspora to relatives in Jordan. The interaction of both external and internal changes following the 1948 war made it possible for Jordan and its ruling dynasty to outlast what has been called 'Britain's moment in the Middle East'.[45]

Abdullah was assassinated by a Palestinian in 1951 for what was viewed by many as his traitorous collusion in the partition of Palestine. It is not clear that at the time of his death he understood exactly what he had achieved – that he had brought together the forces that would provide for the continuity of his state. For he viewed the addition of the west bank to Transjordan as but the first step in the creation of a larger Arab state, and his political ambitions at the end of his life, as in 1921, continued to be focused on Damascus. But although he failed to achieve the goal dearest to his heart, he was nonetheless successful in passing on to his heirs a solid legacy in the form of a community of interests which guaranteed not only the survival of Jordan but of the Hashemite dynasty itself. His grandson Husayn is the longest reigning monarch in the region, outlasting the regimes of Abdullah's Arab nationalist rivals and detractors.

NOTES

1. Elie Kedourie, *Islam in the Modern World and Other Studies* (London, 1980), p. 135.
2. Abdullah was amir of Transjordan until 1946 when Transjordan received its independence and he became king. In 1949 Transjordan was renamed the Hashemite Kingdom of Jordan.

3. 'Note on the position in Transjordan regarding the report of the Royal Commission', by A.S Kirkbride, 17 July 1937, CO 733/351. Since 1967 Abdullah has been credited with political foresight for his early acceptance of the partition. In his own time, however, his advocacy of partition was understood to be motivated by personal ambition, as he was the only Arab leader who stood to gain by it. In 1937 the creation of a Jewish state, much less its later expansion, was not a foregone conclusion.

4. Report on the Political Situation in Transjordan for the month of Sept. 1939, CO 831/51; J.B. Glubb, 'Transjordan and the War', *Journal of the Royal Central Asian Society*, xxxiii (1945), 25-6.

5. For two very different assessments of Faysal's reign and that of his successors see Hanna Batatu, *The Old Social Classes and the Revolutionary Movements of Iraq* (Princeton, 1978), pp. 25-36, and Elie Kedourie, 'The Kingdom of Iraq, a Retrospect', in his *Chatham House Version*, pp. 236-82.

6. Young to Hardinge, 27 July 1920, FO 371/5254.

7. Curzon to Samuel, 6 Aug. 1920, ISA C[hief] S[ecretary's] O[ffice], file 50a.

8. Monckton to Cook, 16 Aug. 1974, SAC Monckton MSS. Monckton was one of the British officers originally sent to Transjordan.

9. Sulayman Musa, *Tasis al-Imara al Urduniyya* (*The Foundation of the Amirate of Jordan*) (Amman, 1971), pp. 11-17.

10. I disagree here with Professor Kedourie's thesis, presented in his book, *In the Anglo-Arab Labyrinth* (Cambridge, 1976), that Great Britain gave no undertakings to the Arabs. See Albert Hourani, 'The Arab Awakening Forty Years Later', in his *The Emergence of the Modern Middle East* (London, 1981), p. 209.

11. 'Awni 'Abd al-Hadi, *Awraq Khassa* (*Private Papers*) (Beirut, 1974), pp. 39-56. Khayr al-Din Zirikli, *'Aman fi 'Amman* (*Two Years in Amman*) (Cairo, 1925), pp. 3-20. Musa, *Tasis*, pp. 44-52.

12. Report on the Middle East Conference held in Cairo and Jerusalem from March 12th to 30th 1921, FO 371/6343.

13. MacMichael to CO, 11 Oct. 1939, FO 371/23281.

14. Antonius to Hodgkin, 24 June 1936, SAC Hodgkin MSS.

15. H. St. John Philby, 'Stepping Stones Across Jordan' (unpublished manuscript), pp. 235-6, SAC Philby MSS.

16. Khayr al-Din Zirikli, *'Aman*, p. 118; Report no. 4 from Amman, 5 June 1921, CO 733/3, and Report no. 5 from Amman, 1 July 1921, CO 733/4.

17. Philby Diary, 22 March 1922, SAC Philby MSS; Samuel to Churchill, 4 April 1922, CO 722/20.

18. The distinction was noted at the time by Fuad Salim who divided Abdullah's constituents into 'leaders of the country' (zu'ama al-balad) and 'men of the awakening' (rijal al-nahda). Musa, *Tasis*, p. 53.

19. Churchill to Samuel, 2 April 1921, CO 733/13.

20. Philby to Gertrude Bell, 17 Feb. 1922, SAC Philby MSS.

21. Philby to Samuel, 17 Sept. 1923, CO 733/50.

22. See Clayton to Abdullah, 14 Aug. 1924, Clayton to CO, 14 Aug. 1924 (two dispatches), and GOC Palestine to air ministry, 14 Aug. 1924, FO 271/10102. Uriel Dann in his article 'The Political Confrontation of the Summer of 1924 in Transjordan' is incorrect in stating that the sending of the Ninth Lancers to Amman was unconnected with the political crisis. British documents make clear that the Lancers were sent precisely because of the political crisis and that the simultaneous Wahabi raid had, by chance, provided a publishable cover story. Dann, *Studies in the History of Transjordan 1920-1949* (Boulder, 1984), p. 89.

23. 'Great Britain and Arab Nationalism', by A.H. Hourani, Aug. 1943, CO 732/87.

24. Estimates vary between 130,000 and 230,000. A. Ruppin, *Syrien als Wirtschaftsgebiet* (Berlin, 1917), p. 8, estimates 131,788, but excludes nomads. Two British officers

serving in Jordan in 1921 put the figure at 230,000. See 'Observations on Dr. Weizmann's letter to the Secretary of State for the Colonies with reference to Transjordania' by Major Somerset (later Lord Raglan) and Captain Peake, 14 March 1921, CO 733/15. A contemporary Arab document puts the population at 225,380, but has excluded the districts of Ma'an and 'Aqaba which were not officially part of Transjordan at the time. See Musa, *Tasis*, pp. 177-8.

25. A. Konikoff, *Trans-Jordan. An Economic Survey* (Jerusalem, 1943), pp. 27-9.
26. Fawzi al-Mulqi.
27. A. Konikoff, *Trans-Jordan*, pp. 71-3.
28. Report on the Middle East Conference held in Cairo and Jerusalem from March 12th to 30th, 1921, FO 371/6343, pp. 8, 98.
29. Samuel to Churchill, 2 June 1921, FO 406/46.
30. When Great Britain first authorized the sending of political officers to Jordan in August 1920, Samuel wrote to his wife: 'I have at last arrived at a settlement with the F.O. about Trans-Jordania – less than I wanted, but 'twill serve. (I am referring not to extent of territory but to manner of occupation.)' Samuel to his wife, 13 Aug. 1920, ISA Samuel MSS.
31. Herbert Young commented acidly on Samuel's campaign for troops for Transjordan: 'I remain unconvinced by the various, and in some cases contradictory, arguments put forward for the military occupation of Trans-Jordania. Sir H. Samuel fears that Palestine is not to get her proper boundaries on the north, and casts longing eyes across the Jordan to make up for it'. Minute of Young on papers submitted on 6 Nov. 1920, FO 371/5289.
32. Churchill to Samuel, 7 Feb. 1922, CO 733/8.
33. British officials noted the number of articles in the Palestine press favourable to Wahabism and acknowledged that although the Palestinians might not normally be attracted to its austere tenets, under the unusual conditions of the British mandate it might well prove a potent ideology. Kamil Budayri, a prominent Palestinian activist, was one of the chief liaisons between Arab nationalist groups in Palestine (notably the Nadi al-'Arabi) and Ibn Saud. He was killed in the desert on one of his journeys between Jerusalem and Arabia in 1922. His friends and partisans suspected that the deed had been instigated by Great Britain.
34. Minute of Young on Milner to Churchill, 3 Sept. 1922, CO 733/38.
35. For texts see Helen Davis, *Constitutions, Electoral Laws, Treaties of States in the Near and Middle East* (Durham, N.C., 1947).
36. G.F. Walpole, 'Land Problems in Transjordan', *Journal of the Royal Central Asian Society*, xxxv (1948), 52-65.
37. British Government Royal Commission on Palestine, *Report*, 22 June 1937, Cmd 5479.
38. Abdullah later published a whole book concerning his claims to Syria. *al-Kitab al-Urduni al-Abyad* (*The Jordanian White Book*) (Amman, 1946).
39. Churchill to Eden, 19 May 1941, FO 371/27043.
40. See Philip S. Khoury, *Syria and the French Mandate: The Politics of Arab Nationalism 1920-1945* (Princeton, forthcoming), ch. 23.
41. See Alec Kirkbride, *A Crackle of Thorns* (London, 1956), p. 2.
42. 'Note on the Possible Political Results of Disbanding the Arab Legion Infantry Companies', by J.B. Glubb, 1946, FO 371/52930.
43. Eric Beckett (legal adviser to the FO) to attorney general, 20 Feb. 1950, FO 371/82714; Kirkbride to Furlonge, 31 March 1950, FO 371/82751.
44. Note by Burrows, 17 Aug. 1948, FO 371/68822.
45. Elizabeth Monroe, *Britain's Moment in the Middle East 1914-1956* (London, 1963).

XII

FRITZ GROBBA AND THE MIDDLE EAST POLICY OF THE THIRD REICH

Francis R. Nicosia

> In the 1930s Germany and Italy – by skilful propaganda,
> by judicious disbursements, by the powerful appeal of
> their efficiency and success – established themselves as the
> champions of, and set the pace for Arab nationalism. And
> yet when one comes to examine what – with their freedom
> from local and imperial responsibilities, and their lack of
> scruple – they were in the end prepared to concede, one is
> struck with their discretion and circumspection, compared
> with the generous and insouciant abandon of British policy.
>
> Elie Kedourie[1]

The Allied victory in the First World War destroyed the considerable
political and economic position that Imperial Germany had built up
in the Middle East before 1914.[2] The defeat and disintegration of the
principal vehicle of German penetration, the Ottoman Empire,
coupled with Germany's own military, political, and economic
collapse in Europe, radically altered the conditions under which
post-war German governments would have to pursue German
interests in the region. For both the Weimar Republic and the
National Socialist regime prior to 1939, the most significant changes
in the post-war world were the loss of German power and dominance
in Europe and the almost supreme power of the British Empire
throughout the Middle East. Although Germany's demise in Europe
naturally became for both the Weimar Republic and the Third Reich
its most critical foreign policy concern, the preservation of British
pre-eminence in the Middle East was quickly perceived to be an
important condition for restoring German power in Europe. Thus,
both the Weimar Republic and the Hitler regime pursued a policy
aimed at restoring some German political and economic influence in

206

the Middle East, while fully accepting Great Britain's dominant role in the region.

That the Weimar Republic would seek to restore some semblance of Germany's pre-war position in the Middle East was evident just two years after the war had ended, as early as September 1920.[3] Karl von Schubert, state secretary from 1924 to 1930, circulated a memorandum advocating strong German support for Zionism and the Jewish National Home in Palestine, noting that this was the best means of promoting German influence both in Palestine and throughout the Middle East.[4] His idea soon became official policy. On 8 May 1922, the German foreign office issued its first comprehensive statement on Palestine and the Middle East to all German diplomatic missions.[5] Although the memorandum concentrated on Palestine, it had policy implications for the whole Middle East. It reflected Germany's acceptance of the post-war settlement in the Middle East, specifically Anglo-French dominance through the Mandates and the Jewish National Home in Palestine, and pointed to the current and potential economic and political advantages for Germany in Palestine and the Middle East offered by the terms of peace.

The most comprehensive account of Weimar policy in the region was to be provided by Moritz Sobernheim, head of the Jewish affairs section of the German foreign office. In a lengthy report on a visit to Palestine in the spring of 1925,[6] he set out as Germany's primary goal the restoration of her great power position in Europe and the world, and as her regional goal the restoration of a strong political, economic, and cultural presence. He also outlined as one means to those ends, full German acceptance of the *status quo* in the Middle East. According to Sobernheim, this included first and foremost recognition of Great Britain's pre-eminence in the region, support for the Jewish National Home in Palestine, and the rejection of Arab demands for independence.

The National Socialist assumption of power in January 1933 did not alter the foundations of German Middle East policy established during the Weimar period. Although the domestic and foreign policy objectives of the new regime changed radically, it maintained the same approach to the Middle East for the rest of the decade.[7] Great Britain continued to be the most critical factor affecting the formulation of German foreign policy. At least since 1923, Hitler had believed some form of Anglo-German understanding, preferably an alliance, to be an essential preparation for the conquest of *Lebensraum* in central and eastern Europe. Such an understanding would include full German support for Great Britain's imperial interests throughout the world, and preclude any support for the independence movements that were becoming more and more troublesome to Great Britain during the 1930s. Hitler's *Englandpolitik* was also fully in keeping with his racial *Weltanschauung* and the tenets of National Socialism, which could only conceive of a world perpetually under white European domination, and which precluded any form of German support for colonial peoples against the racially superior, Germanic, Anglo-Saxons.

The strategic and racial requirements of the Hitler regime in the pursuit of its *Englandpolitik* therefore precluded support for Arab nationalist movements in the Middle East. Arab efforts to enlist German support against the Anglo-French presence in the Middle East were firmly rebuffed, and German political and economic aims in the Middle East were pursued, as they had been during the Weimar period, without any attempt to undermine Great Britain's position in the area. Finally, the German position on Zionism and the Palestine question after 1933 remained the same as before, albeit for different reasons. With the goal of rapidly removing the Jewish community from Germany, the Hitler regime fully supported both Zionist emigration to Palestine, and the continued development of the Jewish National Home embodied in the Balfour Declaration and incorporated into Great Britain's Palestine Mandate. The regime also remained firmly opposed to the establishment of an independent Jewish state in Palestine, as recommended by the Peel Commission in its partition plan of July 1937. In addition to traditional anti-Semitic myths of an international Jewish conspiracy with a possibly independent power base in Palestine, the German government also feared an addition to the growing coalition of states hostile to the new Germany.

These assumptions underlying German policy in the Middle East prescribed the role of Dr Fritz Grobba, the controversial German ambassador in Iraq from 1932 to 1939, and the German representative in the Middle East with the most knowledge of and familiarity with the area. Grobba had been born on 18 July 1886 in Gartz/Oder. He studied oriental languages at the university of Berlin before the First World War, receiving his doctorate in 1913. After working briefly as a translator at the German consulate in Jerusalem in 1913, he served as an officer in the German army in France and on the Palestine front. Working in the German foreign office after the war, he was assigned in 1923 to Abteilung III, the department responsible for the Middle East and south Asia. Later that year, he was appointed German consul in Kabul, where he remained until 1926. From 1926 until 1932 he was back in Berlin in charge of the section Persia/Afghanistan/India in Abteilung III, after which he was assigned to Baghdad.

To estimate Grobba's role in the formulation of German policy in the Middle East during the 1930s is a difficult task for a number of reasons. Given the nature of the National Socialist regime, and the SS practice of spying on German diplomats abroad, official communications between Grobba in Baghdad and, as of 1939, in Saudi Arabia, and the German foreign office in Berlin, are often more reticent than one might otherwise have expected. Grobba's own view of events in the Middle East and German policy in the area was not always explicitly set out, certainly not if it contradicted the prevailing view in Berlin.[8] Second, Grobba's private papers had not at the time of writing been made available to scholars by his family, and his published memoirs, informative and insightful as they are, remain memoirs nevertheless, written some time after the events they describe with an eye on the author's own place in history.[9] Despite these handicaps, one can compose from the official German diplomatic documents a sufficiently detailed account of Grobba's views on the issues and events that dominated the Middle East at the time, and on the role he thought Germany should play. Since the views of the various government and party agencies, and the policies the German government followed in the Middle East, are known, it is possible to establish the extent to which Grobba differed from Berlin, and perhaps more important, how far Grobba himself influenced the formulation of German policy.

That there existed important differences between Grobba and the Hitler regime on Germany's role in the Middle East is strongly implied throughout Grobba's memoirs.[10] He entitled the brief section containing his concluding remarks 'Reasons for not Using the Opportunities Afforded Us by Arab Friendship During the War', and implicit in them is the view that he had favoured a clear German identification with the cause of Arab national self-determination and independence: 'In the last war, we did not take advantage of the opportunities that we had as a result of the friendly attitude of the

Arabs towards us, because we did not promise the Arabs the independence that would have been a precondition for their active *Waffenbereitschaft*'. Although Grobba admits that one reason for Hitler's refusal to endorse Arab independence was his usual reluctance to make long-range promises, he asserts that the major reasons were both strategic and racial. Hitler considered that Germany's strategic interests would be best served before 1939 by supporting Great Britain's imperial position in the Middle East, while the aims of his Italian ally in the eastern Mediterranean after 1939, and those of Vichy France after 1940 in North Africa and Syria, became part of Germany's own war aims. Noting the influence of race on the formulation of German policy, Grobba contemptuously referred to Hitler as the 'preacher of the superiority of the Aryan race who did not want to see that the semitic Arabs could be a very valuable source of support for us'.[11]

Fritz Grobba was appointed German chargé d'affaires in Baghdad in February 1932, and ambassador in October of that year, after Iraq's entry into the League of Nations.[12] For the rest of the decade, he concentrated primarily on expanding Germany's economic position in Iraq and Saudi Arabia, and on avoiding friction with Great Britain in the process. As the decade progressed, however, Grobba was forced to deal with Germany's political and strategic interests in the region, owing to her rapid re-emergence as a great power under National Socialism, and to the growing strength of Arab nationalism and its increasing ability to threaten Anglo-French power in the Middle East. He was drawn furthest into the developing conflict in Palestine.

Grobba's active style in Iraq and the Persian Gulf area, and the naively positive assessment in the Arab world of the Hitler regime in 1933, created opportunities for him to further German economic expansion.[13] In June 1933, Abdul Latif al-Abdul Jalil, a representative of King Ibn Saud, met Grobba at Baghdad to discuss Saudi proposals for involving Germany in the kingdom's economic development, including its search for oil.[14] After expressing Ibn Saud's gratitude for the loan of a German ship to transport Saudi troops to Asir to crush an uprising earlier that year, Abdul Latif told Grobba that Ibn Saud wanted Germany to play an important role in the economic and technological development of Saudi Arabia, helping to make the kingdom less dependent on Great Britain. Germany should compete with Great Britain and the United States for oil concessions in Saudi Arabia and should help to develop Saudi industry and transport, including a railway from Mecca to Medina as well as improved methods of transporting pilgrims to the holy cities from the Persian Gulf. Finally, Abdul Latif expressed an interest in purchasing weapons and munitions, as well as trucks and aeroplanes from Germany.

Grobba lent the Saudi agent a sympathetic ear, promising to recommend his proposals to Berlin, but warning him that Germany's own critical economic position would make it difficult for her to provide that kind of investment and assistance. So it proved, and Grobba later recounted in his memoirs the reasons for Germany's lack of interest in Saudi Arabia. In addition to her own economic problems and consequent lack of the necessary resources, Hitler felt that, in the event of war, Germany would never be able to defend her economic interests in Saudi Arabia, particularly oil concessions.[15] These reasons, however important, were of little consequence compared with Hitler's determination to conquer Germany's 'living space' in eastern Europe as the best source of food and raw materials, including oil, and his willingness to assign the Middle East to his would-be allies, Great Britain and Italy.

German lack of interest in the Saudi proposals in 1933 did not mean that Berlin was opposed to German economic expansion in the Middle East. The Hitler regime was eager to increase German exports to the area, to help bring Germany out of the Depression. The German economy had always been heavily dependent on exports.[16] Under the so-called 'New Plan' of September 1934 devised by Hjalmar Schacht, the minister of economics and director of the Reichsbank, imports were to be severely curtailed, exports were to be stimulated with government support, and Germany's foreign trade was to be steered away from her traditional trading partners in western Europe and North America towards northern, eastern, and south-eastern Europe, the Middle East, and South America – areas providing less competitive and more accessible markets for German manufactured goods, and at the same time sources of much needed raw materials.[17]

Grobba worked tirelessly to expand the Iraqi market for goods imported from Germany. The international boycott against German goods, organized early in 1933 in an attempt to halt the persecution of Jews in Germany, had quickly spread to the Jewish community in Iraq, and in April, Grobba warned Berlin that it could damage

Germany's economic interests there.[18] In July, however, Grobba was able to report that a counter-boycott of Jewish goods, both Iraqi and Palestinian, had been organized by the Iraqi Arab business community in protest against the situation in Palestine.[19] This second boycott served German interests in two ways. The Jews would see that the weapon they were so fond of using against Germany could also be used against them, and the call for the elimination of 'Zionist goods' from the Iraqi market was being accompanied by a call for more German goods. Grobba had made contact with the organizers of the anti-Jewish boycott, and encouraged their efforts.

Grobba also encouraged the extension of the Haavara transfer agreement to Iraq in 1934.[20] Besides promoting Jewish emigration from Germany and German exports to Palestine, the agreement was seen as a means of neutralizing the world-wide anti-German boycott. One of the architects of the agreement, the German consul-general in Jerusalem, Heinrich Wolff, sought to expand the Haavara system beyond the borders of Palestine to other states in the Middle East, particularly to Syria, Egypt, and Iraq.[21] Grobba supported Wolff and reported to Berlin in November 1934, that local Jewish importers who had previously boycotted German goods now showed an interest in importing German goods by means of the Haavara system.[22] Its extension to Iraq might therefore help to compensate for Germany's lack of investment capital, the aggressiveness of other countries in promoting their goods in Iraq, and the anti-German boycott.

Most of Grobba's time through 1935 was spent trying to promote German exports in Iraq. His efforts reflected the priorities for the Middle East and the German economy established in Berlin; they also fitted Grobba's view of Germany's interests, even if they fell short of the more ambitious plans he would have liked to develop. Nevertheless, his efforts did result in expanding Germany's trade with Iraq by 1937, not an easy task in view of Great Britain's natural trade advantages in its former mandate. The trade statistics for the years 1932 to 1937 were bolstered after the commercial treaty with Iraq was signed on 4 August 1935.[23] During those years, the total value in Iraqi dinars of German imports into Iraq tripled from 211,346 to 632,365, while the percentage of German goods in Iraq's total imports rose from 2.91% to 6.6% and Germany's position among countries from which Iraq imported goods rose from seventh to fifth.[24] In 1938, Germany moved into third place behind Great Britain and Japan in exports to Iraq, with German goods amounting to 11.5% of total Iraqi imports.[25] Grobba's export drive in Iraq was particularly aimed at the oil industry. Germany had acquired a 12% share in the British Oil Development Company in Iraq in 1930, and had added a 10% share in Mosul Oil Fields Ltd. in 1932. Germany imported little or no Iraqi oil during the 1930s, but concentrated instead on selling the drilling, railway, and pipeline equipment needed in the search for, production, and transport of Iraqi oil.[26]

If economic questions inside Iraq preoccupied Grobba during his first three years in Baghdad, he became increasingly involved in political questions outside Iraq after 1935. As Iraq had achieved a nominal independence in 1930, it was natural that the unrest and turmoil generated by the intensifying clash between Arab nationalism and Anglo-French imperialism would be more acute in other parts of the Arab world, particularly in Palestine with its unique triangular conflict involving Arab nationalism, Zionism, and British imperialism. The apparently irreconcilable aims of each of the components of the Palestine triangle, coupled with the deteriorating situation in Europe and the threat of war during the second half of the decade, served to increase the importance of Germany's political role in Palestine and the role of Grobba as her most senior diplomat in the area.

It was inevitable that Germany, particularly through her diplomats in the Middle East, would become the target of requests for diplomatic and material support for the Arab cause. The governments of the Weimar Republic had received such requests, as Arab nationalists tended to view Germany as a fellow-victim of the peace settlement, and as the only great power without a history of imperialist domination in the region.[27] Moreover, the nationalist fervour and militaristic pose of the new regime in Germany, its determination to remove what it considered to be the inequities of the hated post-war settlement, and its anti-Jewish philosophy and policies all combined to make Germany appear the natural ally of Arab nationalism.

As much as German representatives in Palestine, Grobba became the target of requests for German assistance.[28] In 1935 and 1936, Grobba was approached by Palestinian, Syrian, and Iraqi Arabs for various forms of German assistance in Palestine, ranging from propaganda, to formal diplomatic support, to the provision of weapons for Arab insurgents in Palestine.[29] His response to these overtures remained consistently negative. He repeatedly expressed Germany's sympathy for the efforts of other people to achieve their rights, but stated that Germany could not actively support Arab efforts in Palestine or elsewhere because of her desire for friendly relations with Great Britain, although he did advise Berlin to maintain unofficial contact with these groups. Prior to the crisis years of 1938 and 1939, Grobba was restricted in his ability to increase German influence by the need to avoid any conflict with the British. He was particularly careful to reject requests for German weapons for the Arabs in Palestine, to limit himself to vague declarations about the right of all people to national self-determination. Despite his own sympathy for the Arab cause, Grobba never forgot that German interests in the Middle East rested on friendship with Great Britain, a realization which fitted Hitler's strategic view that avoiding conflict with Great Britain was a necessary condition for his coming conquest of Europe. In February 1935, Grobba was cautioned by Berlin to avoid even informal, unofficial contact with Arab nationalist groups.[30] Two years later, a German foreign office note generally reinforcing Grobba's refusal of active, official, German support, exemplified both the influence on Grobba of Berlin's view of Germany's overall strategic requirements, as well as the influence on Berlin of Grobba's perception of Germany's interests in the Middle East.[31]

By 1936, with the outbreak of the Arab revolt, developments in Palestine seemed likely to complicate Germany's relations with Iraq. In August, Grobba warned Berlin that as Palestine became increasingly unsettled, public opinion in Iraq might force the government to join the Arab side, something likely to disrupt Germany's friendly relations with Great Britain.[32] Iraq had already joined Saudi Arabia and Yemen in demanding that Great Britain prohibit further Jewish immigration and the sale of Arab land to Jews, send a royal commission to Palestine, and create in Palestine a national Arab government.

Until the publication of the Peel Commission report on Palestine in July 1937, Grobba's communications with the German foreign office regarding Palestine contained virtually no explicit recommendations or personal preferences. He merely reiterated to Iraqi and other Arab representatives that Germany, while sympathetic, must remain strictly neutral owing to her desire for friendly relations with Great Britain. However, the crisis in Palestine in the spring of 1936 led to more vehement demands on Germany by the Arabs for diplomatic and material assistance. More important, the recommendation of the establishment of an independent Jewish state, certainly not in the Nazi interest, led to a complete re-examination in Berlin of the previous German policy of promoting Jewish emigration to Palestine, which had facilitated what Germany now wished to prevent. This debate in Berlin among government and party agencies over German Palestine policy in 1937 and 1938 was bound to affect German policy in the rest of the Middle East, in particular Germany's attitude to Arab nationalism.

That Grobba had not been happy with the Hitler regime's active promotion of Jewish emigration from Germany to Palestine is apparent from his communications with the foreign ministry early in 1937, some months before the publication of the partition plan. As early as January 1937, there was much speculation in Europe and the Middle East, including the German foreign office, that the Peel Commission might recommend an independent Jewish state in some part of Mandatory Palestine. In January, Grobba reported on his discussions in Baghdad with members of the Arab Higher Committee from Palestine.[33] He stressed the warning the members of the committee had given to him, namely that a Jewish Palestine would always be hostile towards Germany, whereas an Arab Palestine would be a natural friend, and that Germany had little choice but to support the Arab cause. He also implied that the Arabs were finally beginning to make the connection between Germany's support for Zionist emigration to Palestine and the demands for a Jewish state. While Grobba answered the Arab spokesmen with the usual protestations of German sympathy tempered by Germany's need of friendship with Great Britain, he did urge Berlin to recognize the importance of their arguments.

In the spring of 1937, Grobba joined forces with the other proponents of change in German Palestine policy, among them the consul-general in Jerusalem, Wilhelm Döhle, and *Referat Deutschland* and the *Auslandsorganisation* in the foreign office, departments which respectively concerned themselves with the foreign policy implications of Nazi Jewish policy and the interests of overseas Germans. Grobba again expressed his alarm over the negative effect of German support for Zionist emigration to Palestine on German prestige among the Arabs, and urged a more sympathetic response, short of material assistance, to Arab national aspirations.[34] Opposed to the creation of an independent Jewish state in Palestine for strategic reasons, Grobba recommended that fewer German Jews should be encouraged to emigrate to Palestine lest a Jewish state become inevitable. In April, he outlined his views on Palestine and the Jewish National Home to General Sir John Dill, the British GOC in Palestine.[35] Grobba told Dill that Great Britain should keep to a strict interpretation of the Balfour Declaration; that the promise of a 'Jewish State' in Palestine should mean a symbolic state, with perhaps a self-governing core along the lines of the Vatican – the city of Tel Aviv and its surroundings, for example. Clearly Grobba was recommending cutting back German promotion of Jewish emigration to Palestine, and a more public posture of sympathy, short of direct diplomatic or material assistance, for the Arab cause.

Grobba's views were in part incorporated into official German policy in response to the expected recommendations of the Peel Commission. On 1 June 1937, the German foreign office informed the German embassies in London and Baghdad, and the German consulate-general in Jerusalem, that a Jewish state in Palestine was not in the German interest, that a strengthening of the Arab position in Palestine to offset the growing Jewish strength was in the German interest, and that Germany should make its position known to the other powers in a way that would not involve Germany in the events in Palestine.[36] The foreign ministry gave special additional instructions to each of the three missions, telling Grobba to give clearer public declarations of understanding for Arab national ambitions without promising active support. Thus, the instructions changed virtually nothing and fell far short of the active involvement, including the diplomatic support and supplies of weapons, the Arabs wanted from Germany. However, the foreign ministry did promise a complete review of emigration policy, specifically the policy of promoting Jewish emigration from Germany to Palestine and the Haavara agreement, to determine their contribution to the pressure for a Jewish state.

From Baghdad, Grobba tried to influence the debate in Berlin over emigration policy and the Haavara by sending frequent reports about the angry reaction in Iraq to the publication on 7 July of the Peel partition plan.[37] He reported his conversations with the prime minister, Hikmet Sulayman, with Iraqi military officials, with leaders of an Iraqi protest committee against the partition plan, and with representatives of the Arab Higher Committee from Jerusalem, retailing their threats and describing their efforts to organize Iraqi intervention in support of the Arab cause to Palestine. In this way, Grobba seemed to be recommending less emphasis on Palestine, the reduction or termination of the Haavara system, and the steering of Jewish emigrants to other parts of the world. His main concern was to sever the obvious link between Germany and the rapid growth of Jewish strength in Palestine in order to preserve Germany's popularity in the Arab world, rather than to stop Jewish immigration into Palestine altogether. He no doubt realized that even a complete end to German-Jewish immigration into Palestine would be offset by an increase in Jewish immigration from other parts of Europe.

Grobba's objectives for Germany in the Palestine crisis did not come close to achievement. The debate in Berlin in the summer and autumn of 1937, and early 1938, was ended by Hitler, who directed that Germany's remaining Jewish population should be forced out of the country, regardless of their destination.[38] In short, despite Grobba's reports to Berlin of Arab anger over German emigration policy and Germany's promotion of Jewish emigration to Palestine,[39] the removal of Jews from Germany took precedence over Middle Eastern policy. Jewish emigration from Germany to Palestine, legal and illegal, continued with active German support in ever greater numbers in 1938 and 1939.

Germany's new, more outspokenly pro-Arab, public posture in 1938 and 1939 did not represent a change in the substance of German policy in the Middle East. For one thing, the possibility of a Jewish state, which had alarmed Germany in 1937, seemed to vanish as the partition plan, rejected by both Arabs and Jews, was dropped by the British government. Yet, German propaganda became more critical of Great Britain and supportive of the Arab cause in Palestine, even though the need to bolster the Arabs as a counterweight to the Jews seemed to have vanished with the partition plan. The reasons for the new posture must be found, therefore, primarily in the needs of German policy in Europe as the Hitler regime prepared for war, as well as in the continuation of its previous policy of promoting exports to the Middle East. If Grobba had been seeking to establish a solid German position in the Arab Middle East, one that was nevertheless compatible with British interests, the German government continued to use the Middle East, if in a different manner from previous years, primarily to influence events in Europe in 1938 and 1939.

Germany's new public posture on the Middle East actually became part of a broader anti-British propaganda campaign in 1938 and 1939, as the Hitler regime sought to distract Great Britain from the crisis in Europe. Much of the ammunition for this campaign was provided by the always volatile situation in the Middle East, particularly in Palestine. Early in 1938, Germany began broadcasting in Arabic from a transmitter at Zeesen, broadcasts which stressed Arab–German friendship and criticized Anglo-French policy in the Middle East.[40] These broadcasts, accompanied by criticism of British policy on German radio and in the German press, with vague references to the legitimate national aspirations of the Arab people, never called for an end to British power in the Middle East, nor did they demand immediate Arab independence. On several occasions, Hitler himself joined the propaganda campaign against Great Britain, particularly as the crisis over Czechoslovakia intensified in the summer and autumn of 1938. In speeches to the Reichstag on 20 February 1938, the Nuremberg party rally in September, at Saarbrücken on 9 October, at the Bürgerbräukeller in Munich on 8 November, and at Wilhelmshaven on 1 April 1939, Hitler reproached Great Britain for her criticism of German racial policy and her resistance to German policy on Austria, Czechoslovakia, and Poland. Each time, he repeatedly referred to Great Britain's problems in Palestine and the Middle East, criticizing the British treatment of the Arabs and their denial of legitimate Arab rights.[41]

That the German propaganda campaign against Great Britain in 1938 and 1939, with its strong and persistent criticism of British policy in Palestine and the Middle East, was neither an attempt to undermine Great Britain's position nor an attempt to bolster the cause of Arab independence, was evident to the British, who concluded that Hitler's sudden interest in the Middle East was designed to put pressure on Great Britain in order to distract the British government from central and eastern Europe.[42] Further evidence of the nature of Germany's new posture in the Middle East can be deduced from Germany's brief intervention in the Palestine crisis during the summer and autumn of 1938, when Germany agreed to provide a small amount of money and arms to be funnelled by German intelligence to Arab insurgents in Palestine.[43] Grobba was used on at least one occasion to relay £800 to Haj Amin al-Husayni, the mufti of Jerusalem, in Damascus, while German intelligence attempted unsuccessfully to channel a few weapons into Palestine by way of Saudi Arabia.[44] The Munich Agreement and the end of the

Czech crisis brought an end, however, to Germany's brief, limited material assistance to the Arabs in Palestine.

Grobba's view of Germany's new, pro-Arab posture in the Middle East was mixed. Generally, there existed an important difference between him and Berlin. For Grobba, the goal of German Middle East policy was in the Middle East itself – increasing German economic and political power and influence in the region – while the goals of the Hitler regime were to be found in Europe, preparing for European war. An important ingredient of both was the avoidance of conflict with Great Britain, while the German government increasingly treated the area as Italy's sphere of interest. Berlin did not pursue Grobba's goal in the Middle East, as the achievement of Germany's goal in Europe would terminate her interest in the region.

Yet the new posture was, in spite of ultimate differences in aims, consistent for the most part with Grobba's view. He enthusiastically reported to Berlin on the positive impact of Hitler's speeches in 1938 on Arab opinion, and of the German press and radio campaign on Germany's standing with Iraqi public opinion.[45] He helped to arrange for an Iraqi youth organization (*Futuwwah*) to attend the Nuremberg party rally in September 1938.[46] It seems doubtful, however, that he favoured the brief attempt to provide money and arms to Arab insurgents in Palestine. While Grobba always favoured a clear and explicit position of public support for the Arab position in Palestine, and thus the retention of Arab friendship by Germany, he was equally opposed to any action that would directly provoke Great Britain by appearing to threaten her imperial interests, as he repeated in a report to Berlin in November 1937 on his talks in Baghdad with Sheikh Yussuf Yassin, Ibn Saud's secretary.[47]

It was in selling weapons to Iraq and Saudi Arabia that Grobba became most active in promoting Germany's interests in the Arab world in 1938 and 1939. Germany again began to export weapons in 1936, largely a reflection of the Hitler regime's policy since 1933 of increasing exports in order to earn much-needed foreign currency to pay for imports of food and raw materials. Of course, in the Middle East as elsewhere in Africa and Asia, export opportunities for Germany were limited by the varying degrees of continued European colonial rule. Moreover, Hitler's massive rearmament programme did not leave many weapons to export, and even if there had been a surplus, none of the states in the area were in a position to pay for

German weapons with the hard cash that Germany required.

Grobba took the initiative in promoting the sale of German weapons in Iraq and Saudi Arabia almost immediately. The resumption of German sales coincided with the *coup d'état* by Hikmet Sulayman in October 1936 which brought to power a regime eager to lessen its dependence on Great Britain, particularly on British weapons, and to move closer to Germany.[48] By the Anglo-Iraqi treaty of 30 June 1930, which replaced Great Britain's mandate by a military alliance, the British had kept their military installations in Iraq and Iraq had been required to purchase its weapons from Great Britain. It was understood, however, that Iraq might look elsewhere when Great Britain was unable to meet Iraq's needs. This loophole enabled Grobba to promote German arms sales in Iraq while avoiding a conflict with Great Britain.

According to Grobba, the new Iraqi regime immediately requested five million marks worth of German military equipment, including anti-aircraft guns and grenades, which prompted two of Germany's leading arms manufacturers, Rheinmetall-Borsig of Berlin and Otto Wolff of Cologne, to send agents to Baghdad.[49] With Grobba's encouragement, the Iraqi government also requested the sending of a German officer to Iraq to assess Iraqi needs. Although not much is known of the visit made early in 1937, Grobba indicates in his memoirs that the officer, Colonel R. Heins, tried to temper the anti-British passions of Bakr Sidqi of the Iraqi army.

It is clear from Grobba's correspondence with the German foreign office that he did everything in his power to arrange for Germany to meet some of Iraq's military needs, albeit with the full knowledge and understanding of Great Britain. In early January, he sent a warning to Berlin that Italy was trying to sell arms to Iraq, implying that Germany might lose a good opportunity.[50] Grobba repeatedly stressed to the reluctant foreign office, which feared provoking London, that Great Britain would not object to Iraqi purchases of weapons from other sources as long as Great Britain, owing to her own rearmament, was unable to provide what Iraq required.[51] He added that Iraq's wish to purchase weapons from Germany was not intended as an attack on Great Britain. Iraq needed weapons primarily to control rebellious tribes, maintain national unity, and defend the country against its natural enemy, Iran. Great Britain understood this and therefore approved of the purchase of German weapons and of Grobba's close relationship with the Iraqi government.[52] Finally, Grobba also sought to reassure Berlin that Iraq could pay cash for any weapons.[53]

So strongly did Grobba believe that Germany should sell arms to Iraq that he disregarded the growing British reservation in the summer of 1937 about an Iraqi–German arms agreement. Grobba reported that the British were worried by the conflict in Palestine, by the renewal of Arab violence after the publication of the partition plan in July, and by Iraq's role as a leading opponent of the plan.[54] On 24 July, he urged Berlin to sign an arms agreement with Iraq, even if Great Britain objected, because Iraq had already ordered fighter aircraft and tanks from Italy, a transaction to which Great Britain had also objected but without any effect.[55] Grobba argued that Great Britain would always resent competition for British goods in Iraq, but that Germany must fulfil Iraq's requests for weapons in order to be perceived by the Arabs as a reliable trading partner in the future. Finally, he claimed that his recommendation was in keeping with Germany's new public posture in favour of the Arabs, would help to counter the plan for a Jewish state, and would stiffen the Arabs' resistance to it.

Aside from the ministry of economics, few in Berlin shared Grobba's enthusiasm for promoting the sale of weapons to Iraq. The ministry of war informed the foreign office in April that Germany could not supply the arms desired by Iraq because of Great Britain's insistence that arms purchased from other countries be of the same calibre as British arms, and because Germany, like Great Britain, was unable to spare many of the weapons Iraq wanted owing to its own rearmament.[56] Even arms producers in Germany such as Krupp and Rheinmetall-Borsig, who took part in the discussions with the Iraqi government, were uncertain whether the Anglo-Iraqi treaty of 1930 permitted them to sell weapons to Iraq, and if so, whether Great Britain would acquiesce in this kind of German economic penetration.[57]

Germany and Iraq finally signed their first arms agreement on 9 December 1937, although for fewer weapons than the Iraqi government and Grobba had desired. Rheinmetall-Borsig would merely supply Iraq with eighteen 2cm. anti-aircraft guns, with ammunition, at a cost of £92,082.[58] Two other arms agreements would be made between Germany and Iraq before the war. In September 1938, Germany sold Iraq eighteen 2cm. machine guns and in April 1939, eighteen more 2cm. anti-aircraft guns.[59] These figures, and the even lower figures for German sales to the other Arab states, clearly illustrate Germany's inability to supply large numbers of weapons owing to her own massive rearmament programme. However, they also demonstrate an unwillingness to alter German policy in the Middle East and thus the complete lack of substance to its apparently pro-Arab public posture after 1937.

Grobba met with similar frustration in 1938 and 1939 as he attempted to promote closer ties between Germany and Saudi Arabia, again by selling weapons. The tone of his correspondence with Berlin, and the intensity of his efforts firmly to establish Germany's position in Iraq and Saudi Arabia seem to show that he assumed that the deepening crisis in Europe was bound to lead to war between Germany and Great Britain.

Grobba and Germany became targets for arms requests from both Ibn Saud and his opponents late in 1937 and early in 1938, about the time Iraq had succeeded in obtaining some German weapons. The king's personal secretary, Yussuf Yassin al-Hud, with Grobba's support, approached representatives of the German firm Otto Wolff in Baghdad, with a request for 15,000 rifles and credits with which to pay for the weapons.[60] In March, al-Hud was sent to Berlin to press the Saudi request for arms, including 25,000 rifles with ammunition, as well as for closer political and economic co-operation with Germany.[61] Both requests were politely rejected by the foreign office, even more reluctant to sell arms to Saudi Arabia than to Iraq. Werner-Otto von Hentig, the head of Abteilung VII, the department in the foreign office responsible for the Middle East after 1936, was firmly opposed to the sale of weapons to Saudi Arabia, as were the economics section of the foreign office and the ministry of economics. Hentig believed that Germany could never protect its interests in Saudi Arabia in opposition to the British and, along with the economic authorities, faulted Saudi Arabia for its inability to pay for German goods in cash.[62] Grobba's only achievement was the establishment of diplomatic relations between Germany and Saudi Arabia and his own accreditation to Saudi Arabia as well as Iraq.

While Grobba did not disagree with Hentig's assessment of Saudi Arabia's vulnerability to British power, he did press the case for meeting at least some of the Saudi requests. Early in 1939, with the threat of war in Europe intensifying, he urged the under-secretary of state in the foreign office, Ernst Woermann, to supply some weapons, along with a general declaration of German sympathy for Arab independence, in order to preserve Saudi goodwill for Germany.[63] Grobba renewed his appeal to Woermann in May, at a time when the crisis over Poland had convinced even Hitler that war with Great Britain was probably unavoidable.[64] Grobba argued that as Germany would soon be at war with Great Britain, the neutrality of Saudi Arabia would be of considerable value, and could easily be obtained in return for the supply of a few weapons. Even Hentig changed his view of German arms sales to Saudi Arabia by May, as he too seems to have accepted the inevitability of war with Great Britain, and thus Grobba's argument that Germany would need friends in the Middle East.[65]

When al-Hud returned to Berlin in the middle of May 1939, he found the foreign office more receptive and was even allowed to meet Hitler. On 17 June, Hitler approved the sale to Saudi Arabia of 8,000 rifles with ammunition, the construction there of a small munitions factory, and the agreement in principle for future sales of anti-aircraft guns and tanks.[66] Although the agreement was extended in July to include anti-aircraft guns, none of the weapons was delivered, owing to the outbreak of war in September. The Hitler regime may never have intended to supply the weapons, but only to use the threat of arms sales to Saudi Arabia as a lever on Great Britain during the crisis over Poland, much as it had used Palestine the year before during the Czech crisis.

Grobba's hopes were dashed, in Baghdad as well as in Berlin, upon the outbreak of war. Hikmet Sulayman's government had been overthrown by Jamil Midfa'i in August 1937, and he in turn by Nuri al-Sa'id in December 1938. Nuri had opposed the drift away from Great Britain towards Germany, and severed diplomatic relations with Germany on the outbreak of war in Europe.[67] Grobba no doubt expected this; he notes in his memoirs that one reason for the decision to open diplomatic relations with Saudi Arabia was to provide Germany, in the event of war, with a neutral haven from which to maintain German influence.[68] However, when the break with Iraq came, Berlin refused to permit Grobba to go to Saudi Arabia, ordering him to return to Germany.[69]

Fritz Grobba was unquestionably the most interesting and controversial German agent in the Middle East during the 1930s, and remains so among scholars today. Much of the controversy has been generated by the aggressive and expansionist character of Nazi foreign policy, the result of the Nazis' determination radically to alter the post-war settlement by force and illustrated in Grobba's active style and tireless efforts to rebuild Germany's economic and political position in the Middle East. Yet Grobba's idea of Germany's proper objectives in the Middle East differed from those of his government.

Grobba's fondest wish was to restore Germany's position as a major political and economic power in the Middle East, within the context of peaceful relations with Great Britain. For Grobba, the Middle East was an end in itself, an area in which he wished Germany to promote her exports and investment, show respect for British interests, place less emphasis on promoting Zionist emigration from Germany to Palestine and more on publicly supporting Arab nationalism, and show much less deference to Italian ambitions. The German government, on the other hand, viewed the region as a convenient means to reach more important goals in Europe. During the 1930s, the Hitler regime sought an alliance, or some form of understanding, with Great Britain as an essential step towards the conquest of central and eastern Europe, the removal of all Jews from Germany, economic recovery in part through a vigorous export drive, and an alliance with Italy. Of course, the objectives of the Hitler regime, and the policies it pursued to achieve them, are what mattered. Even if some of those policies were conducive to Grobba's vision of Germany as a Middle East power, he was bound to be frustrated in the end because his vision was not shared by his government.

NOTES

1. Elie Kedourie, *The Chatham House Version and Other Middle Eastern Studies* (London, 1970), p. 220.
2. There is much literature on German policy and aims in the Middle East before 1914, among them Isaiah Friedman, *Germany, Turkey and Zionism, 1897-1918* (Oxford, 1977); Gregor Schöllgen, *Imperialismus und Gleichgewicht: Deutschland, England und die orientalische Frage 1871-1914* (Munich, 1984); Ulrich Trumpener, *Germany and the Ottoman Empire, 1914-1918* (Princeton, 1968).
3. The only recent attempt to examine German aims in the Middle East during the Weimar period is Francis R. Nicosia, 'Weimar Germany and the Palestine Question', *Yearbook of the Leo Baeck Institute*, xxiv (1979), 321-45.
4. Memorandum of von Schubert, 2 Sept. 1920, PA Pol. Abt. III, Politik 2-Palästina.
5. Foreign office memorandum on Palestine, No. 11b 245, 8 May 1922, PA Gesandtschaft Bern, Palästina 1922-37.
6. 'Bericht über meine Reise nach Palästina in März und April, 1925', III 0 1269, PA Botschaft Ankara, Pol. 3-Palästina, 1924-38.

7. The most recent account of Germany, the Palestine Question, and the Middle East during the 1930s is Francis R. Nicosia, *The Third Reich and The Palestine Question* (Austin, 1985).

8. In an interview in his home in Bad Godesberg on 30 June 1973, Grobba remarked that he and his staff in Baghdad were constantly watched by agents of the Sicherheitsdienst (Security Service) of the SS. Joachim von Ribbentrop, Hitler's foreign minister from 1938 to 1945, also mentions SD activities of this sort in his memoirs. See *Zwischen London und Moskau: Erinnerungen und letzte Aufzeichnungen* (Leoni am Starnberger See, 1953), pp. 128-9.

9. Fritz Grobba, *Männer und Mächte im Orient: 25 Jahre diplomatischer Tätigkeit im Orient* (Gottingen, 1967). The author was granted permission by the Grobba family in November 1985, to examine the papers in May 1986, too late for inclusion in this essay.

10. *Ibid.*, pp. 317-18.

11. Grobba's assessment was echoed by General Franz Halder, chief of the German general staff from 1938 to 1942, in his foreword to a study of Germany's relationship with the Arab nationalist movements, prepared for the United States army by two former German officers who had been involved in the Middle East, specifically in the half-hearted German efforts in Syria and Iraq in 1940 and 1941. Halder concluded that Germany had neglected to prepare the ground in the area for a serious threat to Great Britain before the war. See *German Use of Arab Nationalist Movements in World War II*, by General der Flieger a.D. Helmuth Felmy and General der Artillerie a.D. Walter Warlimont, with a foreword by Generaloberst a.D. Franz Halder, Historical Division Headquarters, United States Army–Europe, Foreign Ministry Studies Branch, n.d., USNA MS/P.207.

12. Majid Khadduri, *Independent Iraq: A Study in Iraqi Politics from 1932 to 1958* (London, 1960), p. 172.

13. For a brief description of the Arab response to the events in Germany in 1933, drawn from German records, see Francis R. Nicosia, 'Arab Nationalism and National Socialist Germany, 1933-1939: Ideological and Strategic Incompatibility', *International Journal of Middle East Studies*, xii (1980), 352-4.

14. Grobba to A[uswärtige] A[mt], No. 754, 15 June 1933, PA Pol. Abt. III-Wirtschaft: Saudi Arabian Wirtschaft.

15. Grobba, *Männer und Mächte*, pp. 94-5.

16. For a complete account of German economic policies under the Nazis see Dörte Doering, 'Deutsche Aussenwirtschaftspolitik 1933-35' (Diss. Berlin, 1969); Dieter Petzina, 'Hauptprobleme der deutschen Wirtschaftspolitik 1932-33', *Vierteljahrshefte für Zeitgeschichte*, xv (1967), 18-55; *idem, Autarkiepolitik im Dritten Reich* (Stuttgart, 1968); Hans-Jürgen Schröder, *Deutschland und die Vereinigten Staaten 1933-39; Wirtschaft und Politik in der Entwicklung des deutsch-amerikanischen Gegensatzes* (Wiesbaden, 1970).

17. See Hjalmar Schacht, *My First Seventy-Six Years*, tr. Diana Pyke (London, 1955), pp. 327-34. See also Petzina, *Autarkiepolitik*, p. 18.

18. Grobba to AA, No. 418, 27 April 1933, PA Pol. Abt. III, Politik 2-Irak.

19. Grobba to AA, No. 940, 19 July 1933, *ibid.*

20. The Haavara Transfer Agreement, concluded by the German government and Zionist groups in Palestine in August 1933, was designed to facilitate Jewish emigration from Germany to Palestine by enabling Jews to enter Palestine with some assets and, at the same time, prevent a flight of capital from Germany. Jewish assets were blocked in Germany and Jewish immigrants entered Palestine with a very small portion of their blocked assets in the form of German goods to be sold on the Palestine market. Thus, the German government facilitated the removal of Jews from Germany and the promotion of German exports, while the Jewish National Home in Palestine was

bolstered by the new immigrants who were saved from the horrors of Nazi persecution. See Werner Feilchenfeld, Dolf Michaelis, and Ludwig Pinner, *Haavara-Transfer nach Palästina und Einwanderung deutscher Juden 1933-39* (Tübingen, 1972); Nicosia, *The Third Reich*, ch. 3; David Yisraeli, 'The Third Reich and the Transfer Agreement', *Journal of Contemporary History*, vi (1972) 129-48.

21. See Wolff to Grobba, No. Empf. 29/34, 16 Aug. 1934, PA Pol. Abt. III, Sonderreferat-W: Finanzwesen-16.
22. Grobba to AA, No. 2687, 8 Nov. 1934, *ibid.*
23. The text of the treaty in German and Arabic can be found in PA HaPol Abt., Handakten Wiehl-Irak (Geheim).
24. 'Der deutsch-irakische Warenaustausch', Reichswirtschaftsministerium v.s No. 35, 5 April 1938, BA R/7-VI: 222/2. The value of the Iraqi dinar in 1932 was £1 or 20 Reichsmarks.
25. 'Wirtschaftsanalyse Irak', in *Deutsche Bergwerks-Zeitung*, No. 199, 27 Aug. 1940, BA R/7-VI: 222/2. German exports to Iraq during those years consisted mainly of cotton and wool textiles, iron and steel, machines, synthetic textiles, cars, electrical equipment and machinery, lumber and cement.
26. 'Jahresbericht 1934 der deutschen Gesandtschaft/Bagdad', 8 Feb. 1935, PA Pol. Abt. III-Wirtschaft, Irak-Allgemeines 3. In his memoirs, Grobba writes that he was active later in the decade in promoting the sale of German drilling, pipeline, and refinery equipment to American and British oil companies in Saudi Arabia, and that the California Arabian Standard Oil Company had been using much German equipment in Saudi Arabia and Bahrein during the 1930s. See Grobba, *Männer und Mächte*, p. 95.
27. See Nicosia, 'Weimar Germany', pp. 339-40.
28. For more on the requests made to German consular officials in Jerusalem, as well as those made to Grobba in Baghdad, see Nicosia, *The Third Reich*, ch. 6.
29. See the following reports by Grobba to the foreign office: Telegram No. 20, 20 Nov. 1934, and III O 574, 2 Feb. 1935, PA. Pol. Abt. III, Pol. 4-Pan Arab.Bund; No. 1335, 30 May 1936, PA Botschaft Rom, Politik 3-Palästina; No. 3121, 17 Dec. 1936, PA Pol. Abt. II, Pol. 3-England, Bd. 1; No. 1671, 30 June 1936, PA Pol. Abt. VII, Politik 5-Palästina, Bd. 1.
30. AA to Grobba. No. 2, 12 Feb. 1935, PA Pol. Abt. III. pol. 4-Pan Arab. Bund.
31. Pilger to Grobba, zu Pol. VII 116, 5 Jan. 1937, PA Pol. Abt. VII, Politik 2-Palästina. Bd. 1.
32. Grobba to AA, No. 2184, 21 Aug. 1936, PA Pol. Abt. VII, Politik 36-Palästina.
33. Grobba to AA, 116-37, 5 Jan. 1937, PA Pol. Abt. VII, Politik 2-Palästina, Bd. 1.
34. Grobba to AA, No. 799, 8 Apr. 1937, PA Pol. Abt. II, Politik 3-England, Bd. 2.
35. *Ibid.*
36. Foreign minister to London, Jerusalem, and Baghdad, 83-21A 25/5, 1 June 1937, *ADAP*, No. 561.
37. See Grobba to AA, No. 1674, 10 July 1937, No. 1692, 13 July 1937, No. 1730, 15 July 1937, No. 1752, 17 July 1937, and No. 1771, 20 July 1937, PA Pol. Abt. VII, Politik 5a-Palästina, Bd. 1.
38. See Nicosia, *The Third Reich*, pp. 126-44.
39. See, for example, Grobba to AA, No. 2950, 16 Nov. 1938, PA Gesandtschaft Beirut, Paket 63, Bd. 2.
40. See Seth Arsenian, 'Wartime Propaganda in the Middle East', *Middle East Journal*, ii (1948), 419-21.
41. See Max Doramus, *Hitler: Reden und Proklamationen 1932-45*, I. ii (Munich, 1965), 904-5, 956, 969; II. i (Munich, 1965), 1121-2.
42. See foreign office memorandum, 22 Nov. 1938, FO 371/21665-C14758; war office memoranda, 2 March, 7 May 1939, FO 371/23232-E2274.
43. See Nicosia, *The Third Reich*, pp. 185-7.

44. Great Britain suspected, but was never quite certain, that some German money was going to the Mufti in 1938. See 'Report of the High Commissioner for Palestine', May 1938, FO 371/21877-E3137; foreign office memorandum, 12 Aug. 1938, FO 371/21887-E4838; foreign office memorandum, 14 Dec. 1938, FO 371/21872-E7560. The United States was convinced that German money was making its way into Palestine. See memorandum of Paul Alling, 21 Oct. 1938, USNA, State Department Decimal Files, 867N.01/1329.

45. Grobba to AA, No. 2471, 4 Oct. 1938, BA R/-II:142143.

46. Grobba to AA, No. 2037, 11 Aug. 1938, PA Inland I-Partei, Bd. 1. The invitation was extended by Baldur von Schirach, leader of the Hitler Youth, during his visit to Iraq in August 1938.

47. Grobba to AA, No. 2633, 9 Nov. 1937, PA Pol. Abt. VII, Politik 2-Palästina, Bd. 1.

48. See Khadduri, *Independent Iraq*, ch. 5.

49. See Grobba, *Männer und Mächte*, pp. 157-8.

50. Grobba to AA, No. 1304, 1 Jan. 1937, PA HaPol Abt., Kriegsgerät: Handel mit Irak (Geheim), Bd. 2.

51. See, for example, Grobba to AA, Telegram No. 6, 8 March 1937, Telegram No. 26, 12 May 1937, *ibid.*, Bd. 1. That the German foreign office had severe misgivings about selling weapons to Iraq due to its fear of antagonizing Great Britain is evident from 'Aufzeichnung zur Randnotiz auf dem Bericht des deutschen Gesandten in Bagdad vom 24 Juli 1937', No. 1823, 29 July 1937, *ibid.*, Bd. 2.

52. See Grobba to AA, No. 679, 20 March 1937, *ibid.*, Bd. 1; same to same, EWB/RO, 19 June 1937, PA Büro des Chefs des AO, Irak, Bd. 92.

53. See Grobba to AA, Telegram No. 25, 12 May 1937, PA HaPol Abt., Kriegsgerät: Handel mit Irak (Geheim), Bd. 1. The German ministry of economics, always a firm supporter of German exports, favoured the sale of weapons to Iraq, but only on the condition that they be paid for immediately in cash. Germany almost never extended credit terms to buyers of its weapons. See Reichswirtschaftsministerium to AA, II301/37g, 29 May 1937, *ibid.*

54. Grobba to AA, No. 1717, 15 July 1937, *ibid.*, Bd. 2.

55. Grobba to AA, No. 1823, 24 July 1937, *ibid.*

56. Reichskriegsministerium to AA, Pol. I I793, 3 April 1937, *ibid.*, Bd. 1.

57. In October 1937, officials of Rheinmetall-Borsig went to London to obtain British approval for its sale of weapons to Iraq, as well as to Egypt, Iran, and Ireland. According to the British embassy in Berlin, Rheinmetall-Borsig was instructed by the German ministry of war to work with rather than against Great Britain and her interests in the Middle East. Great Britain expressed her reluctance to permit German arms into Iraq and Egypt because of treaty arrangements with those countries, and also expressed reservations about the sale of German arms to Saudi Arabia and Afghanistan. Nevertheless, British officials did grant permission to Egypt and Iraq to purchase from Germany arms that Great Britain was unable to provide. See war office memorandum, Oct. 1937, FO 371/20911-J4567 (Secret Papers, 1937). See also Friedrich Krupp AG to AA, No. 32532/Pba/Va, 8 March 1937, PA Hapol Abt., Kriegsgerät: Handel mit Irak (Geheim), Bd. 1.

58. See Grobba to AA, No. 2921, 12 Dec. 1937, *ibid.*, Bd. 2.

59. See 'Kriegslieferungsverträge' (Geheim), e.o. W746g, 10 Aug. 1938, PA Hapol Abt., Kriegsgerät (Geheim): Handel mit Kriegsgerät-Allgemeines, Bd. 3. For a complete list of all German sales of weapons to the Middle East from 1936 to 1939, see Nicosia, *The Third Reich*, appendix No. 13.

60. Grobba to AA, No. 2765, 21 Nov. 1937, PA Pol. Abt. VII, Politik 5-Palästina, Bd. 3.

61. Aktennotiz betr. Besprechungen mit al-Hud, 17 March 1938, PA Parteidienststellen-Aussenpolitisches Amt, Politische Berichte-Saudisch Arabien. The Aussenpolitisches Amt of the NSDAP, the Nazi party agency responsible for foreign policy under Alfred

Rosenberg, became active in Afghanistan and Saudi Arabia in 1938 and 1939, providing Grobba with his only ally in the effort to sell weapons to the Saudis. The APA had virtually no power, however, as Hitler always preferred to use the traditional foreign policy apparatus in the foreign office.

62. See Hentig to Woermann, zu Pol. VII 1263, 6 Sept. 1938, PA Pol. Abt. VII, Politik 2-Saudisch Arabien, Bd. 1; Hentig to Malletke/APA, n.d. *ibid.*

63. Grobba to Woermann, No. Dj.44, 18 Feb. 1939, *ibid.*

64. *ADAP*, D, VI, No. 313.

65. See *ADAP*, D, VI, No. 422; Hentig to Ribbentrop, Pol. VII 949, 9 June 1939, PA Pol. Abt. VII, Politik-2 Saudisch Arabien, Bd. 1.

66. *ADAP*, D, VI, No. 541.

67. See Khadduri, *Independent Iraq*, p. 174.

68. Grobba, *Männer und Mächte*, p. 114.

69. *Ibid.*, p. 183.

XIII

MODERN EDUCATION AND THE EVOLUTION OF SAUDI ARABIA

Mordechai Abir

A university's business is to increase, to safeguard and to transmit learning . . . with this ideal . . . religious tests and political preoccupations are alike incompatible.

Elie Kedourie[1]

Saudi Arabia has a territory of 865,000 square miles and a citizen population of five million.[2] With the exception of Asir in the south and a score of oases, the largest of which is al-Hasa in the east, it is a country of varied desert landscape, in which until recently, the tribe or clan was the most important socio-political structure. At mid-twentieth century more than half the population were still nomads (*badu*), and perhaps thirty-five per cent settled (*hadr*) and semi-settled.[3] Barely ten per cent lived in the kingdom's major towns. The number of bedouin had begun to decline in the first half of the century, a process greatly accelerated after the 1950s by massive urbanization sparked by increasing oil wealth and modernization. By the early 1980s only ten per cent of the population was fully nomadic, and only about twenty-five per cent settled or semi-settled culti-vators.[4] On the other hand, the main urban centres grew dramatically and by 1980 claimed forty-two per cent of the total population, though towns of under 100,000 people had somewhat declined.[5]

Illiteracy in Saudi Arabia at the middle of the twentieth century was said to be as high as ninety-five per cent.[6] Traditionally, the teachers of the devout and of the sons of the ruling élites were the ulema, who taught in addition to their religious and judicial duties. The puri-tanical Wahabi ulema, however, limited themselves to the study of religion and to the interpretation of the *shari'a*, totally rejecting the study of any other subject.

The Hejaz with its holy cities was of old a centre of Islamic scholarship, and in the twentieth century it benefited from the development of 'modern' education in the Ottoman Empire. Yet, except for Arabic and geography, the curriculum of its handful of 'modern' schools remained almost exclusively based on the study of the Koran and related subjects.[7]

In 1926, Ibn Saud created in the kingdom of the Hejaz (conquered in 1924) a directorate of education (*mudiriyyat al-ma'arif*) under his Egyptian adviser, Hafiz Wahba, who opened the first secondary school, reformed the public schools, and introduced modern subjects into the curriculum. For this purpose Wahba hired teachers from Egypt and between 1926 and 1931 sent some young Hejazis to study there. His activities naturally aroused substantial opposition among the ulema, whose leaders strongly protested against his policy. Yet the king supported Wahba's programme, which he considered essential for national integration and his kingdom's development.

Ibn Saud, however, prudently tried to avoid a confrontation with the ulema, and whenever they protested at his innovations, sought a compromise. As his meagre revenues suffered in the 1930s from the world economic recession and its aftermath, until after the Second World War the development of modern education in Saudi Arabia was slow and largely confined to the Hejaz, leaving the ulema with a *de facto* monopoly.

Faced with the challenges of a modern world after he had begun to unify his kingdom, Ibn Saud increasingly recruited Arabs from outside the kingdom to help with the running of his government. He realized, however, that to modernize Saudi Arabia and promote national unity, he needed the support of educated Saudis who would eventually replace the traditional administrators and foreign experts. Accordingly, despite the financial difficulties of the early 1940s, Ibn Saud, in an effort to advance Saudi education, hired many more Egyptian and other Arabic speaking teachers, and sent more Saudis to study in Egypt. Commercial exploitation of oil in Saudi Arabia, after 1946, speeded these efforts which eventually caused the progressive Egyptianization of Saudi education.

In 1949, Aramco launched a five-year plan for the development of the skills of its employees and by 1952, 8,000 company workers had benefited. Not only were handpicked Saudi employees sent for training to the American University in Beirut (AUB) and later to the United States, but Aramco also provided modern education for their children and for other children in the eastern province.[8] Of course, Aramco was not motivated exclusively by philanthropy: its investment in education was necessitated by its operations and the need to Saudiize its workforce. Yet its contribution to the development of modern Saudi education, especially in the eastern province, is very important.

In 1949 and 1952 respectively, an Islamic College and a teachers training college were founded by the directorate of education in Mecca to offer subjects such as Arabic language, history, and civilization. Yet the curriculum of schools and colleges continued to be dominated by religious and Arabic studies.

The ulema, led by the kingdom's grand mufti, countered the administration's move by modernizing and reorganizing the traditional system of education. Thus, the grand mufti founded in Riyadh a college of Islamic jurisprudence (1953) and one for Arabic language (1954) which also offered courses in Arab history and civilization.[9] This pattern of adding related subjects to religious studies and adopting a modern framework became the trend thereafter in secondary and higher religious education; it was also part of a subtle competition between the ulema-controlled educational system and the state system. Eventually, however, the ulema realized that they could not turn the clock back and though they continued their efforts to adapt traditional education to the new situation, they now strove as well to become the supervisors of the development of 'modern' education.

The death of King Ibn Saud and the rise of his son Saud in 1953 signalled the revival of the power of the conservatives on one hand and the emergence of Saudi nationalists on the other. King Saud (reigned 1953-64) is generally described as a reactionary who abrogated some of his father's reforms and even in 1955 instructed all Saudis studying abroad to return home. In this way he gained the co-operation of the ulema, who were suspicious of his heir (and prime minister) Faysal's reformist tendencies.[10]

There were achievements, however. A ministry of education was created in 1953 to replace the Hejaz directorate and although students up to college level in schools abroad were indeed ordered in 1955 to return home, many more were sent to foreign universities. Indeed, the number of schools and students in all levels of education tripled or quadrupled during Saud's reign and the budget for education, $2.8 million in 1953, grew to nearly $100 million in 1964.[11] King Saud, moreover, established the first secular university in the kingdom in 1957 (Riyadh University), and in 1958 adopted a three-cycle sequence of education: six years of elementary school, three years of intermediate, and three years of secondary school.

It would be misleading, of course, to attribute these achievements solely to Saud, because Faysal practically ruled the country during 1958-60 and 1962-4. Although Saud was a conservative and a weak ruler, he nevertheless helped to develop modern Saudi education; paradoxically, he even allied himself in 1960 with the liberal princes and the small new Western-educated élite who were dissatisfied with Faysal's evolutionary reforms.

When Arab nationalism, with its strong anti-colonial and anti-Western overtones, erupted in the early 1950s following the Egyptian revolution, it found immediate support among young educated Saudis. Ironically, Aramco trainees, especially those sent abroad in the late 1940s and 1950s, were in the forefront of the nascent anti-American and anti-monarchy Saudi nationalism; in fact, they led the first strikes in the Saudi oil industry in 1953 and 1956 (claims against Aramco had anti-American overtones) and they joined the ranks of the pro-Nasser new élites in their strange coalition in 1960-2 with King Saud.

Encouraged by events in the region and the split within the royal family between Saud and Faysal between 1953 and 1964, the new Saudi middle class nationalists, though still few in number, attempted to change the character of the Saudi kingdom and its government. Impatient with Faysal's mild reform programme, they, together with the liberal princes led by Prince Talal, supported King Saud's bid to resume full authority in 1960. They hoped, it seems, eventually to oust the House of Saud altogether. Although their quixotic adventure collapsed in 1962, the advent of an educated élite introduced a new factor into the Saudi power equation.

The ulema joined Faysal's camp only in 1961. Their frustration with Saud's incompetence reached its peak when he allied himself with the new élite and the liberal princes, whose reformist zeal they feared. Although he ignored the ulema's opposition to modernization,

Faysal followed his father's policy and tried to win their support for his reforms through concessions and compromises. For example, after pioneering girls' education in 1960 in the face of violent opposition,[12] Faysal placed the new general directorate of girls' education under the grand mufti. Subsequently, ulema-controlled female education became completely segregated and male teachers communicated with women students through closed-circuit television. The more conservative continued to reject girls' education altogether. Thus, only fifty per cent of Saudi girls attended elementary schools in the 1970s and a smaller proportion intermediate and secondary schools.[13] In recent years this tendency has been reversed. More females enrol in schools because educated girls make better marriages.

Because of ulema support in his struggle with his brother Saud in 1961-4 and their acquiescence in his reforms, Faysal in effect granted them the supervision of the modern education system. After his appointment of Sheikh Hassan al-Sheikh minister of education in 1962, the ministry became a stronghold of conservatives and graduates of the Islamic universities. Then in 1970 Faysal established the general directorate of religious institutions and colleges through which the government funded the religious system of education, and in 1975, when the government was reorganized by Prince Fahd and a ministry of higher education created, Sheikh Hassan was appointed its head and a technocrat replaced him as minister of education.

Paradoxically, the ulema, who at first opposed modern education, practically controlled it under Faysal. The curriculum of Saudi schools came to be focused on Islamic and Arabic studies to the point where mandatory Islamic courses comprised a third of the curriculum in elementary schools and nearly a third at the intermediate and secondary levels.[14] Elementary school graduates could opt for a religious stream in separate intermediate and secondary schools, but even if they did not, they would be constantly reminded of the organic relationship between the Saudi state and the Wahabiyya.[15] Consequently, the new generation of Saudis, their minds conditioned by the educational system, were largely conservative in outlook. However, the ulema, though not unaware of the far-reaching social and cultural changes generated by Faysal's modernization programme, continued to co-operate with Faysal, who was careful to preserve the kingdom's puritan-Wahabi framework and their special status within it.

Whatever the achievements of Saud's period, it was Faysal's

accession to the throne in 1964 that facilitated the great leap forward of modern Saudi education. Faysal believed that the modernization of Saudi Arabia was conditional on the emergence of a large educated élite, and was determined to provide, eventually, a minimum level of education for every Saudi. Though he prudently slowed down the expansion of elementary education because of financial constraints in the mid-1960s and shifted the focus to quality from quantity, simultaneously he accelerated the development of secondary and higher education, and the vocational system. Yet, notwithstanding a substantial investment in the latter in the 1960s, and even more in the 1970s, vocational training failed to attract sufficient students, owing to the low prestige of manual work in Saudi society. There were other more attractive opportunities open to young Saudis after the late 1960s.[16]

In the 1970s and early 1980s the mammoth expansion of the Saudi education system was facilitated by the enormous rise in state revenues from the sale of oil, and the planning – with American help – of educational development. The kingdom's first five-year development plan (1970-5), prepared in 1969, had projected a substantial expansion of the different levels of education, but no one envisaged the vast growth of the kingdom's oil revenues after 1973, or the huge budgets for the 'development of human resources'.[17]

The rapid development of modern education, which in fact ensued, necessitated more than ever the employment of foreign teachers and administrators. At first this dependence on foreigners (mainly Egyptians) was nearly total, but after the mid-1960s, when a major effort was made to expand and improve the training of teachers, an increasing number of them were employed in school administration and as teachers at the elementary level. Even so, although today it is claimed that elementary education is practically Saudiized, at the intermediary and secondary levels the dependence on foreigners is very high.[18]

Possibly more serious is the poor quality of the Saudi education system itself. Two major reasons for this are the low standard of foreign teachers and the Egyptian model followed by the Saudis. Saudi teachers who replace foreigners in elementary and secondary schools are generally no better than their predecessors, which is why Faysal's government attempted to improve and expand the teacher training colleges in the late 1960s.[19] The vast expansion of the Saudi education system in the 1970s together with the accelerated development of the economy, however, completely undermined his efforts. As demand for the limited Saudi manpower constantly increased, educated Saudis were being snapped up by the private and public sectors, while the lower levels of the teaching profession were not considered sufficiently prestigious or rewarding. Thus the poor quality of teaching in Saudi schools remains a problem to this day.[20]

When Faysal was assassinated in 1975, Prince Khaled (reigned 1975-82) came to the throne. The true ruler of Saudi Arabia, however, was Prince Fahd, Khaled's heir and prime minister. Fahd's reformist enthusiasm had been restrained by Faysal, whose closest assistant Fahd was, but after Faysal's death Fahd immediately stepped up the modernization programme, which, added to the rapid industrialization of the country, necessitated accelerated manpower training. As there was no shortage of funds, the education system was therefore expanded at an unprecedented rate; by 1983, the total number of students in Saudi schools had risen to about 1,600,000 (thirty per cent of the population) compared to 33,000 in 1953.[21] The fourth development plan (1985-90) projects for 1990 about 2,105,000 students, of whom 937,000 will be girls.[22]

The enormous expansion of modern education and the substantial decline of illiteracy in Saudi Arabia since the 1960s are impressive achievements. Yet, Saudi statistics are often inaccurate, if not misleading,[23] and they do not reflect the low standard of the education system or the social composition of its students. The quality of schools and students varies according to geographical and social environment. Rural and urban lower class students, with relatively backward conservative (largely bedouin) backgrounds, are often unprepared for the systematic approach and foreign philosophy of modern education. In the rural areas, where the standard of teaching is even lower than in the cities, the number of dropouts and repeaters in the first years of elementary school is exceptionally high. Beyond these first years, education has no economic value for rural students who do not wish to change their way of life. The same is true, to a lesser degree, of many lower class students in the poorer sections of the big cities, largely populated by the newly urbanized who, despite generous grants, are incapable of, or uninterested in, continuing their studies beyond the first grades. An exceptional case is that of the Shiites of the eastern province, who until the 1980s were intentionally discriminated against by the Wahabi kingdom. Their best chance to acquire education above the elementary level then was through the Aramco schools, and the few who studied in Saudi or foreign universities did so, in most cases, on Aramco scholarships.[24]

Not surprisingly, only about one-third of elementary school students reached the intermediate level in the 1970s and less than six per cent of those who had entered first grade reached a secondary level.[25] Saudi statistics take no account of the middle and upper classes' disproportionate benefits from subsidized education, and other government services. Middle and upper class children, especially from the major towns in the Hejaz, were better prepared for modern education and also had access to better schools with more qualified teachers. Children of the Nejdi *hadr* and aristocracy were not far behind them. These groups also dominated secondary education and enrolment in Saudi or foreign universities in the 1960s and 1970s.

However, the government is not unaware that the first two development plans (1970-80) favoured the urban population, especially the middle and upper classes. One of the aims of the third and fourth development plans (1980-90) is to improve the standard of living in the rural areas, where traditional social differences are polarized by modernization, particularly modern education. Although such aims often remain unfulfilled, the numerous successful lower class entrepreneurs have not been constrained by their minimal education, or social background. Their children have made good students in the last decade and are considered part of the new middle class.

Determined not to remain completely dependent on foreign higher education, Ibn Saud established in Mecca a college of *shari'a* in 1949 and a teacher training college in 1952. These colleges, and their Taif extension, opened the first period of Saudi higher education (1949-57).

Evidently in competition with this government system, the grand mufti established in Riyadh a *shari'a* college in 1953 and an Arabic language college in 1954, which, as they offered more generous scholarships, attracted students away from government institutions. Their growth was so rapid that by the early 1960s they had graduated over 2,000 students with 1,000 more on the way, which helped prolong somewhat the conservatives' hegemony in education and in the Saudi administration.[26]

At this stage, both state and ulema-controlled colleges, despite the use of modern terminology, were still traditional institutions. The government, because of its growing need for modern bureaucrats, continued therefore to send young Saudis to study in Egyptian and other Arab universities and, from the 1950s, increasingly to European and American ones. This costly, and to the Wahabi ulema undesirable, solution was considered by the authorities an interim measure, and in 1957 King Saud founded in Riyadh the first Western-type university.

The establishment of Riyadh University ushered in the second period in the development of Saudi higher education (1957-75). Older colleges were consolidated into, or merged with, full scale universities, while new ones were opened elsewhere in the kingdom, in a rapid development of higher education intended to facilitate Saudi Arabia's modernization and economic development. King Faysal, who dominates this period, appears to have hoped to offset the tensions arising from this rapid modernization and social change by enabling talented Saudis to acquire university education and so benefit from their country's prosperity.

The accelerated development of the universities was made possible by the increasing availability of funds. Numerous Egyptian and other Arab professors and administrators were hired, and most new universities adopted an Egyptian model based on the British system of higher education. Although the influence of the many US-trained bureaucrats caused the Egyptian/British format to be replaced in 1974-5 by an American one, Egyptians and other foreigners continue to dominate the faculties of most Saudi universities.[27] As in other aspects of the Faysal era, the path of development was facilitated by concessions to the ulema; thus, Islamic universities and schools became government funded and religious courses were mandatory in the curriculum of the 'secular' universities.[28]

Riyadh University (in 1980 King Saud University – KSU) is the stronghold of the Nejdi 'aristocracy'[29] and is somewhat more conservative than other 'secular' universities. It grew from 21 students in 1958 to 5,600 in 1975, to about 17,000 in 1984-5,[30] and has several campuses, including one in Asir.

The Islamic University of Medina was established in 1961 following consultations between foreign fundamentalists (mainly Egyptians), Wahabi ulema, and the Saudi authorities. It was hoped that it would eventually replace Al-Azhar (following its reorganization by Colonel Nasser in 1961) as an international Islamic university: in fact, ninety per cent of its staff and the majority of its students are foreign Muslims.[31]

The University of Petroleum and Minerals (UPM) in Dhahran (eastern province) is the best and most prestigious university in the country. Established by Aramco in 1963 as the College of Petroleum and Minerals (P&M), it became a university in 1975. The UPM is a US enclave in Saudi higher education: its teaching language is English, its faculty is largely American, and it is the least constrained by Wahabi custom. Unlike other Saudi universities, its students (1,000 in 1974, 3,000 in 1980) are admitted solely on merit.[32]

Supported by Faysal since the mid-1960s the ulema-controlled Riyadh colleges became in 1974 The Imam Muhammad Ibn Saud Islamic University. A stronghold of Nejdi-Wahabi conservatism, this university was given the task of co-ordinating all Saudi religious schools and studies. In 1980-1, it had about 6,000 students of which twenty per cent were foreigners.[33]

King Abdul Aziz Ibn Saud University at Jedda was established in 1967-8 by local philanthropists as a Western-oriented business institution. In 1971, it became a state university ('secular') and the two Mecca colleges and their offshoot in Taif were temporarily affiliated with it (they became the nucleus of Umm al-Qura University in 1980). Thereafter, its orientation became more Arabic-Islamic, and in 1977 it opened a new campus in Medina. From 90 students in 1967-8 it grew to 2,500 in 1974-5 and 17,000 in 1980-1.[34]

King Faysal University (KFU), the fourth and smallest 'secular' university, was established in 1974-5. Its main campus in Hufuf (eastern province) specializes in agriculture and veterinary science and medicine; while in Dammam is a medical campus with a programme in medical science. Its international faculty is largely American; after 1980, it established a full range of faculties; and its student body grew from 1,430 in 1980-1 to nearly 5,000 in 1985.[35] KFU was intended to provide for the special needs of the agricultural and bedouin population of the eastern province and to supply some of the trained manpower required for its sophisticated new industries. Since 1980, because of the regime's efforts to mitigate the traditional discrimination against the Shiite minority, the university has enrolled a growing number of Shiite students.

Umm al-Qura University (Mecca) was formed in 1980, its nucleus the colleges founded in 1949 and 1953. In so far as Medina University is an international Islamic institution, Riyadh, it seems, intended Umm al-Qura to serve the conservative population of the Hejaz. A synthesis of the traditional and the modern, Umm al-Qura's enrolment requirements and standards are even lower than is usual in Saudi universities. In 1983 it had nearly 6,000 students of which about one-quarter were foreigners.[36]

By 1975, there were nearly 20,000 students in Saudi universities, yet despite the intention of reducing the number of Saudis in foreign universities, there were more than 5,000 Saudis studying abroad. Some, mainly offspring of wealthy merchants (largely Hejazis, but also Nejdi *hadr*) and Nejdi aristocrats, studied at their own expense, many others, mostly of middle class background, were given government stipends throughout their graduate and postgraduate studies.[37] On their return to Saudi Arabia, these graduates of foreign universities were often appointed to important positions in Faysal's new administration and even in his government. Graduates of the 'secular' domestic universities (mostly of *hadr* or urban middle class background), if they did not choose the private sector, were appointed to lesser but still prestigious positions. Subsequently, bureaucrats of middle and upper class background, largely Hejazis and to a lesser degree Nejdis, came to dominate the Saudi administration (with the exception of the ulema-controlled ministries and legal system, where the trainees of the Wahabi ulema were preferred), at the expense of traditional bureaucrats and graduates of religious institutions.

The third period in the development of higher education in Saudi Arabia (1975-84) coincides with the rise to power of Prince Fahd (king in 1982) and the second and third development plans. Although this was a period of almost uncontrolled growth in the existing universities, it saw a further decline in their standards. The substantial acceleration of Saudi modernization and economic development from 1974 increased the demand for educated Saudi manpower. Budgets for the 'development of human resources' became enormous: multi-billion dollar campuses were built for the universities and for women's colleges, and thousands of foreigners, again mainly Egyptians, were hired to teach in them.

Not only were 'campus mercenaries', as foreign faculty are called by Saudi intellectuals, usually not of the highest quality;[38] but Saudis who opted for a university career were also, in many cases, poorly qualified. As in the past, teaching still focused on 'cramming' and memorizing, rather than on evaluation and analysis.[39] The transformation in 1974-5 from the Egyptian–British structure to the

American one introduced the semester system and credit hours, but that was not enough to improve the universities' standards. Indeed, Egyptian and other foreigners have remained the backbone of the faculty in most universities to this day.

The rapid expansion of Saudi higher education after the 1960s was partly facilitated by the growth of secondary education, mainly in urban centres. In 1974, enrolment requirements in the 'secular' universities were noticeably lowered 'by order of the government' to provide higher education to more students,[40] who in addition to free education, housing, stipends, and other privileges, were assured of government employment on graduation. Such concessions were obviously motivated by the regime's need to defuse socio-political tensions. The majority of students normally opted for the less demanding humanities and social sciences; only a small minority chose engineering and sciences, which were badly needed in the kingdom's developing economy. Therefore, although the number of graduates rose quickly in the 1970s, it could not satisfy the demand. Nevertheless, women graduates were discouraged from seeking work and no more than 50,000 women were employed in the Saudi economy in 1980-1.[41]

Meanwhile the Saudi bureaucracy continued to absorb all the graduates of domestic and foreign universities who applied for government service. The great majority of these flocked to the ministries and government agencies in Riyadh, avoiding appointments in rural areas, and rejecting any connection with manual labour. By the early 1980s large sections of the administration had become inflated with university-trained bureaucrats which exacerbated the prevailing inefficiency.[42]

In 1985, Saudi Arabia's seven universities and fourteen women's colleges have a total student population of approximately 80,000. The number of Saudi students abroad continues to rise and is estimated at about 20,000. Moreover, additional universities are scheduled to open soon in Riyadh (women), Taif, and Abha (Asir). Indeed, the total number of students in Saudi Arabia is projected to rise by 1990 to 108,000 with 20,000 graduates annually.[43]

In addition to Aramco, the growing American involvement in Saudi education arises from the strong ties developed by Faysal's reformist government with the United States since 1958. American influence in Saudi education was formalized through bilateral agreements, the most important of which was the establishment of the United States–Saudi Arabia Joint Commission on Economic Co-operation in 1975, which, *inter alia*, deals with Saudi education.

American influence was absorbed and later spread by the increasing number of Saudi students enrolled in American universities in the 1960s and 1970s whose number surpassed 15,000 by the early 1980s.[44] Subsequently, an office was set up in the Saudi consulate-general in Houston (moved to Washington in 1984) to help Saudi students and co-ordinate and supervise their studies. Those who returned to Saudi Arabia in the 1960s and early 1970s, mainly those with Ph.D. and Masters degrees, were appointed to key positions in the government's bureaucracy and education system. The second wave of foreign-trained graduates returning home since the mid-1970s has dominated most of the middle level of the civil service and government agencies, and increasingly the staff of the 'secular' universities. Besides their influence on the central government and its policy, their manners, ideas, and way of life have been copied by many others. Thus, the formal transformation of the universities from the Egyptian to the American system in 1975 seemed to the conservatives another aspect of the growing 'Americanization' of Saudi Arabia.

Frustrated by what they perceived as the Westernization of the Wahabi kingdom through uncontrolled modernization, many conservatives accused the government and its US-educated technocrats of helping to supplant Wahabi puritanism and 'the Saudi way of life' with Western culture and 'the American way of life'.[45] Even before the Mecca incident in 1979, Prince Fahd had come under growing pressure from the more extreme ulema and Saudi middle class nationalists to reduce Western influence in the kingdom. By the early 1980s, with the completion of the third development plan, even some American trained Saudis, unhappy with the impact of rapid modernization on their society and culture, began to question Western values and the aims of modern Saudi education which they had helped develop.[46] Indeed, after the Mecca incident, the influence of the ulema seemed again to be on the rise.[47]

As in other fields, Riyadh has tried to bridge centuries of backwardness by allocating larger and larger budgets for education. Certainly, for a nation whose illiteracy rate was ninety-five per cent thirty years ago, the development of Saudi education has been phenomenal. Yet its quality leaves much to be desired. Moreover, it is absurd that Saudi Arabia, experiencing an acute shortage of manpower and employing millions of foreigners, maintains a third of its population in school, some for indefinite periods. Indeed, for a nation of this size, the number of its students in domestic and foreign universities seems excessive.

Saudi Arabia's oil revenue has declined from about $108 billion in 1981-2 to about $37 billion in 1984-5.[48] Consequently Riyadh has been trimming its expenditures on one hand and drawing on its financial reserves on the other. For obvious reasons the allocations to services and subsidies, which benefit all Saudis, have been reduced only marginally, but Saudi Arabia will not be able to maintain its present level of expenditure and continue to drain its financial reserves for long. Thus, the education budget, a significant proportion of the total, could be noticeably reduced in the future.[49]

Nevertheless, the Saudi regime still employs all the university graduates who decide to go into administration. Now, however, unless graduates are from the UPM, with a badly required speciality, or are well connected, they must be satisfied with whatever job they get. Indeed, students have begun to adapt their studies to their country's needs. The question remains, however, whether Saudi Arabia can afford its extensive, wasteful, and inferior education system. Further economies may make it difficult to provide suitable employment for 20,000 university graduates annually.

Modernization, education, and the rapid urbanization of the rural population did not erase traditional differences, which already existed in the Saudi society (*hadr* and *badu*, Nejdi and Hejazi, Sunni and Shiite); rather they polarized them. Yet all this seemed irrelevant as long as oil revenues on a vast scale were pouring in.

The relatively small but growing proportion of lower class students with secondary education in the last decade often chose the Islamic universities with their traditional character and curriculum, easy admission requirements, and higher stipends.[50] Lower-class graduates from both Islamic and nonreligious universities, unless well connected, rarely reached high positions in the administration. This undoubtedly contributed to their interest in fundamentalist (neo-Ikhwan) ideologies and, since the 1960s, to the tension between graduates of Saudi religious universities and the 'secular' ones – and between both these groups and their Western-trained colleagues, who have captured most of the key positions in the central government and its agencies.[51]

As for the Shiites, who were not even permitted to enter government service or the armed forces until the 1980s, only a few advanced through the Aramco hierarchy and reached positions of importance in the administration and the economy. Frustration made them an easy target for fundamentalist Shiite propaganda from Iran and radical leftist ideologies to which they became exposed in the oilfields and in foreign universities. But theirs is a separate problem because even the lower class Sunnis would not associate with them.

As the number of university graduates continued to grow in the early 1980s, the three-sided competition for jobs has been extended to the lesser positions in the middle hierarchy of the civil service, and with economic recession, may eventually become explosive, accompanied as it is by social nuances and conflicting philosophies.

The rise of the Saudi middle class has been ably discussed by William Rugh[52] in the early 1970s. However, the dramatic growth of Saudi oil revenues and the acceleration of the kingdom's modernization in the 1970s on the one hand, and the dramatic rise in the number of educated Saudis on the other, have given new dimensions to this phenomenon. Faysal's policy in the 1960s and early 1970s, which enabled the new élites to participate in his government and share in the country's wealth, encouraged them to co-operate with his regime and, to some extent, to join its power base. Thus, notwithstanding two abortive attempts at coups in 1969 and a third rumoured in 1977, social unrest among the new middle class was avoided in the 1970s and early 1980s. Yet, despite the decisive role played by the new élites in their country's modernization and the dramatic expansion of their ranks, it is the Saudi aristocracy who still monopolizes the kingdom's decision and policy making. It remains to be seen how the new élites will react to the changes in their country's economy and position in the world, and whether social unrest can be avoided in the future. Continuous expansion of university education in Saudi Arabia while the economy is declining, is bound to exacerbate these problems.

NOTES

The author wishes to thank the Woodrow Wilson International Center for Scholars for a fellowship in 1982-3 which facilitated the research for this chapter.

1. Elie Kedourie, *Arabic Political Memoirs and Other Studies* (London, 1976), p. 66.

2. *Area Handbook Series: Saudi Arabia A Country Study* (Washington D.C., 1982), pp. 45, 63; Ramon Knauerhase, *The Saudi Arabian Economy* (New York, 1975), p. 13. Saudi statistics are often untrustworthy.

3. Ahmed A. Shamekh, 'Spatial Patterns of Bedouin Settlement in Al-Qasim Region Saudi Arabia' (Ph.D., Kentucky, 1975), pp. 247, 249; Motoko Katakura, *Bedouin Village: A Study of a Saudi Arabian People in Transition* (Tokyo, 1977), p. 6; George Arthur Lipsky, *Saudi Arabia: Its People, Its Society, Its Culture* (New Haven, 1959), p. 24.

4. Estimates for nomads range from five to twenty-five per cent. Ralph Braibanti and Fouad Abdul-Salam Al-Farsy, 'Saudi Arabia: A Development Perspective', *The Journal of South Asian and Middle Eastern Studies*, i (1977), 13; Fouad Abdul-Salam Al-Farsy, *Saudi Arabia: A Case Study in Development* (London 1982), p. 78; Abdulrahman H. Said, 'Saudi Arabia: The Transition From a Tribal Society to a Nation' (Ph.D., Missouri, 1979), pp. 115, 137, 156-7; Helen Lackner, *A House Built on Sand: A Political Economy of Saudi Arabia* (London, 1978), p. 175; 'Abd al-Amir al-Rikabi, 'Al-dawla wal da'awa fi al-'Arabiyya al-Sa'udiyya al-iftiraq shart al-tahaquq', *Qadaya 'Arabiyya* (June 1980), p. 73.

5. Kingdom of Saudi Arabia, Ministry of Planning: *Third Development Plan 1400-1405 A.H. – 1980-1985 A.D.*, p. 56.

6. Lackner, *House Built on Sand*, p. 74; Othman Al-Rawaf, 'The Concept of the Five Crises in Political Development: Relevance to the Kingdom of Saudi Arabia' (Ph.D., Duke, 1981), p. 244; John P. Entiles, 'Oil Wealth and the Prospects for Democratization in the Arabian Peninsula: The Case of Saudi Arabia', in *Arab Oil: Impact on the Arab Countries and Global Implications*, ed. Naiem A. Sherbiny and Mark A. Tessur (New York, 1976), p. 91.

7. Hafiz Wahba, *Arabian Days* (London 1964), p. 50; Said, 'Saudi Arabia', p. 75.

8. *Aramco Handbook* (Netherlands, 1960), p. 161; Najmudein Abdulghafour Jan, 'Between Islamic and Western Education: A Case Study of Umm Al-Qura University, Makkah, Saudi Arabia' (Ph.D., Michigan State, 1983), pp. 30, 33; Mohammed Eisa Faheem, 'Higher Education and Nation Building: The Case of King Abdul Aziz University' (Ph.D., Illinois at Urbana-Champaign, 1982), p. 3; Said, 'Saudi Arabia', p. 81; Leonard Mosley, *Power Play: The Tumultuous World of Middle East Oil 1890-1973* (Birkenhead, 1973), p. 327.

9. See below, higher education.

10. James Buchan, 'Secular and Religious Opposition in Saudi Arabia', in *State, Society and Economy in Saudi Arabia*, ed. Tim Niblock (New York, 1982), p. 108; *Jerusalem Post*, 1 July 1956; Fatina Amin Shaker, 'Modernization of the Developing Nations. The Case of Saudi Arabia' (Ph.D., Purdue, 1972), pp. 171, 222, note 48.

11. See Table 4; also Faysal M. Zedan, 'Political Development of the Kingdom of Saudi Arabia 1932-1975' (Ph.D., Claremont Graduate School, 1981), pp. 73-6; Ahmed Assah, *Miracle of the Desert Kingdom* (London, 1969), pp. 80, 298-307; Shaker, 'Modernization', pp. 170-1.

12. Before he was replaced by Saud at the end of 1960.

13. See *Third Development Plan* (Education), pp. 309-12. The number of female students has increased in the 1980s.

14. Donald Powell Cole, *Nomads of the Nomads: The Al Murrah Bedouins of the Empty Quarter* (Chicago, 1975), pp. 141-2, 153; Katakura, *Bedouin Village*, pp. 64, 115, 118, 157-9, 168-9; *Area Handbook*, p. 105.

15. *Ibid.*, pp. 102-3, 105. Also Said, 'Saudi Arabia', p. 111; Faheem, 'Higher Education', p. 77; Al-Farsy, *Saudi Arabia*, p. 166.

16. Mahmoud Mohammed Kinsawi, 'Attitude of Students and Fathers Towards Vocational Education in Economic Development in Saudi Arabia' (Ph.D., Colorado at Boulder, 1981), pp. 9-10, 90-1, 104; Said, 'Saudi Arabia', pp. 94-5; F[inancial] T[imes], 5 May 1981, supplement.

17. For instance $22.8 billion in the second development plan (1975-80). See Table 5.
18. Sixty-three per cent in intermediate and eighty-two per cent in secondary in 1981-2. Faheem, 'Higher Education', p. 137, note 56; *Area Handbook*, p. 100.
19. Assah, *Miracle*, p. 298; Entiles, 'Oil Wealth', p. 91; Shaker, 'Modernization', p. 222, note 48. On the Egyptian influence see Al-Farsy, *Saudi Arabia*, pp. 164-5; also Manfred W. Wenner, 'Saudi Arabia: Survival of Traditional Elites', in *Political Elites and Political Development in the Middle East*, ed. Frank Tachau (New York, 1975), p. 176.
20. *Area Handbook*, pp. 100-1, 112.
21. See Table 1.
22. King Fahd's speech, 21 March 1985, Foreign Broadcasting Information Service (FBIS), 22 March 1985; Alec Thomas, *FT*, 22 April 1985, supplement, p. ii.
23. For conflicting figures for elementary, intermediary, and secondary education see Kingdom of Saudi Arabia, Ministry of Finance and National Economy, Central Department of Statistics: *Statistical Year Book 1400 A.H. – 1980 A.D.*; Kingdom of Saudi Arabia, Ministry of Finance and National Economy, General Department of Statistics: T*he Statistical Indicator, Sixth Issue 1401 A.H. – 1981 A.D.*; *Third Development Plan* (education).
24. Shiites make up about seven per cent of Saudi Arabia's population, but they are about forty per cent of the population of the eastern province. Michael Field, *The Merchants: The Big Business Families of Arabia* (London, 1984), pp. 81-4. See also King Faysal University below.
25. *Area Handbook*, p. 105. See Abdullah Ali Al-Ibrahim, 'Regional and Urban Development in Saudi Arabia' (Ph.D., Colorado at Boulder, 1982), for instance pp. 151, 153-5, 211.
26. Center for Statistical Data and Educational Documentation: *Development of Education in the Ministry of Education . . . 1954-78* (Riyadh, 1978), pp. 13-15; Abdul Latif Tibawi, *Islamic Education: Its Traditions and Modernization into the Arab National System* (London, 1972), p. 182; William Rugh, 'Emergence of a New Saudi Middle Class in Saudi Arabia', *The Middle East Journal*, xxvii (1973), ll; Jan, 'Umm Al-Qura', pp. 55-7.
27. *Ibid.*, pp. 58-9; Tibawi, *Islamic Education*, p. 183.
28. Al-Farsy, *Saudi Arabia*, pp. 166-7; Said, 'Saudi Arabia', p. 111; Faheem, 'Higher Education', p. 77; Tibawi, *Islamic Education*, pp. 182-3.
29. The Nejdis, who dominate the Saudi regime, look down at the Hejazis whom they consider of mixed blood, whatever their socio-cultural background. Michael Field (*The Merchants*, pp. 30, 71-4, 83-4) suggests an interesting stratification of Saudi society.
30. Jan, 'Umm Al-Qura', p. 59; *Statistical Year Book*, p. 87; Kingdom of Saudi Arabia, Saudi Arabian Monetary Agency (SAMA), Research and Statistics Department: *Annual Report 1401(1981)*, (Riyadh, 1981) (henceforth, SAMA Report 1981), p. 89.
31. SAMA Report 1981, p. 92; Buchan, 'Secular and Religious Opposition', p. 123; Al-Farsy, *Saudi Arabia*, p. 156; Ibrahim M. al-Khudair, 'Islamic University at Madina, the Kingdom of Saudi Arabia: A History and Evaluation' (M.A., California State, 1981); Jan, 'Umm Al-Qura', pp. 61-3.
32. Fahad S. al-Hazzam, 'The College of Petroleum and Minerals, the Kingdom of Saudi Arabia' (Ph.D., Arizona State, 1975); Jan, 'Umm Al-Qura', pp. 63-6; John Shaw and David E. Long, The Washington Papers: *Saudi Arabian Modernization: The Impact of Change on Stability*, lxxxix (1982), 81-3.
33. SAMA Report 1981, p. 89; Al-Farsy, *Saudi Arabia*, pp. 156-7; William Ochsenwald, 'Saudi Arabia and the Islamic Revival', *International Journal of Middle East Studies*, xiii (1981), pp. 281, 283; *Statistical Year Book*, pp. 92-3.
34. Faheem, 'Higher Education', pp. 115-16, 141-51, 153-71, 180, 183; Jan, 'Umm

Al-Qura', pp. 66-8, 77-80; *Statistical Year Book* , pp. 88-9; SAMA Report 1981, p. 91.

35. *Third Development Plan* (education), pp. 322-33; Jan, 'Umm Al-Qura', p. 75; Al-Farsy, *Saudi Arabia*, p. 157; SAMA Report 1981, p. 89; Shaw and Long, *Modernization*, p. 81.

36. *Al-Nadwa* (Mecca), 25 March 1983, pp. 11-12; *Middle East Economic Digest (MEED)*, 29 March 1985; Jan, 'Umm Al-Qura', pp. 80-100, 105-8, 114-20.

37. The author's impression based on the study of over 120 theses written by Saudis for American and European universities. Hejazi and, to a lesser degree, Nejdi middle class and aristocracy practically monopolized Saudi secondary and higher education in the 1950s and 1960s and were the first to return to the kingdom with Masters and Ph.D. degrees from Western universities.

38. Faheem, 'Higher Education', p. 137, n. 56; also pp. 167, 172-3.

39. *Ibid.*, pp. 81, 124, 127, 177, 185-6; *Area Handbook*, p. 112; Anthony McDermott, *FT*, 22 April 1985, supplement, p. xi.

40. Faheem, 'Higher Education', p. 159.

41. *FT*, 26 April 1982, supplement; 8 *Days* (Beirut), 16 May 1981; *MEED*, 12 Oct. 1984, p. 47.

42. Faheem, 'Higher Education', p. 109; *MEED*, 30 April 1982; Rostam Kavoussi and Ali Reza Sheikoleslami, *The Political Economy of Saudi Arabia* (Seattle, 1984), p. 14-15; David Holden and Richard Johns, *The House of Saud* (London, 1982), p. 459; Al-Rawaf, 'Five Crises', p. 494; Amr al-Faruq Sayd Ragib, 'Nizam al-ta'alim wa-mutatallabat al-umalah fi al-mamlaka al-'Arabiyya al-Sa'udiyya', *Dirasat al-Khalij wal-Jazira al-'Arabiyya* (Jan. 1983), pp. 53-61.

43. Fourth development plan 1985-90, *MEED*, 29 March 1985, p. 33; *FT*, 22 April 1985, supplement, p. ii; Faheem, 'Higher Education', p. 4.

44. See Table 3.

45. James Buchan, *World Press Review* (July 1981), p. 30; Peter Mansfield, *FT*, 15 May 1981, supplement, p. xx; Faheem, 'Higher Education', pp. 111-12.

46. Faheem, 'Higher Education', pp. 111-12, 117-18; Jan, 'Umm Al-Qura', p. 31; Marguerite M. Marks, 'The American Influence on the Development of the Universities in the Kingdom of Saudi Arabia' (Ph.D., Oregon, 1980).

47. *I[nternational] H[erald] T[ribune]*, 22 Nov. 1983, 6 Aug. 1984, 16 April 1985; *Al-Madinah* (Saudi Arabia), 30 Nov. 1983; *Ma'ariv* (Israel), 22 March 1984; *FT*, 23 May 1984.

48. Probably less than in 1985-6. *Wall Street Journal*, 8 Jan. 1985; *FT*, 29 March 1985; *IHT*, 1 April 1985.

49. See Table 4. The allocations for education in the 1985-6 budget were already reduced substantially.

50. Nazih N. M. Ayubi, 'Vulnerability of the Rich: The Political Economy of Defense and Development in Saudi Arabia and the Gulf', a paper prepared for The Gulf Project, Center for Strategic and International Studies, Georgetown University (Washington D.C., May 1982), p. 19; Buchan, 'Secular and Religious Opposition', p. 123; Holden and Johns, *House of Saud*, pp. 516-17; *Al-Mawqif al-'Arabi* (Beirut), 20 April 1981.

51. Ochsenwald, 'Islamic Revival', pp. 278-9.

52. Rugh, 'Emergence'.

TABLE 1

Number of students in modern education system
1950s-1984

Year	No. of students	Level	Source
1953	33,000	All	(1)
1960	113,176	All	(2)
1970-1	512,071	All	(2) (3)
1973-4	698,519	All	(4) (5)
1975-6	1,057,994	All	(6)
	889,803	Primary, secondary & intermediate	(7)
1977-8	1,214,457	All	(6)
	1,020,509	Primary, secondary & intermediate	(7)
1979-80	1,452,856	All	(6)
	1,201,038	Primary, secondary & intermediate	(7)
1980-1	1,528,431	All	(8)
	1,287,183	Primary, secondary & intermediate	(7)
1982-3	1,600,000	Primary & secondary	(9)
1984	2,100,000	All	(1)

(1) King Fahd, *Sunday Times*, 2 Dec. 1984.
(2) Lackner, *House Built on Sand*, pp. 67, 79.
(3) Wenner, 'Saudi Arabia', p. 176.
(4) Lackner, *House Built on Sand*, p. 79.
(5) Entiles, 'Oil Wealth', pp. 91-2.
(6) *Statistical Year Book*, p. 40.
(7) *Statistical Indicator*, pp. 175-7.
(8) SAMA report 1981, p. 86.
(9) King Fahd's budget speech, Radio Riyadh, 13 April 1983, FBIS, 14 April 1983.

TABLE 2

Number of students in institutions of higher education
in Saudi Arabia 1955-1985

Year	Students	Graduates	Source
1950-4		31	Rugh, 'Emergence', p. 11.
1955-9		211	Rugh, 'Emergence', p. 11.
1960-1	1,300		Anthony McDermott, *FT*, 22 April 1985, supplement, p. xi.
1960-4		1,202	Rugh, 'Emergence', p. 11.
1969-70	6,942	488	Jan, 'Umm Al-Qura', p. 1; Rugh, 'Emergence', p. 11.
1974-5	18,966	1,885	*Third Development Plan*, p. 315.
1975-6	26,437		*Statistical Indicator*, p. 182.
	26,338	2,485	*Third Development Plan*, p. 315.
1976	14,500		Braibanti & Farsy, *Saudi Arabia*, p. 23.
1978-9	44,101		*Statistical Indicator*, p. 182.
	36,112	3,779	*Third Development Plan*, p. 315.
1980-1	54,397	5,448	SAMA report 1981, p. 89.
	56,252		*Statistical Indicator*, p. 182.
	42,957		Faheem, 'Higher Education', pp. 115-16.
1982-3	63,000		King Fahd's budget speech, 13 April 1983, FBIS, 14 April 1983.
	68,892		*Al-Riyadh*, 22 June 1983, p. 11.
1983-4	75,000	7,500	King Fahd's budget speech, 1 April 1984, FBIS, 2 April 1984, Riyadh SPA in Arabic.
1984	80,000		Alec Thomas, *FT*, 22 April 1985, supplement, p. ii.
1984-5	95,000		Anthony McDermott, *FT*, 22 April 1985, supplement, p. xi.
1990	108,000	20,000	*MEED*, 29 March 1985, p. 33, fourth development plan.

TABLE 3

Estimated number of Saudi students studying abroad*

Year	All Countries	In the US	Source
1947		7	Fahd Mohamed Al Nassar, 'Saudi-Arabian Educational Mission to the US', (Ph.D., Oklahoma, 1982), p. 44.
1953-4	43		Al Nassar, 'Mission', p. 32.
1961		200 (B.A.)	Assah, *Miracle*, p. 311.
1963-4	1,058		*Ibid.*
1964-5	393		Al Nassar, 'Mission', p. 32.
1973-4	944		*Ibid.*
1974-5	2,122		*Ibid.*
1975	5,108	2,003	*Ibid.*, p. 19.
1976	approx. 8,000	4,350	Braibanti & Farsy, *Saudi Arabia*, p. 160.
1979-80	10,035	6,896	*Statistical Year Book*, p. 107.
1980		13,000	*Washington Post*, 22 July 1980; *Al Fajr*, (Jerusalem), 26 Oct.-1 Nov. 1980.
		11,022	Al Nassar, 'Mission', p. 70.
1981	18,000		*The Middle East* (July 1981), p. 63
		14,000	*World Press Review* (July 1981), p. 70.
1982	over 15,000		Al Nassar, *Mission*, p. 3.
		13,000	Faheem, 'Higher Education', p. 131.
	30,000		Shaw and Long, *Modernization*, p. 26.
1983	12,505		*Al-Riyadh*, 22 June 1983, p. 11.
1983-4		20,000	*FT*, 22 April 1985, supplement.

*The number of privately financed students in the 1970s and 1980s is quite large but impossible to follow.

TABLE 4

Allocations for education in budgets 1952-1953 – 1985-1986
(in million Saudi Riyals) (1)

Year	Ministry of Education			Women's Education		Universities	
1952-3	12.5	($2.8m)	(2)				
1957		($33m)	(3)				
1960	122.0			2.0	(4)		
				(less than $1m.)	(3)		
1963-4	301.0		(3)	12.4	(5)		
		($78.7m)	(6)				
1965-6	473.0		(3)				
1970	665.0	($148m)	(2)				
1974-5						682.1	(7)
1975-6		($597m)	(8)			1,780.5	(7)
1976-7		($3.3bn)	(8)			2,666.7	(7)
1979-80						5,471.8	(7)
1981-2	9,835.0			4,867.0		8,333.0	(9)
1982-3	13,239.0			6,738.0		9,003.0	(9)
1984-5	11,535.0			6,535.0		9,840.0	(10)
1985-6	10,427.0			5,916.0		6,145.0	(11)

(1) US dollar denomination when available or when rate of exchange is known.
(2) Wenner, 'Saudi Arabia', pp. 175-6.
(3) Said, *Saudi Arabia*, p. 94.
(4) Assah, *Miracle*, p. 313.
(5) *Ibid.*, p. 314.
(6) Entiles, 'Oil Wealth', pp. 91-2.
(7) *Statistical Year Book*, p. 445.
(8) Ghassan Salameh, 'Political Power and the Saudi State', *MERIP Reports*, xci (1980), p. 15.
(9) *MEED*, 30 April 1982.
(10) FBIS, 4 April 1984.
(11) *MEED*, 29 March 1985.

TABLE 5

Allocations for Education in Five Year Development Plans (1)

Plan	Total budget	For education		%
First Plan 1970-75	SR56,223.0m	SR10,007.7m		17.8
Second Plan 1975-80	SR498,230.2m	SR74,161.0m		
	$142bn	$22.7bn	(2)	16
Third Plan 1980-85	SR782.8bn	SR101,171.0m		13
	$285bn	$54.15bn	(3)	19
	$268bn (4)			
Fourth Plan 1985-90	SR1,000,000m	SR125,523.0m		12.5
	$277bn	$34.8bn	(5)	12.5

(1) Sources: Kingdom of Saudi Arabia, Ministry of Planning: *Second Development Plan 1395-1400 A.H. – 1975-1980 A.D.*; *ibid.*, *Third Development Plan 1400-1405 A.H. – 1980-1985 A.D.*; *ibid.*, *Fourth Development Plan 1405-1410 A.H. – 1985-1990 A.D.* For first development plan see: Mohamed Mohsen Ali Assad, 'Saudi Arabia's National Security: A Perspective Derived from Political, Economic and Defense Policies' (Ph.D., Claremont Graduate School, 1981), pp. 109-10.
(2) Ghassan Salameh, 'Saudi Arabia: Development and Dependence', *Jerusalem Quarterly*, xx (1981), 113.
(3) Thomas A. Sams, 'Education and training in Saudi Arabia', *Business America* (13 July 1981), p. 12.
(4) Al-Ibrahim, 'Urban Development', p. 95.
(5) *FT*, 29 March 1985.

XIV

THE POLITICAL RELEVANCE
OF THE DOCTRINE OF JIHAD
IN SADAT'S EGYPT

Rudolph Peters

It is common knowledge that religion and politics in Islam
are closely related, and that in this relationship the
prevalent mode has been for the man of the sword to
dominate the man of the pen.

Elie Kedourie[1]

Since the beginning of the 1970s the doctrine of jihad has made a comeback in the Islamic world. While in previous decades it appeared to have faded to a mere theory – mainly a topic for academic discussion – occasionally it was allowed to play a marginal role in politics when Islamic dignitaries invoked it to spur on the fighting spirit of Muslim soldiers in the Arab–Israeli wars. However, since the beginning of the 1970s this has changed, and Islamic symbols and idioms have become more central to political discourse as Islamic movements have reappeared on the political scene. As a consequence, the doctrine of jihad has returned to favour.

The following paper deals with the political role of the jihad in Egypt under Anwar Sadat (1970-81). The word jihad has many meanings, usually connected with an effort towards a commendable aim, which is as a rule religious (such as the struggle against Satan or one's own evil inclinations) but need not be so. Ten years ago for instance, jihad for cleanliness of public places and the removal of garbage from the streets was proclaimed by the authorities in Cairo. The term will be discussed here, however, in its sense of fighting and armed struggle, which is its principal meaning in traditional Islamic law. Indeed, it seems appropriate to use the term in this way here,

252

as the period under consideration was terminated by a violent act that was justified by the doctrine of jihad.

When is violence permissible and against whom? These practical and concrete questions regarding the application of jihad doctrine are the central ones in this paper. The abstract and theoretical aspects of jihad are of minor importance, as hardly any novel points of view have been put forward on the subject during our period. The traditionalists copy the phrases of the classical works on *fiqh*; the modernists emphasize the defensive aspect of jihad, regarding it as tantamount to *bellum justum* in modern international law; and the fundamentalists view it as a struggle for the expansion of Islam and the realization of Islamic ideals.[2]

After a survey of the growth of Islamic movements in Egypt,[3] two discussions of jihad doctrine will be analysed here. The first is a debate on the application of the rules of jihad to the Camp David Agreement between Egypt and Israel. The other revolves around the question of whether jihad against the Egyptian government is allowable under the present circumstances.

The Arab–Israeli war of 1967 is usually regarded as having been crucial to Islamic revival in the Middle East. It marked not only the defeat of Israel's Arab neighbours, but also that of two radical Arab nationalist regimes, the result of which was to discredit the secular nationalist and socialist ideologies they espoused. One response was the rise of leftist radicalism, claiming that the defeated regimes had not been radical enough and represented by groups of intellectuals and university students, and by the various Palestinian nationalist organizations. Between 1967 and the October War of 1973 both were repressed: the leftist groups of intellectuals and students were dealt with locally, while King Husayn of Jordan acted as the proxy of the other Arab states in the region in subduing the Palestinian National Movement in 1970 and 1971.

The containment of the left was a corollary of the realignment of forces in the Middle East, another more lasting result of the 1967 defeat. If only for financial reasons, Egypt and Syria had to come to terms with the conservative Arab oil-producing countries, by abandoning their radical stance and bringing their policies more in line with the wishes of their patrons. As a result, a certain Islamization of political vocabulary and symbolism in political discourse took place, particularly evident in the October War of 1973 ('Operation Badr'), when religious images and concepts were much more frequently used than they had been in 1967.

Perhaps an even more important aspect of the new state of affairs in the region was the *rapprochement* between the erstwhile radical regimes and the United States. President Nasser's acceptance of William Rogers's plan for a settlement in the Middle East in 1970 anticipated Sadat's pro-Western policy, which – via the expulsion of the Soviet military advisers, the removal of the pro-Soviet faction in the state-apparatus, and the crack-down on Communist and Nasserist students – ultimately led to the Camp David Agreement in March 1979.

Connected with the establishment of American hegemony in the Middle East was the economic integration of the Arab states, especially Egypt, into the capitalist world market. After 1967, in order to gain the support of the middle and upper classes who had been alienated from the regime by its socialist economic policies, Nasser had inaugurated a policy of producing and importing more consumer goods. Sadat not only continued this policy, but gave it more prominence by announcing his Open Door Policy in 1975. The effect of all this was the rise of a section of the bourgeoisie that profited from the increased import trade of luxury consumer goods and, above all, from the increased economic links with other countries. This group delighted in the ostentatious display of its rapidly-acquired wealth, while the overwhelming majority of Egyptians was obliged to live off extremely meagre public sector salaries, or eke out a scanty livelihood as agricultural wage labourers. Such conspicuous consumption by the newly rich sharpened the social and economic contradictions in society.

Heightened social and economic tensions provide a fertile soil for radical movements militating against the established order for a just society. Such tensions are emphasized in the idioms in which radical movements express themselves, whether they derive from secular ideologies like socialism, anarchism, or fascism, or from religious thought. The ideology to which a specific movement subscribes is therefore contingent on the prevailing cultural and political conditions, and it is to these we must look for an explanation of why most of the Egyptian radical movements in the 1970s were inspired by Islam.

One important cause was the tension that existed in Egyptian culture. In the wake of reorientation towards the West, Western consumer goods and living styles had invaded certain sections of Egyptian society, via the mass media. In short, Western popular culture was much more in evidence in 1975 than in the preceding quarter of a century, and posed a threat to many people, especially those who lacked the financial means to join in, and thus felt themselves excluded. At the same time, the introduction of Islamic norms and ideals into politics and public life was stimulated by the government, which hoped to use Islam as a weapon against the left and simultaneously to curry favour with the Arab oil states. This contradiction between Western culture and the Islamization of public life and political discourse, in addition to the disparagement of leftist ideas in the wake of the 1967 defeat, and the government's persistent attack on the evils of 'atheist ideologies', created the conditions for the rise of Islamic movements, which sought to reform society in the direction of the Islamic norm.

The first movement of this kind consisted of the *Jama 'at Islamiyya* (Islamic Groups) at the Egyptian universities. They were founded around 1972 with active support from the government, in the hope of their countering the Communist and Nasserist student organizations then dominating political life at the universities and since 1968 the source of frequently staged protest meetings, demonstrations, and sit-ins against the government. However, though they were backed by the regime, the *Jama 'at Islamiyya* were not mere instruments with no will of their own. They had their own ideas and objectives, as is evidenced by their falling-out with the government over Sadat's journey to Jerusalem in 1977.

By then they had acquired a large following among students, as a result of assiduous work and clever organizing which, together with discreet government backing, had enabled them to take over the student unions in 1976-7. Part of their popularity was due to their ability to provide Islamic solutions to common problems such as transportation for women students, who were being harassed in the overcrowded buses of the Cairo public transport system. The condition in this case, however, was that women must thereafter wear Islamic dress. As an alternative to the expensive private lessons necessary to pass examinations, study groups were organized in mosques. Cheap copies of textbooks were distributed, and efforts made to improve student housing. At the same time the *Jama 'at Islamiyya* militated at the universities for the application of Islamic norms such as the separation of the sexes in lecture halls, the banning of film shows and singing, and the establishment of prayer rooms. As a demonstration of their popularity, they organized mass prayer meetings in large squares or in stadiums. Like all Islamic movements, the *Jama'at Islamiyya* wanted to create a truly religious society. They tried to mainly by peaceful means, which is to say by preaching, by creating a large following, and by themselves attaining influential positions in society.

The year 1977 was a turning-point for the *Jama'at Islamiyya*. Because of their critical stance towards Egypt's new policy *vis-à-vis* Israel, the government withdrew its support and began to work against them. It withheld subsidies from the student unions they dominated and tried to rig the unions' elections. Finally, in 1979, all student unions were banned, which deprived the *Jama'at Islamiyya* of their legal cover, their organization, and their funds. Many of their militants became more radical and in 1979 and 1981 were implicated in sectarian violence in Upper Egypt and Cairo. Their activities came to an end when many of their active members were arrested during Sadat's crack-down on religious groups in September 1981.

A second tendency within the Egyptian Islamic movement is represented by the group supporting the old magazine of the Muslim Brotherhood, *al-Da'wa*, which was allowed to resume publication in 1976. This group considers itself as the rightful heir of the Muslim Brotherhood of the 1930s and 1940s, and Hasan al-Banna's portrait is prominently featured on the magazine's pages. The social background of its following, however, is totally different. Whereas the membership of the Muslim Brotherhood of old was drawn chiefly from the lower and middle classes, the *al-Da'wa* group represents the interests of the section of the bourgeoisie that has profited from the Open Door Policy and has close economic ties with the Arab oil countries. This group wants Egypt to forge tighter political and economic links with oil countries, and is therefore against any *rapprochement* between Egypt and Israel.

It also wants to realize the ideal of the Islamic state by the introduction of Islamic Law, the *shari'a*, not by the overthrow of the state, but rather by means of press campaigns and lobbying, by legal means, and adherence to the established political conventions. A number of the group were arrested in September 1981 and their organ was banned. However, the group remained in existence and came to an agreement with the opposition Wafd party to join its election platform, with the result that the *al-Da'wa* group is now represented in the People's Assembly.

Both the *al-Da'wa* group and the *Jama'at Islamiyya* operated legally. As they were committed to the Islamization of state and society by peaceful means, they represented the reformist trend in the Islamic movement. The revolutionary trend consisted of a number of radical organizations that did not eschew the use of violence as a means of realizing their aims. They justified this by the doctrine of *takfir*, the view that in spite of all appearances, the rulers or even society as a whole is godless (*kafir*), an idea whose origins can be traced back to heretical sects in the early centuries of Islam and has recently been revived among the Muslim Brothers detained in the Egyptian prisons and detention camps.[4] The members of these organizations were mainly students and young university graduates with rural backgrounds. Entangled in the contradictions between their conservative background and university life in the big cities, they would frequent mosques and religious gatherings, where they could easily be recruited by the leaders and older members of these organizations.

There have been, and probably still are, several of these groups. But as they work clandestinely it is difficult to keep track of and get information about them. However, three of them have attained notoriety, being implicated in bloody incidents, after which their membership and leaders were tried and sentenced. In April 1974, a group led by Salih Sirriyya, a young Palestinian with a doctorate in science, carried out an attack on the Military Academy in Heliopolis, as the first stage in a planned *coup d'état*. The organization, named *Munazzamat al-Tahrir al-Islami*, but later commonly referred to as the Military Academy Organization (*Munazzamat al-Fanniyya al-'Askariyya*), was started in 1971 when Sirriyya came to Egypt. The plan – an act of violence – *ghadba lillah* (an outcry for the sake of God) – was to topple the government and establish a true Islamic state. The attempt was foiled, however, and the members of the group arrested and brought to trial.

Three years later, in July 1977, the members of another group, calling itself 'The Association of Muslims' (*Jama'at al-Muslimin*), but better known as *Jama'at al-Takfir wa-l-Hijra*, were arrested for having kidnapped and assassinated the minister of *Awqaf*, Muhammad Husayn al-Dhahabi. This organization was also established around 1971. Its leader, Mustafa Shukri, an agricultural engineer, had recruited members both in Upper Egypt and in Cairo and Alexandria. There is a curious contradiction between the basic tenets of the movement and the violent acts that marked its end. As had many other groups, it considered all outsiders as unbelievers (*takfir*). However, as it realized it did not yet have the strength to fight the prevailing unbelief, it saw its duty as separation from society (*hijra*) and building a genuine Islamic community. After the growth of this community and the attainment of a position of strength, it would wage the struggle against the rest of society with the object of establishing a totally Islamic society and state. It was a typical long-term strategy. However, when in the beginning of 1977 a number of the organization's members were arrested, many others pressed for immediate action to free their imprisoned brethren. They kidnapped al-Dhahabi – in their view a prominent representative of the corrupt establishment of official ulema – and demanded that the government set their comrades free, publish their statements widely in the media, and pay them a large sum of money. When these demands were not met, they killed their hostage.

The last of these three groups is the Jihad Organization (*Tanzim al-Jihad*), which was responsible for President Sadat's assassination. This group only recently established itself in Upper Egypt and Cairo and was not fully organized before 1980. It prepared for a *coup d'état*, which in its opinion would almost automatically be followed by a popular revolt. There were some soldiers among the organization's members and one of them, Khalid al-Islambuli, was directly responsible for the murder of Sadat in October 1981.

In many countries of the Islamic world it is common practice for governments to seek endorsement of important or controversial policies by the official ulema, in order to show that these policies conform to or, at least, do not run counter to the prescriptions of Islam. This is exactly what Sadat did when he prevailed upon the Al-Azhar University and the religious institutions connected with it to issue statements on the legality according to the *shari'a* of the Camp David Agreement of March 1979. Apparently, it took some time to convince them to endorse this new policy – in the past they had often issued declarations to the effect that war against Israel was obligatory and that the conclusion of a peace treaty forbidden[5] – for the *fatwa* was not drafted before 9 May 1979. For reasons unknown, this *fatwa* seems not to have been published.[6] On 10 May, however, a declaration by the Azhar sheikhs was published in both *al-Ahram* and *al-Akhbar*, summarizing the arguments of this *fatwa*.[7] Eight days later it was followed by an elucidation by the minister of *Awqaf*, 'Abd al-Mun'im Nimr, in response to criticism by ulema in other Arab countries.[8] Much later, on 16 November 1979, the state mufti (*Mufti l-Diyar al-Misriyya*) issued a *fatwa* on the subject.[9] The discussion here is based on the declarations of the Azhar sheikhs and the minister of *Awqaf* published on 10 and 18 May 1979.

The official ulema's arguments in support of the agreement derive from the classical doctrine which teaches that the head of an Islamic state (*al-imam*) may conclude an armistice with the enemy whenever he deems one to be in the interest of Muslims. However, they do not refer to the duration of the armistice, which, according to most legal schools, must be limited in order to keep the jihad obligation alive. This omission may have been merely political, but could also be a consequence of the ulema's modernist position that peaceful co-existence is the normal state of affairs between *Dar al-Islam* and *Dar al-Harb*, a view different from the classical doctrine that holds that war, jihad, is the natural relationship between the Islamic and non-Islamic worlds. In the latter doctrine, a peace treaty between an Islamic and a non-Islamic state is allowed only in case of necessity, as a temporary suspension of hostilities.

The evidence the ulema adduce for the general permissibility of treaties with the enemy is similar to that found in the standard texts on *fiqh*:[10] they cite K 8:61 ('And if they incline to peace, do thou incline to it') and the examples of the Prophet in concluding a treaty with the Meccans at Hudaybiyya and in planning to conclude an agreement with the Ghatafan tribe to the effect that, for a consideration, they would abandon the confederacy of tribes then laying siege to Medina.

The ulema's point of view was severely criticized in *al-Da'wa*[11] by 'Abd al-'Azim al-Mata'ni, who defends the view that in the present circumstances a peace treaty with Israel is not allowed according to Islam.[12] The circumstances under which the Prophet concluded the treaty of Hudaybiyya were so different from the present situation, he argues, that this comparison cannot be offered as evidence for the lawfulness of the treaty with Israel. And what is more, the treaty of Hudaybiyya was to last only ten years. The intended pact with Ghatafan was never made and cannot, therefore, in al-Mata'ni's view, count as evidence. As for K 8:61, he argues that this verse has no general validity, and must be read in combination with K 47:35 ('So do not faint and call for peace; you shall be the upper ones'). The former verse is applicable when the enemy recognizes all Muslim rights, whereas the second verse obtains when this is not the case – as in the present situation according to al-Mata'ni. Moreover, many jurists have taught that K 8:61 has been abrogated by the Verses of Fighting, such as K 9:5 ('Then, when the sacred months are drawn away, slay the idolaters wherever you find them, and take them, and confine them, and lie in wait for them at every place of ambush'). But even if K 8:61 has not been abrogated, al-Mata'ni maintains, the Koran makes fighting incumbent in a number of specific instances – as in the situation of an oppressed Muslim people asking for help – on the strength of K 4:75 ('How is it with you, that you do not fight in the way of God, and for the men, women and children who, being abased, say, "Our Lord, bring us forth from this city whose people are evildoers, and appoint to us a protector from Thee, and appoint to us from Thee a helper"?').

Interestingly, al-Mata'ni does not mention the role of the head of the state in deciding when to wage war and when to accept peace, something which is an essential and realistic element in the classical theory. He was therefore an easy prey for the official ulema. The main thrust of the Al-Azhar's counter-attack was directed against this politically sensitive issue, and in his reply al-Mata'ni was forced to recognize the head of state's authority in these matters.[13] His criticism consequently emasculated, he tried to present it as counsel to the ruler, similar to advice offered by the Companions to the Prophet. The Al-Azhar scholars also charged that al-Mata'ni had misunderstood why the examples of the treaty of Hudaybiyya and the intended pact with Ghatafan were cited. It was not in order to prove by analogy that the conclusion of the Camp David Agreement was permitted, but in evidence of the principle that peace treaties between Islamic and other states are permissible.

It is not surprising that the attack against the Camp David Agreement should come from the *al-Da'wa* group. They had criticized the Egyptian-Israeli *rapprochement* from the very beginning. This was consistent with their close ties to the conservative Arab oil states and an ideology that ascribed all evils in Egyptian society to four external enemies: Judaism, the Crusades, Communism, and Secularism.[14] As peace with Israel thus would mean surrender to one of the main enemies of Islam, it is intolerable.

Moreover, depicting Jews as intrinsically untrustworthy and wicked, *al-Da'wa* reasons that any pact with them would be precarious.

Occasionally *al-Da'wa* refers to the effort of introducing Islamic law and Islamicizing society as jihad. From the context, however, it is clear that no armed struggle is meant: 'Our country is an Islamic country and Islam must return to it through *our* jihad. He who claims that it is *dar harb* only wants to surrender it as an easy prey to the enemies of Islam'.[15] The contributors often mention that jihad signified much more than fighting and that spreading the message of Islam by peaceful means is also a form of jihad. Obedience to the ruler is regarded as a natural necessity: 'Obedience is following orders ... if there is no obedience, civil war will break out ... Obedience then is obligatory as long as it does not constitute disobedience to God's commands'.[16] These attitudes clearly reflect the social background of the *al-Da'wa* group, whose economic position is linked to the Open Door Policy and who are not committed to radical political and socio-economic change in Egyptian society.

If the word jihad is used in *al-Da'wa* to mean fighting, this is (apart from occasional references to the freedom struggle of oppressed Muslim peoples like the Afghans, the Muslims of the Soviet Union, or those of the South Philippines), always done in the context of the Arab–Israeli conflict. But anyone joining this struggle must await the orders of the head of state, as is clearly shown in the following words of the editor-in-chief, 'Umar al-Tilmisani, written in October 1978, with reference to the Camp David talks:

If asked for an alternative I would say that I am ready, and, I believe, all Muslims and non-Muslims of Egypt are ready to place themselves to-day and tomorrow under the command of the president of the state. If he appeals to God's Book, demands from us the austerity required by the nature of the situation, and prepares us dogmatically, morally and militarily for the decisive stand, we shall not bargain or demand a price. Because then we shall enlist ourselves for jihad in the way of God, because jihad in the way of God is the only way to reduce every aggressor to his natural proportions.[17]

There is nothing here that reminds us of the zeal of the Muslim Brothers in 1948, when they sent guerrilla bands to Palestine to aid the Palestinian people before the war between Israel and the Arab states had broken out. On the contrary, jihad against Israel is not envisaged as something immediate or pressing:

We shall seek its [the Jewish occupation of Jerusalem] remedy only in devotedness and sacrifice, and in the training for the holy jihad (*al-jihad al-muqaddas*), which we must promote with the youth of the present generation, so that they can teach it to those who come after them. We shall be victorious through God's favour and power: 'And they will say, "When will it be?" Say: "It is possible that it may be nigh"'. (K 17:51.)[18]

For the other Islamic political groups war against Israel is of only secondary importance. Foremost on their agenda is the struggle in their own country to establish an Islamic government or society. The issue is lucidly dealt with in *al-Farida al-Ghaiba* (The Absent Duty), a booklet written by Muhammad 'Abd al Salam Faraj, the ideologue of the Jihad Organization and our main source for the discussion on internal jihad.[19] The author adduces three arguments in order to refute the view that the jihad duty requires that Jerusalem be liberated before anything else. In the first place, he argues, the Jews are in the present situation the further enemy, whereas the rulers of Egypt are the nearer one. According to the prescriptions of the Koran the nearer enemy ought to be attacked first (cf. K 9:123: 'O believers, fight the unbelievers who are near to you and let them find in you a harshness'). His second point is that the struggle for the liberation of Jerusalem can only be waged under the banner of Islam, not under the leadership of impious rulers. Finally he maintains that the colonial presence of Israel in the Islamic world is completely the fault of the rulers of the Muslims. These must therefore be replaced before Jerusalem can be set free.

The standpoint of the Association of Muslims (*al-Takfir wa-l-Hijra*) is similar on this score, except that, as we shall presently see, they not only abominate the rulers, but Egyptian society at large, with all its institutions. They therefore keep aloof from the struggle between Israel and Egypt in its present state and are not inclined to fight in order to rescue Egypt and Egyptian society. Their leader, Mustafa Shukri, expressed himself as follows on this point: 'If the Jews or others would arrive here, the movement should not participate in combat within the framework of the Egyptian army, but, on the contrary, go to a safe place. In general our line is to flee from both the external and the internal enemy and not to offer resistance'.[20]

The well-known fundamentalist thinker and militant, Sayyid Qutb (hanged in 1966), used to elucidate the concept of jihad by saying that it is the permanent revolution of the Islamic Movement. This is an indication of the centrality of the concept in Islamic activist thought. This notion of jihad, that is internal jihad, the struggle within one's own society in order to change it according to the Islamic ideals, has also been the subject of heated discussions. The analysis here concentrates on the definition of the enemy and the permissibility of the immediate use of violence, and draws on two texts: the booklet 'The Absent Duty' (al-Farida al-Ghaiba) by Muhammad 'Abd al-Salam Faraj, which expresses the views of the Jihad Organization and also expounds the ideas of other groups and organizations in order to rebut them, and its refutation by the Sheikh al-Azhar, Jad al-Haqq 'Ali Jad al-Haqq.[21] The booklet consists of an introduction and three parts. Part One deals with the definition of the enemy and tries to demonstrate that the present rulers of Egypt are unbelievers and must therefore be fought. In Part Two, a number of contrary positions, which actually represent the points of view of the whole spectrum of Islamic organizations and groups, are systematically refuted. The last part is of less interest to us; it mentions a number of instances of the Prophet's and the Companions' use of tactics and enumerates the rules of warfare.

The title of the book refers to the jihad duty. According to the author, the command to take part in jihad is no longer observed and is even denied by some. In his introduction the author stresses that jihad is the method by which to establish an Islamic government, a duty for all Muslims because God orders men to judge and govern according to His revelation: 'So judge between them according to what God has sent down, and do not follow their caprices'. (K 5:48.) Finally, the author cites traditions, some of which are clearly millenarian and connected with the coming of the Mahdi, in order to demonstrate that after a period of tyranny an Islamic state, encompassing the whole earth, will soon be established.

Jihad is basically a struggle of Muslims against unbelievers who are not protected by a treaty of dhimma or an armistice. An appeal to the doctrine of jihad to justify a struggle waged against people who are to all appearances Muslims and consider themselves so, requires some reasoning. This is done in the first part of 'The Absent Duty'. The props of the author's disquisition are two fatwas by the well-known fundamentalist scholar Ibn Taymiyya (1263-1328) dealing with the consequences of Mongol or, as he calls it, Tartar rule in the Middle East.[22] The first fatwa addresses itself to the question of whether these rulers are Muslims as they claim to be, and the second explains the position of Muslims under their rule.

In spite of their profession of faith (shahada), it is beyond dispute for Ibn Taymiyya that these Mongol rulers must be fought because they are unbelievers. For they venerate and obey Genghis Khan and consider him of the same rank as the Prophet Muhammad; they take unbelievers as allies against Muslims; and, what is of the utmost importance, they do not apply the *shari'a*, but judge according to their own law (*yasaq* or *yasa*). Even if it is held that they are not unbelievers, this last charge justifies that they be fought on the strength of K 2:278 ('O believers, fear you God; and give up the usury that is outstanding, if you are believers. But if you do not, then take notice that God shall war with you, and His Messenger'), which was directed against the inhabitants of Taif, who first refused to abide by the *shari'a* and abandon their usurious practices. Territory under their rule where Muslims live is, according to Ibn Taymiyya, neither *dar harb* nor *dar silm* [*dar islam*]. It is a category of its own, 'where both Muslims and those who deviate from the *shari'a* must be treated each according to what they deserve'. Muslims are certainly not allowed to help such rulers.

For 'Abd al-Salam Faraj it is not difficult to find parallels between the Middle East under Mongol rule and present-day Egypt: the Egyptian rulers apply laws made by unbelievers instead of the *shari'a*, they take unbelievers as their allies, and they are venerated even more than their Creator: 'Therefore the rulers of these days are apostates. They have been brought up at the tables of colonialism, no matter whether of the crusading, the communist, or the zionist variety. They are Muslims only in name, even if they pray, fast, and pretend that they are Muslims'.[23] He then continues and expounds in detail that apostasy is much more serious than just unbelief, because the *shari'a* prescribes that the apostate must be killed unless he repents, whereas unbelievers may escape this fate by, for example, accepting *dhimma* or an armistice.

Having thus established that jihad against the government is incumbent immediately, the author devotes Part Two to refuting alternative arguments. He first tackles those who maintain that an Islamic society and an Islamic state can be brought about through individual piety, obedience to God, and by establishment of pious associations (*jam'iyyat khayriyya*). Piety and obedience, he argues, can only mean jihad under the present circumstances, and founding pious associations is out of the question because they perforce must collaborate with the infidel state.

Next he addresses the *Jama'at Islamiyya*, without, however, mentioning their name. That they want to realize their ideals simply by propaganda (*da'wa*) and by creating a broad base is only a consequence of their cowardice, because populism cannot be a substitute for jihad. Moreover, the Koran teaches that the establishment of an Islamic regime is the work of only a very small group: 'For few indeed are those that are thankful among My servants' (K 34:11); 'If thou obeyest the most part of those on earth they will lead thee astray from the path of God' (K 6:116); and 'Yet, be thou ever so eager, the most part of men believe not' (K 12:103). This minority, the author goes on, must first try to get control of the mass media by force, and the rest will then follow automatically: 'The effort that is really useful is the one for the sake of setting free these mass media from the hands of these... It is well known that as soon as we are victorious and have command, there will be a response, for He Who must be praised and is exalted says: "When comes the help of God, and victory, and thou seest men entering God's religion in throngs"' (K 110:2).[24] As can be imagined, Faraj makes short shrift of the view that was sometimes brought forward by the *Jama'at Islamiyya*, according to which a real Islamic state could eventually be founded by the pious and devoted after having won positions of influence in society. From such people, he asserts, nothing can be expected, as they will have had to collaborate with the existing state in order to establish themselves, and will have been corrupted in the process.

Another target of his attacks is the Association of Muslims (*al-Takfir wa-l-Hijra*). This group considers not only the rulers as unbelievers, but also the entire Egyptian society (*takfir*). However, being well aware of the balance of power between their small band and the rest of society, their tactics differ from those of the Jihad Organization. Their solution is to withdraw or emigrate from society (*hijra*), either geographically by going to live in small settlements along the edge of the desert, or socially by founding a community within, but totally separated from, society at large. They compare their lack of power with that of Muhammad and the first Muslims during the earliest Meccan period, when Muhammad only preached in secret to friends and relatives. Their strategy is a long-term one. They want to create a counter-society which, once it has acquired power, would proclaim jihad and take over the country.

After a short exposé of the theory of *hijra* in Islam and under what conditions emigration is compulsory, Faraj ridicules their notions: 'There are also those who say: The way to establish the Islamic state is by emigrating to another place, establishing the state there and coming back again victoriously. But in order to save effort, they should establish the Islamic state in their own place and then leave victoriously'.[25] Neither does he approve of their view that jihad is not (yet) obligatory since, as *al-Takfir wa-l-Hijra* maintain, their position is to be compared with that of the first Muslims in Mecca. The consequence would be, he argues, that all other prescriptions, for example fasting, that were revealed after this Meccan period, would not be applicable either. This is obviously not the case. Moreover God has said: 'Today I have perfected your religion for you' (K 5:3).

The jihad obligation can take different forms. In general it is a collective duty (*fard kifaya*), for example a duty of which the fulfilment by a sufficient number of believers is the responsibility of the whole community. Only under special circumstances can the jihad duty become an individual obligation (*fard 'ayn*) for everybody who is capable of going to war. One such case occurs, however, when enemies attack and occupy Islamic territory. Thus, in the concluding sections of Part Two the author demonstrates that under the present circumstances jihad has indeed become an individual duty, as the enemies, the infidel rulers, have taken over the country and are occupying it. He further deals with some modernist positions on jihad, now held by many official ulema. The first view he attacks is that jihad is only defensive warfare:

This is a false opinion . . . The correct point of view is to be found in the answer given by the Messenger of God – may God bless him and preserve him – to the question: 'What is jihad in the path of God?' He said: 'Who fights in order that God's word be uppermost [cf. K 9:40], is on the path of God'. The aim of fighting in Islam is therefore raising God's word on earth, both by attacking and by defence . . . Islam was spread by the sword, against the leaders of unbelief who tried to keep it [Islam] away from humanity, and therefore nobody is forced [to accept Islam] . . . Therefore it is obligatory for the Muslims to raise their swords against the leaders who hide what is true and divulge what is false. Otherwise the truth will not reach the hearts of the people.[26]

In addition, he argues, quoting a host of classical texts, that the Sword Verses or the Verses of Fighting (K 9:5 and 2:216) have abrogated all other verses concerning relations with unbelievers. Modernist writings often emphasize that jihad covers a much wider set of meanings than merely fighting. They explain that there are spiritual and moral forms of jihad which are more important than fighting and that the jihad duty can also be performed by the tongue or the pen (*jihad al-da'wa*) or by financial support. Faraj rejects all this. God has said: 'Prescribed to you is fighting [*qital*, not: *jihad*]' (K 2:216); just as He has said: 'Prescribed for you is the Fast' (K 2:183). This proves that fighting is obligatory and that one cannot just discharge one's duty by preaching or propaganda, or by any other means apart from combat.

The Sheikh al-Azhar's *fatwa* against *al-Farida al-Ghaiba* is long and detailed. Much of it is taken up by discussion of the authenticity of certain Traditions or interpretation of particular words and expressions in the Koran and the Hadith in order to sap the foundations of his adversary's positions. Occasionally there are interesting remarks that show how close ulema thought is to the official political ideology. The ruler in Islam is described as 'the representative of the nation (*wakil al-umma*)', which has the right to choose its rulers and to depose them.[27] With regard to our interest here, the *fatwa* deals with two issues: the question of when and under what conditions a Muslim, and especially a Muslim ruler, becomes an unbeliever, and second, the jihad doctrine and its application.

The first debate is a very old one in Islam. It goes back to the first century when the Kharidjites justified their revolt by pointing out that the caliph had committed grave sins and could therefore no longer be considered a Muslim. This, however, was not the generally accepted position, which held that a Muslim would be regarded as an apostate only when he expressly abjured Islam or denied axiomatic articles of faith (*ma 'ulim al-din daruratan*) in act or speech.[28] Non-observance of the *shari'a* is not enough. There must be an explicit act or utterance which denies the obligatory character of certain prescriptions. There is, of course, much room for interpretation, and one might argue that a ruler who does not apply parts of the *shari'a* denies its binding character and is therefore an apostate. Jad al-Haqq, however, does not go into this question. Instead, he formulates a totally new principle in this matter, namely that one becomes an apostate only by renouncing the *shari'a* in its entirety and he toils mightily to explain in this sense the verse: 'Whosoever judges not according to what God has set down – they are the unbelievers' (K 5:44). Finally he asserts that judging a Muslim's belief or unbelief is not the task of a layman, but exclusively the task of the ulema. His conclusion is that 'accusing a ruler of unbelief because he does not enforce some of God's prescriptions and ordinances, is founded on no text in the Koran nor on the Sunna'.[29]

Having argued that under these circumstances a ruler is not an unbeliever, he then tackles the question of whether a rebellion against him might be allowed on other grounds. After quoting a host of Traditions, he declares:

> On the strength of these and other authentic Traditions we must conclude that Islam does not allow rebellion against nor the assassination of a Muslim ruler as long as he sticks to Islam and acts according to it, even if this is only by performing prayer. If the ruler acts contrary to Islam, the Muslims must take care of him by counsel and sound and sincere appeal... Whenever a ruler does not administer God's ordinances nor enforce His law in any way, he loses the right to demand obedience with regard to such commands as are sinful or blameworthy.[30]

Jad al-Haqq's treatment of the jihad doctrine conforms completely with the writings of the Modernists. He states clearly that there are many forms of jihad apart from fighting and that, if combat is necessary in order to protect Islamic territory or the religion of Islam, the jihad duty can also be performed by financial support, by the tongue, or by the heart. Islam, he argues, has not been spread by the sword, Orientalist slander notwithstanding. This would be contrary to verses like: 'No compulsion is there in religion' (K 16:25); 'Call thou to the way of thy Lord with wisdom and good admonition, and dispute with them in the better way' (K 16:125); and 'Wouldst thou then constrain the people, until they are believers?' (K 10:99). As for the Sword Verse, he asserts that it has not abrogated all other verses regarding the relationship between Muslims and unbelievers, which are all applicable under specific circumstances. Jihad is, then, essentially defensive warfare, and when the need for jihad exists, it is to be carried out by the regular army to which the nation has entrusted this task.

The discussions summed up above demonstrate that the jihad doctrine is still very much alive and the subject of fierce controversies. This, however, does not tell us anything about the actual impact of jihad doctrine on Egyptian politics. In order to clarify this issue we shall first have a look at Egypt's foreign policy and, more specifically, her relations with Israel. Even without going deeply into the motives underlying the change in Egyptian policy towards Israel, it is evident that they were not religious. However, in order to confer greater legitimacy on the Camp David Agreements, especially in the face of the Islamic opposition, the government invited a number of religious institutions and religious dignitaries to pronounce on the matter from the point of view of the *shari'a*. Not surprisingly these *fatwas* and declarations lent full support to Sadat's policy, stating that termination of jihad on the strength of a peace treaty was under the present circumstances permitted. As for the Islamic opposition to the new relationship with Israel, represented by the *al-Da'wa* group, their stance was not based on the jihad doctrine. Going through the editorials of *al-Da'wa*, it becomes clear that their main motives for opposing the Camp David Agreement were Islamic solidarity with the Muslim Palestinians and aversion to and mistrust of the Jews. References to jihad are rare, and the jihad doctrine is only invoked to counter the legal arguments of the official ulema and to demonstrate that a peace treaty is not allowed under the given circumstances and war continues to be obligatory. From the foregoing, it appears that in Egyptian foreign policy the jihad doctrine does not play an independent role, not for the government, as could be expected, and not for the Islamic opposition. Its role is only marginal or complementary; and it is interpreted in different ways in order to justify political stances that have already been taken for other reasons, religious or otherwise.

In national politics there is more room for Islamic discourse, which by increasingly employing Islamic symbols and idioms the state has tried to dominate and even to monopolize. For obvious reasons the doctrine of internal, revolutionary jihad is not mentioned except to refute its legitimacy; this form of jihad is an essential part of the ideology of the opposition Islamic movements. To them it is identical with revolution, which like jihad, is an instrumental or tactical concept, covering all kinds of activities conducive to the ultimate objective: the overthrow of the established order and the restructuring of the state and society.

Only for the most radical organizations does internal jihad require actual fighting and the use of violence, themselves calling for considerable doctrinal acrobatics, as the enemies to be fought are to all appearances Muslims. However, by applying a very strict definition of Islam, the radicals' enemies are excluded and regarded as unbelievers. Differences among the various groups with regard to the application of this definition are related to differences in strategy. Some organizations see only the rulers and their supporters as being beyond the pale of Islam. They are in favour of an immediate struggle to topple the government, and count on popular support for their cause once they have seized power. Others see only themselves as true Muslims and regard anybody not belonging to their organization as an unbeliever. For them, being only a small minority in society, immediate jihad is out of the question; by conversion and recruitment they hope to create a position of power which will ultimately enable them to wage a successful jihad against their adversaries.

Thus it is clear that jihad is a concept with a wide semantic spectrum, and its actual meaning differs from organization to organization. Even if there is agreement among some groups that jihad signifies armed struggle only, these groups disagree on strategy and the immediacy of the struggle. The concept and doctrine of jihad, it appears, do not give clear and unambiguous directives; their interpretation and application depend very much on the political and strategical positions taken by the Islamic opposition groups. Jihad, therefore, cannot be considered as an independent driving force in Egyptian national politics. But like the notion of revolution, it can be used to justify positions that have already been taken and, what is perhaps more important, to enhance the loyalty and devotion of an organization's followers.

NOTES

1. Elie Kedourie, *The Chatham House Version and Other Middle Eastern Studies* (London, 1970), p. 177.
2. See Rudolph Peters, *Islam and Colonialism: The Doctrine of Jihad in Modern History* (The Hague, 1979), ch. 4.
3. This survey is based on the following literature: Nabil 'Abd al-Fattah, *al-Mushaf wa-l-Sayf: Sira' al-Din wa-l-Dawla fi Misr, Ruya Awwaliyya* (Cairo, 1984); Hamied N. Ansari, 'The Islamic Militants in Egyptian Politics', *International Journal of Middle East Studies*, xvi (1984), 123-44; Fouad Ajami, 'In the Pharaoh's Shadow: Religion and Authority in Egypt', in *Islam in the Political Process*, ed. J.P. Piscatori (Cambridge, 1983), pp. 12-36; Nazih N.M. Ayubi, 'The Political Revival of Islam: The Case of Egypt', *International Journal of Middle East Studies*, xii (1980) 481-90; O. Carré and M. Seurat, 'L'utopie islamiste au Moyen-Orient arabe et particulièrement en Egypte et Syrie', in *L'Islam et l'état dans le monde d'aujourd'hui*, ed. O. Carré (Paris, 1982), ch. l; R. Hrair Dekmejian, 'The Anatomy of Islamic Revival: Legitimacy Crisis, Ethnic Conflict and the Search for an Islamic Alternative', *Middle East Journal*, xxxiv (1980), 1-12; Ali E. Hillal Dessouki, 'Islamic Organizations in Egypt', in *Islam and Power*, ed. Alexander S. Cudsi and Ali E. Hillal Dessouki (London, 1981), pp. 107-18; Saad Eddin Ibrahim, 'Anatomy of Egypt's Militant Islamic Groups: Methodological Note and Preliminary Findings', *International Journal of Middle East Studies*, xii (1980), 423-53; *idem*, 'Islamic Militancy as a Social Movement: The Case of Two Groups in Egypt', in *Islamic Resurgence in the Arab World*, ed. Ali E. Hillal Dessouki (New York, 1982) pp. 117-37; *idem*, 'Egypt's Islamic Militants', *MERIP Reports*, ciii (1982), 5-14; Gilles Képel, *Le Prophète et le Pharaon: Les mouvements islamistes dans l'Egypte contemporaine* (Paris, 1984).

4. *Takfir* or accusing of unbelief is a practice going back to the early Islamic sects like the Kharidjites. More recently the Wahabi and the Sudanese Mahdi movement used it in order to justify war against their Muslim adversaries. In the Egyptian context the discussion goes back to the prison terms of the Muslim Brethren under Nasser. For a survey of the various answers to the question of who exactly were to be regarded as unbelievers, see Salim 'Ali al-Bahbasawi, *al-Hukm wa-qadiyyat takfir al-Muslim* (Cairo, 1397/1977).

5. See Sabine Hartert, 'Ein Aegyptisches *Fatwa* zu Camp David', *Die Welt des Islams*, xxii (1982), 139-42; Peters, *Islam and Colonialism*, pp. 106-8.

6. A German translation was published by Sabine Hartert in the above mentioned article.

7. Italian translation in I. Camera d'Afflitto, 'Traduzione e commento del communicato emesso dagli 'ulama di al-Azhar, relativo all' accordo di pace tra Egitto e Israele', *Oriente Moderno*, lx (1980), 79-84.

8. *al-Ahram*, 18 May 1979.

9. *al-Fatawa l-Islamiyya min Dar al-Ifta al-Misriyya*, x (Cairo, 1403/1983), 3621-36.

10. See Peters, *Islam and Colonialism*, p. 33.

11. *Al-Da'wa*, July 1979, pp. 58-9.

12. 'Abd al-'Azim al-Mata'ni is a professor in the faculty of Arabic Linguistics of al-Azhar University and the editor of the *fatwa* section of *al-Da'wa*.

13. The reaction of al-Azhar, written by Muhammad Husam al-Din at the instruction of the Sheikh al-Azhar, 'Abd al-Rahman Baysar, was published in *al-Da'wa* of Sept. 1979, pp. 30-3, followed by al-Mata'ni's reply.

14. See Képel, *Prophète et Pharaon*, p. 108.

15. *Al-Da'wa*, Jan. 1977, p. 47 (a reaction against radical Islamic movements).

16. *Ibid.*, May 1978, p. 41.

17. *Ibid.*, Oct. 1978, p. 3.

18. *Ibid.*, May 1980, p. 7.

19. Text published in *al-Ahram*, 14 Dec. 1981, and in *al-Fatawa l-Islamiyya min Dar al-Ifta al Misriyya*, x (Cairo, 1403/1983), 3762-92; Parts of the text (about one third) published in *Jamal al-Banna, al-Farida al-Ghaiba: Jihad al-Sayf...am Jihad al-'Aql...? Ma' fusul kamila min kitab "al-Farida al-Ghaiba" al-Mansub li-l-muhandis Muhammad 'Abd al-Salam Faraj* (Cairo, 1984). I quote from the text published in *al-Fatawa l-Islamiyya*.

20. Képel, *Prophète et Pharaon*, p. 83.

21. Text in *al-Fatawa l-Islamiyya*, x. 3726-61; French tr. in G.C. Anawati, 'Une résurgence du Kharijisme au XXe siècle: L'Obligation absente', *Mélanges de l'Institut dominicain d'Etudes orientales*, xvi (1983), 191-228.

22. For the texts of these *fatwas* see Ibn Taymiyya, *al-Fatawa l-Kubra* (Repr. Beirut, 1397/1978), iv. 331-58.

23. *al-Fatawa l-Islamiyya*, x. 3766.

24. *Ibid.*, p. 3773.

25. *Ibid.*, p. 3774.

26. *Ibid.*, pp. 3776-7.

27. *Ibid.*, p. 3750.

28. See R. Peters and Gert J.J. de Vries, 'Apostasy in Islam', *Die Welt des Islams*, xvii (1976-7), 1-25, and the *fiqh* literature quoted there.

29. *al-Fatawa l-Islamiyya*, x. 3743.

30. *Ibid.*, p. 3745.

INDEX

INDEX